Research Skills for Psychology

Research Skills for Psychology

Rebecca Wheeler-Mundy
and Stacey Bedwell

Los Angeles | London | New Delhi
Singapore | Washington DC | Melbourne

Los Angeles | London | New Delhi
Singapore | Washington DC | Melbourne

SAGE Publications Ltd
1 Oliver's Yard
55 City Road
London EC1Y 1SP

SAGE Publications Inc.
2455 Teller Road
Thousand Oaks, California 91320

SAGE Publications India Pvt Ltd
B 1/I 1 Mohan Cooperative Industrial Area
Mathura Road
New Delhi 110 044

SAGE Publications Asia-Pacific Pte Ltd
3 Church Street
#10-04 Samsung Hub
Singapore 049483

Editorial arrangement © *Rebecca Wheeler-Mundy and Stacey Bedwell*, 2020
Chapters 1, 21 © Rebecca Wheeler-Mundy and Stacey Bedwell, 2020
Chapter 2 © SAGE Publications, Inc., 2020
Chapter 3 © James Stiller and Philip Banyard & Sarah Buglass, Lydia Harkin, Peter Macaulay, Luke Vinter and Rosie Daly, 2019
Chapter 4 © Chris Fife-Schaw, 2012
Chapter 5 © Virginia Eatough, 2012
Chapters 6, 8, 16, 20 Tom Burns and Sandra Sinfield, 2016
Chapters 7, 12, 13, 15 © Pete Greasley, 2016
Chapters 9, 10, 11 © Phillip Chong Ho Shon, 2015
Chapter 14 © Gary Thomas, 2017
Chapters 17, 18 © Diana Ridley, 2012
Chapter 19 © S Alex Haslam and Craig McGarty, 2019
Chapter 22 © Andy Field, 2018

Throughout the book, screenshots and images from IBM® SPSS® Statistics software ('SPSS') are reprinted courtesy of International Business Machines Corporation, © International Business Machines Corporation. SPSS Inc. was acquired by IBM in October 2009.

First published 2020

Typeset by: C&M Digitals (P) Ltd, Chennai, India
Printed and bound in the UK

ISBN 978-1-5297-5968-6

At SAGE we take sustainability seriously. Most of our products are printed in the UK using responsibly sourced papers and boards. When we print overseas we ensure sustainable papers are used as measured by the PREPS grading system. We undertake an annual audit to monitor our sustainability.

Contents

Welcome to Research Skills

Wheeler-Mundy, R. & Bedwell, S. R.

We are very excited to bring you our unique edited collection, designed exclusively for the level 4 Psychology Research Skills module at Birmingham City University. The following chapters have been complied by Dr Stacey Bedwell and Dr Rebecca Wheeler-Mundy specifically to aid your journey in becoming a scientific researcher.

Throughout the module you will be working your way through the book, covering topics such as *Psychology as a Science, Psychology Study Skills, Critical Analysis & Adopting a Perpective and Research Ethics*. Each chapter is linked to your assessment in Psychology Research Skills and will provide an important basis for your development as a psychologist.

As you progress through the module we will be working on a range of research skills and activities designed to complement lecture materials and your reading. Together these will set you on the path towards becoming a successful researcher.

Rebecca Wheeler-Mundy and Stacey Bedwell

2 Psychological research: the whys and hows of the scientific method

McBride M. D.

Consider the following questions as you read Chapter 1

- What is the value of research in psychology?
- Why do psychologists use the scientific method?
- How do psychologists use the scientific method?
- What are the canons of the scientific method?
- What is the difference between basic and applied research?
- How do basic and applied research interact to increase our knowledge about behavior?

LEARNING OBJECTIVES FOR CHAPTER 1

- Understand that knowledge of research in psychology has value beyond careers in research
- Understand what it means to learn about behavior through observation
- Evaluate research in terms of the basic–applied distinction

As an instructor of an introductory psychology course for psychology majors, I have asked my first-semester freshman students the question, "What is a psychologist?" At the beginning of the semester, students typically say that a psychologist listens to other people's problems to help them live happier lives. By the end of the semester and their first college course in psychology, these same students will respond that a psychologist studies behavior through research. These students have learned that psychology is a science that is used to investigate behaviors, mental processes, and their causes. That is what this book is about: how psychologists use the scientific method to observe and understand behaviors and mental processes.

The goal of this text is to give you a step-by-step approach to designing research in psychology, from the purpose of research (discussed in this chapter) and the types of questions psychologists ask about behavior, to the methods used by psychologists to observe and understand behavior, and to how psychologists describe their findings to others in the field.

WHY SHOULD I CARE ABOUT RESEARCH
IF I DON'T WANT TO DO RESEARCH IN MY CAREER?

Throughout my years of teaching psychology methods courses, this question is often asked by students who don't think they want to conduct research in their careers. A few of you might be bitten by the "research bug," as I was as an undergraduate, and find research to be an exciting way to answer questions you have about behavior. Knowing the process of research can help you better understand the topics presented in other psychology courses you may take because you will have the knowledge of how this information was gained. However, a majority of students majoring in psychology are interested in working as practitioners of psychology or may be completing a psychology minor that is related to another career they want to pursue (e.g., education, social work) and do not understand why research methods courses are part of their curriculum. In fact, most people who hold a degree in psychology do not conduct research in their jobs. Instead, the majority of individuals working in psychological areas are in helping or other applied professions. However, what we know about behavior in everyday settings comes from research findings. For example, effective treatments and counseling techniques come from research in these areas. When a new treatment technique is tested, its effectiveness is determined by the research conducted on it. Thus, just as medical doctors do, clinicians and counselors must evaluate the latest research in psychology to determine whether a new treatment is one they should adopt. Knowledge of how research is conducted can help them evaluate this research more effectively to aid their practice. In addition, other popular applied areas, such as industrial-organization psychology and human factors, use research findings to help address issues in everyday life. Industrial-organizational psychologists help organizations hire effective employees, prevent job dissatisfaction, and explore the best training methods for new employees using research findings on these topics (see Photo 1.1). Human factors professionals use research to help understand the best way to design products and interfaces (such as an airplane cockpit—see Photo 1.2) to make them easier to use and prevent errors. Finally, it is important that we as individuals understand how to interpret the vast amounts of information we take in each day through media sources. Research findings are reported by the media every day. Knowing the basics of how research is conducted can help you decide which of those reports you should listen to and which are best ignored.

To give you a recent example, in debates about global warming and the seriousness of the problem, many opponents of global warming solutions point out that there is disagreement among scientists about the cause. My own father once told me that this is the reason that he doesn't believe global warming is caused by human activities—some scientists have stated that there isn't enough evidence. As voters and consumers, it is important that we understand which evidence from research is the most valid (i.e., accurate) and that there will almost always be disagreement among researchers in an area because no single study can fully answer a research question. In order to understand what answers research provides on a question, we must consider the accumulation of data in many research studies (and

PHOTOS 1.1 AND 1.2: Knowledge of research can aid in applied areas of psychology, such as industrial-organizational psychology and human factors.

this is what I told my father when he stated his reasoning to me about his beliefs). We must also understand that new knowledge is always being discovered, and we must be flexible in our conclusions about an issue when new data suggest a different answer. Remember, there was a time when most humans believed the sun revolved around the earth. Scientific study revealed this idea to be false, and over time, humans adapted their beliefs to the new knowledge. We must do the same when we learn new findings about the best everyday behaviors, such as how to prevent Alzheimer's disease or how to keep our hearts healthy and live longer.

Understanding research methods can also help you better interpret research study results that are reported in the media. In almost all cases, media sources present concise and simplified reports of a research study and its results, leaving many questions about the quality of the study still to be answered. When one encounters reports of research in the media, some important questions should come to mind. Who were the research subjects? Was an appropriate sample tested? Was an appropriate method used to investigate the question? Were the results published in a high-quality source where other researchers were able to critique the work? How do the results correspond to past studies on this topic? The topics covered in this text and in your methods course will help you ask and answer these questions as you evaluate reports in the media you can use to make decisions about your life.

Finally, the new knowledge you gain from your study of research methods can help you decide how to evaluate claims made by others in general. When you see an ad on television for a new miracle diet pill that the ad claims has helped people lose weight in studies, should you buy the pill? When your friends tell you that drinking energy drinks helps you study better and achieve higher scores on exams, should you follow their advice? Should you believe claims that vaccines cause autism? (You shouldn't: There's no good research evidence that vaccinations cause autism.) Hopefully, one of the things you will consider as you learn about research is to be skeptical about claims that seem too good to be true. A good researcher uses the data to decide what the best thing to do is rather than using unsubstantiated advice from others who just sound knowledgeable about a topic but who cannot provide evidence beyond an anecdote or two. Examples of how to evaluate claims and research reported in the media are given in the *Using Research* sections found at the end of some of the chapters in this text.

WHY PSYCHOLOGISTS CONDUCT RESEARCH

Think about how you know the things you know. How do you know the earth is round? How do you know it is September? How do you know that terrorist threats are increasing around the world? There are probably many ways that you know these things. In some cases, you may know things because you used your **intuition** or previous knowledge to **deduce** these facts. For example, you may know from past experience that where you live, in the month of September, days tend to be warm but start to get cooler, especially at night. Therefore, remembering the characteristics of the weather you are experiencing and knowing you are still living in the same location as past years, you can deduce that the month is September from your knowledge base. You may have first learned that the earth is round from an **authority** figure like your parents, teachers, or text authors. You may have also observed that the earth is round by viewing photographs of the earth taken from space. You may know that terrorist threats are increasing from authority figures as well (e.g., magazine and newspaper reporters, your country's leaders' statements). These are the primary ways that we learn new facts: intuition, deduction, authority, and **observation**.

Suppose something occurred that caused you to suspect that the authority figures you have learned these facts from are not reliable sources of information. Perhaps they have been caught lying about other facts. You might also consider a situation where you do not have enough previous experience with a topic to use your intuition to determine the information for yourself. In these situations, what is the best way for you to find the facts? The answer is observation. If you had reason to believe, for example, that an increase in terrorist threats is not being represented accurately, you could examine the incidence of terrorist attacks (e.g., from public records) over a period of time to find out if people are representing the true conditions. Observing the world directly is going to give you the most accurate information because you are directly gaining the knowledge yourself—you are not relying on possibly faulty reasoning on your part or information someone may be giving you that is false or misleading. See Table 1.1 for some examples of the different ways of knowing information.

This is why psychologists conduct behavioral research; it is the best way to make certain that the information they have about behavior is accurate. By conducting careful and systematic observations, they can be certain that they are getting the most accurate knowledge they can about behavior. This does not mean that every study conducted will yield accurate results. There are many cases where the observations collected by different researchers conflict, but this is an important part of the process. Different ways of observing a behavior may yield different observations, and these different observations help us to better understand how behaviors occur. Over time, with enough observations, a clearer answer to the question can be found. But no single research study can "prove" that something is true. Researchers are not able to "prove" facts with a study; the best they can do is support an idea about behavior

intuition: relying on common sense as a means of knowing about the world

deduction: using logical reasoning and current knowledge as a means of knowing about the world

authority: relying on a knowledgeable person or group as a means of knowing about the world

observation: relying on what one observes as a means of knowing about the world

TABLE 1.1 ■ Examples of Ways of Knowing Information	
Way of Knowing	**Example**
Intuition	I'm trying to go someplace I've never been, but I do not know the way. I decide to turn left because it just "feels like" that's the right way to go.
Deduction	I want to know which direction I am facing. The sun is setting to my right, and I know the sun sets in the west, so I know that south is the direction I am facing.
Authority	I want to know what my pancreas does. I know that my pancreas produces hormones important for digestion because that is what my high school biology teacher told me.
Observation	I want to know how much sleep on average Americans get per night. I determine this by conducting a survey of Americans to learn that most Americans get an average of 6 to 8 hours of sleep per night (e.g., Moore, 2004).

with their data. Despite the limits of observation as a way of knowing, it is superior to the other methods because it allows for a more objective way of gaining knowledge. Relying on the other ways of gaining knowledge can be misleading because they can be more easily influenced by biases that people have.

Using Science to Understand and Explain Behavior

Observation is really what sets scientific fields apart from other fields of study. Someone who wants to know about the political situation during the Civil War may read historical documents and use his or her intuition to describe the situation based on these documents. He or she might also read books by experts (authority figures) on the Civil War period or books on important figures who lived during that time. However, historians typically cannot observe the historical event they are studying. Psychologists have an advantage in that the behavior they want to learn about is happening in humans and other animals in the world around them. The best way to learn about it is to just observe it (see Photo 1.3).

Some behaviors, such as mental processes, cannot be directly observed (e.g., thoughts or memories). Thus, psychologists have developed techniques for inferring information about mental processes through observation of specific behaviors that are affected by the mental processes.

© andresr/iStock Photo

PHOTO 1.3: If we want to know how much sleep people get, we can use scientific methods to measure this directly or ask people to report this behavior on a survey.

Psychologists then attempt to understand mental processes through observation of these behaviors and the investigation of the factors that influence those behaviors. That is what this book (and the course you are taking) is all about—understanding the methods psychologists use to observe, measure, and study behavior and mental processes.

Research is the foundation of the field of psychology. Many people think of the *helping* professions when they think about what psychologists do. This is because most people with a graduate degree in psychology work in these helping (or related) professions (American Psychological Association, 2003). However, to do their jobs well, helping professionals, such as clinicians and counselors, need to understand the findings from research about behavior so that they know what types of treatments and therapies can best help their clients. The research studies conducted in psychology also help clinicians and counselors understand what constitutes "normal" behavior and what behaviors might be considered "abnormal."

Thinking about the field of biology may help you understand how influential research is in the field of psychology. In the biological field, there are researchers who investigate the way our bodies react physically to the world around us (e.g., after being exposed to a virus). This knowledge helps other researchers determine which drugs may be effective in helping us improve these physical reactions (e.g., reduce our symptoms as we fight the virus). Finally, the knowledge gained in biological research helps doctors correctly diagnose and treat their patients (e.g., what symptoms indicate the presence of a particular virus and which drugs are most effective in treating these symptoms). The field of psychology works a lot like the field of biology (although the term *psychologist* applies to both scientists and practitioners in psychology, sometimes causing confusion). Some researchers investigate what causes certain types of behaviors (e.g., distraction in people with attention-deficit/hyperactivity disorder ADHD). Other researchers investigate what treatments are effective in reducing these behaviors (e.g., rewarding someone for staying on task). Finally, some psychologists work with clients to help them deal with problem behaviors. For example, school psychologists work with teachers and parents to develop a reward system for students with ADHD who have difficulty completing work in class because they become easily distracted. The research that investigated the behaviors associated with ADHD and the factors that can reduce those behaviors was necessary for the school psychologist to be able to develop an effective treatment plan for the student.

STOP AND THINK

[1.1] Think about some things you know are true about the world. For each of these facts, try to determine the way you know that information (intuition, deduction, authority, or observation).

[1.2] Suppose you wanted to know about the factors that cause college students to become anxious. Describe how you might learn about these factors using the observation way of knowing.

[1.3] Explain how the fields of psychology and biology are similar.

HOW PSYCHOLOGISTS USE
THE SCIENTIFIC METHOD

Our starting place for conducting research studies in psychology is an understanding of the assumptions that come along with the methods of science. We need to keep some concepts in mind when we use the scientific method to understand behavior. As discussed earlier, scientific study requires observations. It is the primary aspect of the scientific method. However, there are actually four primary facets or *canons* (i.e., rules or principles that guide a field of study) that define the scientific method. They are empiricism, determinism, parsimony, and testability.

Empiricism

The first canon is empiricism, and this is just what we discussed above—that the scientific method relies on observations. We have several important people to thank for the empirical nature of science. Galileo, for example, was an influential scientist who used observations to understand the world (Sharratt, 1996). Much of the learning up to Galileo's time (1564–1642) had relied on authority figures, such as Aristotle and Plato, and their ideas about the world to understand how the world worked. However, Galileo and his contemporaries (e.g., Copernicus, Newton) claimed that to learn how the world works, one should observe it. When Galileo wanted to understand how our solar system worked, he *observed* the movement of the planets around the sun through a telescope, instead of simply accepting the authoritative position held by Aristotle that the earth was the center of the solar system and everything revolved around it. He made careful, systematic observations of the phenomena of interest to better understand those phenomena. What we do in psychology is not very different from what Galileo did. If developmental psychologists want to know about bullying behaviors in elementary school children, they go out and carefully observe specific playground behaviors among these children or systematically observe the behaviors of children who have been identified as bullies.

Why do psychologists observe behavior? Observing behavior gives researchers a more accurate understanding of the causes of behaviors than other methods of gaining knowledge. Relying on an authority to learn about behavior, for example, greatly limits our understanding of behaviors across large groups of individuals because not all authority figures are equally reliable and some may have faulty information.

How do we use empiricism to learn about behavior? There are many different ways to do this. We can simply observe people in their normal environment (e.g., children on a playground at recess). We can ask them to complete a survey (e.g., have the participants respond to items that help us measure their mood). We can ask them to come into a lab and complete a task on a computer (e.g., test their memory for different types of information). Each of these methods allows us to gather empirical measurements of behavior (observation techniques are discussed further in Chapter 4).

One thing to keep in mind is that one observation (either from one individual or from one study) is never enough for us to be sure that the knowledge we are gaining is real. Chance factors can cause a particular behavior, which will not be clear if we observe it only

empiricism:
gaining knowledge
through systematic
observation of the
world

once. Therefore, it is important to replicate our observations, both across multiple individuals within a study and/or across multiple studies using different sets of subjects and, oftentimes, different procedures. This replication of results assures researchers that the behaviors they observe are not just because of chance factors and that the results they find can be used to make more confident conclusions about how behavior works. We will discuss the importance of replication across individuals further in our discussion of sampling in Chapter 6.

Determinism

Another important aspect of the scientific method is the adherence to **determinism**. This is the concept that phenomena in the world (and human behaviors) occur naturally and have identifiable causes (in extreme cases, determinism can indicate a denial of free will). In other words, by conducting studies to observe behavior, we can understand the factors that *cause* those behaviors to occur. One goal of psychological research is to be able to explain behavior by understanding the causes of different types of behavior. For example, why do people get depressed? What causes false memories? Does sleeplessness cause anxiety? Does anxiety cause sleeplessness? The assumption of determinism in psychological research is that each of these behaviors (depression, false memories, anxiety, and insomnia) has a specific cause or set of causes, and we can understand these causes through observation of behavior in different circumstances. For many behaviors studied by psychologists, multiple causes may affect the behaviors. However, not all research is conducted to directly test causes of behavior. In some cases, the behavior first must be described and related factors identified. Although these types of studies do not directly test a cause of behavior, they do contribute to our knowledge of the behavior, which is one step in the scientific process of understanding its causes. We will discuss the different ways we conduct psychological studies and the different goals researchers may have in their studies in Chapter 4.

How is determinism used in psychological research? Because the overall goal of research is typically to gain a better understanding of behavior and its causes, researchers design their studies to contribute to this goal through the description of behaviors (e.g., How common is anxiety among college freshmen?), through the identification of factors related to the behaviors (e.g., Are students who are younger more anxious their freshmen year in college than older students?), and through the testing of specific causes of the behaviors (e.g., Does technology use in coursework reduce anxiety in college freshmen?).

Parsimony

In the 1997 film *Contact,* Jodie Foster's character, Dr. Ellie Arroway, attempts to explain her beliefs as a scientist to Matthew McConaughey's character, Palmer Joss (see Photo 1.4). She tells him that simpler explanations of the world are preferred over more complex explanations, particularly if there is no scientific evidence that a complex explanation is correct. She uses the term "Occam's Razor" (after the Franciscan friar who suggested it as an important part of the scientific method). **Parsimony** is what Arroway is speaking of when she talks about the preference for more simple explanations. In psychological research, we develop explanations of behavior starting with the simplest descriptions

determinism: the assumption that phenomena have identifiable causes

parsimony: the assumption that the simplest explanation of a phenomenon is most likely to be correct

PHOTO 1.4: In the movie *Contact*, Jodie Foster's character, Dr. Arroway, describes the concept of parsimony, which means, in science, we prefer simpler explanations of a phenomena as a starting assumption.

and expanding those descriptions only when it becomes clear that the behavior is more complex than our original description of it. In other words, simple explanations are preferred. It is assumed that the simpler explanation is more likely to be correct. More complex explanations should be developed only after simpler explanations have failed to be supported by research studies.

Why is parsimony useful in psychological research? Parsimony helps scientists test their ideas because it is easier to develop a study that might falsify a simple explanation than to develop a study that might falsify a more complex explanation. Falsification is an important part of the research process. This idea is relevant to the concept of testability as well and will be discussed further in the next section.

Testability

The fourth canon of science is **testability**. The scientific method can only be used to examine ideas that can be tested through observation. The only explanations of behavior that can be tested with the scientific method are those that can be contradicted with observations of behavior. *Why* is falsifiability important? It is important because a test of an explanation of a behavior that allows that explanation to be falsified provides a stronger test of that explanation. If we look only for evidence to support our explanations of behavior, we are likely to find that evidence and hold on to those explanations longer even if they are wrong. Seeking only confirmatory evidence and ignoring contradictory evidence is known as **confirmation bias**. If, instead, we design research studies that can show us behaviors inconsistent with our explanations, we are more likely to find evidence against them, if such evidence exists. It takes only a few studies with results inconsistent with an explanation of behavior to falsify it. However, it takes many studies conducted in many different contexts to produce results consistent with an explanation of behavior to support it.

testability: the assumption that explanations of behavior can be tested and falsified through observation

confirmation bias: seeking only evidence that supports our beliefs and ignoring evidence that contradicts those beliefs

Testability is one of the reasons why many of Sigmund Freud's ideas have not had more influence on current clinical and personality psychology theories—they are difficult to test using the scientific method. For example, Freud proposed that many of our personality traits are a product of a struggle between constructs of our minds (id, ego, and superego) that we do not have full conscious access to (Nairne, 2009). It is difficult to test this theory because the constructs Freud proposed are difficult to connect to observable behaviors. Thus, it is difficult to systematically observe behaviors in a research study that would contradict the theory. We can, however, answer questions about other types of mental processes that are indicated by observable behaviors. For example, we can test the idea that anxiety causes sleeplessness. We can observe behaviors of sleeplessness in situations where people are placed in anxiety-provoking situations with anxiety verified by self-report. If anxious people are sleeping well, this contradicts our explanation of sleeplessness (i.e., anxiety) and provides us with a good test of our explanation (although this particular result is unlikely to be found). As psychologists using the scientific method, it is important that we ask questions and test explanations about behavior that can be falsified by observations of those behaviors.

How is falsifiability used in psychological science? As indicated above, falsification of explanations of behavior advances psychological science much more than supporting explanations (Platt, 1964). Whenever researchers can show that an accepted explanation is not supported, it changes the direction of investigation in an area of research and moves psychological science forward in gaining new knowledge about behavior. Making predictions about the results they will find in their studies helps researchers contribute to the testability of their observations. With clear predictions made before a study is conducted, researchers can design good tests of their ideas about behavior, which helps them avoid falling prey to the confirmation bias—believing the results are consistent with their ideas regardless of how they turn out.

The canons of science provide a general "how to" guide for psychologists designing research studies because they help us conduct good tests of our explanations of the causes of behaviors and further our understanding of why certain behaviors occur. The rest of this text describes more of the details of how psychologists apply these canons in designing and conducting research and walks you through the process of developing research studies of your own.

STOP AND THINK

(1.4)   Which assumption of the scientific method suggests that simple explanations are most likely to be correct? Which assumption of the scientific method suggests that observation is the best means of learning about the world?

(1.5)   Explain how confirmation bias could affect your decision-making.

(1.6)   Explain why replication of results is an important part of the scientific process.

BASIC AND APPLIED RESEARCH

As you begin to consider the types of questions that can be answered in psychological research studies (a topic that will be discussed more in Chapter 2), it is important to keep in mind the goals of two major categories of research: **basic research** and **applied research**.

The goal of basic research is to understand the most fundamental processes of behavior and how they operate. Research questions in basic research are typically about how a behavior works. How much information can we store in short-term memory? Who exhibits more symptoms of depression: men or women? Do we have implicit stereotypes that affect our social behavior?

Applied research is generally focused on answering questions related to solving real-world problems. What type of automated teller machine (ATM) is the easiest to use?

basic research: research conducted with the goal of understanding fundamental processes of phenomena

applied research: research conducted with the goal of solving everyday problems

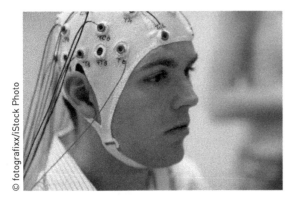 

PHOTOS 1.5 AND 1.6: Both basic (left - measuring brain activity) and applied (right - observing workplace behaviors) research studies contribute important knowledge about behavior.

Are drug treatments most effective in helping people who are depressed? What type of work environment increases productivity of employees? What sorts of treatment programs best prevent relapse in drug addiction? See Photos 1.5 and 1.6 for examples of each type of research.

Typically, basic research provides fundamental knowledge of how behaviors operate that is useful to researchers conducting applied studies. For example, suppose that a researcher finds that people who report having insomnia also report symptoms of anxiety (a similar result was reported by Morphy, Dunn, Lewis, Boardman, & Croft, 2007). A conclusion from this study might be that anxiety and sleeplessness are related in some way (note that this does not mean that anxiety *causes* sleeplessness, only that they are related). This conclusion represents basic knowledge about the connection between emotional state and sleeplessness or insomnia. Researchers interested in the more applied question of how we help people with sleep problems may use this basic knowledge to test treatments for sleeplessness that focus on reducing anxiety to determine whether the relationship found in the above study is causal or not. The basic research in this case is vital for the development of applied studies that address a real-world problem (i.e., insomnia). Table 1.2 provides some additional examples of basic and applied research studies.

An important example of how basic research can inform on a real-world issue is in eyewitness testimony in the legal system. According to The Innocence Project, 70% of exonerations from DNA evidence in the United States have included a false eyewitness identification (www.innocence project.org). In the 1970s, Elizabeth Loftus (see Photo 1.7) began conducting research looking at how accurate memory is for an eyewitness. Along with her colleagues, she conducted studies looking at how the wording of questions asked about an event can affect the way someone remembers the event (e.g., Loftus, 1975; Loftus & Palmer, 1974). Over time, applied work in this area followed these early, basic studies that developed and tested new techniques of questioning witnesses that have been adopted by many police departments across the world (e.g., the cognitive interview, Fisher & Geiselman, 1992; Geiselman, Fisher, MacKinnon, & Holland, 1986). Research (both basic

TABLE 1.2 ■ Examples of Basic and Applied Research Studies
Basic Research
• Researchers investigated the process through which visual memories are stored and strengthened in memory (Ricker & Hardman, 2017).
• Making choices leads people to think more analytically (Savani, Stephens, & Markus, 2017).
• Participants were randomly assigned to mixed-race groups while their brain activity was recorded to investigate brain areas involved in in-group biases (Van Bavel, Packer, & Cunningham, 2008).
Applied Research
• Researchers showed that writing to-do lists helps people fall asleep faster than making a list of completed tasks (Scullin, Krueger, Ballard, Pruett, & Bliwise, 2018).
• Experienced border officers detected fraudulent passports based on face-matching more often than novices but still missed a high ratio of the inaccurate passports (Wirth & Carbon, 2017).
• Specific warnings increased memory accuracy compared with general warnings when inaccurate information was presented to eyewitnesses (Higham, Blank, & Luna, 2017).

and applied) continues today to help us better understand how accurate eyewitnesses' memories really are (e.g., Wixted & Wells, 2017).

It is also important to remember that the applications of basic research may not be obvious when the research is initially conducted. The utility of such research to real-world problems may not be revealed until much later when enough is known about an issue to apply the knowledge gained in the basic research studies. For example, early neuroscientists (e.g., Santiago Ramón y Cajal, as cited in Meyers, 2007) conducted basic research studies to understand how neurons function. The applications of this knowledge were not clear until much later when neuroscientists better understood how this neural functioning affected behavior. For example, we now know that some types of disorders (e.g., depression) are linked to neural functioning that is abnormal (e.g., higher levels of serotonin than are typical; Barlow & Durand, 2008), and drugs have been developed to alter neuron functioning to help individuals with such disorders. The basic knowledge of neural functioning became useful in helping individuals with disorders long after this research had been completed. Thus, basic research is important to conduct, even if an application is not immediately clear.

PHOTO 1.7: Elizabeth Loftus conducted basic research on eyewitness memory that has influenced applied research on this topic and changes in the way eyewitnesses are questioned.

© Don Tormey/LA Times/via Getty Images

Because applied research investigates realistic problems, applied researchers are often concerned with the **external validity** of their studies. This means that they attempt to observe behaviors that can be applied to real-life situations. This is important because these researchers want to be able to apply their results to a problem that generalizes to individuals who are not participants in their study (as well as to those individuals who were observed in the study). External validity is also a consideration in basic research but, in some cases, can be less important than it is in applied research.

In turn, knowledge gained in applied studies can also help basic researchers refine their theories about how behavior works. Suppose in the above example regarding anxiety and insomnia, the applied studies showed that treatments reducing anxiety did not reduce the symptoms of insomnia (similar results were reported by Morin, Belanger, & Fortier-Brochu, 2006). In this case, the basic researchers may use this knowledge to hypothesize that the link between anxiety and insomnia may not be a simple causal relationship and conduct further studies to better understand the causes of insomnia and how it is related to anxiety. In this way, the two types of research, basic and applied, interact with each other, showing that both types of research are critical to the field of psychology.

As you encounter descriptions of psychological research, you may find that not all research fits neatly into basic or applied categories. Some research can both answer fundamental questions about behavior and help solve a realistic problem. It may be better to think about research as primarily basic or applied. In other words, basic and applied descriptors may be end points in a continuum of types of research studies with each research study falling somewhere between these end points.

external validity: the degree to which the results of a study apply to individuals and realistic behaviors outside the study

STOP AND THINK

[1.7]   Explain how external validity differs for basic and applied research studies.

[1.8]   In what way(s) can knowledge of the scientific process help you in your daily life?

THINKING ABOUT RESEARCH

A summary of a research study in psychology is given below. As you read the summary, think about the following questions:

1. What behaviors did the researchers observe?

2. How were the observations recorded by the researchers?

3. Were the researchers able to identify a cause of behavior from this study?

4. Were the researchers able to answer their research questions with the observations they collected? How?

5. What results would have falsified the explanation of behavior the authors tested?

6. Do you think this study qualifies as primarily basic or applied research? Why?

7. What are some examples of real-world behaviors that the results of this study might apply to?

Research Study. Strayer, D. L., & Johnston, W. A. (2001). Driven to distraction: Dual-task studies of simulated driving and conversing on a cellular phone. *Psychological Science, 12,* 462–466.

Purpose of the Study. The researchers were interested in how use of a cell phone while driving influences driving performance (see Photo 1.8). They describe previous studies that have shown that devices that require one's hands while driving (e.g., the radio, temperature controls, etc.) can reduce driving performance. In this study, they predicted that cell phone use would reduce driving performance. They tested two ideas about how cell phone use could decrease driving: (1) that the use of a hand-held phone would interfere with driving and (2) that the attention requirements of a phone conversation would interfere with driving.

Method of the Study. Forty-eight undergraduates (half male, half female) participated in the experiment. Each of the students was randomly assigned to one of three cell phone conditions: hand-held phone, hands-free phone, and no phone (radio control only). The participants performed a computer-simulated driving task where they moved the cursor on the screen to match a moving target as closely as possible, using a joystick. Red and green lights flashed periodically during the task and subjects were instructed to press the "brake" button as quickly as possible when the red light flashed. They performed this task on its own in a practice segment and two test segments, with a dual-task segment placed between the two test segments. In the dual-task segment, they were given an additional task that included one of the following to match the conditions listed above: hand-held phone conversation with another person (who was part of the research team) about a current news story, hands-free phone conversation with another person about a current news story, or controlling a radio to listen to a broadcast of their choice. The frequency of missing red lights and the reaction time to hit the "brake" button when a red light appeared were measured and compared for the three phone conditions.

Results of the Study. The two cell phone use conditions did not differ in their results, suggesting that driving performance in response to red lights is similar for hand-held and hands-free phone use. Figure 1.1 shows a graph for each of the measures according to the phone (combined for hand-held and hands-free conditions) and no-phone conditions. The data are shown in each graph separately for driving performance in the driving only segments (single task) and for the phone/radio task while

PHOTO 1.8: Strayer and Johnston's (2001) study examined whether talking on a cell phone while driving decreases driving performance.

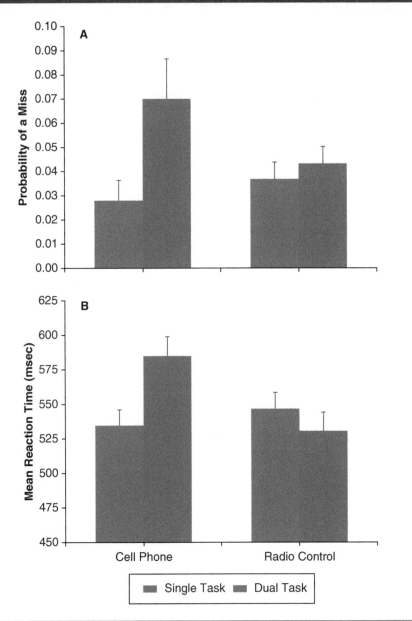

FIGURE 1.1 ▪ Driving Performance as Measured by Responses to Red Lights in the Driving Task While Performing the Driving Task on Its Own (Single Task) or While Also Performing the Phone or Radio Task (Dual Task)

Source: Figure 1 from Strayer and Johnston (2001).

driving (dual task) segment. The graphs show that more red lights were missed and time to press the "brake" button was longer when subjects were talking on the phone (compared with when only driving), but there was no difference in driving performance when subjects listened to the radio while driving and when they just performed the driving task on its own.

Conclusions of the Study. The authors concluded that phone use, regardless of whether it requires one's hands, interferes with driving performance more than just listening to the radio. This suggests that the attention component of phone use is the key factor in the driving performance interference.

CHAPTER SUMMARY

Reconsider the questions from the beginning of the chapter:

- Why do psychologists use the scientific method? Psychologists use the scientific method because it provides the best way to gain new knowledge about behavior.

- How do psychologists use the scientific method? Psychologists use the scientific method to observe behaviors as they occur in everyday life and in situations researchers are interested in learning about.

- What are the canons of the scientific method? The canons are empiricism, determinism, parsimony, and testability.

- What is the difference between basic and applied research? Basic research is designed to answer fundamental questions about behavior. Applied research is designed to gain solutions to everyday problems.

- How do basic and applied research interact to increase our knowledge about behavior? Basic research advances our understanding of the causes of behavior. In applied research, these explanations are tested in everyday situations to inform researchers about the best solutions for everyday problems. Knowledge gained about these problems in applied research can then inform basic researchers about how explanations of behavior may need to be revised to explain behaviors that occur in everyday life.

COMMON PITFALLS AND HOW TO AVOID THEM

Problem: Assuming that psychology equals practice in a *helping* profession, ignoring or dismissing the scientific aspect of psychology.

Solution: Understand that science and practice are both important aspects of the field of psychology. In addition, although there is debate about this issue, many psychologists find it important that practitioners of psychology stay abreast of current research findings to ensure that they are using the most effective treatments.

Problem: Positive test bias—designing studies that provide supportive evidence of an explanation of behavior without including the possibility for contradictory evidence.

Solution: Carefully design studies to allow collection of data that can support or contradict explanations of behavior.

Problem: Misinterpretation of causation—study of cause and effect relationships requires manipulation (e.g., randomly assigning participants to different situations), but many people confuse reports of relationships with evidence of causation. In other words, correlation does not equal causation, but many people assume a link between two things means one caused the other.

Solution: Do not assume a reported relationship between factors is evidence that one factor causes another unless the study has been designed in such a way that other noncausal relationships can be ruled out.

Problem: Dismissing basic research—some people dismiss basic research as unimportant because it is not designed to solve a real-world problem.

Solution: View the "big picture" of knowledge in psychology to see how basic research informs applied research by providing fundamental knowledge of behavior that guides research questions and interpretation of results in applied studies. In addition, for a basic research study, do not assume that because an application is not immediately evident the study is not valuable. Applications of basic research findings are often not clear until long after the basic research has been conducted.

APPLYING YOUR KNOWLEDGE

On Facebook one day, you see a post from one of your friends that they have found the most amazing vitamin supplement. They claim that they have taken the vitamin once a day for the past few weeks and they have more energy and feel great. They are passing on the information to their friends (including you) and urging you to try the vitamin for yourself.

- Why should you be skeptical of the claim you read from your friend?

- What other information would you want to have before deciding if you should try the new vitamin your friend is so excited about?

- Suppose you came across a news item reporting that thousands of people have been trying the new vitamin (they include interviews with some of these people) and that overall, these people have reported positive results. Would this convince you to try the new vitamin? Why or why not?

TEST YOURSELF

Match each canon of science below with its correct definition.

1. Determinism
2. Empiricism
3. Testability
4. Parsimony

(a) The scientific method can be used to test descriptions and explanations of the world that can be contradicted by observations.

(b) The scientific method is used to examine phenomena that have an identifiable cause.

(c) An assumption of science is that simpler explanations are more likely than complex explanations to be correct.

(d) Knowledge is gained in science by systematically observing the phenomenon being studied.

5. Freud hypothesized that many of our personality traits are controlled by an unconscious conflict between aspects of ourselves—the id, ego, and superego—that we are not consciously aware of (Nairne, 2009). Using what you know about the scientific method, explain why this hypothesis is difficult to support with observations of behavior.

6. Explain how parsimony is helpful in psychological studies.

7. For each reference listed below, decide whether the study is primarily basic or applied.

   a. Drews, F., Pasupathu, M., & Strayer, D. (2008). Passenger and cell phone conversations in simulated driving. *Journal of Experimental Psychology: Applied, 14,* 392–400.

   b. Roediger, H. L., III, & Geraci, L. (2007). Aging and the misinformation effect: A neuropsychological analysis. *Journal of Experimental Psychology: Learning, Memory, and Cognition, 33,* 321–334.

   c. Wagman, J. B., Langley, M. D., & Farmer-Dougan, V. (2017). Doggone affordances: Canine perception of affordances for reaching. *Psychonomic Bulletin & Review, 24,* 1097–1103.

   d. Smith, A. M., & Thomas, A. K. (2018). Reducing the consequences of acute stress on memory retrieval. *Journal of Applied Research in Memory and Cognition 7,* 219–229.

   e. West, R. (2007). The influence of strategic monitoring on the neural correlates of prospective memory.

   Memory & Cognition, 35, 1034–1046.

   f. McClernon, C. K., McCauley, M. E., O'Connor, P. E., & Warm, J. S. (2011). Stress training improves performance during a stressful flight. *Human Factors, 53,* 207–218.

   g. Weaver, J. R., & Bosson, J. K. (2011). I feel like I know you: Sharing negative attitudes of others promotes feelings of familiarity. *Personality and Social Psychology Bulletin, 37,* 481–491.

   h. Blanchette, I., & Leese, J. (2011). The effect of negative emotion on deductive reasoning: Examining the contribution of physiological arousal. *Experimental Psychology, 58,* 235–246.

8. I believe that the best way to study for exams is to reread my notes three times from start to finish because last semester I did that and I got an A on my psychology exam. I believe this despite the fact that I have tried this method before and did not receive an A on an exam. I am falling prey to the _____.

9. The scientific method relies on which way of knowing information about the world?

10. If I am concerned about whether the behavior exhibited in my research study maps on to the everyday behaviors of individuals, I am considering the _____ of my study.

Answers can be found at **edge.sagepub.com/ mcbride4e.**

STOP AND THINK ANSWERS

(1.1)   Answers will vary—should use some of the ways of knowing: intuition, deduction, authority, and observation.

(1.2)   Answers will vary, but should include a measure that will indicate anxiety based on some type of observation.

(1.3)   Psychology and biology both have research and practice areas, where the two areas inform each other.

(1.4)   Parsimony, empiricism

(1.5)   Confirmation bias can hinder decision-making in keeping you from considering all evidence for something because you are focused on finding evidence to support your own beliefs.

(1.6)   Replication is important because each individual study is based on just a small subset of subjects, and chance factors could be causing the results obtained.

(1.7)   External validity is typically higher in applied studies than basic studies, because applied studies are designed to solve a real-world problem, whereas basic studies are designed to understand a fundamental process of behavior with control over extraneous factors.

(1.8)   Answers will vary, but will be focused on considering evidence for something before deciding on things relevant for your life.

$SAGE edge™

Visit **edge.sagepub.com/mcbride4e** to help you accomplish your coursework goals in an easy-to-use learning environment.

How psychology became a science

3

Stiller, J. and Banyard, P.

of survival and greater reproductive success. Therefore, having the associated cognitive hardware to replicate memes and imitate behaviour would have been advantageous and provided behavioural flexibility, making those individuals thrive.

Similar to Dunbar's (1998) social brain hypothesis, the human cognitive system has evolved to deal with complex social information, but it is the ability to imitate cultural elements (which arguably could require gossip as a key transmission mechanism) that is driving reproductive success and therefore creating a strong meme–gene interaction. So, although the actual meme might not be an evolved trait, the ability to propagate culture and imitate can be seen as an adaptive trait. However, as Dawkins (1989) points out, it is important to note that some memes can actually be detrimental to an individual's fitness, for example, some religious practices that involve chastity or abstinence. However, the benefits of the associated hardware (big brains) outweigh the costs of these anomalies in terms of the overall inclusive fitness of the gene pool at large.

Although the memetic approach to culture can provide a mechanism for understanding how the brain acts as a meme replication machine, allowing for cultural transmission, Boyd and Richerson (2005) provide a useful framework for examining how biologically-based mechanisms and the cultural ideas can both be seen as adaptive traits. According to the dual-inheritance model, culture is inherited in parallel with genetic inheritance. This frees up the concept that human evolution is solely the product of genetic change. In this model, there is an evolved social learning mechanism that will have developed as a result of natural selection, whereby it is beneficial to use a low-cost learning strategy such as imitation (rather than learning by individual trial and error).

There is also the cultural evolution process which is not genetically-based but follows the methods of transmission outlined earlier (horizontal and vertical). However, we now have to consider what affects the replication of specific behaviours. Two key biases are conformist bias and prestige bias, both of which provide a simple, low-cost heuristic (rule of thumb) for adopting specific cultural traits. *Conformist bias*, whereby the most common behaviour within a group is imitated, results in the adoption of a particular behaviour or cultural trait based on the heuristic that an action can be perceived as advantageous if the majority of people use it. *Prestige bias* shifts the focus away from conforming with the group towards the characteristics of a particular person carrying out the behaviour, whereby if an individual appears to be successful (e.g. they might be wealthy, have many mates), then the way these individuals are acting could contribute to their perceived prestige.

So far, the relationship between genetics and culture has been unidirectional, in that the cognitive hardware is selected and this allows for the epiphenomenon of culture to evolve. However, when looking at the adaptive properties of cultural activities, it is clear that culture can influence our genetic evolution too. So many cultural practices, such as cooking, using tools and wearing clothes, can be seen as practices that, once adopted by the group, can change our environment or the extent to which the environment impacts upon our lives. This in turn is changing our resource requirements and the environmental pressures that natural selection acts upon, and therefore can impact on our phenotype.

Henrich and McElreath (2009) provide a nice example that summarises this. At some point in our ancestral past, the practice of cooking meat would have spread by social learning. This trait in itself is adaptive as it makes food easier to chew, easier to digest and kills harmful parasites. Over subsequent generations, the requirements for large teeth and large intestines to break down the food are no longer needed or favoured by natural selection, freeing up energy that can be used to develop larger brains. In this way, a cultural practice has modified the biology of the organism, and therefore the cultural evolution and natural selection are working reflexively with each other in changing the human phenotype.

Finally, it is important to note that not all cultural traits are adaptive. Examples of maladaptive cultural practices abound, and again many of these maladaptive traits can be acquired via inappropriate adoption of a conformist or prestige bias.

1.5.3 Epigenetics

Over the past few decades, there has been a wealth of studies looking at identical twins and to what extent certain traits (ranging from depression to vulnerability to diseases) are inherited due to shared genes. However, more recently it has been acknowledged that the old-fashioned view of one gene coding for one protein is actually wrong. One gene can account for several proteins and, as such, it becomes increasingly difficult to suggest that there are specific genes for specific traits. However, perhaps due to selective reporting, there has been an emphasis on the similarities between identical twins in terms of behaviour, personality and psychiatric disorders. What is often neglected is why in identical twins, who by definition should have identical sets of genes, there are so many differences. One argument is that this is due to the environment and that not all traits are inherited; some are acquired via experience. However, this does not explain why certain traits then appear to be inherited in later generations. Traditional gene–behaviour arguments would suggest that life experience cannot be inherited. Another argument is that some of these differences are **epigenetic**.

The epigenetic argument suggests that genes can be effectively switched off by a process called methylation. So, for example, let us say there is a set of identical twins where both individuals share a gene that is associated with happiness, yet only one of the twins actually exhibits the trait (i.e. is happy). The relevant gene in one of the twins could have been 'switched off' so they do not show the happy trait. This could be the result of methylation of the associated gene due to some life experience (e.g. a traumatic childhood accident).

EXERCISE

WHAT INFLUENCES YOUR ADOPTION OF CULTURAL PRACTICES?

Consider the following cultural traits and decide whether your adoption of these traits is due to a conformist bias or prestige bias and whether or not they are adaptive or maladaptive (or perhaps neither adaptive nor maladaptive). Just to make you feel better, we will give you an example of a prestige bias in the 1970s, when there was a trend for wearing ridiculously high platform boots. Many celebrities and pop acts of the time wore them and, as such, there was prestige associated with them, with many people consequently adopting the trend (including one of the editors, ahem, PB), despite this being a maladaptive trait – as wearing these skyscraper heels increased the risk of falling over, vertigo and hitting your head on low doors.

So, looking at the list below, are you showing a conformist or a prestige bias when you make the following decisions?

1. Your choice of clothes to wear in the morning
2. Whether you choose to drink alcohol or not
3. Your choice of food in the evening
4. The music you listen to
5. Your religious beliefs

What is interesting is that for a few generations this trait might be passed on in its shutdown form to offspring. Therefore, the happy twin will have happy children and the traumatised twin will have less happy children. If we revisit the yellow dung fly from the earlier example, it could be argued that perhaps the increase in testes size across the generations is an epigenetic response. In other words, the environment has had an effect on gene expression that is inherited. This does not mean the fly has lost the gene for normal-sized testes, but simply that it has been switched off in response to environmental pressures.

Epigenetics The study of heritable changes in gene expression that occur without changes to the genotype (DNA). So, traits (these can be physical and/ or behavioural) that are inherited via epigenetics are not due to changes in the gene combinations, but are due to changes in whether a gene is actively expressed or not.

In evolutionary terms, epigenetic traits are of particular interest as they highlight how some traits can be temporarily passed on without an actual change in genes. Therefore, there has not been an evolutionary change in response to the environment as there is no mutation or change in genetic material across the generations, but instead some genes might not be expressed.

1.6 CHAPTER SUMMARY

We have seen how the development of science enabled people to explain the world around them, drawing upon empirical data. This allowed them to challenge superstitious beliefs with evidence gained from the natural sciences. Psychology has, at its heart, a commitment to empiricism. It also draws significantly from the sister biological disciplines of palaeo-anthropology, neo-Darwinian evolutionary theory and behavioural genetics. The story of human evolution is the story of how our brain and our psychology have evolved alongside each other. Communication, problem solving and tool making are key abilities within our species. Evolutionary psychology can provide a framework for understanding why certain human behaviours have become widespread, and how our cognitive hardware has evolved in response to our physical environment, limited resources and social environment.

WHAT DO PSYCHOLGOISTS DO?

Evolutionary psychologists are interested in the biological and cognitive evolutionary explanation of human behaviour. While much of this research is conducted on humans, they will often take a comparative approach and look at how human behaviour differs from our closest non-human primate relatives. This can involve field research and observing primate behaviour in the wild. For example, for many decades Jane Goodall has observed the behaviour of chimpanzees, our closest relative in evolutionary terms, at the Gombe Nature Reserve in Tanzania. Her research has provided us with valuable insights in their tool use, family life and social behaviour, much of which has changed what behaviours we see as exclusively human and has lead to the development of a clearer understanding of observational methods within comparative studies.

CRITICAL EVALUATION

A major challenge for evolutionary psychologists is that it is difficult to find evidence within the fossil record or archaeological digs to justify some of the claims that psychological traits have been inherited and evolved over time as universally human traits. Therefore, the area can be subject to ethnocentric biases (much of the research is conducted by researchers in the US and Europe) and perhaps over-generalises some proposed universal traits, in particular in relation to areas such as mate choice. When researching, we have to acknowledge our own potential cultural biases in what we value as important, for example, is kinship really about genetic relatedness or is it about marital status or social rankings or social proximity. There can also be an over-reliance on behaviours being solely linked to reproductive success. Currently, with over seven billion people on the planet, we can be confident that somewhere our genetic code is represented within the human gene pool and therefore perhaps the genetic imperative to reproduce is not as strong. Perhaps the evolution of human culture is more important than the traditional biological benchmarks of reproduction and maybe we have largely broken free of our selfish genes.

In Video 1.2 Leda Cosmides discusses evolutionary psychology and how it relates to psychology in general.

DISCUSSION QUESTIONS

Can you think of examples of our own, contemporary behaviour that may be explained from an evolutionary point of view? To help, think of what men tend to look for in their partners if they are attracted to the opposite sex, and contrast this with the signals women use to select men. To what extent do both sexes rate features in the same way? If not much, is this a case of different natural selection pressures applying to the sexes in making a mate choice?

SUGGESTIONS FOR FURTHER READING

Buss, D. (2008). *Evolutionary psychology: the new science of the mind* (3rd edn). Harlow: Pearson Higher Education.

David Buss is one of the key people in the field of evolutionary psychology. The book is written in a style that engages you to consider the argument as an active reader. You are not told what to think but are invited to apply what you are reading to a range of questions that arise from the work he covers.

Dawkins, R. (1989). *The selfish gene* (3rd edn). Oxford: Oxford University Press.

The modern evolutionary approach continues to have a significant impact on how behavioural scientists, including psychologists, think about the function and maintenance of behaviour. This is a classic and very readable text that helped promote the importance of neo-Darwinian thinking in relation to behaviour.

www.apa.org/science/genetics/.

If you are interested in exploring further the relationship between genetics and behaviour, we recommend you visit the very helpful website hosted by the American Psychological Association.

Still want more? For links to online resources relevant to this chapter and a quiz to test your understanding, visit the companion website at **https://study.sagepub.com/banyard3e**

HOW PSYCHOLOGY BECAME A SCIENCE

2

Lead authors Sarah Buglass, Lydia Harkin, Peter Macaulay, Luke Vinter and Rosie Daly

CHAPTER OUTLINE

2.1 INTRODUCTION

Chapter 1 considered how we came to be human. In this chapter, we look at how we a
humans came to develop theories regarding ourselves and our behaviours. The origin:
of psychology can be traced back as far as the philosophical thinkers of Ancient Greece
However, the purpose of this chapter is not to provide you with an account of over 200(
years of psychological musings. Instead, we offer an insight into the emergence of moderr
psychology. To do this we only need to go back approximately 150 years. What follows
therefore, is not *the* history of psychology but *a* history of the main issues, concepts, peo
ple and debates that have helped shape and define a fascinating and varied modern-da
discipline. We have devised a chapter to help you navigate some of psychology's ke:
moments, but please note that this is not always a linear journey. At the heart of thi
chapter, we consider how psychology became a science.

FRAMING QUESTIONS

◀ What have been the main stages in the development of psychology as a science?
◀ How has psychology developed as a natural science and as a social science?
◀ How has the social and political landscape influenced psychology's development
  over time?
◀ What does the future hold for psychology as a science?

2.2 WHAT IS A SCIENCE?

To help us understand psychology as a discipline, it is important to address the meanin
of science itself. Science helps us to determine our understanding of the universe ar
observed phenomena. It provides a collective understanding and knowledge of how th
universe works. Science is not defined by the type of experimental tools used or the sul
ject matter under observation. Rather, it is the integration of scientific principles that ca
be applied to a particular subject matter, to help provide a further understanding of ph
nomena (Tyson, Jones & Elcock, 2011). The principles that disciplines follow in ord
to achieve scientific status can be referred to as the 'scientific approach'. Modern-da
psychology, as a relatively new science, has adopted the scientific approach to gain stat:
as a scientific discipline.

2.2.1 What is the scientific approach?

Objectivity is the foundation of science. The scientific approach follows three key stage
systematic observation, testable predictions and verification of scientific facts (Stanovi
& Stanovich, 2013).

Systematic observation Observations of
subject matter need to be empirical. This
means that they must be structured in
order to provide a systematic account of
observed phenomena.

The public perception of psychology as a science
much debated. In Sir Isaac Newton's (1642–1727) time, t
idea of **determinism** in science emerged and went on to
a strong influence on psychology. Determinism is the id
that the universe and its behaviour is predetermined bas

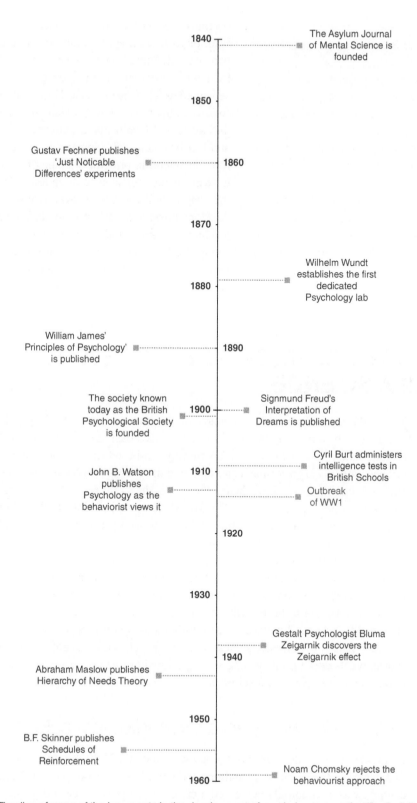

Figure 2.1   Timeline of some of the key events in the development of psychology as a scientific discipline

Testable predictions Through controlled settings, it should be possible to test these systematic observations. This is also referred to as falsification and allows researchers to test hypotheses about the way the world works.

Verification of scientific facts The systematic observations and testable predictions are reviewed and even replicated to verify scientific facts. It is the *replication* that confirms scientific knowledge for public understanding, providing sense to a particular observed phenomenon. This is often called the 'peer review' stage.

on rules. Just as Newton developed the theory of gravity from observing an apple falling to the ground, determinism suggested that human behaviour could be understood by making observations and testing theories. Determinism separated us from the universe. However, serious questions followed about the 'mind' and human experiences. Where did we fit in? Could our experiences of love, prejudice, and fear be quantified? Nonetheless, determinism, with its roots in scientific principles, helped psychology to join a growing gang of scientific disciplines. The remainder of the chapter will provide an overview of how psychology developed from this early position to become the scientific discipline we know today (see Figure 2.1 for a timeline of some of the key events). We will guide you through the way in which the changing social and political landscape has influenced psychology's past, present, and future.

2.3 THE DEVELOPMENT OF PSYCHOLOGY AS A SCIENCE

The word *psychology* means 'a study of the mind or soul'. Early psychologists had to decide how best to study this subject matter. Two basic models presented themselves. On the one hand, there was Newton's determinism-based model, also known as the natural science model. This prioritised counting and measuring behaviours that could be observed and verified. You may have heard these methods referred to as **quantitative research methods**, which pursue **nomothetic** knowledge as a priority. On the other hand, a social science model was also a possibility. This approach predominated in the humanities and was embodied by the German word *Geisteswissenschaft* (which means 'science of the spirit'). Under this model, the aim was to study humans, human life and human events by re-creating their meaning for the actors involved. This approach prioritised discovering peoples' *reasons* for doing what they were doing and focused on their *lived experience*. You may have heard these methods referred to as **qualitative research methods**, which explore **idiographic** knowledge. It is important to consider the relationship these methods have had in the broader societal context. Psychology has not developed in a vacuum. World events and a transforming socio-political climate have shaped the development of psychology as a scientific discipline.

2.3.1 Why did we need a psychological science?

Many key developments in psychology were a result of the emergence of social problems that demanded scientific explanations and solutions. An example of this, in the nineteenth century, was a commonly perceived increase in the prevalence and incidence of '*insanity*' and other psychopathological issues, such as **hysteria**, habitual drunkenness, violence and criminal responsibility, which were deemed as bordering upon insanity.

ASIDE

HYSTERIA

Hysteria is a term which stems from the Greek and Latin phrase for the womb. The medical condition has appeared throughout history but was most commonly used to diagnose ill-health in nineteenth-century women. Hysterical women displayed a range of physical symptoms, including convulsions, delirium, mania, and even possession by the devil!

At the time, clinical theories suggested that the uterus caused this behaviour in unmarried women of low morals. Indeed, Sigmund Freud (1856–1939) initially proposed (*very* controversially) that all hysterics had suffered sexual abuse in childhood. He later retracted this 'seduction theory' of hysteria. He nonetheless retained the belief that many of the hysteric's 'potentially damaging' ideas and desires were of a sexual nature and that much of everybody's behaviour was driven by the repression of sexual desires.

Today, hysteria might well be called a dissociative disorder. In Freud's time, only women were thought to be hysterical. Nice. This is a prime example of the masculine bias which has long afflicted psychology.

To tackle the growing societal concern and social problems caused by the 'insane', legislation was passed in 1845 (The Act for the Provision and Regulation of Lunatic Asylums for Counties and Boroughs), which made it compulsory for English counties to establish lunatic asylums. Asylums housed and treated those deemed to be insane.

The expansion of these asylums across the country gave rise to new practical demands, challenges and questions on how to effectively manage 'the insane'. Asylum medical officers not only began to research ways to tackle these issues, but also began to share their research with others. The *Asylum Journal of Mental Science* was founded in 1841 as a means of information sharing and became an early form of dissemination for psychological research. Interestingly, while asylums gradually faded out, this journal remained, later becoming the *Journal of Mental Science* in 1855, which transformed again into the *British Journal of Psychiatry* in 1963, a journal that is still published to this day.

The initial intention of establishing asylums was to tackle a social concern: removing those deemed to be insane from mainstream society. As time went on, medical officers shifted in focus and began to consider the social problems that had inspired the establishment of asylums, such as habitual drunkenness (or alcoholism) and hysteria, from a different perspective. These social problems began to be interpreted as having psychological dimensions, rather than merely a moral failing or lack of free will.

The psychological explanations for insanity were often interlaced with scientific physiological explanations. In addition to deterministic ideas spreading among scientists, Charles Darwin (1809–1882) had published ground-breaking theories of evolution in *The Origin of Species* (1859). Scientists (and psychologists) looked to this for inspiration when interpreting maladaptive behaviours such as insanity. This jarred with core Victorian values of moral responsibility and Christian purity. On the one hand, were the mentally ill born that way? Or, on the other hand, were they influenced by their poor judgement and temptations? This blending of psycho-physiological approaches posed a problem: if human behaviours were caused by genetics, then all people may lack volition for their actions, and not just those who were deemed to be insane.

Asylums and the study of mental illness is one example of how psychology could provide an explanation for the dominant societal concerns of the time. While science became increasingly valued and encouraged in the nineteenth century as a means of progress, it was not exempt from the pressures felt by society as a whole. Progress would be met with fierce opposition if it appeared to violate the dominant views of society at that time, such as the importance of moral responsibility and perceptions of women. For example, a key figure at the time, Henry Maudsley (1835–1918), weaved moral concerns into his accounts of insanity, particularly in women (Ussher, 1992). Maudsley posited that female insanity was exacerbated during menstruation. Therefore, for psychology to provide a socially acceptable explanation of these behaviours, the methods evolved to suit the contemporary thinking of the time. For nineteenth-century psychologists, this meant a focus on the observable and quantifiable.

2.3.2 Counting and quantifying: towards a behavioural science

Why did nineteenth-century psychologists focus on quantifying behaviours? At the time, natural scientific methods were 'the only reliable methods for securing useful and reliable knowledge about anything' (Danziger, 1990: 41). In order to flourish, psychology *had* to align itself with the methods of the natural sciences.

So, psychology went along with the idea that all mental phenomena could, in fact, be explained in terms of physiological causes. This double whammy of **reductionism** and **materialism** reduced the psychological world to a by-product of the physiological properties which produced it. As a by-product, subjective mental phenomena were no longer psychology's primary subject matter; physiology was. And natural scientific methods operated very comfortably in this physical domain. As Leahey puts it:

> 'by insisting that the nervous system is the basis of all mentality, and by defining psychology as the investigation of the physiological conditions of conscious events, the new field … could establish itself as a [natural] science.' (Leahey, 2004: 235)

But defining psychology in this way was not enough. Establishing psychology as a natural science also demanded that psychological experimentation is carried out in the same way as the natural sciences, and this, in turn, demanded that psychological phenomena be mathematically measured and described. This was now to involve the investigation of the physiological conditions of conscious events (rather than the events themselves), yet those conditions would still have to be counted and measured.

The first attempts at counting and measuring in psychology, otherwise known as quantification, were developed by a number of people in a number of different ways.

In 1850 **Hermann von Helmholtz** (1821–1894), an eminent natural scientist, demonstrated that nerve impulses travelled at finite speeds which could be measured in terms of *reaction times*. He did this by passing electric currents through the severed leg of a frog. He also established the psychological principle that human perception (by which he implied the psychological reality we experience) was not a simple replication of the physical reality captured by our senses. Helmholtz proposed instead that sensations were *transformed* into perceptions in a mechanical and lawful fashion by the machinery of our minds.

F.C. Donders (1818–1889) built upon Helmholtz's reaction-time work. Donders realised that the time between the presentation of a stimulus and a person's response to it could be used as a quantifiable measure of the speed of physiological and mental processes (processes which could not otherwise be observed). It was even possible, by making a person choose between two stimuli, to ascertain the exact duration of a mental judgement. This act of quantification (which became known as *mental chronometry*) was exactly what psychology needed if it was to distinguish itself as a natural science.

Gustav Fechner (1801–1887) quantified psychological phenomena in a different way. Like Helmholtz, Fechner had noticed that the information gathered by our senses was processed and transformed *before* it reached conscious awareness. In particular, he observed that the *perceived* intensity of a physical stimulus did not perfectly reflect its *physical* intensity. A lighted match would, for example, appear to be brighter when it was placed against a dark background. Fechner surmised that if we could somehow measure the physical *and* the perceived intensity of the stimulus, it might become possible to mathematically determine their relationship (and hence to mathematically connect the psychological and physical worlds).

But how could we measure the perceived intensity? Fechner realised that you could not quantify it directly or as an absolute value. What you could do, however, was quantify the point at which people recognised differences. In other words, the smallest *perceptual discrimination* people are capable of making. You could do this by calculating a function of changes in the physical intensity itself. Let us say, for example, that I put a weight in your right hand and its physical intensity is 100 grams. What is its perceived intensity? There is, of course, no pure mathematical answer. So, suppose I start putting weights into your left hand, one by one – 101 grams, 102, 103, and so on. The question becomes, 'At what weight can you perceive a difference (or discriminate) between the two weights?' Thanks to Fechner, we know the answer. On average it is when the weight in your left hand is 1/30th (or 3.33%) heavier or lighter than the weight in your right (or, in our example, when the weight in your left hand is 103.33 grams or more). Fechner called this perceived change in intensity a 'just noticeable difference' (or JND) and it constituted a quantitative measure of perceived intensity.

Fechner was able to measure the JND across a range of sensory functions and to graphically represent the relationship between physical and perceived stimulus intensities in each case. He also demonstrated that the relationship between physical and perceived intensity could *always* be expressed via a single mathematical formula. In truth, this law was anything but perfect. Nonetheless, Fechner's psychophysical experiments had clearly shown that:

EXERCISE
HEADS, SHOULDERS, KNEES AND TOES

Can you quantify your sense of touch? Some areas of the human body are more sensitive than others. The differences in sensitivity can change your perception of your everyday interactions with the world.

Blindfold a friend (ask them first!). Find a selection of household objects of different size, shape and texture (for instance, a kitchen spatula, an apple, a paintbrush and a toilet roll tube). Gently press each item onto different parts of their body.

Can your friend identify the objects? Are some areas of the body more sensitive than others? Do their guesses differ depending on the part of the body? Which area of the body produced the most accurate results?

the content of the psychological world could be manipulated by controlling the stimuli presented to it;

while such content might actually represent a subjective 'distortion' of the physical world, such distortion was nevertheless carried out (by our physiology) in a mechanical and lawful fashion;

the content of the psychological world could be shown to have a lawful and quantifiable relationship with the content of the physical world.

Other important work on counting and measuring psychological qualities was occurring at roughly the same time. Perhaps the most notable was the development of mental and intelligence testing procedures, via the work of **Francis Galton** (1822–1911) in Britain (see Chapter 22), **Alfred Binet** (1857–1911) in France (see Chapter 22) and America, and later **William Stern** (1871–1938) in Germany.

However, despite the careful scientific applications of these quantitative measures, the methods were still closely tied to the social concerns of the time. This can be illustrated by psychology's approach to education and personality testing in the late 1800s.

Quantifying intelligence

In the nineteenth century, like never before, large groups of children were brought together in academic environments (in some countries school attendance became compulsory by law). As a result, differences in ability among children started to become clear and apparent. This also brought to light children who had difficulty keeping up with schoolwork. These children did not always possess obvious physical problems. Feeblemindedness was introduced as a term to describe such children (Rose, 1985). There was a broader social concern that, if not tackled, the issue of feeblemindedness could become more problematic, threatening social stability and progress. At this time, abilities and deficiencies alike were considered to be inheritable (a genetic trait). There was a growing fear that feeblemindedness would become more prevalent in the lower social classes than the middle social classes (particularly because they were thought to reproduce much more than middle/ upper classes). In response to this, professionals and politicians became more motivated to examine and assess the population, in order to protect and manage it effectively.

Therefore, psychology needed an approach which observed the quantifiable actions of the children and inferred their underlying psychological abilities. Initial approaches involved medical examiners seeking to identify physical signs that could indicate feeblemindedness. These attempts were largely unsuccessful. Physical signs alone could not adequately explain the phenomena.

In the early twentieth century, the French government appointed Alfred Binet and Theodore Simon to develop a method to detect sub-normality in children, including feeblemindedness. In 1905 they devised and published their first series of intelligence tests and age norms for intelligence. The development tests had a significant effect on the establishment of psychology in Western Europe and the United States, and they were quickly adopted in Britain after being translated into English in 1908. The Binet and Simon tests were brought to the attention of the London County Council in 1909, which resulted in the appointment of a psychologist, Cyril Burt (1883–1971), to administer those tests to children joining schools, to identify children who were *mentally defective* (a term that had come to replace feeblemindedness).

While psychological testing and assessment, in Britain, began primarily as a means of identifying a specific problem, feeblemindedness, which was seen as a national concern, it soon expanded into a field that sought to study variation in the population as a whole. Work began on the standardisation of tests. The psychological research sought to develop tests to identify not only problems or weakness but also exceptional ability, and to grade the entire population of children to establish what constituted average performance. As you can see, the quantifying and measurement approach in psychology was politically popular. However, there was some objection that reliance on objective tests was oversimplifying complex issues, such as supposed mental defectiveness. In time, this would become a problematic issue for psychology (see Critical Psychology). This opened the door to the social scientific model being incorporated.

CRITICAL PSYCHOLOGY

DID YOU KNOW THE EUGENICS MOVEMENT BEGAN IN ENGLAND?

While **Eugenics** is commonly associated with Adolf Hitler and Nazi Germany, the idea and term were actually first coined by English psychologist and statistician Francis

(Continued)

Galton (1822–1911). In pursuit of a measure of ability, Galton became interested in individual differences in the population. In particular, he became concerned with the spread of 'feeblemindedness' and an advocate of state-directed selective breeding to identify and promote exceptional ability (positive eugenics). This also meant eradication of weak genetic material (negative eugenics). Galton founded the British Eugenics Society in 1907.

Meanwhile, in Nazi Germany, eugenics was implemented in a sinister way. An extreme case of this was in the selective killing of children who had been identified as disabled. This had ramifications for German researchers in the field of developmental psychology, such as Hans Asperger (1906–1980).

Asperger was one of the first to identify autism as a distinct condition. However, the dissemination of his research was likely to have been heavily influenced by the Nazi's eugenics regime. Asperger was well aware that the lives of his young patients were at stake. Therefore, it has been suggested that his findings emphasised the beneficial symptoms of autism, such as autistic children as 'mini-professors'. This also meant refraining from focusing on potential impairments. However, the nature of Asperger's relationship with the Nazi regime continues to be an area of contention and historical debate to this day (see Suggestions for Further Reading).

WHAT DO YOU THINK?

If you read some of Asperger's work today, would you find it trustworthy? Would it provide a complete account of autism?

2.3.3 Bridging the gap

This distinction (between the social and natural sciences) was popularised by the historian **Wilhelm Dilthey** (1833–1911). Dilthey offered clear advice to psychology. First, he acknowledged that humans and human events both possess important physical properties. As an example, your brain is a physical object and its physical properties are going to be pretty important if you want to think. However, observing the physical brain alone may only give an indication of what your actual thoughts and cognitions are. While psychology cannot avoid our physical or somatic properties (the latter means 'of the body'), Dilthey warned that:

> explaining human actions is fundamentally different from explaining physical events. A woman shooting a man is a physical event. However, understanding the event in human terms involves more than tracing the path of the bullet and showing how the bullet caused the man's death. We need to know why she shot the man, not just how she did so. (Leahey, 2004: 248)

Introduction to quantitative research

Fife-Schaw, C.

CONTENTS

AIMS OF THIS CHAPTER

This chapter is about the idea of quantification as used in psychological studies and it explains why psychologists might want to use numbers to test hypotheses and develop theories. It covers some of the basic ideas surrounding hypothesis testing and describes the traditional categories of measurement used in psychological science. This traditional categorisation system is important for understanding how to conduct good research but is also key to making decisions about how to analyse the data generated by a study. The chapter also briefly describes some of the challenges to this orthodox view.

KEY TERMS

approximate value	mutual exclusivity
continuous variables	population
discrete variables	real limits
exhaustiveness	replication
falsifiability	sample
hypothetico-deductive method	type I error
measurement	type II error

2.1 **INTRODUCTION**

Many of the nineteenth and early twentieth century pioneers of psychology thought that psychological phenomena were in principle no different from any other phenomena in the natural world and that they therefore ought to be open to scientific study in ways similar to those used by biologists and physicists. Sigmund Freud, probably the most famous psychologist of them all, was convinced that by systematically observing his patients, much like a biologist observes plants and animals, he could generate scientific theories about why people do what they do. Although Freud's theories have subsequently been criticised for not being good scientific theories – more on what a 'good scientific theory' is later – he nonetheless felt that following the principles of scientific investigation used in other disciplines would be the best way forward, and this would certainly be better than sitting around speculating on people's behaviour.

Deciding on what counts as 'science' and what is 'scientific' is not quite as straightforward as it might first seem and there is a vast literature on the philosophy of science which attempts to pin these things down. For the early psychologists the model of good science was physics, where careful and ostensibly objective observations were made which allowed physicists to produce theories which in turn led to predictions or hypotheses which could be tested by making observations in the future. If these observations produced data consistent with the hypotheses we would be more inclined to believe the theories that generated the hypotheses in the first place. If many different sets of observations and experiments produced data consistent with a theory we would conclude, by a process of induction that the theory is probably true and applies both now and in the future. A classic example would be the relationship between the orbits of the moon and the earth and the size and timing of the tides in the oceans. Once scientists were able to predict the orbits of the earth and the moon and measure tidal heights accurately they observed the correlation between the phase of the moon and the size of the tide, and they were able to induce 'laws' linking the tides to the phases of the moon which allowed them to produce tide tables that have helped save countless thousands of lives since.

While this seems a much more reasonable way to establish knowledge than wise men (for historically it was usually men with women's views being largely ignored) speculating on the nature of life, the universe and everything it has its problems as a model of good science. Perhaps the most fundamental is that induction works on the basis that what has happened in the past – that is, when we were making our observations – will happen in the future and there will no be exceptions. The particular observations we make in our studies lead us to general 'laws' or theories. Sir Karl Popper (1963) introduced a very important idea – falsifiability – which points out that a single counter example to a theory can render a theory either totally wrong or in need of serious modification. The classic example used is that of the naturalist who is studying swans and notices that in a lake all the swans are white. From this a proposition is induced that all swans are white and as the naturalist continues to travel and continues to see white swans this firms up the belief in the proposition which is gradually edging towards the status of a 'true' theory. If, however, the naturalist went to a lake and saw a single black swan then the proposition 'all swans are white' can no longer be true and has thus been falsified.

For Popper the thing that distinguishes scientific theories from non-scientific ones is that scientific theories produce propositions or hypotheses that are at least in principle falsifiable. If they are stated in such a way that any observation would be consistent with the theory (a charge that was levelled at many of Freud's theories) then the theory cannot make useful predictions and thus should not be treated as scientific. If I came up with a theory that said that people who were punished harshly when they were children might commit violent crimes when they are teenagers this would be essentially unfalsifiable. If I find a violent teenage criminal who was not harshly punished that would not challenge my theory, and neither would finding adults who had never committed violent crimes as teenagers who had nonetheless been punished harshly as kids. If I recast the theory to say that harshly punished children become violent teenagers this would become potentially falsifiable, as the finding of single harshly punished person who had gone through their teenage years non-violently would falsify the theory. This is almost certainly not a true hypothesis and you might ask whether this requirement for potential falsifiability severely limits the possibility of asking interesting questions. It can in certain circumstances, but in this example it would be perfectly reasonable to rephrase the theory to predict that early harsh punishment increases the likelihood of later teenage violent criminality. Here there is a possibility of falsification since if the proportion of violent teenagers is higher among the less harshly punished the proposition will have been falsified.

A second problem with induction is that in practice scientists rarely start their work with no prior expectations about what it is that they are hoping to find out. Popper calls these expectations 'conjectures' and the argument is that scientists do not really sit around waiting to observe relationships between just any sets of phenomena; they go out intentionally to study something and have some implicit theories (conjectures) that guide what questions they ask and how they will make their observations. In my punishment example I presumably looked at this because I had a hunch that harsh parents produced violent teenagers. In setting out to study this I would have to decide on what counted as harsh punishment in childhood and I would have to decide which crimes counted as violent ones and collect observations accordingly. Deciding on what counts as harsh punishment involves me in making a range of quite subjective and historically time-bound judgements. In the eighteenth century, for instance, children could expect to be physically chastised by a whole range of adults pretty much as a matter of course, and even adults could be subjected to floggings by their betters for what we would now regard as relatively minor transgressions; harshness is therefore a relative concept. The point here is simply that the process of induction rarely if ever proceeds without there being some element of subjective input from the scientist; it is not the entirely neutral and objective process that early psychologists hoped for.

Popper's requirement that theories produce hypotheses that are potentially falsi-fiable is still regarded by many as the mark of a good scientific theory, but it is focused on proving theories wrong rather than on knowing when we are right or how to choose between two competing theories that try to explain the same thing. The most common approach used in psychology today is to combine inductive pro-cesses acknowledging the potentially subjective aspects of this in what has come to be known as the hypothetico-deductive method. In the hypothetico-deductive method predictions or hypotheses are formally stated and subjected to some form of empirical test. Often this will be in the form of an experiment (Chapter 3), a quasi-experiment (Chapter 4) or it could be in an observational study (Chapter 14). The precise technique used is not important but what is important is that deduc-tions are made about the theory that generated the hypothesis based on the results of this test. If the study data are consistent with the hypothesis (the predictions) this is good news for the theory. If they are not then this casts doubt on the theory.

The hypothetico-deductive method is in fact really a process since no single test of a hypothesis would usually be enough to establish whether a theory is true or totally false. Various different studies are conducted and if the body of evidence in favour of the theory builds up over time it is more likely that we will believe that it is worth keeping. If the various studies produce negative or mixed results for the theory we will probably want to reject it or at least revise it. We then need to come up with a new/revised theory – possibly by induction, possibly by intuition – and develop new tests of the hypotheses generated by this new or revised theory. Thus the process is an iterative one and the hope is that, provided the quality of the research is high, we will gradually end up with theories that seem to survive all fair attempts to falsify them (see Figure 2.1). Thus repeating studies – replication – is a valuable scientific activity even if it may not seem as exciting as conducting a com-pletely new study. We never get to a point, however, where we know for certain that our theory is definitely true and will be so for all time and in all circumstances, but the weight of evidence supporting it will lead us to *act as if* to all intents and purposes it is true.

There are critics of the hypothetico-deductive approach and of falsification. Strict falsificationists would expect scientists to abandon theories in the face of *any* theo-retically inconsistent observations and the evidence is that quite often they do not. For example, had early hydrographers abandoned their tide tables the first time that their tidal height predictions were wrong marine navigation would be a much more hazardous activity than it is now. The basic premise of tidal theory, that the phase of the moon determines the height of the water over the seabed, is regarded as

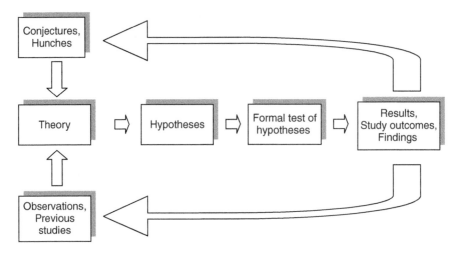

Figure 2.1 The cycle of induction and deduction in the hypothetico-deductive approach

essentially correct, but tidal height is also influenced by other things like atmospheric pressure – when there is high pressure the sea is squashed onto the seabed – which was not recognised initially. It would have been a big mistake to reject the 'phase of the moon causes the tides' theory outright on the basis of this theory-inconsistent evidence. The theory just needed modification. So, while the possibility of falsification is always desirable we need to be wary of rejecting theories outright too early – they may be partially correct.

2.2 STATISTICAL INFERENCE AND HYPOTHESIS TESTING

Whenever we run an empirical study like an experiment or an observational study we will almost always be studying a sample of people (or animals, or dyads or whatever the focus of the study is) rather than observing all members of the population. For my theory predicting that early harsh punishment increases the likelihood of later teenage violent criminality I will not be able to study all teenagers from the UK, let alone the rest of the world, so I will inevitably have to draw on a sample of teenagers and hope to make valid inferences about all teenagers based on my findings from this sample. I will nonetheless want to draw conclusions about all teenagers and not just the ones I have studied so I will have to find some way of saying how confident I am in my inference that what I find in my particular sample of teenagers – whether my hypothesis should be rejected or retained – should be applied to the population of all teenagers.

Box 2.1 On confusing terminology in statistics books: populations and samples

In the section on statistical inference I referred to getting samples from populations and wrote about this in the sense of you getting a sample of people from the relevant population and getting them to participate in your study. This is what most people understand when taking samples of things and most of us are aware of the idea of samples of members of the public being asked questions in polls in order to gauge 'public opinion'. In many statistics books you will see the terms 'sample' and 'population' used in a somewhat more precise way. Strictly speaking, inferential statistical tests make inferences about a population of *scores* on some variables from the sample of *scores* on these variables. The sample of people you have in your study generates a sample of scores on the variables of interest and they might produce a different set of scores had you tested them on another day. This may seem like a very subtle point, and for many purposes it makes no difference to what you will do, but there are occasions when the same sample of *people* will generate multiple *samples of scores*, so be aware of this distinction.

One way to improve my confidence is to make sure that my sample of teenagers is very large for, as we find out in Chapter 9, the closer in size the sample is to the size of the population, the more confidence we can have in any conclusions we draw from the sample data. However, increasing the size of the sample is both costly, eventually prohibitively so, and after a point the added confidence brought about by increasing the sample size ever further is not that great – how much more confident will I be if I study 1.1 million teenagers than if I study just one million? To get over this problem statistical inference tests have been developed that allow us estimate how confident we can be in accepting or rejecting a hypothesis.

The classical statistical inference tests proceed by identifying two kinds of hypothesis relating to a study – the null hypothesis and the alternative hypothesis. The null hypothesis is what the inference tests actually test and this appears slightly odd at first sight. The null hypothesis in an experiment is the statement that the independent variable (the thing we manipulate in the experiment – see Chapter 3) has *no effect* at all on the dependent variable (the thing that the independent variable is supposed to influence) *in the population*. In a correlational study the null hypothesis would normally be that two variables are not associated, or correlated, with one another *in the population*. In my punishment study the null hypothesis is that there is no difference in the likelihood of criminality between harshly and less harshly punished teenagers *in the population*. It is sometimes casually referred to as the 'no effect' hypothesis. Note that what happens in the *sample* is not what we are really interested in. The null hypothesis is usually referred to as H_0.

The alternative hypothesis is our 'hunch' hypothesis: that the independent variable does indeed affect the dependent variable *in the population* or that two variables are correlated with one another *in the population* – that harshly punished children are more likely to become criminal teenagers *in the population*. However, this is only one hypothesis in a range of possible alternative explanations about what is actually going on in our studies and we cannot treat our preferred alternative hypothesis as absolutely true even if we reject the null hypothesis. In an experiment, for example, it may be that some third, unmeasured variable affects both our independent and dependent variables but we were simply unaware of it. The alternative hypothesis is referred to as H_1.

It is easier to show that a hypothesis is false than it is to show that a hypothesis is true. As we saw from the work of Popper on falsifiability there is a philosophical argument that says that we can only ever prove that something is not true: we can never show that something is absolutely true. It is for this reason that inference tests focus on testing the null hypothesis. If we can show that the 'no effect' null hypothesis is not true then there is something going on and an alternative hypothesis, hopefully our preferred hypothesis, may be a more accurate reflection of reality. We never end up saying that our preferred hypothesis is true, however, as it has not been tested directly.

Statistical inference tests will tell us how confident we can be that we have made the right decision when we make our judgement about the null hypothesis. If you think about it, there are two kinds of mistake or error we could commit when we make this decision.

A type I error would have occurred if you rejected a true null hypothesis. This is where you conclude that the independent variable did affect the dependent variable when, in fact, it did not. This can happen when, by chance, you allocate people who were already high scorers to one condition in your experiment and low scorers to another. When you measure scores on the dependent variable, the difference between the conditions is due to the fact that the people were different before you started, *not* because the independent variable had any effect. In terms of correlational analyses, type I errors occur when you say that the two variables were related to one another when, in fact, they were not.

Most common statistical tests give you an estimate of the probability of having made a type I error. They do this by using information about the size of relationships between the observations you have made, the size of the sample and the design of your study. If the probability of having made a type I error is high then you should not throw away the null hypothesis just yet. If the probability is very low (conventionally less than 0.05, a 1 in 20 chance) then it is probably safe to reject the null hypothesis, in which case some other alternative hypothesis must be true, quite possibly your preferred alternative hypothesis but not necessarily so.

The probability of making a type I error will never be exactly zero; that is, there is no chance of being wrong about rejecting the null hypothesis, since your data will have come from a sample and you do not know whether there are exceptional cases that you are unaware of in the unsampled part of the population.

A type II error occurs when you fail to reject a false null hypothesis. You conclude that the independent variable has no influence on the dependent variable when it actually does. This happens sometimes because the size of the treatment effect is very small and hard to notice in your sample. It can also happen when you get the opposite of the example given for type I errors. Here, by chance, you allocate people who were already high scorers on the dependent variable to the treatment condition that actually lowers scores and vice versa. The effect of the experiment is to level up the two groups so that there is now no difference between treatment groups on the scores and you accept the null hypothesis of 'no differences' between groups. In fact, the independent variable had a big effect but your sampling obscured this. With correlational designs, type II errors have occurred when you conclude that there is no relationship between your two variables when, in fact, there is. If you publish such 'non-findings', then it may discourage people from investigating a potentially important effect in the future.

Estimates of the likelihood of having made these errors allow us to have varying degrees of confidence in making inferences about what is happening in the population from what is happening in our samples. To estimate these probabilities we obviously need to have our measurements in the form of numbers, and it is partly because of the need to get good estimates of the confidence we can have in making inferences that so much effort has been devoted to developing good numerical measures of the variables we are interested in. Chapter 9 deals with statistical inference and hypothesis testing in much more detail, but in the next section we look at ways in which measurements are conceived.

2.3 QUANTIFICATION AND LEVELS OF MEASUREMENT

It is often incorrectly assumed that 'proper' scientific studies have to involve numbers in some way or another. This is partly a function of the need to quantify our confidence about inferences we make from sample-generated findings (the probabilities of making type I and type II errors) but as you will see from Part 3 of this book it is perfectly possible to advance knowledge and develop useful theories without recourse to numbers. While there are many aspects of the research process that do not involve measurement using numbers and, indeed, some fields of enquiry where explicit measurement is avoided altogether, the majority of current research studies in psychology do involve it in some form.

Measurement here is defined as the assigning of numbers to objects, events or observations according to some set of rules. Sometimes these numbers will be used just to indicate that an observation belongs to a certain category or has a certain quality; at other times these numbers will mean that the observation has more of some property than an observation that is given a lower number. These observations could be generated directly by the research participants (e.g. people's ratings of certain stimuli) or by the researcher by, for example, observing the participants' behaviours in different situations. For many studies, whether a research hypothesis stands or falls will depend on how well the key concepts have been measured, independently of whether or not it is a worthy hypothesis. It is also the case that before we can construct grand psychological theories we must first be able to measure and describe things in these theories validly and with reasonable accuracy (Cattell, 1981).

In much of psychology we have to measure psychological properties indirectly because we have no direct access to the mental constructs we want to measure. It is a straightforward matter to measure length and we can do this fairly directly by offering up our measuring instrument (e.g. a ruler or tape measure) to the object we want to measure. However, in the case of IQ, for example, we can only infer levels of intelligence from tests that ask people to solve problems of varying difficulty. We assume that people who solve more of the more-difficult problems are more intelligent than people who get them wrong, but we cannot yet see intelligence in any more direct way than this. The existence of something called intelligence is itself a hypothesis and the debate about what IQ tests *actually* measure has often been a heated one. While few people would argue about what a ruler measures, the quantities measured by many psychological measurement instruments are more open to debate and much more obviously depend on the theoretical perspective of the researcher than is perhaps the case in the physical sciences.

This does not mean that psychological measurements are arbitrary or of little value. A great deal of effort has been expended in establishing the reliability and validity of psychological measures over the last century. There are now libraries of well-validated tests for all sorts of psychological phenomena which can be used very effectively as long as the manuals are used appropriately. Chapter 7 outlines the principles involved in test construction and development commonly used in psychology.

While many established tests exist, psychologists are often confronted by the need to create their own measures to deal with the specific problems they have. This may be because nobody has yet developed a test for the particular kinds of phenomena they are interested in. It may be that they are measuring something which has not been measured before or, perhaps, that the existing tests are too cumbersome for their purposes. In these cases more attention has to be paid to the precise meaning and nature of the new measures.

It goes without saying that the goal is always to measure things as well as possible but there are often trade-offs that have to be made. Measurements that demand lots of time and effort from participants may induce fatigue and boredom that may simply introduce unwanted 'noise' into the measurements. On the other hand, measurements that are very simple and quick to make can be crude and inaccurate. Ultimately judgements have to be made as to whether the measurements are 'good enough' for their stated purposes.

2.4 CLASSIFYING MEASUREMENTS

Whether you use a ready made measure or create your own, you will need to know what class of measurement you have used, as how you classify a measurement will have an impact on the kinds of numerical analyses you can perform on the data later on. S.S. Stevens (1946) proposed that all measurements can be classified as being of one of four types. This system has become dominant within psychology and no methods textbook would be complete without describing it. There are, however, other important alternative conceptualisations of measurement such as those of Luce *et al.* (1990) and Adams (1966) and objections to the way psychologists think (or rather, do not think) about their measures (see Box 2.2). Stevens' classification remains the best known but it is only one way of thinking about measurement.

2.4.1 Nominal/categorical measurements

Nominal or categorical measurements (variables) reflect qualitative differences rather than quantitative ones. Common examples include categories like yes/no, present/absent, pass/fail, male/female or Conservative/Liberal/Labour. When setting up a categorical measurement system the only requirements are those of mutual exclusivity and exhaustiveness. Mutual exclusivity means that each

---

Box 2.2 Are we deluding ourselves about our measures? A word of caution

The beginning of this century has seen a challenge to the orthodoxy on measurement presented in this book coming most notably from Joel Michell (e.g. Michell, 2000). Michell's arguments are highly detailed philosophical ones and it is difficult to represent them fairly in a short space; however, a key idea in his work is that in the rush to appear to be 'hard' scientists like physicists, psychologists have failed to consider some fundamental questions about what they are assuming when they attempt to measure psychological attributes. When coming up with a quantitative measure of some attribute psychologists are assuming that the attribute concerned has a quantitative structure, yet this is rarely, if ever, tested even though Michell argues that this is in principle an empirical question that is open to investigation. When trying to measure job satisfaction, say, psychologists rarely stop and ask the question, 'Is job satisfaction really a quantitative attribute?' – it is already assumed to be quantitative and indeed it is necessary to assume this if the quantitative test scores are to have any sensible meaning. The focus usually moves directly on to how satisfaction test scores are quantitatively related to other variables even though the quantitative nature of satisfaction was never actually established. Satisfaction could be a categorical state for instance – people could be

---

Box 2.2 (Continued)

either satisfied or not and there might be no sense in which someone who has been satisfied can become even more satisfied. A crude example might be that you could be 'satisfied' (in the sense of being satiated) after having a very big meal but having another big meal would not make you any more satisfied. Also, it is far from proven that dissatisfaction is the dimensional opposite of satisfaction.

The existence of a test that produces numbers does not establish that the attribute being 'measured' is really quantitative and a lot of bogus 'science' may be built on flawed measurement assumptions. Although Michell speculates about why psychologists and psychometricians have not bothered with establishing that given attributes are quantitative, doing this is not a simple matter. Conjoint measurement theory (e.g. Luce and Tukey, 1964) offers one of the few ways to address this at the moment and Michell (2000) gives a nice illustrative example. Other methods have proven illusive yet the need for them is clear – we should not be attempting to present psychology as a rigorous science that measures quantitative things if we cannot establish that the things we want to measure are actually quantitative in the first place.

---

observation (person, case, score) cannot fall into more than one category; somebody cannot, for example, both pass and fail a test at the same time. Exhaustiveness simply means that the category system should have enough categories for all the observations. For example, when asking people about handedness, a category system of left-handed and right-handed would not be exhaustive since some people might say they were ambidextrous.

A key feature of categorical measurements is that there is no *necessary* sense in which one category has more or less of a particular quality: they are simply different. Males are different from females (at least at some biological level) and northerners come from the north and southerners do not. Sometimes, however, this will seem like an odd assumption. Surely 'passing' something is better than 'failing', for example? Well, yes, in certain cases this would be so, but this would depend on what your *a priori* theory about the measure was. If you believed that 'passing' was more valuable and reflected more positively on somebody (that they were more intelligent, paid more attention, etc.) then that is a matter for you as a researcher; the use of a pass/fail category system itself does not inherently contain any notion of greater or lesser value.

To allow us to use computers to help with analyses, we commonly assign numbers to observations in each category. For instance we might assign (code) a value of 1 for males and 2 for females. The important point is that although females have a numerically larger number there is no suggestion that being female is somehow better or has more value. Again, this can cause confusion, especially as computers deal only with numbers and not their meanings. You could, for instance, ask the computer to calculate the mean sex of your participants and it might come up with a figure like 1.54; clearly this is pretty uninformative.

Although the categories of a categorical variable do not necessarily have any value associated with them, this does not mean that they cannot reflect some underlying dimension in some circumstances if this is what you want to do. As an example, you might classify people you are observing in the street as 'young' or 'old' because you do not want to approach them to ask their ages directly. While this is likely to be an extremely rough and ready classification, this system implies an underlying continuous dimension of age even though we place people in only two categories.

The criteria for categorical measurement do not rule out the possibility of having a category of 'uncategorisable'. If you did have such a category you would satisfy both the mutual exclusivity and exhaustiveness criteria, but if there were a lot of 'uncategorisable' observations then the value of the categorisation system might be questionable. How useful is it to have a variable on which the majority of observations are 'uncategorisable'? This can only truly be answered with reference to the research question.

2.4.2 Ordinal level measures

This is the next level of measurement in terms of complexity. As before, the assumptions of mutual exclusivity and exhaustiveness apply and cases are still assigned to categories. The big difference is that now the categories themselves can be rank ordered with reference to some external criteria such that being in one category can be regarded as having more or less of some underlying quantity than being in another category. A lecturer might want to rank order their students in terms of general ability at statistics. They could put each student into one of five categories: excellent, good, average, poor, diabolical. Clare might fall into the 'excellent' category and Jane into the 'good' category. Clare is better at statistics than Jane, but what we do not know is just how much better Clare is than Jane. The rankings reflect more or less of something but not *how much* more or less.

Most psychological test scores should strictly be regarded as ordinal measures. For instance, one of the subscales of the well-known NEO PI-R personality test (Costa & McCrae, 1992) is designed to measure extroversion. Like other extroversion measures this one allows us to infer levels of extroversion from responses to items about self-reported behaviours and preferences, it does not measure extroversion in any direct sense. Years of validation studies have shown how high scorers will tend to behave in a more extroverted manner in the future, but all the test can do is rank order people in terms of extroversion. If two people differ by three points on the scale we cannot say *how much* more extroverted the higher scoring person is, just that they are more extroverted. Here the scale intervals do not map directly on to some psychological reality in the way that the length of a stick can be measured in centimetres using a ruler. The fundamental unit of measurement is not known.

Since many mental constructs within psychology cannot be observed directly, most measures tend to be ordinal. Attitudes, intentions, opinions, personality characteristics, psychological wellbeing, depression, and so on, are all constructs which are thought to vary in degree between individuals but tend only to allow indirect ordinal measurements. This conclusion is a point of contention for many researchers, since one of the implications of assuming these measures to be ordinal is that some parametric statistical tests should not be used with them. Indeed even the humble mean is not used appropriately with ordinal measures (the median is a more appropriate measure of central tendency). This sits uneasily with what you will see when you read academic journal articles, where you will regularly find means and parametric statistics applied to ordinal measures. We will deal with this issue later in this chapter (see also Chapter 9).

2.4.3 Interval level measures

Like an ordinal scale, the numbers associated with an interval measure reflect more or less of some underlying dimension. The key distinction is that with interval level measures, numerically equal distances on the scale reflect equal differences in the underlying dimension. For example, the 2°C difference in temperature between 38°C and 40°C is the same as the 2°C difference between 5°C and 7°C.

As we will see later, many psychologists are prepared to assume that scores on psychological tests can be treated as interval level measures so that they can carry out more sophisticated analyses on their data. A well-known example of this practice is the use of IQ test scores. In order to treat scores as interval level measures, the assumption is made that the 5-point difference in IQ between someone who scores 75 and someone who gets 80 means the same difference in intelligence as the difference between someone who score 155 and someone who scores 160.

2.4.4 Ratio scale measures

These differ from interval level measures only in that they have a potential absolute zero value. Good examples of ratio scales are length, time and number of correct answers on a test. It is possible to have zero (no) length, for something to take no time, or for someone to get no answers correct on a test. An important corollary of having an absolute zero is that, for example, someone who gets four questions right has got twice as many questions right as someone who got only two right.

The ratio of scores to one another now carries some sensible meaning which was not the case for the interval scale.

The difference between interval and ratio scales is easiest to explain with an example. Say we measure reaction times to dangers presented to people in a driving simulator. This could be measured in seconds and would be a ratio scale measurement, as 0 seconds is a possible (if a little unlikely) score and someone who takes 2 seconds is taking twice as long to react as someone who takes 1 second.

If, on average, people take 800 milliseconds (0.8 of a second) to react we could just look at the *difference* between the observed reaction time and this average level of performance. In this case the level of measurement is on an interval scale. Our first person scores 1200 ms (i.e. takes 1200 ms longer than the average of 800 ms) and the second person scores 200 ms (i.e. takes 200 ms more than the average). However, the first person did not take six times longer (1200 ms divided by 200 ms) than the second. They did take 1000 ms longer, so the *interval* remains meaningful but the ratio element does not.

True psychological ratio scale measures are quite rare, though there is often confusion about this when it comes to taking scores from scales made up of individual problem items in ability tests. We might measure the number of simple arithmetic problems that people can get right, for instance. We test people on 50 items and simply count the number that are correct. The number that are correct is a ratio scale measure since four right is twice as many as two right, and it is possible to get none right at all (absolute zero). As long as we consider our measure to be *only* an indication of the number correct there is no problem and we can treat them as ratio scale measures.

If, however, we were to treat the scores as reflecting ability at arithmetic then the measure would become an ordinal one. A score of zero might not reflect absolutely no ability at all, as the problems might have been so difficult that only those with above average ability would be able to get any of them right. It would also be a mistake to assume that all the items were equally difficult. Twenty of the questions might be easy and these might be answered correctly by most people. Getting one of these correct and adding one point to your score would be fairly easy. The remaining items may be much more difficult and earning another point by getting one of these correct might require much more ability. In other words, the requirement that equal intervals between scores reflect equal differences in ability is not met and we should strictly speaking treat the scores as an ordinal measure of ability. Even when doing this we are assuming that ability is a quantitative entity though we will not have established this directly (see Box 2.2).

As will hopefully have become clear, there is a hierarchical distinction between the types of measurement described in this section. Nominal measures give information on whether two objects are the same or different, ordinal measures add information concerning more or less of a quantity, interval measures add information on the distance between objects and ratio scale measures add the absolute zero standard.

2.5 DISCRETE VERSUS CONTINUOUS VARIABLES

Many types of measurement result in indices that consist of indivisible categories. If someone scores 13 on our 50-item arithmetic test, they might have scored 14 on a better day but they could never have scored 13½. The score 13½ was not possible as the individual questions can be marked only correct or incorrect. Measures like this are called discrete variables since they can have only discrete, whole number values.

Some variables like height and time are referred to as continuous variables since they could be divided into ever smaller units of measure. We could measure height in metres, then centimetres, then millimetres, then micrometres, then nanometres and so on until we got to the point where our measuring instrument could not make any finer discrimination. There are an infinite number of possible values that fall between any two observed values. Continuous variables can be divided up into an infinite number of fractional parts. Ultimately it is the accuracy of our measuring instrument that puts limits on the measurement of continuous variables. If our ruler can only measure accurately to the nearest millimetre we must settle for that degree of precision.

When measuring a continuous variable you end up recording a single figure but this really represents an interval on the measurement scale rather than a single value. It is therefore always an approximate value. If we time someone doing a task to the nearest second, say it takes them 20 seconds, we are really saying that the time taken lies somewhere in the interval between 19.5 and 20.5 seconds. Had it actually taken them 19.4 seconds we would have rounded the time to 19 seconds, not 20 seconds (note: when rounding a number that ends with a numeral 5, round to the nearest even number). Similarly, an elapsed time of 20.6 seconds would have been rounded to 21 seconds. This is shown in Figure 2.2.

In this example we are deliberately recording times only to the nearest second but, in principle, the choice of any measurement tool carries with it a limit to the degree of accuracy that can be achieved and thus the rounding process will have to happen even if we are unaware of it. We will still be reporting a time that corresponds to an interval and not a discrete value. If our stopwatch could record times to the nearest 100th of a second, say, and we recorded a time of 20.12 seconds, this would still mean we were saying that the time taken lies somewhere in the

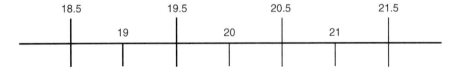

Figure 2.2   Real limits on a continuous variable

interval between 20.115 and 20.125 seconds. These boundary values are referred to as real limits.

It is always desirable to use the most accurate measure practicable. Any calculations done using approximate values necessarily include that approximation in the final result. If you use two or more approximate values in a calculation the scope for misleading results increases dramatically. So it is always preferable to use approximate measures associated with the smallest intervals possible so as to minimise this problem. Although our variables might be theoretically continuous, like time and length, the act of measurement always reduces the measure to a discrete one.

2.6 MEASUREMENT ERRORS

The goal of all researchers should be to minimise measurement errors. Put formally, these are the discrepancies between the observed value of your measurement and the 'true' value. There is a simple formula to illustrate this:

observed score = true score + error

The 'error' term may be positive or negative. Obviously it would be nice to have the error term as small as possible. If you were measuring people's heights with a ruler marked off in inches then you could probably only measure accurately to within half an inch. Having a ruler marked off in millimetres would give rise to much more accurate measurement and finer distinctions between individuals could be made (see the previous section). In a similar way, psychological measures should strive to make as fine a set of distinctions between people as possible. Assuming your measure is valid, it makes sense to have more points on your measurement scale rather than fewer.

This holds true only so long as you believe the individual points on the scale carry the same meaning for all participants. When it comes to ratio scale and interval level measures, such as time, this is not a problem. You could measure time to the nearest millionth of a second, though you might find the timing equipment a bit expensive. For most psychological research, timing to the nearest millisecond is accurate enough. Things get much more difficult when you have ordinal measures, and problems crop up when you try to label individual responses on your ordinal scale. For example, say you have an attitude statement about a political issue and you would like people to tell you how much they agree or disagree with it. You could provide a five-point scale as follows:

1   strongly agree
2   agree
3   neither agree or disagree
4   disagree
5   strongly disagree

Most respondents would know what they were required to do with such a response scale. While you could not be certain that all those who 'agreed' had agreed to the same extent, you would probably feel reasonably happy that they did not intend to tell you they had very strong views on the topic. Similarly it is probably safe to assume that they are not entirely equivocal about the issue either.

If you gave this question to several hundred people in a survey, however, you would find that so many people had the same score on the item that it did not discriminate very much between people. In this situation you might want to increase the number of response options available. A seven-point scale could be used and it would be reasonably easy to label the response options. You might even think a nine-point scale was appropriate, though labelling all the points might prove more of a challenge. Indeed you could simply label the end- and mid-points, leaving the rest unlabelled.

Why not opt for a 29-point scale instead? This would give even greater discrimination, surely? The answer, unfortunately, is no. People would now have trouble working out where they should indicate their response on the scale. Should it be the 18th or the 19th point or even the 20th? Such a response format increases the scope for confusion and will introduce, rather than reduce, measurement error. There is also the problem that we still do not know that all people responding at point 19 agree to the same extent. Multi-point ordinal scales can introduce an unfortunate illusion of precision.

2.7 CHOICES OVER LEVELS OF MEASUREMENT

In the previous and very traditional section I have implicitly suggested that ratio and interval level measurement is to be preferred over ordinal or categorical measures. The reason for this is that in most cases a good ratio scale measure will contain more information about the thing being measured than a good ordinal measure. You would probably rather have temperature reported in degrees Celsius than on a scale of very cold, cold, neither warm nor cold, warm, hot, very hot. You should always strive for greater accuracy of measurement where possible.

Naturally some kinds of variable are always going to be categorical (e.g. gender) and some are always going to be ordinal (e.g. most scaled psychological measures). In these cases you should not regard your measures as somehow inferior. Whilst it would be nice to think that ultimately we will have much more direct measures of attitudes and personalities, for example, these are not likely for the foreseeable future.

There are some common practices which should be discouraged, however. The most notorious of these is the collapsing of ordinal measures into categorical ones. It is quite common to see researchers take an attitude item with a seven-point agree/disagree response format and collapse the data into a simple three-point scale of agree/uncertain/disagree. This practice degrades the measurement by removing the extremity information. There are three kinds of motive for collapsing data in this way. One is the desire to use simpler statistical procedures; a second is to make graphs and tables clearer; and the third is that you might not believe that your seven-point measure is very accurate or valid. With the ready availability of comprehensive statistics books and computer programs the first problem is easily overcome. While clarifying graphs and tables is an admirable aim it would be desirable to collapse the scores only for this purpose and to conduct statistical analyses on the un-collapsed data. The third justification is also a 'justification' for not using the measure at all! If you doubt the validity or accuracy of a measure then you should think twice about using it in the first place.

2.8 THE RELATIONSHIP BETWEEN LEVEL OF MEASUREMENT AND STATISTICS

Most statistics textbooks present readers with 'decision trees' which help you select the correct statistical test to use providing you know the answers to a number of simple questions about your data and research design. These are very useful, and some are provided in Chapter 9.

These decision trees ask about the level of measurement for your data as well as the nature of the distribution of scores on the measure that you expect in the population from which your sample scores were drawn. The topic of distributions of scores is dealt with in Chapter 9 but the level of measurement issue is relevant here, particularly at the boundary between ordinal and interval level measures.

The attraction of parametric tests, ones that assume something about the distribution of scores in the population (e.g. the t-test, ANOVA), is that there are many more of them than non-parametric tests. They often allow you to ask interesting questions about your data that are not easily answered without using such parametric procedures. To say that your measure is 'only' ordinal, rather than interval level, usually rules out many of these useful procedures. Two views have developed over the appropriateness of treating ordinal measures as interval ones. Those interested in reading more on this debate should see Henkel (1975), Labovitz (1975), Townsend and Ashby (1984), Stine (1989) and Davison and Sharma (1990), among many others.

One view states that, most of the time, providing the quality of an ordinal measure is good, you will arrive at the same conclusions using parametric techniques as you would have using more appropriate non-parametric tests (assuming there was one available). It is argued that while most psychological measures are technically ordinal measures, some of the better measures lie in a region somewhere between ordinal and interval level measurement (see Minium *et al.*, 1993).

Take a simple example of a seven-point response scale for an attitude item. At one level this allows you to rank order people relative to their agreement with the statement. It is also likely that a two-point difference in scores for two individuals reflects more of a difference than if they had only differed by one point. The possibility that you might be able to rank order the magnitude of *differences,* while not implying interval level measurement, suggests that the measure contains more information than merely how to rank order the respondents. The argument then runs that it would be wasteful to throw away this additional useful information and so unnecessarily limit the possibility of revealing greater theoretical insights by using more elaborate parametric statistical procedures.

The more traditional and strict view (e.g. Henkel, 1975; Stine, 1989) says that using sophisticated techniques designed for one level of measurement on data of a less sophisticated level simply results in nonsense. Computer outputs will provide you with sensible-looking figures but these will still be nonsense and should not be used to draw inferences about anything. This line of argument also rejects the claim that using parametric tests with ordinal data will lead to the same conclusion *most of the time* on the grounds that you will have no way of knowing when you have stumbled across an exception to this 'rule'.

The debate on this issue continues. The safest solution, advocated by Blalock (1988), is to conduct analyses on ordinal measures using both parametric and non-parametric techniques where possible. Then, where both procedures lead you to the same substantive conclusion, when reporting parametric test results, you will at least know that you are not misleading anyone. You should be guided more by the non-parametric procedures if the conclusions are contradictory. What would be unacceptable would be to select the statistical procedure that leads to results that support your hypothesis. It is important to be consistent in reporting findings, so you must decide that either your data meet the assumptions for parametric procedures or that they do not.

Ultimately, whether this issue matters depends on the seriousness of making a mistake and who the audience for this research is likely to be. Research on a drug or an intervention that may change people's lives demands the most strict and conservative approach to the analysis. On the other hand, if your research topic is more esoteric and your audience is restricted to researchers in a field that has regularly used (abused?) parametric techniques on ordinal data, then you may find it difficult to get a hearing if you do not report findings in the accepted way.

2.9 CONCLUSION

This chapter has described the main issues surrounding levels of measurement and quantification in psychology as well as briefly looking at the logic behind quantitative hypothesis testing. In time, the research community may come to an alternative system of measurement classifications (cf. the debate discussed above). However, the Stevens system described here remains the dominant one in psychology for the time being. Chapter 9 takes this a step further by looking at the principles of statistical inference in more detail.

2.10 EXERCISES

1 Take three psychological research questions that you are interested in. Can you formulate hypotheses relating to each question that could be tested in a study? What kinds of results would falsify these hypotheses?
2 Think of a psychological variable that you are interested in. Can you create a nominal, ordinal, interval and ratio-scale version of it? If not, why is this?

2.11 DISCUSSION QUESTIONS

1 Should psychologists abandon attempts to mimic the 'hard' sciences? If they did, what would be the implications?
2 Is it going to be possible to find 'laws' of psychology in the same way as we have laws of physics?
3 Are there constructs in psychology which cannot in principle be measured by an instrument on one of Stevens' four measurement levels? Why is this?

2.12 FURTHER READING

All good statistics textbooks explain Stevens' classification system and the relationship levels of measurement and statistics, though few books will go much beyond what has been presented here and in Chapter 9. Many of the key papers on the debate about measurement and statistics have appeared in the *Psychological Bulletin* and are likely to continue to appear in that journal. Chalmers' (1999) *What is this thing called science? An assessment of the nature and status of science and its methods*, 3rd edition, is a classic textbook on the philosophy of science and although it is oriented towards the physical sciences it still gives a good introduction to the philosophy of science.

Introduction to qualitative methods

Eatough, V.

CONTENTS

AIMS OF THIS CHAPTER

This chapter offers an overview of the field of qualitative research in psychology. After reading the chapter you should have some understanding of the following aspects of qualitative psychological research:

- the history and philosophical origins of qualitative research;
- characteristics of qualitative research;
- contemporary qualitative research in psychology.

KEY TERMS

epistemology	reflexivity
human sciences	relativism
meanings	social constructionism
realism	subjective experience

13.1 **INTRODUCTION**

In recent years, psychology has seen the steady development of a range of qualitative research methods. All British Psychological Society (BPS) accredited undergraduate degree programmes offer (at least some) qualitative research instruction alongside training in quantitative methods. It is also the case that the use of qualitative methods at postgraduate level and the number of journals publishing qualitative research is increasing. 2005 saw the formation of the BPS Qualitative Methods in Psychology Section, which is the largest section of the BPS at present (Madill & Gough, 2008).

This chapter aims to provide a broad-brush background to the field of qualitative research in psychology. It does not aim to convince you that qualitative methods are 'better' than quantitative ones (or vice versa). Rather it attempts to show you where qualitative research fits within psychology and its contribution to a versatile psychological 'tool-kit' (Hayes, 2000, p. 165) which assists psychologists to ask different questions about the topics they study.

For qualitative psychologists, a key interest is 'people's grasp of their world.' (Ashworth, 2008, p. 4). In other words qualitative researchers are interested in people's subjective experience as well as the resources available to them to make sense of and understand their world. This interest can lead to a focus on how people *construct* their world (including the relationships they have and the objects they encounter) through the social, cultural and linguistic practices they are born into. Alternatively, it can lead to an emphasis on how it is through our perceptions and the meanings we attribute to events that we come to understand our personal and social world. Reicher (2000) classifies these different approaches as *discursive* and *experiential* respectively. The following chapters will introduce you to specific methods which are underpinned by these different (yet overlapping) approaches to how people understand their worlds.

13.2 **SHORT HISTORY OF QUALITATIVE RESEARCH**

From its development in the late nineteenth century to the present day, psychology has endeavoured to be a natural science discipline. This means it has adopted both the methodology (logical positivism) and the methods of the natural sciences (hypothetic-deductive). Perhaps not surprisingly, the emerging discipline of psychology was dazzled by the achievements and insights of the natural sciences and sought to emulate these by adopting their methods. For example, the systematic manipulation of variables under controlled experimental conditions. Yet, from the outset, there has been a persistent and significant challenge to this conception of psychology and this section traces this challenge through the history of the discipline.

Importantly, some of the early psychologists you are probably familiar with as belonging to the experimental tradition were open and responsive to the value of understanding subjective experience as well as the need for appropriate methods to investigate it. It might surprise you to know that Wilhelm Wundt (1832–1920) who established his experimental laboratory in 1879 at the University of Leipzig, Germany, envisaged psychology as 'a hybrid discipline, representing a combination of a natural science and a human science' (Kendler, 1987, p. 27). Early psychologists such as Wundt and William James (1842–1910) were interested in the conscious mind and individual subjective experience rather than behaviour and sought to establish psychology as a science of experience. Wundt's introspectionist method trained research participants in the technique of self-observation and aimed to get close to their experience of the phenomenon being studied. His experiments were not natural science experiments and he was doubtful whether experimentation could provide the answers to all of psychology's questions (Danziger, 1990; Schneider, 1998).

The philosopher and psychologist, William James, understood experience holistically and described it metaphorically as a rhythmic stream of consciousness. To understand the richness and complexity of our experiential life required techniques which focused on concrete experiences in their entirety rather than breaking them down into discrete parts. For James, studying the particularities of concrete experiences was an essential first step for a proper understanding. Like Wundt, he used introspectionist methods as well as analysing documents such as personal letters, autobiographies and diaries. James recognised that understanding the subjective life of individuals required the fledgling discipline of psychology to be creative and flexible in how it investigated its subject matter.

Similarly, Edward B. Titchener (1867–1927) recognised the value and legitimacy of qualitative research and advocated a psychology which drew on its strengths as well as those of quantitative research; namely both *description* and *measurement*. Questions that began with 'how much?' left 'what?' and 'how?' questions unanswered. Thus, Titchener proposed experiments which had both qualitative and quantitative dimensions:

> The experiments are complementary, each sacrificing something, and each gaining something. The qualitative experiment shows us all the detail and variety of the mental life, and in so doing forbids us to pack its results into formulae; the quantitative experiment furnishes us with certain uniformities of the mental life, neatly and summarily expressed, but for that very reason must pass unnoticed many things that a qualitatively directed introspection would bring to light.
>
> Titchener, 1905, p. vi

Almost half a century later, both Solomon Asch (1907–1996) and Gordon Allport (1897–1967) echoed these voices. Asch believed that psychology's willingness to treat its subject matter (people) like the subject matter of the natural sciences (e.g. rocks) meant that most psychology paid insufficient attention to developing methods which harnessed and made use of our particularly human qualities – language and self-reflection:

> In their anxiety to be scientific, students of psychology have often imitated the latest forms of sciences with a long history, while ignoring the steps these sciences took when they were young. They have, for example, striven to emulate the quantitative exactness of natural sciences without asking whether their own subject matter is always ripe for such treatment, failing to realize that one does not advance time by moving the hands of the clock. Because physicists cannot speak with stars or electric currents, psychologists have often been hesitant to speak to their human participants.
>
> Asch, 1952/1987, pp. xiv–xv

Like James and the Gestalt theorists, Allport took a holistic stance and was a strong proponent of *idiographic* research which studies the individual person in all her/his complexity and richness. In today's terminology, people are embodied, situated and historical beings who cannot be studied in isolation from the social and material world in which they live out their lives. Also like James, Allport saw the value of using a variety of documents as important sources for acquiring knowledge about subjective life. Many more familiar names (e.g. Piaget, Mead and Kelly) could be mentioned to support the claim that, historically, a significant minority of psychologists were committed to a psychology which viewed subjective experience as worthy of study.

More recently, the 1970s saw a number of critical perspectives develop in opposition to mainstream psychological research and which proposed that qualitative methods were both more relevant and naturalistic ways to understand people. It was argued that people should be studied in their everyday social settings and a shift away from measurement and quantification was needed if psychology was to advance (Gergen, 1973; Harré & Secord, 1972). However, many of these writers were less concerned with developing alternative methods than they were with highlighting the limitations of a discipline which drew its methods almost solely from the natural sciences. A notable exception was the US psychologist Giorgi who, working from within the humanist tradition, developed the descriptive phenomenological method as a way of going beyond a theoretical critique of quantitative research (Giorgi, 1970, 2009). During the 1980s discourse analysis emerged as a specific qualitative method with its particular focus on the role of language and discourse for understanding psychological phenomena. By the 1990s psychologists interested in qualitative approaches engaged with grounded theory and the different forms of narrative analysis as well as seeing the development of new psychological research approaches such as Interpretative Phenomenological Analysis (IPA) (Smith, 1996). The contemporary picture of qualitative research 'is one of heterogeneity, with qualitative research best conceptualized as a fuzzy set.' (Madill & Gough, 2008, pp. 254–255).

Hopefully, this brief sketch has illustrated the historical thread that can be traced with respect to alternative ways of thinking about psychology's subject matter. We turn now to the philosophical origins of these different ways of thinking.

13.3 PHILOSOPHICAL ORIGINS OF QUALITATIVE RESEARCH

13.3.1 Human sciences for human kinds

Underpinning qualitative research is the belief in a human sciences tradition with its own set of methods and techniques to answer those questions which are not amenable to quantitative research perspectives. Many of the things that make us human are not receptive to measurement and objective mathematical precision. Furthermore, with respect to human beings, the universal laws that might be established are likely to be very small in number. Psychology from a human sciences perspective aims to understand human actions, human intentions and the meanings people impute to these actions and intentions in the context of their lives. To paraphrase the philosopher Wilhelm Dilthey (1976), 'No real blood flows in the knowing subject' when examined from a natural science perspective.

As human beings there are certain types of behaviour and actions which we can exert on ourselves and others. For example, we have a tendency to classify people into different groups on a wide range of characteristics such as gender, ethnicity and social class (not to mention more psychological classifications such as high/low IQ, neuroticism, levels of self-esteem, and so on). We are affected by these classifications not least because we experience ourselves in particular ways because of them. Such classifications *matter* and are meaningful for us. We interact with them in ways that natural kinds do not because they are not aware of how they are classified. This does not mean that human kinds are not real:

> Human kinds definitely are real, but it is a reality in which they themselves are deeply involved. It is a reality of which they are a part ... Human psychological beings require sociocultural, biological and physical reality for their existence, but they are not entirely determined by their sociocultural, biological and physical constitution.
>
> Martin & Sugarman, 2001, p. 194

This view of people as human kinds not natural kinds (Hacking, 1995; Van Langenhove, 1995) encourages qualitative researchers to concentrate on the things that make us human – the tangled, messy and multifaceted aspects of experiences – so that research findings connect to peoples' attempts to make sense of their lives and which cannot be captured in experimentation for example. In terms of real-life relevance and applicability, one might argue that there is little in common between the frustration induced in laboratory-based aggression experiments and the intense slow burning rage felt by a woman who, whilst chopping vegetables, contemplates stabbing her husband.

13.3.2 Epistemology, realism and relativism

Epistemology is a philosophical term concerned with how, and what we can say we know about the world; in other words, epistemological issues deal with the nature of knowledge. Realism and relativism are epistemological perspectives and they refer to the different ways that psychologists approach these questions both intellectually and in a more practical sense in terms of the methods they use.

The differences between realism and relativism are best understood as a continuum with psychologists positioning themselves and the perspectives they subscribe to at various points along it. At one end of the continuum is naive realism whilst at the other is radical relativism. Positions in between include critical realism and less extreme forms of relativism. However, as you might imagine, there is sometimes disagreement over where particular perspectives are situated:

> The classification of epistemological perspectives into distinct positions necessarily requires a degree of simplification and homogenizing of perspectives. A label such as 'realist' or 'relativist' is unable to capture the true complexities and ambiguities that characterize the various epistemologies. Furthermore, the categorization of any particular method(ology) is itself a matter of judgment. Most approaches combine a number of features that are compatible with more than one epistemological position. In addition, most methods evolve over time and may modify their epistemological assumptions accordingly.
>
> Willig, 2001, p. 149

Furthermore, it is worth remembering that very few psychological researchers would adopt the extreme ends of the continuum, with most falling somewhere in between.

Naive realism refers to the perspective that we have unmediated access to the world: there is an uncomplicated relationship between our perceptions of the world and the world itself. Acquiring knowledge of the world is a matter of discovering what is already 'out there'. No qualitative researcher (indeed, very few quantitative researchers) is likely to commit to such an extreme form of realism.

In stark contrast, radical relativism proposes that there are multiple competing knowledges of the world and that these knowledges are socially constructed solely from available linguistic and discursive resources. Very simply, the only reality we can know is one which has arisen out of the language we use. A small but significant number of qualitative researchers support the view that our psychological and social worlds are derived from nothing more than the linguistic resources available to us.

Alternatively, critical realists adopt a more or less middling and pragmatic position. They acknowledge the existence of an objective and real world but argue that our access to it is mediated through a lens of social, cultural and historical practices which includes the linguistic and discursive practices we are born into. Thus, a critical realist position believes in an 'extra-discursive' world which consists of objects and entities which have an independent existence and which is partially accessible to us. Earlier in the chapter it was mentioned how the qualitative approaches you will be introduced to in the following chapters can be described as either *experiential* or *discursive*. In terms of the realist–relativist continuum, experiential methods are located variously between critical realism and realism whilst discursive methods line up towards the relativism pole.

13.3.3 **Phenomenology**

Phenomenology is an approach which was very influential in Continental European twentieth century philosophy but less so in the UK which arguably was dominated by analytic philosophy. As a philosophical approach it has influenced a number of qualitative psychological methods (one of the most well-known being IPA (Smith, 1996) which is the focus of Chapter 18) for which the fundamental unit of analysis is experience. Phenomenology is interested in how things *appear* to us through our conscious experience; reality is experiential and we experience the world through a practical and meaningful engagement with it.

'To the things themselves' is the rallying call of Husserl, whom many people consider to be the founding father of phenomenology. The aim of the phenomenological project is to describe and understand the 'things themselves' as they are meaningfully lived. This requires what we think we know already about the phenomenon (such as preconceptions and presuppositions) to be put aside so that it can be examined 'as it appears to our flesh-and-bone selves' (Varela, 1999, p. 267). Contemporary qualitative researchers recognise the impossibility of carrying out a piece of research in a neutral fashion, arguing that there is no 'view from nowhere'. Thus, throughout the research they strive to make themselves aware of the values and beliefs they bring to the process and reflect on how they might have influenced it.

Phenomenology aims to clarify, illuminate and elucidate the meaning of people's experiences in the context of what is often referred to as the lifeworld. The lifeworld is an important concept because it refers to the world we live in and experience – a world of mountains, colours, people, objects and sounds – rather than a world of scientific abstraction. This is the world in which we think, feel and practically engage with, both by ourselves and with other people. It is a subjectively lived world rather than the world of objective science. This does not mean that phenomenology rejects modern science but it does argue that the scientific world presupposes the experienced world:

> [Phenomenology] attempts to show that the exact, mathematical sciences take their origin from the lived world. They are founded on the lifeworld. The exact sciences are a transformation of the experience we directly have of things in the world; they push this experience to a much higher level of identification, and correlatively they transform the objects we experience into idealized, mathematical objects. It may seem that the exact sciences are discovering a new and different world, but what they are really doing, according to phenomenology, is subjecting the ordinary world to a new method. Through this method, the exact sciences merely increase the knowledge we have about the world in which we live; they provide a greater precision in our dealings with things, but they never abandon or discard the world that is their basis. Such sciences are nested within the life world; they do not enter into competition with it.
>
> Sokolowski, 2000, p. 147

Therefore, for phenomenology, there are not two worlds with one being more real than the other.

13.3.4 **Hermeneutics**

Hermeneutics is the established name used to describe the skills of interpretation, a practice which began with the interpretation of biblical texts. Much later, Enlightenment thinkers set about systematising this practice into a general method of understanding (Moran, 2000) whilst contemporary qualitative researchers use it to denote how understanding is a matter of interpretation. Humans are by nature 'self-interpreting beings' (Taylor, 1985) and how we ascribe meaning to an event, person or object is always filtered through an already existing experiential knowledge. This experiential knowledge is acquired through living our lives in a particular place and time and as such it is constrained by cultural context and historical specificity.

Thus, there are many ways to interpret life's happenings and how you do so is dependent, at least in part, on your particular perspective. For example, Gallagher (2004) suggests, somewhat provocatively, that science is simply one perspective one can subscribe to:

> The practice of science is itself hermeneutical. That is, scientists make interpretations, and their interpretations are biased in a very productive way by

the scientific tradition to which they belong, and the specific kinds of questions that they ask. Explanation is no less interpretation than understanding. The interpretation of quantitative data, for example, relies on certain developments in the history of science, and on qualitative judgments amongst scientists.

Gallagher, 2004, p. 164

Qualitative researchers of a hermeneutic persuasion do not subscribe to a false objectivity, rather they recognise how reality is contingent on sociocultural practices, individual psychological contexts and human agency. Psychological research (like all science) is a social and interpretive practice (Fowers, 1998) and psychologists 'are not, and cannot become, the neutral dispassionate observers that both empiricism and rationalism would have us be' (Packer & Addison, 1989, pp. 19–20)

None of this should be taken to mean that all perspectives have equal value. Rather it means that when we examine existing understandings we need to have both an open mind and a questioning stance: open to alternative ways of looking at things and willing to question the underpinnings of particular standpoints. Indeed, throughout our daily lives, several interpretations can often be applied to a single human action. Even when supplied with most (if not all) the facts of an event, several conclusions may be drawn. Imagine a group of psychologists of different persuasions who witness an aggressive interaction between two men and are asked to explain what is going on. The social psychologist is likely to focus on situational factors whereas the individual differences theorist might emphasise stable personality traits.

13.3.5 Social constructionism

Social constructionism is a body of postmodern thinking and practice which has had considerable influence on qualitative researchers in psychology. Discursive psychologists (see Chapter 20) whose epistemological underpinnings are relativist in orientation (see previously) are its strongest advocates while more experiential researchers tend to adopt a weaker version of its principles. Burr (1999) describes the main features of social constructionism as:

- a critical approach towards taken for granted knowledge and a corresponding concern with historical and cultural specificity;

- a belief that knowledge is constructed between people;

- a conviction that language has a privileged status in constructing the world.

The first feature clearly rejects the naive realist position described above, arguing that what we come to know of the world is not acquired through objective neutral

observation which uncovers the world as it really is. Importantly, social constructionism challenges us to question this knowledge for the assumptions that lie behind
it and the implications it has for how might people live their lives. For example, the
ways we classify and divide people and objects say more about the specific cultures
we live in than about any real divisions:

> Social constructionism bids us to seriously question whether the
> categories 'man' and 'woman' are simply a reflection of naturally occurring
> distinct types of human being. This may seem a bizarre idea at first, and of
> course differences in reproductive organs are present in many species.
> But we become aware of the greyness of such categories when we look at
> practices such as gender reassignment surgery and the surrounding
> debate about how to classify people as unambiguously male or female. We
> can thus begin to consider that these seemingly natural categories may be
> inevitably bound up with gender, the normative prescriptions of masculin-
> ity and femininity in a culture, so that that whole categories of personhood,
> that is all the things it means to be a man or a woman, have been built upon
> them.
>
> Burr, 2003, p. 3

Once we begin to question the nature of our knowledge about the world it is clear
that categories (e.g. what it means to be a child, a drunk, a mad person) changes over
time in response to shifting social and cultural practices.

The second feature acknowledges the intersubjective nature of knowledge. Social
constructionists argue that our knowledge of the world comes not from the world
as it really is, but arises out of our daily ongoing social interactions with one another
as well as the social practices we engage in. In other words, knowledge is co-
constructed through exchanges between people. For example, psychologists tend
to produce a different sort of knowledge from that produced by biologists or even
sociologists. This is because they are, in many ways, different communities
with different practices which are constituted out of a shared stock of concepts and
meanings.

This perspective highlights the third feature of social constructionism – the
importance of language and its constructive nature. Traditional psychology views
language as a vehicle which simply describes and reflects reality in an unproblematic manner. In contrast, social constructionists propose that it is through language,
talk and discourse that we fashion our worlds and identities. We cannot pre-date
language because it is language which brings us into being, we are born into a pre-
existing language. For the social constructionist, our emotions and desires are not
an essential part of human nature which would be there whether or not we had
language; rather it is through language that they are available to us and hence
structure our experience.

13.3.6 **Narrative**

In recent years, qualitative psychologists have shown an increasing interest in narrative and the role it plays in our lives. Narrative researchers point to how our lives are storied, meaning 'we are born into a narrative world, live our lives through narrative and afterwards are described in terms of narrative' (Murray, 2008, p. 111). This fundamental inclination for story telling allows us to impose a coherence and order on the events in our life, assume temporal continuity and define our sense of self.

Narrative theorists think about narratives in different yet overlapping ways. Gergen and Gergen (1986) state that narratives are social constructions that arise out of linguistic interactions enabling us to make sense of the world. Sarbin (1986, p. 301) ascribes a more ontological status to our narrative capacity: 'We are always enveloped in stories. The narrative for human beings is analogous to the ocean for fishes.' Thus, although Sarbin recognises the socially constructed nature of narratives, he does not simply reduce them to linguistic output but argues that the storied form of our lives is part of what makes us human.

Hermeneutics has also played an important part in the development of narrative psychological research. Qualitative researchers have drawn from the philosophical thinking of Paul Ricoeur, in particular his ideas about the relationship between time, meaning making and narratives:

> Human time ... is neither the subjective time of consciousness nor the objective time of the cosmos. Rather, human time bridges the gap between phenomenological and cosmological time. Human time is the time of our life stories; a narrated time structured and articulated by the symbolic mediations of narratives.
>
> Zahavi, 2008, p. 106

Narrative theorists also stress how it is through narrative that we gain self- knowledge and come to understand ourselves. The events and happenings in our lives (especially those which are most significant and/or disruptive) are placed into a 'life story' in which we have the starring role – that of both narrator and main character. Our sense of self is constituted out of the stories of our life and it is through these stories that we come to know our self. However, our starring role is supported and enhanced by the presence and actions of others. For example, the beginning of our story is put in place for us by others and how our stories develop and move along various paths is a consequence of us being embedded in a web of relationships and shared community:

> [W]e are never more (and sometimes less) than the co-authors of our own narratives. Only in fantasy do we live what story we please. In life, as both

> Aristotle and Engels noted, we are always under certain constraints. We enter upon a stage which we did not design and we find ourselves part of an action that was not of our making.
>
> MacIntyre, 1984, p. 213

To conclude this section, it has introduced you to several related epistemological perspectives which underpin to varying degrees the specific qualitative approaches explained in the subsequent chapters.

13.4 CHARACTERISTICS OF QUALITATIVE RESEARCH

13.4.1 The 'essence' of doing qualitative research

Many qualitative researchers talk about research being a 'voyage of discovery' (Finlay & Evans, 2009), an 'adventure' (Willig, 2001). By this they mean that qualitative researchers deliberately adopt an attitude of openness towards the topics they investigate. Their focus on understanding people as embodied situated persons means that they expect to encounter unknowns and contradictions along the way. They do not seek to exclude these, rather they are to be accounted for in order to do justice to the phenomenon being investigated. This is one of the reasons why qualitative psychologists do not (typically) make predictions and test hypotheses. Open research questions are preferred in the attempt to achieve a more holistic understanding. Nonetheless, it should be remembered that no matter how open a research question is, it will inevitably exclude the exploration of some dimensions of the phenomenon one is interested in.

The act of carrying out a qualitative study is often described as a 'craft' (Miles & Huberman, 1994). This points to how qualitative research is a set of skills and techniques which are to be used flexibly and creatively. Qualitative researchers aim for a position of immersion, informed curiosity and careful receptivity to the research process. This is in contrast to their quantitative counterparts whose methods require detachment, prediction and control. Inevitably this leads to different sorts of questions being asked, and qualitative researchers argue that the more interesting questions are the ones which are not easily apparent nor which lend themselves readily to measurement:

> Progress in science is won by the application of an informed imagination to a problem of genuine consequence; not by the habitual application of some formulaic mode of inquiry to a set of quasi-problems chosen chiefly because of their compatibility with the adopted method.
>
> Robinson, 2000, p. 41

Qualitative researchers aim to remain open to uncertainty and ambiguity throughout the research process because their research designs are grounded in the reality of peoples' lives which, more often than not, are disordered, multifaceted and complex. This requires them to be resourceful throughout the research process as well as responsive to situations that might arise.

All of the above means that the laboratory is not a suitable context for carrying out qualitative research. The preference is for studying the topics of interest in the context in which they occur or at least in environments which are familiar to participants rather than unknown and artificial. For instance, researchers using interviews often prefer to carry these out in participants' homes or a venue of the participants' choice. Of course, naturalistic settings and an emphasis on real-worldness comes at a price; what is gained in terms of richness and relevance is at the expense of control and certainty.

Qualitative researchers are usually not very much interested in the quantity and measurement of a particular phenomenon but the qualities and features which make a phenomenon what it is. Qualitative researchers collect languaged data (Polkinghorne, 2005) rather than numerical data. It is worth noting that a considerable amount of quantitative data begins as languaged data (e.g. verbal reports) and is transformed into numbers. Qualitative data is analysed by employing various systematic techniques which reflect the epistemological underpinnings of a particular approach. These techniques are described in detail in subsequent chapters. Table 13.1 provides a useful summary of the main features of qualitative and quantitative research.

13.4.2 Evaluating qualitative research

Qualitative researchers, like their quantitative colleagues, are concerned with evaluating the quality, validity and value of their empirical work. However, given that the specifics of the two approaches are very different (see Table 13.1), it makes no sense to employ the same set of evaluative criteria. As Coyle (2008) suggests, this would be akin to evaluating the music of opera using the criteria applied to heavy metal or folk.

At present, there is some debate within the qualitative community as to which criteria are most useful and appropriate for gauging the quality of their work. For example, given the range of qualitative approaches with their different epistemological and philosophical orientations, is it possible to have a single set of criteria? Even if the answer is 'only with difficulty', it is important to agree a set of criteria which act as guidelines for what constitutes best practice in qualitative research. However, a note of caution is needed:

> Simply following guidelines cannot guarantee good research; qualitative research is not simply a descriptive science but also relies on the capacity to

Table 13.1   Typical features of qualitative and quantitative research

Features	Qualitative	Quantitative
Key concepts	Experience, meaning, understanding, intersubjectivity, reflexivity	Prediction, probability, reliability, replication, operationalisation
Designs	Flexible, evolving, open, not prescriptive	Controlled, formal, predetermined
Sampling	Small, purposive selection, theoretical sampling	Representative, large, control groups, random selection
Methods	Participant observation, semi- and un-structured interviews, focus groups, diaries, documents	Experiments, surveys, structured observation and interviewing
Data	Words, interview transcripts, naturally occurring conversations, documents, media text	Numbers, measuring, counting, quantifiable coding
Tools	Research diaries, audio visual equipment, software analytic packages	Test scores, scales, psychometric measures
Data analysis	Systematic operations like coding, clustering and abstraction, iterative, inductive	Statistical, deductive, takes place at the end of data collection
Strengths	Detailed and in-depth, participant led, meaningful, high in ecological validity	Standardised procedures, fast, researcher control, possibility of large sample sizes
Limitations	Difficulty extrapolating to populations, unwieldy complex data, time consuming	Low ecological validity, participants constrained

evoke imaginative experience and reveal new meanings – and this core quality is not easily captured by check-list criteria.

Yardley, 2008, p. 239

Several sets of guidelines have been developed and published in recent years (see for example, Elliott *et al.*, 1999; Yardley, 2000, 2008) with some emphasising scientific rigour while others highlight the creativity and personal tone of most qualitative research. Others try to address both and a good example of this is the '4 R's criteria' (Finlay & Evans, 2009). These include *rigour, relevance, resonance* and *reflexivity* with researchers attending to each one differentially depending on the stage of the research as well as the aims and values of the researcher.

In brief, *rigour* assesses whether or not the research has been carried out competently and systematically. Is the write-up of the research understandable and decisions with respect to sampling, depth/breadth of analysis set out clearly? Are the interpretations suitably contextualised, justified and plausible? *Relevance* refers to what sort of contribution the research makes to the existing body of knowledge. Good research makes a difference in some way, whether that is practically or theoretically. *Resonance* addresses whether or not the findings of the research chime with and 'speak' to the reader. Much qualitative research deals with events which not only have personal significance for those taking part in the research but which resonate with many people's experiences. This criterion is related to trustworthiness of the findings (Polkinghorne, 1983). Many issues are raised under *reflexivity* so this is dealt with in a separate section below.

13.4.3 **Reflexivity**

Being a qualitative researcher means being a reflexive researcher. It involves adopting an attitude of self-awareness and active reflection throughout the research process. More specifically, it means thinking about the 'baggage' that you bring to the process and questioning how it has shaped and moulded the research. Willig (2001) talks about personal and methodological reflexivity. The former refers to how the researcher should examine her/his background, values and beliefs for how they might have influenced the research question(s) asked or the interpretation of the findings. Additionally, being personally reflexive might involve examining how the research has changed the researcher. The latter requires researchers to examine their assumptions about the nature of knowledge and how these, for example, will have led to particular questions being asked whilst others were excluded.

Engaging in the reflexive process is not something that is simply done before and at the end of the research. Indeed, you might not be aware of some assumptions until you are part way through the research. For instance, during the data analysis, you may become aware of a dormant preconception because something in the data brings it to the fore. Two practical ways of ensuring that reflexive attention is ensured throughout the research is by keeping a reflective diary and maintaining an audit trail (Shaw, 2010). The diary should be used to make personal notes of decisions made, problems encountered and how they were resolved, and more personal notes reflecting on their preconceptions and how they are having an effect on the research. The audit (or paper) trail is a complete record of the procedures carried out throughout the data analysis. A thorough and full audit trail means that an observer should be able to examine it and see how you moved from the raw data to provisional claims and interpretations to final conclusions.

13.5 **MAPPING OF CONTEMPORARY QUALITATIVE RESEARCH**

At the start of this chapter, I mentioned how the different qualitative approaches can be mapped onto an experiential-discursive dimension (Reicher, 2000). This is the simplest mapping and other researchers have proposed more substantive ones (Madill & Gough, 2008; Willig, 2001). Another way of illustrating the different approaches is to show how the differences lead to different sorts of research questions and different research designs. Box 13.1 provides examples of the types of research questions the approaches ask while Box 13.2 illustrates how different methodologies lead to different aims for a research study. For example, researchers committed to a phenomenological methodology will approach the research with a very different set of assumptions and concerns from those of a researcher who adopts a discursive approach.

The following chapters will describe in detail some of the qualitative methods of data collection and data analysis available to researchers. Here I will briefly map these methods to set the scene. The first four deal with the different ways qualitative researchers collect and elicit data whilst the remaining chapters describe four widely used data analysis approaches.

Box 13.1   Types of research questions

Interpretative phenomenological analysis (IPA):
What does it mean to become a parent?
What is it like to live with Parkinson's disease?
How does an athlete come to terms with a career-threatening injury?

Grounded theory:
How does a person become a member of a terrorist group?
How do people become proficient at playing a musical instrument?
What is the role of punishment in the teacher–pupil relationship?

Discourse analysis:
How do mediators construct 'conflict' in their interactions with clients?
How does racist discourse operate in the workplace?
How do women talk about and negotiate the menopause?

Content analysis:
What are the dominant themes in young children's storybooks?
What do nurses think when patients become angry?
How do newspapers report anti-social behaviour?

Box 13.2 Researching the topic of binge drinking using different qualitative approaches

IPA: The IPA researcher aims to elicit a rich detailed description of the lived experience of binge drinking for participants. Questions aim to draw out examples of specific times participants carried out binge drinking, prompting for details which keep participants focused on the concrete rather than the general. Other questions will tap into the personal meanings attached to the experience of binge drinking.

Grounded theory: The grounded theory researcher aims to understand the processes and mechanisms involved in binge drinking. Questions will focus on the specific times and contexts in which binge drinking takes place and how they manage their binge drinking over time. For example, the specific social situations that facilitate or inhibit binge drinking.

Discourse analysis: Discursive psychologists examine how people 'do binge drinking' in their talk allowing them to construct particular versions of reality and manage account-ability. This includes identifying aspects of talk such as rhetoric. The Foucauldian analyst focuses on the cultural discourses (eg binge drinking is a normal part of British youth culture vs. binge drinking is a sign of a self-indulgent degenerate society) available to people, and how they take up and challenge these in their lives.

Content analysis: The content analyst collects qualitative data and analyses it by establish-ing common categories in the data or by converting it into quantitative data, e.g. num-bers. Most commonly the content analyst will have a number of predetermined categories and they will examine the data to see how many examples of each category can be identified in the data. So, in the case of binge drinking they may use the catego-ries 'normal behaviour' and 'helps to relax'.

Chapter 14 introduces you to observational methods. Observation is an everyday skill which is employed systematically in qualitative research. These methods can be used by themselves or alongside other types of data collection such as interviews. Often observation is used to examine how people behave in specific situations and the social roles and cultural practices which influence behaviour. However, more controlled and artificial settings can also be the focus. The role of the researcher can range from being an active participant observer to a non-participant one.

Chapter 15 describes another form of data collection, that of interviewing. Interviews are a widely used and very flexible data collection tool, and like observation they can be used with other techniques. Research interviews are a form of conversation (another everyday skill we have) which have a specific structure and purpose. The researcher must be a careful and attentive listener in order to gather knowledge about the topic they are interested in. Interviews sit on a continuum from structured through to semi-structured and finally unstructured. Often the metaphor of a traveller on a journey is used to describe the role of the interviewer.

Chapter 16 addresses the use of diaries and self-narratives as another way to elicit qualitative data. Diaries and narratives have a particular concern with identity issues and emphasise the storied nature of human life. Moreover, they are very good at capturing changes over time. Diary records are very versatile in terms of structure and what participants are required to do. For example, participants might be asked to keep a daily record of a specific aspect of behaviour such as recycling, or school teachers might be requested to keep a weekly diary for a term on how they managed classroom behaviour. Self-narratives often involve asking people to relate or write their life story; for example, asking a person for the story of how they became a priest or doctor or criminal.

Chapter 17 discusses the use of focus groups in qualitative research. They are often described as focus group interviews or group interviews and involve one or more discussions between selected participants on a topic chosen by the researcher. The topic to be discussed can be presented in a number of different ways: through a film or video, other media such as newspaper reports or advertisements, vignettes, or a set of questions. The method can be particularly useful for conducting research with children where games, role-play and drawing exercises can be used with good effect.

Chapter 18 introduces interpretative phenomenological analysis (IPA) which is an approach to data analysis grounded in phenomenology and hermeneutics. IPA adopts an explicitly idiographic stance aiming to understand in detail personal and lived experience. IPA studies typically use semi-structured interviews because researchers are interested in the real-time sense-making of individuals with respect to a particular aspect of their experience. To put it another way, IPA is concerned with the ways in which people ascribe meaning to the events in their lives. Often, IPA studies address events of change, transition and disruption. Through its hermeneutic focus IPA pays particular attention to the role of the researcher in co-creating these meanings.

Chapter 19 describes the grounded theory approach originally developed in sociology in the late 1960s. It aimed to develop new theories of social processes which were 'grounded' in the data and which emerged from a number of systematic analytic steps. So the process is one from the local and particular to the abstract and conceptual. This early formulation has now given rise to several 'versions' of grounded theory known as social constructivist (Charmaz, 2006), methodical hermeneutic (Rennie, 2000) and postmodern (Clarke, 2003). A key feature of grounded theory approaches is the use of theoretical sampling which develops theory by using new samples of data as the analysis progresses.

Chapter 20 gives an account of the two forms of discourse analysis, which are discursive psychology and Foucauldian discourse analysis. At the heart of both approaches is the view that language constructs our psychological and social reality. People are born into a specific language and have a finite range of linguistic resources with which to construct their worlds. Discursive psychology regards language as a form of social action through which, for example, people manage their accountability and negotiate their social interactions. Foucauldian discourse analysis emphasises the discursive resources available to people and how such discourses are involved in identity construction and power relations.

Chapter 21 addresses how content analysis can be used both quantitatively and qualitatively. Typically, studies with a content analysis design use language data but then convert it into numbers by identifying recurrent themes in the data. In a quantitative study the occurrence of clearly defined categories will be analysed statistically. In a qualitative study, there will be some counting of categories followed by an interpretive commentary. Often, categories are identified prior to beginning analysis but the category system can be developed after data collection.

13.6 CONCLUSION

In conclusion, qualitative research aims to understand the relations between people, objects and the world they inhabit without losing the complexity of these relations. It should not be regarded as a 'methodological deviation' (Kidder & Fine, 1997) but as a form of enquiry which makes a valuable contribution to understanding the topics of interest to psychologists.

13.7 EXERCISES

Develop a list of research questions on the topic of being single in one's thirties which reflect the various qualitative approaches discussed in the chapter.

13.8 DISCUSSION QUESTIONS

1   How do different qualitative researchers think about the nature of reality?
2   What are the key differences between qualitative and quantitative research approaches?

13.9 **FURTHER READING**

Ashworth (2008) and Van Langenhove (1995) discuss the development of qualitative research and the limitations of experimental psychology respectively. Martin and Sugarman (2001) describe the relationship between hermeneutics and psychology and Zahavi (2008) discusses subjectivity and the self, including ideas about the experiential and narrative self. For those who want to read more about social constructionism and the turn to language, then Burr's (2003) text *Social constructionism* (2003) provides an excellent introduction. Finlay & Gough (2003) offer an accessible and practical guide to issues of reflexivity and reflexive practice.

How to learn, how to study

Burns, T. and Sinfield, S.

We're not born knowing how to study – these learning and studying strategies will help you make the most of the study aspects of university.

Introduction

In this chapter we bring together arguments about learning with an exploration of how to study – and how to study at university. We begin by asking you to examine your past learning experiences – and consider a multi-sensory approach to learning and how to harness this. We explore when, where and how to study – with a focus on how universities organise their teaching and learning; assessment is tackled in Chapters 11 and 12. As always – think: what do I know? What do I need? How will I harness this information to promote my active learning and study success?

Past learning experiences

Before moving on, we'd like you to think back to your own past learning experiences. In particular, think about the conditions that helped you to learn – and the things that got in the way of your learning. Make brief notes to answer the questions below – then read what another student has said.

- Think back to a previous successful learning experience. It does not have to have been at school – it could be learning to drive or sky dive. Why was it successful – why did you learn?
- Now think back to an unsuccessful learning experience. What was it? Why did little or no learning take place?
- Looking over these good and bad experiences of yours – can you sum up: 'Things that help learning to happen' and 'Things that prevent learning'?
- If you wish, use your notes to free write quickly on 'Things that help me learn – and things that stop me from learning'.
- Once you have completed your own thoughts, compare your thoughts with those written by another student, below.

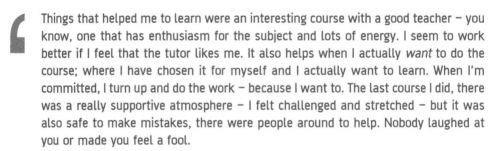

Things that helped me to learn were an interesting course with a good teacher – you know, one that has enthusiasm for the subject and lots of energy. I seem to work better if I feel that the tutor likes me. It also helps when I actually *want* to do the course; where I have chosen it for myself and I actually want to learn. When I'm committed, I turn up and do the work – because I want to. The last course I did, there was a really supportive atmosphere – I felt challenged and stretched – but it was also safe to make mistakes, there were people around to help. Nobody laughed at you or made you feel a fool.

The worst learning experience I had was at school. I had to be there – it was compulsory – but I never really saw the point of it. I just felt so powerless all the time. I never knew what we were doing or why or when or how. It was a nightmare and one of the reasons that I left school the minute I could!

Do you recognise some of yourself in the responses? What might this tell you? One thing we can see is that if we are going to be successful when learning, then we must want to learn: we must be interested and motivated.

On the other hand, what seems to stop people from learning is feeling unmotivated, confused, unhappy, fearful and powerless. These are some of the reasons that compulsory education does not work for some people.

TIP

Whenever you start to study, sit down and write your own personal goals for that course. Put them on Post-its and display them over your desk. Cut out pictures that represent your success to you and stick these up also. Use these to keep you motivated and interested.

What is learning?

Learning is not about the empty student coming to university to be filled with knowledge and wisdom – though some people might wish that it was! Learning is active and interactive; it is a process. Learning involves engaging with ideas – and engaging with other people as they engage with ideas (Wenger-Trayner, 2014). An early author on study skills, Devine (1987), describes learning as a series of processes:

- gathering new ideas and information
- recording them
- organising them
- making sense of and understanding them
- remembering them
- using them.

Learning is about gathering new ideas and information – engaging with and acquiring information from classes, lectures, seminars, tutorials, discussions, practical activities, reading (textbooks, journals, newspapers and more). It is notemaking – recording what is important. We encounter information in many forms, in many places and at different times – we have to reorganise the information to make sense of it for ourselves and remember it. Finally we have to be able to use the information – we have to be able to discuss it with other people and use it in our assignments. Learning also changes us, once truly learned something cannot be unlearned – we have crossed a threshold and become someone slightly different (Land, 2010).

- Before you can forget your lecture or class, don't rush home, go to the canteen and talk about it.
- Get a study partner or form a study group: discuss lectures and seminars. Discuss your reading.
- Write before you know or understand it all.
- Discuss your writing.

Harness a multi-sensory approach to learning

So learning is active and social and it also involves all the senses. If you went to a Montessori primary school, you would already have been encouraged to see, hear, say and do in order to learn effectively; for we learn some of what we see, we learn some of what we hear, we learn when we speak or discuss (when we say) and we learn when we do (when we make something or engage in an activity) – but it is argued that we can learn most when we see, hear, say *and* do. Here we explore visual (sight based), auditory (sound based) and kinaesthetic (touch, feel or movement based) learning.

- *Sight*: to learn by seeing, enjoy learning by reading and by watching television, film or video. Enjoy watching your lecturer and seeing how they convey information – how they show you what is important. Use pictures in your learning and revision activities: draw cartoons and pictures to illustrate your points, draw pattern notes, put in colour, and put in memory-jogging cartoon images or visuals. (See also Chapters 5 and 6.)
- *Sound*: to learn by hearing and speaking, enjoy learning through listening and joining in discussions. You will learn as you explain things to other people. Make audiotapes to support your learning using songs, rhymes and jingles that you write yourself as learning and revision aids. Tape yourself and sing along. Talk yourself through your assignment.
- *Feel*: to harness the kinaesthetic, enjoy practical learning activities, from making something, to performing a science experiment to role-playing. Make charts and patterns of the things you want to remember – role-play ideas or act them out in some way. Care about your subject – find meaning and value in your course.

Activity

Watch, listen, learn: Barbara Oakley has given an interesting TED Talk on 'How to learn' (https:// youtu.be/O96fE1E-rf8). Watch the video and make notes whilst thinking, 'How will I use this information to become a better student?' Reflect: How much of the information did I hear? How much did I see? How much of it did I feel was right?

Studying: when, where and how

 I'm a mum, I work, I've got my parents to look after ... I guess I'm organised!

Studying is more formalised learning – and it tends to be hard work. We are going to explore when, where and how to study and provide you with very practical advice and tips.

When should I study?

I know we are supposed to start work weeks before the deadline, but I usually start two or three days before.

Many students do not start work until a deadline really frightens them – they need the hit of adrenalin to get them over their study fears and into working. The trouble is that whilst adrenalin is great for getting you out of a burning building – it does not help you develop the depth and breadth you need for university level thinking and writing.

 The best tip I ever got was to do at least half an hour's work each day. This has put me on top of all my studies ... And usually once I start I get a little bit more done and I feel so much better.

I know what I should do, I really know ... but I just can't face it.

Studying can feel unbearable, un-do-able, like climbing a mountain. But there is more than one way to face a mountain. For some a mountain is so large and dangerous that they are afraid of it. For some a mountain is an exciting challenge. For some a mountain is just a thing to be tackled sensibly one step at a time. If you normally fear or dread your assignments – change the way you see them. Adopt a 'one step at a time' approach. Look at assignment questions at the beginning of a course. Think about the question before lectures and classes and before you start reading. Break the question down into manageable chunks. Read about one 'chunk' at a time. Write one paragraph at a time – then revise and improve as you do more reading.

 I never seem to feel like studying.

Nobody leaps out of bed in the morning going, 'Wheee – this is the day that I tackle that huge assignment!' So do not rely on feeling like studying. You have to make the time to study – you need a system. Every university student has to work out for themselves just how much time they are prepared to give to their studies – but it should be 35 hours or more each week. You have to decide how much work you are prepared to put in, to get the results – the grades – that you want. Study five days a week – plan and use your time – even when you don't feel like it.

When planning out your time think about:

- *Best time of day?* Are you a morning, afternoon or evening person? Try to fit your study times around your maximum performance times. Work with your strengths.
- *Travel time*: reading on the bus or train is a really effective use of time.
- *Friends and family time*: your studies are important – but most of us would like to have friends and family still talking to us when our studies are over. Help them to help you be a successful student.
- *Housework time*: we need to keep our homes at least sanitary. Watch out though – housework and all chores can become excellent excuses for not working. They become displacement activities – sometimes it feels as though it is easier to completely re-build the house rather than write an essay!
- *Paid work time*: these days we need to earn money whilst we study – we have to work – and still fit in 35 hours of study each week. Sometimes universities help by fitting lectures and other classes into one or two days a week. Beware – this does not mean that all your studying can fit into two days a week! Remember you have to give 12 to 16 hours to classes – and another 20 or so hours to independent study – *each week*. If you cannot do this, you will be in trouble.
- *Rest and relaxation time*: studying is hard work – it can also be very stressful. It is important to get sufficient rest whilst you study and it is useful to build stress relief activities – dancing, exercise, gym, meditation, massage, yoga – into your timetables right at the beginning of your studies.

TIPS

- Find paid work at your university – this helps you be there more.
- Join your university gym – use it at least once a week.

- *Prioritise time*: make lists and prioritise tasks. Keep a diary – note when you are going to read; note which assignment you are writing – when.

- *Study timetables*: timetables give you a strong guide to your work – if you keep to them. But more than that, without timetables you may feel that every time you are not working you ought to be studying. You may not do that studying, but you worry – and this exhausts you. Eventually it may feel that your whole life is work, work, work. Something will have to go – and it could be your studies! Use the timetables at the end of this chapter – plan when you will study – and when you will not study.

Where to study

Everyone deserves a nice place to study, but real life is not always like that; sometimes we just have to adapt to what we have and make it work. Here are some tips about making a study space work for you.

- Negotiate a space with family or flatmates. Creating a study space helps everyone in your life – including you – realise just how important your studies are.
- A good place to study needs light and air – you need to see and breathe – but does not necessarily have to be a completely quiet place. Work out what works for you.
- You will need space to lay out your work, pin up your timetables, deadlines and notes. Have your textbooks out and open.
- Pin up all the new words that you are learning, immerse yourself in your learning.
- Do not tidy your work away. Having your work visible keeps it alive in your mind whereas putting it all away can give the impression that you're finished.
- Have pens and pencils, also highlighters, a stapler and staples, paper clips, correction fluid, Post-its, coloured pens – and all sorts of different sizes of paper. Play around with materials and colour, get an injection of energy and enthusiasm.

Practise being positive: 'Now I am working', 'I enjoy being a student'. Avoid those old negative thoughts: 'I don't want to be here', 'This is too hard'. Negative thoughts have a negative effect – positive thoughts have a positive effect. Give 100% whenever you sit down to study. Act as if you and your studies are important – they are – so are you.

What other students have said:

It felt really good having my own study space. It made me feel like a real student.

I felt that at last I could settle down to some real work.

I felt a bit frightened at first – you know? Like now I couldn't put it off any longer! I'd have to take it seriously.

> Sometimes I use my space to sort of trick myself into working. I think, I'll just sit there for a minute ... Next thing I know I've been working away for an hour and I feel really good.
>
> I felt guilty at having to cut myself off from the kids. It just felt so selfish. I have to work really hard at still giving them some time.
>
> I used to get so frustrated; it was like every time I sat down to work they would start demanding things from me. Now we all sit down to work at the same time – even if they are just crayoning or reading a storybook. This has helped us all feel better.
>
> I still like going to the library to work – but it's great having a proper place for my stuff at home. It really does help.

Experiment with working at home, in the library and when you travel – being a commuter adds hours of study time to your week, if you use it. But whether you want to work in a library or on a bus, you will also need a study space at home.

TIP

If you have children, try to make a family study time – so you all work together.

How to study

University is supposed to be a full-time occupation – using up to 35–40 hours of your time per week. You are supposed to be studying and learning full time, through lectures, seminars, tutorials, the virtual learning environment (VLE) and through your independent study. Here's how:

The lecture

One lecturer plus a large group of students – can be 150 or more. The lecturer is an expert, a researcher at the cutting edge of the subject. The lecturer gives a short-cut to key information – and successful students make notes – and use those notes to seed further reading, thought and writing. Always prepare before you attend a lecture. Always think – what is it about? What do I know already? Why this topic? How will it help me with my assignment?

The seminar

A seminar usually consists of a lecturer plus 10–30 students. A seminar is supposed to seed your thinking and develop your ideas through discussion – it is active learning. Join in the discussions. Prepare beforehand: read, watch or write what you are supposed to.

Learn seminar survival strategies: know how to present your opinions assertively, not aggressively; learn how to interrupt the person who never stops talking; and learn how to draw out quiet people who may actually have much to offer. Don't worry whether people are making friends with you – you make friends with other people.

The tutorial

A tutorial is like the seminar but with one tutor to four or five students. There is definitely no hiding place in a tutorial. You will have to be prepared and you will have to join in.

The VLE

Universities include virtual, blended or e-learning experiences as part of their teaching and learning practices. Find out how your course is going to be delivered – and how to make the most of it. Even though the information is 'virtual' – the work is still real – and the learning is still social and interactive.

TIP

Be prepared to join in with online conversations about the work. If you are expected to post comments or blogs in the VLE – do so; and remember to read and 'like' the comments left by your peers – be supportive, encouraging and friendly. See also Chapter 10.

Independent learning

In the UK we 'read for' our degrees – that is, our thinking and learning is seeded by lectures and seminars – and then we are expected to read and read and read. There is much emphasis on independent learning. That is, you will be expected to follow up ideas in various ways, including reading around a subject, on your own and on your own initiative. For more on academic reading, see also Chapter 4.

TIP

Be an interdependent learner: have a study partner or group.

A beginner's guide to taking control of your studies

This whole book is designed to get you studying in more successful ways, but here are some very practical things to do right now.

Want it: you will not learn anything unless you want to. Know what you want from each course that you are studying. Know how your life will be changed when you reach your goals.

─TIP───

Write your goals on Post-its and stick them up in your study space. Write your learning contract (below) for each course, module or unit that you do.

Get the overview (Chapter 11.1): read and understand the aims and the learning outcomes. Know what you have to do and learn to pass your course – and how you will be assessed.

Epistemology: every course has its own theory of knowledge – what counts as argument and evidence – its epistemology. Make sure you know the what, why and how of all your subjects. Read the journals to get a model of how to argue and write in your subject.

Be positive: just as an athlete will perform better if they think they can win – so a student will learn more if they can adopt positive attitudes; if your motivation runs low, act like a successful student, believe that you can succeed.

Pace yourself: work for an hour – take a break. We concentrate best in 15-minute bursts. When we study we have to get into the habit of regularly recharging our mental batteries to wake up our brains. We can do this by:

- taking a short rest
- changing what we do
- making the task very important
- making the task interesting, stimulating or more difficult.

Prioritise time: be strategic – do first the assignments that carry the most marks or whose deadlines are coming first.

Use time: we know students who sit down to study – out come the pens and paper – they get rearranged. Out come the books and the highlighters – they get rearranged. They go for a coffee. They go for a glass of water. They put one lot of books away and get out another set. They look at the clock – oh good! An hour has passed – they put their materials away. But they have done no work. Before you study – set goals. Afterwards – reflect. Make the learning conscious.

Worry about one assignment at a time: put up a set of shelves in your brain. Put all your different worries on the shelves. Learn to take down one thing at a time and give it your total concentration. When you have finished with that, put it back on the shelf and take down something else.

Be active: listen/read actively, asking questions as you go. What does it mean? Do I understand it? If not, what am I going to do about that? How does it connect with what I already know? How will I use it in my assignment?

Review actively: at the end of each study session – reflect on what you have read or heard.

TIP

Write a blog post at the end of every day.

Study partners and groups: for many, study is best when undertaken actively, interactively and socially; this is where a friend, study partner or a study group can be invaluable.

Don't end on a sour note: try not to end a study session on a problem – it is demotivating and it can make it that little bit harder to start studying again. Use a study partner, friend or online discussion space to talk it over.

Relaxation and dealing with stress: make time to rest, relax and let go of stress. When we are stressed our body releases cortisol – a hormone that has a direct impact on the brain causing the cortex to shrink – and adrenalin – the flight or fight hormone. The combination of these hormones eliminates short-term memory and produces the narrow, tunnel vision necessary for fight or flight. This might save our lives when escaping from a burning building, but works against us when studying where we need breadth and depth of vision.

TIPS

- **Make a note of the problem and sleep on it – sometimes the solution comes to you when you wake up. But don't lie awake fretting all night; this does not solve the problem and you have made everything worse by losing sleep and gaining stress.**
- **Join the gym. Take up yoga. Practise meditation.**

Organisation and time management: if you are now feeling overwhelmed by all your responsibilities as a student, try this five-step plan to tackling those worries – and getting things done:

1. List everything that you need to do: this may feel like a really bad idea and that you'll be even more frightened; but the opposite is true. Once you write the list, and you can see the reality of the 'problem', it becomes more manageable and less overwhelming.
2. Divide each big task that you have to do into smaller steps. So do not just put down: 'write essay'. Break it down: 'brainstorm question', 'read up on …', 'write a paragraph on …', etc.

3. Organise your big list into things that must be done now; soon; later.
4. Do one of the *now* tasks immediately and cross it off. You will instantly feel more calm and in control.
5. Prioritise your list and put it into a 'to do' order.
   (With thanks to our colleagues at Reading University.)

Still procrastinating? You have to be organised – you have to be methodical – do not procrastinate – just do it! Try this activity suggested by Michelle Reid of Reading University. Work with a group of friends, especially if they are fellow students. You will need Post-it notes and pens.

Activity

The time sponge

Everybody takes one large Post-it and writes their biggest time sponge at the top (a time sponge is anything you find yourself doing instead of working – checking your phone, messaging friends, etc.).

Everybody passes their Post-it to the person on their left. You all read someone else's time sponge problem and write a possible solution.

Pass to the left again and write another solution to another problem.

Keep going until you have run out of space on the Post-its.

Everybody takes a turn to read out the problem on the Post-it they have been left with – and the various solutions offered.

Everybody says one thing they will now do differently after listening to all the sponges and solutions.

When planning your time – think about these:

- *Study timetable*: this is a 24/7 timetable (24 hours a day, seven days a week) that covers how many hours per day go to non-study and how many go to your studies. It is where you can plan which subjects to study and for how long. It takes some trial and error and experiment to get this right – so do give it that time.
- *Assignment timetable*: this is a record of all the assignment deadlines that are coming up either in a term, a semester or across a whole year. Fill in deadlines and pin it up on your wall and place a copy in your folder and diary. Never let a deadline take you by surprise.
- *Exam timetable*: similar to the assignment timetable, this is a record of all the exams you will be taking. Note dates, times and locations. It is all too easy to turn up at the wrong time, on the wrong day and in the wrong place!

- *Revision timetable*: at the appropriate time, each student should devise their own revision timetable where they work out when they are going to test their knowledge and practise for the exams that they are going to sit

Photocopy the timetables below: experiment with using them to help you focus on your work and get the most from your time.

Summary

We have looked at learning and considered when, where and how to study; some authors call this SHAPE: style, habit, attitude, preference and experience. The trouble is that we may stay with unsuccessful study habits even when they do not work, just because they are that – a habit or a preference. None of the good practice in this chapter will mean anything unless and until you put the ideas into practice. Until you push through your discomfort and learn new, successful practices.

Further reading

BBC Scotland's Brain Smart website: www.bbc.co.uk/scotland/brainsmart/.
Devine, T.G. (1987) *Teaching Study Skills*. Newton, MA: Allyn and Bacon.
Wenger-Trayner, E. (2014) Key note at ALDinHE Conference, Huddersfield University, 2014.

Activity

Two key things to do right now: learning contract and timetables

1 Write a learning contract
Reflect on what you have read so far and write a brief learning contract saying what you want from your course: what you're prepared to do to achieve your goals, what might stop you, and what's in it for you (what will change about your life when you achieve your own goals).

- What I want from this course is ...
- What I'm prepared to do to make this happen is ... (Use the six steps to success like this ... Build on my visual strategies like this ... Visit the library ... Write for half an hour every day ...)
- What might stop me is ... (Note the issues in your life: work, family, friends ... How might these affect your studies? What are you going to do about that?)
- What's in it for me (WiiFM) is ... (Knowing WiiFM can help motivate you on those cold, wet days when it feels too hard to get out of bed ...).

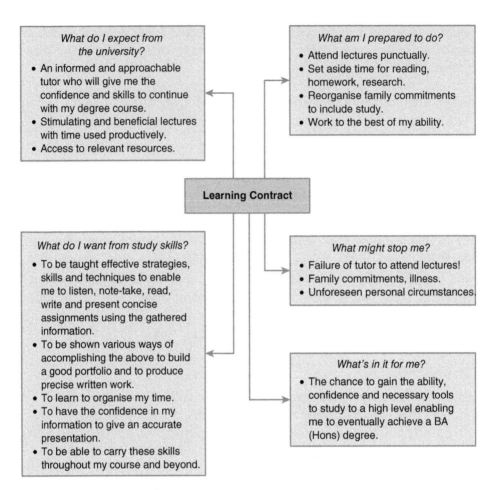

What do I expect from the university?

- An informed and approachable tutor who will give me the confidence and skills to continue with my degree course.
- Stimulating and beneficial lectures with time used productively.
- Access to relevant resources.

What am I prepared to do?

- Attend lectures punctually.
- Set aside time for reading, homework, research.
- Reorganise family commitments to include study.
- Work to the best of my ability.

Learning Contract

What do I want from study skills?

- To be taught effective strategies, skills and techniques to enable me to listen, note-take, read, write and present concise assignments using the gathered information.
- To be shown various ways of accomplishing the above to build a good portfolio and to produce precise written work.
- To learn to organise my time.
- To have the confidence in my information to give an accurate presentation.
- To be able to carry these skills throughout my course and beyond.

What might stop me?

- Failure of tutor to attend lectures!
- Family commitments, illness.
- Unforeseen personal circumstances.

What's in it for me?

- The chance to gain the ability, confidence and necessary tools to study to a high level enabling me to eventually achieve a BA (Hons) degree.

FIGURE 2.1 An example of a learning contract

2 Fill in your timetables

Take some time to complete the following timetables – and experiment with them – see how to use them to organise and motivate yourself.

---TIP---

We have put in *two* blank 24/7 timetables – complete one as a *plan*; complete the other as a *review*. Then decide how you will need to adjust your plans to be more successful.

Filling in the 24-hour timetable:

- Fill in the first one, indicating when you expect to work, sleep, do chores and so forth. Think about the time that you have left. Put in times for study and relaxation. Think about it – are you being realistic? Make sure that you are not under- or over-working yourself. Run that programme for a few weeks.

- After a couple of weeks, review your success in keeping to the study times that you set and in achieving the goals that you had in mind.
- Change your timetable to fit in with reality. Use the second blank timetable for this.
- Remember to do this every term, semester, year.

Time	Monday	Tuesday	Wednesday	Thursday	Friday	Saturday	Sunday
1.00							
2.00							
3.00							
4.00							
5.00							
6.00							
7.00							
8.00							
9.00							
10.00							
11.00							
12.00							
13.00							
14.00							
15.00							
16.00							
17.00							
18.00							
19.00							
20.00							
21.00							
22.00							
23.00							
24.00							

FIGURE 2.2   Blank 24-hour timetable – plan

Time	Monday	Tuesday	Wednesday	Thursday	Friday	Saturday	Sunday
1.00							
2.00							
3.00							
4.00							
5.00							
6.00							
7.00							
8.00							
9.00							
10.00							
11.00							
12.00							
13.00							
14.00							
15.00							
16.00							
17.00							
18.00							
19.00							
20.00							
21.00							
22.00							
23.00							
24.00							

FIGURE 2.3 Blank 24-hour timetable – review and improve

Events and deadlines				
Write down the dates of the following events each term:				
	Course 1	Course 2	Course 3	Course 4
Course title				
Exam(s)				
Essay deadline(s)				
Laboratory report deadline(s)				
Seminar presentations				
Field trips/visits				
Project report or exhibition deadlines				
Bank holidays or other 'days off'				
Other events (specify)				

FIGURE 2.4 Course events and deadlines timetable

	Term plan – what is happening over your terms/semester?						
	Monday	Tuesday	Wednesday	Thursday	Friday	Saturday	Sunday
Week 1							
Week 2							
Week 3							
Week 4							
Week 5							
Week 6							
Week 7							
Week 8							
Week 9							
Week 10							
Week 11							
Week 12							
Longer term deadlines:							

FIGURE 2.5 Term plan timetable

Keep a weekly plan: key events and activities each week							
Week Number:	Monday	Tuesday	Wednesday	Thursday	Friday	Saturday	Sunday
8am							
9am							
10am							
11am							
12 noon							
1pm							
2pm							
3pm							
4pm							
5pm							
6pm							
7pm							
8pm							
9pm							
10pm							
11pm							
12 midnight							
1am							

FIGURE 2.6   Weekly plan timetable

7

Group project work, or 'hell is other people'

Greasley, P.

It was the existentialist philosopher Jean-Paul Sartre who coined the phrase 'hell is other people' in his play *No Exit*. Three people are sent to Hell expecting to be tortured for their sins, but are surprised to find themselves simply left in a room together. As they begin to get on each other's nerves, one of the characters realises that *they* are the instruments of torture – that hell is other people! Group work can feel like this, particularly when your degree classification depends on the performance of others. I can still recall as an undergraduate witnessing a classmate scrambling over chairs and desks in a desperate bid get as much distance between himself and a particularly vociferous student who happened to be sat next to him. If group work is on the agenda, choose where you sit wisely.

On a more positive note, working with others provides the opportunity to share ideas, skills and expertise and learn from each other. Collaboration and teamwork are essential for many tasks in the real world; it would have taken one person a very long time to achieve President Kennedy's aim of 'landing a man on the moon and returning him safely to the earth'. As an old African proverb puts it: 'If you want to go fast, go alone; if you want to go further, go together.'

The key stages of project work are:

1. Define and plan
2. Assign roles and tasks
3. Monitor progress and completion of tasks
4. Review, evaluate and reflect on the project

But it is people who implement projects; so, above all, it is crucial to maintain good relationships within the group.

Tip 128: **Projects fail at the start not at the end – have clear aims and objectives**

The importance of a clear aim and objectives has already been discussed in Chapter 15 (Tips 108 and 109). Just to recap, the aim should be a general statement outlining the ultimate purpose of the project (e.g. the aim of this project is to produce an information leaflet for people with diabetes); and the objectives are the means used to achieve this aim. Try to make them as SMART as possible:

- **S**pecific: clearly defined with completion criteria
- **M**easureable: clear targets so you can measure progress
- **A**chievable: attainable (and agreed – so people can own them)
- **R**ealistic: given resources – time, money, equipment
- **T**ime-bound: clear timeframes

It sounds simple, doesn't it? But it isn't. Consider the project outline in Figure 18.1, where the brief is to produce a stall for a health promotion event. Are you clear from this what the aim and objectives of the project are? I wasn't. This is because the students have not spelled out a clear and simple aim. Indeed, the objectives are more like broad, vague aims; they certainly don't specify how the project will achieve them. For example, *how* will they 'educate people about obesity'? Will they be producing leaflets, doing a play, providing a video with some information about what constitutes obesity and some statistics about the associated risks? If you don't start with clear aims and objectives, your project will be like setting out on a journey without a clear destination or map.

But let's assume you have identified an aim and the relevant objectives for achieving this. What happens next? You should then be asking whether

---

Project specification

Obesity

Brief description of project

According to NHS UK obesity is the accumulation of excess fat in the body and this arises as a result of an imbalance between energy expenditure and energy intake. Obesity has a serious implication on health, such as cancer, type 2 diabetes, high blood pressure, depression, short life, mental illness. Obesity is mostly dictated by measuring body mass index (BMI). The Obese BMI is between 30 and 39.9.

Project objectives

- Educate people about obesity causes and its cost. BBC, 2012 stated that obesity cost NHS at least 500 million a year and it's growing rapidly.
- To empower people on how to eat healthy
- Motivate students on healthy lifestyle
- Keep them informed, alert, and aware of the risks associated with obesity.

Figure 18.1 A project outline with unclear aims and objectives

the aim is worthwhile. In other words, is the project worth doing? As the 'management guru' Peter Drucker (1909–2005) once remarked: 'There is nothing so useless as doing efficiently that which should not be done at all.'

Tip 129: **Plan to avoid the known unknowns and the unknown unknowns**

When the then US Defence Secretary Donald Rumsfeld was asked in 2002 about the lack of evidence linking the government of Iraq with the supply of weapons of mass destruction to terrorist groups, he famously replied:

> Reports that say that something hasn't happened are always interesting to me, because as we know, there are known knowns; there are things we know we know. We also know there are known unknowns; that is to say we know there are some things we do not know. But there are also unknown unknowns – the ones we don't know we don't know. And if one looks throughout the history of our country and other free countries, it is the latter category that tend to be the difficult ones.

Projects rarely go to plan, so it's important to build in time to deal with 'known unknowns' and 'unknown unknowns'.

There are various techniques to help you plan a project, but the Gantt chart is the most commonly used visual device, providing a list of the tasks that need to be completed, and by when. There is a simple example of a Gantt chart for completing an assignment in Chapter 4 (Figure 4.2), but for more complicated projects you will need to be more specific about the sub-tasks as well as identifying the people responsible for completing the tasks. For example, Figure 18.2 details the tasks involved in planning a charity event attempting to break the Guinness world record for the most people you can fit in a Mini (adapted from Maylor, 2010).

Comments from survey of tutors

- Ensure that the group has key objectives/targets to meet, clear deadlines, and particular people responsible for achieving particular tasks
- Set out ground rules and agree responsibilities and allocate tasks at the outset
- Ensure that the workload is divided fairly
- Share out the work and agree/assign clear roles
- Keep a record of meetings – who attended and what was said – and, most importantly who is going to do what

						Weeks						
Activities	1	2	3	4	5	6	7	8	9	10	11	12
Obtain car												
Contact local dealers												
Visit dealers to negotiate borrowing car												
Collect car day of event												
Arrange insurance												
Meet with university department												
Arrange insurance for driving car to site												
Continued...												

Activities	**Person responsible**
Obtain car	John
Contact local dealers	
Visit dealers to negotiate borrowing car	
Collect car on day of event	
Arrange insurance	Paul
Meet with university department	
Arrange insurance for driving car to site	
Organise barbeque	George
Contact university catering	
Obtain barbeque	
Ask supermarkets for free food	
Collect/purchase food day of event	
Collect BBQ day of event	
Satisfy health & safety	Ringo
Meet with health & safety	
Carry out risk assessment	
Promote event	John/Paul
Design and produce posters	
Alert local radio and newspaper	
Set up university stall on walkway	
Arrange venue	George/Ringo
Look for suitable venues	
Select venue and back-up venue	

Figure 18.2 Gantt chart and task allocation for charity event attempting to break the Guinness world record for most people you can fit in a Mini (adapted from Maylor, 2010)

Tip 130: **Assigning roles and tasks: people are better at some things than others**

When allocating tasks try to take into account the preferences and abilities of each member of the group. In this respect Meredith Belbin's nine team roles, summarised in Table 18.1, are a popular management tool for identifying the strengths and weaknesses of people working in teams. Which one are you?

Table 18.1   Belbin's nine team roles

Team Role	Contribution	Allowable Weaknesses
Plant	Creative, imaginative, free-thinking. Generates ideas and solves difficult problems	Ignores incidentals. Too preoccupied to communicate effectively
Resource Investigator	Outgoing, enthusiastic, communicative. Explores opportunities and develops contacts	Over-optimistic. Loses interest once initial enthusiasm has passed
Co-ordinator	Mature, confident, identifies talent. Clarifies goals. Delegates effectively	Can be seen as manipulative. Offloads own share of work
Shaper	Challenging, dynamic, thrives on pressure. Has the drive and courage to overcome obstacles	Prone to provocation. Offends people's feelings
Monitor Evaluator	Sober, strategic and discerning. Sees all options and judges accurately	Lacks drive and ability to inspire others. Can be overly critical
Teamworker	Co-operative, perceptive and diplomatic. Listens and averts friction	Indecisive in crunch situations. Avoids confrontation
Implementer	Practical, reliable, efficient. Turns ideas into actions and organizes work that needs to be done	Somewhat inflexible. Slow to respond to new possibilities
Completer Finisher	Painstaking, conscientious, anxious. Searches out errors. Polishes and perfects	Inclined to worry unduly. Reluctant to delegate
Specialist	Single-minded, self-starting, dedicated. Provides knowledge and skills in rare supply	Contributes only on a narrow front. Dwells on technicalities

Source: www.belbin.com

Belbin defines these team roles as: 'a tendency to behave, contribute and inter-relate with others in a particular way' (www.belbin.com). He found that teams with a good balance of these roles worked best:

> For example … a team with no Plants struggled to come up with the initial spark of an idea with which to push forward. However, once too many Plants were in the team, bad ideas concealed good ones and non-starters were given

too much airtime. Similarly, with no Shaper, the team ambled along without drive and direction, missing deadlines. With too many Shapers, in-fighting began and morale was lowered. (www.belbin.com)

Now obviously, you may not have the luxury of picking the members of your team according to the criteria proposed by Belbin (which requires completing an assessment), but it is important to think about who does what according to their strengths and weaknesses as group members.

Comments from the survey of tutors

- Different people have different strengths and styles with respect to group working so, where possible, work with them rather than against them

- Teamwork is the key. Make sure you consult with all members of your team regularly

Tip 131: Beware of 'social loafers'

The most common complaint about group work is directed at certain members who don't contribute and leave others to do most of the work. There is a term for these people – 'social loafers' – because they tend to put in less effort when part of a group and they can produce a great deal of resentment amongst team members.

So what should you do if certain members of the group are shirking the work? Well, after complaining first to the student and then to the tutor, you could suggest some kind of peer evaluation for the project – where each member of the group awards marks to all the other members of the group reflecting their contribution to the project, in terms of attending group meetings, contributing to discussions, and completing tasks well and on time. There are various ways to do this. If it's not already in place, ask your tutor about it.

Tip 132: Be nice - be polite

Imagine that you want someone to open a door. How are you going to ask them? Which option would you select from the following:

1. Open the door.

2. I would like you to open the door.

3. Can you open the door?

4.   Would you mind opening the door?

5.   May I ask you whether or not you would mind opening the door?

Personally I would probably go for option 3, but it would depend on the context. If I were asking a stranger to let me into a building because I am holding a large heavy object I might opt for 4, but if I were being chased by an angry student wielding a machete I would more likely go for 1.

The issue is one of politeness, which sometimes has to be balanced against directness: option 1 is the most direct; option 5 is the most polite. No matter how many Gantt charts and task allocation tables you produce to make sure your project is well planned, the most common issue that can scupper a project is poor relationships with other people. Successful group project work depends on fostering good relationships, so consider setting some team values at the outset – for example, to show respect and consideration; to listen to what others have to say; to contribute equally; to avoid negativity. I'm sure there are others you would like to add.

Tip 133: Keep tabs on progress: monitor and control

Try to plan your project in stages with tasks and sub-tasks, like those in Figure 18.2, so that you can monitor progress at key junctures. Keeping tabs on progress may be done by email or phone, but it is also important to schedule meetings in your plan (Gantt chart) so that you can review progress at key stages (milestones). This is a very important control mechanism for ensuring the project is still on track to achieving its objectives and ultimately fulfilling the overall aim.

Comments from the survey of tutors

- Plan your meetings, deadlines and targets in advance
- Arrange a clear schedule for the project with small achievable targets to aim for
- Illustrate tangible outputs
- Set targets for the group and individuals
- Keep evidence of plans and schedules
- Hold regular group meetings to review progress
- Check in regularly with each other and reassign tasks if key tasks haven't been completed
- Don't assume anything

Tip 134: Know how to work out the overall module mark

Feelings can run high when your mark depends on the performance of others. I recall one group of students continually bickering about the direction of their project and allocation of tasks, and when I heard one say to another 'It's no wonder you're bald, with the amount of stressing you're doing', I knew it wouldn't be long before I'd be called in to mediate.

Working out how much damage might be done by the group project to your degree classification (and hence your choice of career, and therefore your life generally) is important: you need to know how much the group project work actually accounts for the overall module mark, which often consists of an individual assignment and a group work assignment. There are various ways to allocate marks, but below I've provided a simple example.

Imagine that the group assignment is going to account for 20% of the module marks, and your own individually written assignment will account for 80%. In order to work out the mark you simply need to multiply your mark by the percentage allocated to it. Here are two illustrations.

Scenario 1. The group task is going to bring down your individual mark: you've done worse in the group task than the individual assignment:

Assignment $= 70\% \times 0.8 = 56\%$

Group Project $= 50\% \times 0.2 = 10\%$

Total $= 66\%$

In this case, you got 70% for your individual assignment (well done) but only 50% for your group assignment (those b******s have ruined your life!). So the group task has reduced your individual assignment mark by 4%.

Scenario 2. You've done better in the group task than the individual assignment:

Assignment $= 58\% \times 0.8 = 46\%$

Group Project $= 70\% \times 0.2 = 14\%$

Total $= 60\%$

In this case, you've improved your mark by 2% (well done for aligning yourself with a good group!).

Tip 135: Remain optimistic

Projects rarely go to plan and regularly overrun in terms of time and cost, so try to keep the following advice in mind:

- When things are going well, something will go wrong. When things cannot get any worse, they will. When things appear to be going better, you have overlooked something.

- A carelessly planned project will take three times the time expected to complete. A well-planned one will take twice as long.

Finally:

- Whatever you did, that's what you planned.

summary

The tips in this chapter outline the key ingredients for successful group projects. These require clear aims and objectives, appropriate allocation of tasks, and milestones for monitoring progress towards objectives. Most crucially though, group projects require good communication skills to promote, rather than hinder, collaboration.

8

The ten step approach to better assignments

Burns, T. and Sinfield, S.

Assessment can seem mysterious and daunting — we look at the why, what and how of assessment with a ten step approach to taking control of all your assignments.

Introduction

Nobody really enjoys being assessed, being judged, it means that we can fail; we can make mistakes – mistakes that reveal us to be foolish or inadequate. Funnily enough, that is not really the point of assessment. Assessment is designed to be *of*, *for* and *about* learning. That is, a good assessment is designed to provoke active learning as we produce an assignment that 'shows what we know'. University assignments contribute to our final qualification – the final tally of your grades is used to award the level of your degree. Essays, reports, presentations, seminars … are some of the major forms of assessment used in universities; they each have their own structure and function. We look at these common assessment forms – and then offer a ten step approach to succeeding in any assignment that you are set. We conclude by discussing feedback and how to use it.

University assessments

As you read these, work out how knowing the information might help you to be a more successful student.

The essay

An essay (Chapter 12.1) is a discursive tool – you are supposed to argue for and against a topic and come to a reasoned conclusion using mainly theoretical evidence (what you have read). The essay demonstrates your analytical and critical thinking. One of the most formal academic forms, essays are typically written in the third person, past tense with extensive accurate references to supporting arguments and evidence taken from the key players in your discipline.

The report

A report (Chapter 12.2) is a practical document where you write up the findings of your investigation into real-world problems – think scientific experiment or business report. Reports are written for specific readers, in the third person, past tense and are signposted with headings and sub-headings.

The dissertation

A dissertation (Chapter 12.5) is an extended piece of writing associated with Honours level projects or postgraduate study – Masters or PhD. The dissertation records the findings and conclusions of independent research into specific phenomena. The typical dissertation structure is like that of a formal report, but it has an extended literature review and is written discursively like the essay.

The literature review

The literature review (Chapter 12.5) can be part of a dissertation – though some courses set a literature review as an assignment in its own right. The literature review demonstrates your exploration and understanding of the most up-to-date literature and research in the area that you are studying. The process of reading for and writing a literature review is designed to enable you to gain deep knowledge of the key issues and debates. Your literature review becomes your analysis of the most up-to-date and relevant knowledge-claims in your area and becomes a measuring stick against which you can compare your research findings.

The presentation

A presentation (Chapter 12.3) is a talk of a set length, on a set topic – to a known audience. It is similar in structure to the essay – but is supported by audiovisual aids. The purpose of the presentation is usually to demonstrate the student's subject knowledge and their oral communication skills.

The seminar

The seminar combines written and oral elements. The seminar giver has to present their research, normally to a group of fellow students. The research is discussed and new ideas generated. The workshop is becoming more popular than the seminar – here you teach something to a group of your peers and in a very interactive and creative way. (For both see Chapter 12.4.)

The exam

The exam (Chapter 12.6) is designed to test learning. Students use information learned on a course in new situations. Exams can be open or closed book, time or word length limited, or other variations. Always know what sort of exam you are preparing for.

The reading record

A reading record is not an essay or a literature review. It is designed to be an annotated account of the reading a student has undertaken on a particular course. The annotations are not supposed to be descriptive: 'This book was about ...' but analytical: 'This text is key for this topic outlining the major theoretical perspectives of ...' or 'This text could be used to support the arguments of ...' or 'However, Y and Z would take issue with the following aspects of the major arguments ...'. A tutor might set a reading record to test that students are reading in an active and analytical way (Chapters 4 and 7) – thus your annotations should demonstrate your understanding of the text and its relationship to the key debates in your subject.

The annotated bibliography

An annotated bibliography is a condensed version of the reading record. A conventional bibliography records author (date) *title*, place of publication: publisher, in alphabetical order, by author's surname. In an annotated bibliography, you also note down information on a text's strengths or weaknesses; on how useful it was and why – in relation to the aims and learning outcomes of the module and the key theoretical debates of the discipline.

The digital artefact

A digital artefact (Chapter 10): as universities enter the digital age, some tutors are setting digital rather than written assignments. The most typical one that we have encountered is where students are asked to produce an artefact that could be used to teach or revise some part of the course. If set a task such as this, discover whether there are certain tools that you have to use – investigate just how creative you are allowed to be.

A beginner's guide to better assignments: ten steps ...

We have looked at the *why* and the *what* of assessment, so let's now move on to *how* to prepare and write your assignments. We have broken this down into ten key stages.

1 Preparation

> The Americans talk about the five paragraph essay. This is where a typical 1,500 word essay has an introduction; three paragraphs and a conclusion. You are looking for one big idea per paragraph.

Start to work on an assignment as soon as possible: week one or two of your course would be good. Open a folder or an A4 envelope for every module that you do – and every question that you have to answer. Open the folder early and put information in there. Start collecting information from week one. Allow several weeks for reading and writing – and several more weeks to re-draft and refine your work. Work on it for half an hour a day and your academic life will be turned around.

PLANNING TIPS

- Write the whole question out exactly as it is.
- Put the question in your own words and say it back to another student or a tutor.
- Free write before you read.
- Underline every important word in the question – each is a research opportunity.
- Be creative: brainstorm and question matrix the key words (Chapters 6 and 7).
- Make sure that you do something about every word – don't leave any out.
- Add key words from the aims and learning outcomes module – research these as well (Chapter 11.1).
- Action plan: what will you now read? If working with a study partner or group – who will read what, when?

2 Targeted research and active reading

Once you understand the question and know what you are doing, read actively and interactively, using your active reading technique (Chapter 4) and asking questions as you go. Remember to get physical with the texts – mark them up, annotate, make comments and cross-reference. You will get much more from your reading when you do this.

Don't look for the whole answer to the question in any one piece of reading. When reading, look for references to plug the gaps in your free writing – or the answers to the questions generated by your brainstorm or question matrix (Chapters 6 and 7). Be generally alert and make notes of useful things you see, read and hear, and put the notes in your research folder. Record the source on the outside of the envelope – write: author (date) *title*, place of publication: publisher ... and you will build up your bibliography as you go.

3 Make paragraph patterns

Gather information by topic – rather than by source. That is, as you read, do keep an index card record of everything that you read (Chapter 4) – but also put ideas and information straight into paragraph patterns. Paragraph patterns save time. Use the flowing steps to make paragraph patterns:

- Use really large sheets of paper – A1 rather than A4.
- Write on one side of the paper only – this way you can see all of your notes.
- Remember to put author (date) *title*, place of publication: publisher, and page numbers for quotes.
- Put a key word or phrase from the question in the centre of each sheet: your *paragraph pages*.
- Collect notes from different sources onto each paragraph page – once you have a few ideas or references – you can turn each paragraph pattern into a paragraph.

4 Write – read – write

As you are reading and making notes (and building your paragraph patterns) – take the time to draft possible paragraphs for your assignment. Do not wait until you have finished reading to start the writing.

TIPS

- **You are not looking for the one right answer that already exists – there are usually several ways of tackling a question.**
- **Write your 'favourite' paragraph first to get you started.**
- **Free write a conclusion to get an idea of where you want your answer to go – change the conclusion later.**
- **Write ideas on separate pieces of paper. Move these around to discover the best structure for the answer.**
- **Remember a reader who keeps saying, 'What if ...?' Your reader will be thinking of the opposite arguments and evidence: do not just ignore inconvenient or contradictory evidence – know what it is and argue against it.**
- **Remember a reader who keeps saying, 'So what?' Make points – remember the question (see Chapter 12.1).**

5 Settle on a first draft

After you have struggled to write, read and write – settle on a first draft. Then and only then write a draft introduction and a draft conclusion to this first draft.

An introduction should acknowledge what an interesting or useful question it was – and should give the agenda of your essay – you should indicate how you are going to answer the question.

A conclusion has to prove that you have answered the whole question. Use the words from the question in your conclusion. Remember – do re-state main points; do not introduce new evidence.

6 Leave it!

Once you have achieved a first draft you feel great, your answer is great, your friends are great and life is great. Do not believe this! Put the work to one side and leave it for a while. This will give you some distance and objectivity, but more than this: your unconscious mind will seek to close the gaps that you left. The brain likes closure and will not be happy with all the gaps in your assignment. Thus your brain will struggle to close the gaps that you have left. If you allow a break in your writing process you are allowing the brain to close the gaps – you are working with your brain.

7 Review, revise and edit: struggle to write

This is the stage where you go back over your work and struggle to make it the very best it can be. Here you have to re-read what you have written – and change it. Sometimes we have to change everything – and nothing of our first draft gets left. This does not matter. We are writing to learn, so our thoughts *should* change as we write. Also, we would never get to a good version if we did not go through our rough versions.

Be prepared to draft and re-draft your work. Don't even try for perfection on a first draft – it is bad technique and it can actually stop you writing anything. On your first review, you might read from the beginning of your essay and improve, polish, as you go. After that, try to concentrate on one paragraph at a time – and not always in the order it is written but in any order.

TIPS

- Allow plenty of time for revising.
- Revising is where you go back and put in the 'best' word. This is where you put in the verbs. This is where you shorten long sentences so that you make clear, effective points.

- **Index surf to brush up your paragraphs. That is, once you have completed your major research, and you are happy with it, you can index surf to get little extra bits and pieces to take your work that little bit further.**
- **When you have finished polishing paragraphs, check the 'links' between paragraphs – make sure that they still connect with each other.**

8 Proof read

Once you are happy with your assignment, you are ready to stop revising it and to say: 'This is the best I can do'. Sometimes we are never really 'happy' with our work, but there still comes a time to stop and move on to the next task. At this point you have to proof read the final version.

Proof reading is not editing: you are not looking to make huge changes to what you have written, you are going through looking for mistakes, grammatical errors, tense problems, spelling mistakes or typographical errors.

You know that the brain likes closure – it will work to fill the gaps. This works against us when we are proof reading, it can mean that our eyes will 'see' what *should* be there rather than *what is there*. To get over this we have to make our proof reading 'strange'.

TIPS

- **Read your assignment aloud (if it is a presentation, rehearse before a critical friend).**
- **Swap assignments with a friend – proof read each other's work.**
- **Cover the assignment with paper and proof read one sentence at a time.**
- **Proof read from back to front.**
- **Proof read from the bottom of the page to the top.**
- **Proof read for one of 'your' mistakes at a time.**
- **Like everything else we do, proof reading gets better with practice.**

9 Hand it in – celebrate

You should now be ready to hand your work in on or before the deadline. And remember that deadline. On most university programmes a late submission is awarded an automatic fail – at best many marks are deducted. This is serious.

So once your assignment is done – congratulations! But before you rush off and celebrate remember to always keep copies of your work. Never hand in the only copy.

Obviously if you are writing on a computer, save your work to the hard drive and to a memory stick and email it to yourself and save in a 'cloud' – you can't be too careful!

If writing or producing something by hand – photocopy. And if the assessment unit loses your assignment, do not hand in your last copy – photocopy that. A student of ours came back and told us that the assessment unit lost her essay – the same one – three times!

10 Getting it back

When we get work back, we look at the grade, feel really happy or really unhappy, throw the work to one side and forget all about it. This is not a good idea.

What is a good idea is to review what you have written, and see if you still think it is good. As an active learner, you should try to take control of your own work and you have to learn how to judge it for yourself and not just rely on the tutor's opinions.

At the same time, you should also utilise the feedback that you get from the tutor. Be prepared to use that feedback to write a better essay next time. So a good thing to do is to perform a SWOT analysis of our own work, that is, look for the:

- Strengths
- Weaknesses
- Opportunities
- Threats.

When you SWOT your work look for the things that you think you did well or not so well. Then look for the things that the tutor appears to be telling you that you did well or not so well. Resolve to do something about your strengths and your weaknesses.

It's a struggle – and then there's the feedback

So assignments provide evidence of your achievement, but most importantly, the *process* of preparing an assignment is heuristic – it brings about powerful active learning. That is, as you wrestle with a question and struggle to read and write about it, you learn your subject. The learning cycle is completed when we receive and act upon feedback on our assignments.

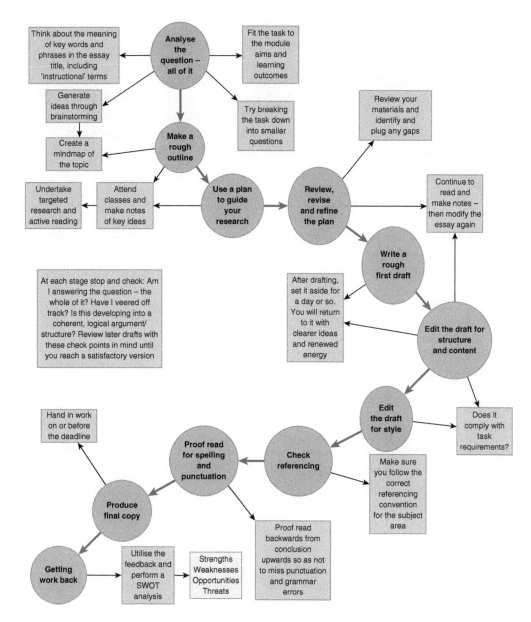

FIGURE 11.3.1   The assignment journey

Assessment and feedback

- Formative assessment is developmental. Designed to measure a student's progress at a particular moment in a subject, there should be an emphasis on tutor feedback where that feedback is designed to help you do better in the summative assessment.

- Summative assessment is final. Usually at the end of a programme of study, it is designed to measure the student's overall achievement in the unit, course or programme.
- Feedback. The best forms of assessment bring about learning in the student – especially when you can use the feedback that your tutors provide. Whether the assessment itself is formative or summative, most tutors will give you feedback on what you have written. This is a critical commentary designed to show you what you have done well (look for the ticks) – and what not so well (look for the advice about what you should have read – or referenced ...). Most students look at the grade – but forget to look at or use the feedback.

—TIPS—

Always try to find three things that you did well in an assignment – and three things that you could have done better.

It helps if you view assessment in a positive light. Try to see assessment as a chance to:

- **be dynamic and creative and show what you know**
- **write to learn your material**
- **write often – for 30 minutes a day**
- **use the feedback (see below).**

Dealing with feedback

It's hard to take feedback – it can feel like a personal attack or rejection. We have to learn how to use the feedback that we get. Here is how one student responded to some short sharp feedback. (Examples taken with permission from 'An Essay Evolves': http://evolvingessay.pbworks.com/w/page/19387227/FrontPage.)

The assessor's feedback on the assignment:

> ... could be improved by having a clearer focus and a stronger take-home message, which could perhaps be achieved by interpreting the title in a narrower way.

The student's response:

> I feel that in this case (and in some others!) I slipped away from my main task which is usually identified by a thorough question analysis. Looking back, instead of presenting the strengths and weaknesses of Freud's theory of personality as measured against the yardstick of evidential science I decided at too early a point to become an advocate for it. I tried also to question the appropriateness of the

> paradigm often used to assess Freud when it might have profited me (in terms of more marks) to stick with it. It may have helped me achieve the stronger take-home message counselled by the assessor. And interestingly, in this case I carried out my question analysis belatedly.

That's a brilliant way to respond to what must have felt like really negative feedback. She had worked long and hard on that task – and then it must have felt like it was being attacked. Would you have been able to do that? It is something we all have to learn – how to listen to feedback whilst not taking offence – not taking it personally – but thinking of what to do differently next time.

For more of this student's essay, search online for 'An Essay Evolves' – and read the essay as it developed – and the student's blog about her thoughts and feelings when writing the essay.

Summary: becoming a successful writer

We have considered the what, why and how of assessment – arguing that the assessment *process* is part of becoming a graduate whilst the *products* provide tangible evidence of your work. We stressed the active learning aspects of assessment: all the reading, thinking, discussing and struggling that you do to produce an assignment. We divided the assignment process into ten manageable stages – and considered how to approach feedback. You should now feel in a better position to approach your assignments.

Activity

Use the paragraph questions to prompt your writing

For each paragraph that you write – answer the following questions:

- What is this paragraph about?
  - introduce topic (and claim)
- What exactly is that?
  - define/clarify/explain
- What is your argument?
  - give argument in relation to question

- What is the evidence? What does it mean?

  - offer evidence and discuss it

- What is the opposing evidence? What does that mean?

  - Therefore …?

- What is your final point (in relation to the question)?

  - tie what you have written to the question. It is not down to your reader to guess what you are try-ing to say — or to think 'I wonder how this relates to the question?' If your reader has to do that then something is missing from your answer.

Access the companion website to this book and find helpful resources for this chapter topic:
https://study.sagepub.com/burnsandsinfield4e

9 Should I even Read This? How to Read the Abstract, General Introduction and Methods Section

Ho Shon, P. C.

Let's assume that you – the student – have searched a database of some sort (e.g., Psychinfo, Social Science Citation Index) to check the number of articles that have been published within the past 20 years on the topic you have selected for a research paper, and the results appear to be unwieldy. For the sake of illustration, let's assume that you get 200 'hits' from the topic words you searched. That is too many to manage, let alone read, so you narrow the search terms and now the results page indicates 70 hits. That is much more manageable. So you peruse the titles; some of the recent works definitely appear to be related to the topic you want to write about – the title is unmistakable. We will say that 40 articles will be included in your literature review because the titles are relevant or because you are sufficiently familiar with the research area to know that certain scholars who have appeared on the list are always cited in relation to the topic you searched and need to be included. Ten articles appear to be irrelevant to your topic, so they are excluded. You are not sure about the remaining 20 articles. From the titles of the papers, they appear to be related to your topic, but you are not sure. What to do at this point? One, you could just go with the 40 articles that you found and ignore the remaining 20, and risk missing out on some important and relevant points – points that might have altered how you might frame your research. Or, you can read the abstract, and then determine if the article is worth including in your literature review or not. Others have called this practice 'skimming' or 'scanning'; however, those terms do not do justice to how the abstract should really be read.

An abstract is a very, very brief summary of a journal article. Most journal publications require an abstract of some sort, which range from 100 to 200 words. Reading through an abstract is less time-consuming than reading the full-length article. An abstract contains enough essential information about the article to be able to assess its merit and relevance. In the less than two minutes it takes to read through an abstract, you can discern and anticipate the logic of the author's argument before even reading through the full article. Even in medical and hard science journals, the format of a research article is similar to that of a social science article: background, materials and methods, results, discussion, and conclusion. In an abstract, those five components are covered in one way or another. And whether the student is reading the article as part of the literature review or trying to decide if the article is pertinent enough to the chosen topic to be included, reading should begin with the abstract. While reading the abstract, the reading codes ought to be written where relevant in the right margin of the hard copy of the article. There is a reason why the codes should be written in the right margin. After the reading is completed, thematic codes will be written in the left margin as a way of classifying and organizing recurring patterns and themes in the literature. The right margin is reserved for the reading codes while the left is reserved for thematic codes.

How to Read the Abstract

In the section below, the abstracts of four published articles from reputable journals have been reproduced. To describe the function of the words in the abstract, and for accessibility, clarity, and ease of reference, each sentence has been numbered consecutively.

The abstract in DiCataldo and Everett's (2008) article on 'Distinguishing juvenile homicide from violent juvenile offending,' published in *International Journal of Offender Therapy and Comparative Criminology*, is exactly 151 words. The abstract is composed of seven sentences. Now, consider the type of information that is contained in the abstract:

(1) Juvenile homicide is a social problem that has remained a central focus within juvenile justice research in recent years. (2) The term juvenile murderer describes a legal category, but it is purported to have significant scientific meaning. (3) Research has attempted to conceptualize adolescent murderers as a clinical category that can be reliably distinguished from their nonhomicidal counterparts. (4) This study examined 33 adolescents adjudicated delinquent or awaiting trial for murder and 38 adolescents who committed violent, nonhomicidal offenses to determine whether the two groups differed significantly on family history, early development, delinquency history, mental health, and weapon possession variables. (5) The nonhomicide

group proved more problematic on many of these measures. (6) Two key factors did distinguish the homicide group: These adolescents endorsed the greater availability of guns and substance abuse at the time of their commitment offenses. (7) The significance of this finding is discussed, and the implications for risk management and policy are reviewed.

Sentences #1–3 do the type of work that could be described as Summary of Previous Literature (SPL). This type of a sentence provides a general background on the topic you have selected, and summarizes the results from previous studies. In this abstract, the previous literature has been framed along the theme of (#1) time, (#2) definitions, (#3) distinguishing characteristics. Sentences #2 and #3 tacitly hint at a Critique of Previous Literature (CPL), but those missing gaps (GAPS) are not explicitly stated. In a CPL, the author you are reading is providing a critique and pointing out a limitation of the previous and existing works; GAP highlights missing elements, deficiencies, and limitations in the current state of knowledge in some systematic way.

Sentences like #4 in the abstract convey what the authors of the paper are doing. Those types of sentences in general are best represented by the reading code WTD: What They (the authors) Do. This code captures the main research question that the authors pose and resolve in their text. In abstracts, WTDs not only describe the main problems the papers address but they also describe the materials and methods used for the study. Simply put, WTDs are what the article is about. WTD sentences usually begin with phrases like, 'This paper examines …' 'In this paper …' 'This paper attempts to …' WTDs generally appear in three places in most social science journal articles: abstract, introduction, and conclusion (WTDD: What They Did).

There is a reason that the code WTD is used rather than the more accepted 'thesis' or 'thesis statement.' Some use thesis statement to indicate a conclusion of sorts – 'a case developed using existing knowledge, sound evidence, and reasoned argument' (Machi & McEvoy, 2012, p. 1). If the thesis statement refers to a conclusion of sorts, then what is an appropriate way to describe the conclusion section that always appears at the end of journal articles? Some use the term 'argument' or 'main idea' to refer to a similar point (Lipson, 2005; Osmond, 2013). Finally, the term thesis is used to indicate the final product that undergraduate and graduate students produce as part of their requirements to fulfill their degrees (i.e., BA, MA, and PhD). The words 'thesis' and 'thesis statement' have too many meanings: they are likely to lead to confusion. Hence, I have avoided the terms.

Sentences #5 and #6 present the Results of Findings (ROF). ROFs describe the primary results – main claims – of the journal article that you are reading. This code is usually found in three places in a social science journal article: abstract, results section, and the discussion/conclusion. There are two main

ROFs that are noteworthy in the preceding article. The ROFs should tell you if the article you are reading is relevant to your own research topic or not. In scanning an article and reading through an abstract, the ROF should be the nugget that ought to be mined for, as this will tell you if the article is related to your own paper and topic. If the ROF suggests that the article you are reading is not pertinent to your topic and the paper you are writing, then that article probably should not be included in your literature review, and you should not read on any further. Sentence #7 discusses the implications of the findings. Readers are not told what the implications are, just that implications exist. Those implications are not revealed because the authors are constrained by the space and word limits imposed on abstracts.

In reading through one 151-word abstract, we have at least a general idea of what the paper is about. The readers are introduced to the background (SPL), possible critiques (CPL/GAP), what the authors are doing in their work

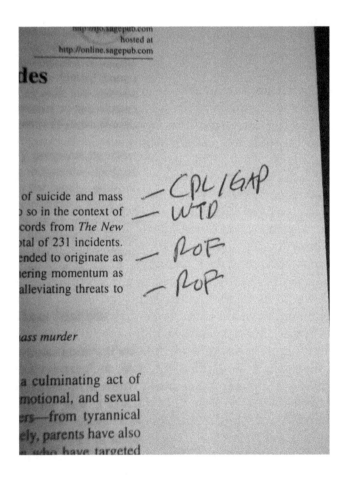

FIGURE 2

as a way of improving the gap in the literature (WTD), and the results of their findings (ROF). These reading codes ought to be marked in the right margin of the text, next to the sentences that exemplify that code (Figure 2). Therefore, sentences #1–3 should be bracketed and the code SPL written in the right margin. Next to sentence #4 the code WTD ought to be inserted; next to sentences #5 and #6 the code ROF ought to be inserted.

The abstract in Hattie and Timperley's (2007) article 'The power of feedback,' published in *Review of Educational Research*, is exactly 145 words. The abstract is composed of six sentences. Again, consider the type of information that is contained in the abstract:

(1) Feedback is one of the most powerful influences on learning and achievement, but this impact can be either positive or negative. (2) Its power is frequently mentioned in articles about teaching, but surprisingly few recent studies have systematically investigated its meaning. (3) This article provides a conceptual analysis of feedback and reviews the evidence related to its impact on learning and achievement. (4) This evidence shows that although feedback is among the major influences, the type of feedback and the way it is given can be differentially effective. (5) A model of feedback is then proposed that identifies the particular properties and circumstances that make it effective, and some typically thorny issues are discussed, including the timing of feedback and the effects of positive and negative feedback. (6) Finally, this analysis is used to suggest ways in which feedback can be used to enhance its effectiveness in classrooms.

Sentence #1 describes what could be called an SPL, for the authors are simply providing background information on the previous literature. In the first sentence, the authors summarize the literature on feedback into one concise sentence, telling readers that feedback can work in positive and negative ways. Sentence #1 should be bracketed and the code SPL should be written in the right margin. In the very next sentence, the authors mention that the power of feedback is often noted in articles related to teaching, again signaling that the clause is performing the work of an SPL, but the disjunction marker 'but' hints that something else may be emerging.

What appears in the second clause is the following assertion: 'surprisingly few recent studies have systematically investigated its meaning.' Clauses like that do not summarize the previous literature. The second clause points to what has not been done in the literature on feedback. Clauses and sentences like that point to a negation – what is not being done – and illustrate a Critique of Previous Literature (CPL) that the authors are pointing out. Logically, that critique leads to a shortcoming or a GAP in the literature. The code CPL/GAP should be written in the right margin. Within the first two

sentences, the authors have summarized the literature on feedback and identified a shortcoming within that literature.

What happens after a GAP is pointed out? Sentence #3 introduces the
reader to what the paper is about or what the authors will do in their paper
(WTD). Again, phrases like, 'This paper examines ...' 'In this article ...' 'This
article provides ...' tell the readers the main research question that is being
asked in the text. If we were to frame this WTD into a standard research
question, it might look like the following: 'How does feedback impact student
learning and achievement?' The question is elegantly simple, but profoundly
meaningful, for in their article, Hattie and Timperley (2007) will review
existing works and provide a conceptual analysis of how feedback affects
students. According to the authors, such a question has not been asked in
previous literature.

And in sentence #4 the authors provide the Results of their Findings (ROF),
that type of feedback and the way it is delivered have different effects; in sentence #5, the authors propose a conceptual model of effective feedback. Both
sentences describe an ROF; those sentences should be highlighted and the
code ROF should be written in the right margin. The ROF should be highlighted because it is the most significant piece of information from that article.
This main finding – claim – should determine if this article should be included
in a student's review of the literature or not.

The abstract in Pritchard and Hughes's (1997) article on 'Patterns of deviance in crime news,' published in the *Journal of Communication*, is exactly
133 words. Consider the work that the sentences in the abstract perform:

(1) Existing research has failed to develop a satisfactory theoretical explanation for journalists' decisions about which crimes to highlight and which
to ignore. (2) We proposed that four forms of deviance (normative deviance,
statistical deviance, status deviance, and cultural deviance) account for
much of the variation in decisions about crime news. (3) To test deviance-
based explanations for crime news, we conducted a comprehensive
investigation of Milwaukee, WI, homicides and how two newspapers covered them. (4) We used content analysis and interviews with journalists.
(5) The results showed that the newsworthiness of a homicide is enhanced
when Whites are suspects or victims, males are suspects, and victims are
females, children, or senior citizens. (6) We concluded that status deviance
and cultural deviance are important components of newsworthiness and
that statistical deviance (unusualness) may be much less important than
commonly assumed.

The presence of the word 'failed' after 'existing research' should be a clue
that sentence #1 is pointing out a CPL/GAP of some sort; in the sentences
that follow, that is what the readers are told. Sentence #1 is an example of

CPL/GAP. What is the missing element in the existing literature? A 'satisfactory theoretical explanation' that explains why journalists highlight some crimes while ignoring others. Sentences #2–4 describe the WTD, for they describe the materials and methods as well the main research questions being addressed in their study. Sentences #5–6 describe the ROF. The SPL is implicitly contained in the words 'commonly assumed,' but readers are not explicitly told what it is. The codes, CPL/GAP, WTD, and ROF ought to be written in the right margin of the article next to the respective sentences. Again, even without adequate background knowledge of the literature or SPL, the ROFs ought to tell you – the reader – if the main claims made in the article are pertinent for your ends. Readers know that status deviance and cultural deviance constitute 'important components of newsworthiness.'

The abstract in Kim, Hogge, Ji, Shim, and Lothspeich's (2014) article, 'Hwa-Byung among middle-aged Korean women: Family relationships, gender-role attitudes, and self-esteem,' published in *Health Care for Women International*, is exactly 100 words. Notice how their abstract is organized:

> (1) We surveyed 395 Korean middle-aged women and examined how their perceptions of family relationships, gender-role attitudes, and self-esteem were associated with Hwa-Byung (HB; Korean Anger Syndrome). (2) Our regression analyses revealed that participants who reported worse family relationship problems experienced more HB symptoms. (3) Having profeminist, egalitarian attitudes toward women's gender roles was also associated with more HB symptoms. (4) Self-esteem was not significantly associated with HB. (5) Based on the results, we suggest that what is crucial to understanding HB is not how women evaluate themselves, but rather the level of stress caused by family relationship problems and their perception of women's roles.

Sentence #1 does not summarize or critique the previous literature; rather, it tells the reader what the article is about. Therefore, the most appropriate code to write in the right margin is WTD. Again, notice how the research question is embedded in the WTD. If we were to turn this assertion into a research question, it would resemble the following: 'How are middle-aged Korean women's perceptions of their family relationships, gender-role attitudes, and self-esteem associated with Hwa-Byung?' In sentences #2 and #3, the authors provide the results of their study (ROF). These two sentences should be highlighted, for they constitute the important pieces of information to be gleaned from this article. After reading the abstract, readers ought to be able to tell if the full paper is relevant to their own projects. If a student is writing a paper about mental illness and women's mental health, this article should be included in her literature review.

As one can observe, there is some variance in the way the abstracts are composed. Some abstracts provide SPL and CPL while others do not; some abstracts use two sentences to describe their ROFs while others expend one to do the work. And when students are not sure whether or not an article should be included in their literature review – and the title of the paper does not provide adequate clues about the paper's pertinence to their chosen topic – the abstract should be read to discern if the primary findings (ROF) of the studies being read are consistent with the proposed topic and aim of the student's paper. Furthermore, even after an article has been deemed to be relevant for inclusion in one's literature review, the abstract should be read first so that the logic of the author's argument embedded in the article can be rehearsed and anticipated in the subsequent sections.

As stated earlier, certain components of an article will appear more than once throughout the article. For example, ROFs are found in the abstract, the results, and the discussion and conclusion. Similarly, the rationale (RAT) for why a particular study is necessary and warranted cannot appear randomly and out of the blue. It has to follow a logical, linear, and anticipatable path of reasoning and argumentation (Jordan & Zanna, 1999). This logical 'set-up' unfurls in the literature review section; its shadow is implicitly cast in the abstract.

The use of reading codes can also serve as a guide to students for how to construct an abstract. One sentence can describe the SPL, another the CPL. The SPL and the CPL ought to at least tacitly suggest a GAP, which logically leads to the WTD. One to two sentences can be used to describe the WTD, including the materials and methods. One to two sentences could be used to describe the ROF, with a final sentence for implications of results. With a minimum of five sentences, then, a student ought to be able to craft an abstract of her own, without wondering about its constitutive elements.

By noting the primary function of words, sentences, and paragraphs in texts, readers are able to structure their reading so that the contents of what they have read can be organized and classified along predictable, anticipatable, and recurring patterns. In this section, I have shown students how to read abstracts. In subsequent sections and chapters, I will show how to read much longer blocks of text using the reading codes. Thus, rather than reading social science articles without boundaries (unstructured reading), the reading codes provide textual, cognitive, and conceptual boundaries so that readers do not engage in mindless and meandering reading. By actively engaging with the text (and the author), readers of social science articles should not ask, 'What did I just read for the past 30 minutes?' Those types of questions arise because texts are too difficult to decipher (e.g., Jacques Lacan, Immanuel Kant, Judith Butler) or the mind has wandered away during the act of reading because of an absence of structure to the reading.

By identifying the function of texts and writing the codes in the right margin, readers achieve three objectives.

1. Slowing down the act of reading. The use of reading codes structures the mind toward a purposive task, thereby delineating cognitive boundaries.
2. Organizing the contents of the reading into recurring themes (e.g., SPL, CPL, GAP, ROF) that can be easily retrieved for writing purposes.
3. Identifying potential GAPs so that the reader could anticipate the RAT (see Chapter 5) from the given CPL and GAP for use in their own papers.

How to Read the General Introduction

An introduction, as the word denotes, appears at the beginning of something; it does not appear at the end, for that would make it a conclusion. An introduction in a social science journal article is like a blueprint and a map: it lays out the itinerary of an article's path of logical travel. Introductions are longer than abstracts but shorter than literature review sections. Introductions tend to be between two and four paragraphs; they are also organized and structured into predictable patterns. Consider the following introduction from Gruenewald, Pizarro, and Chermak's (2009) article on 'Race, gender, and the newsworthiness of homicide incidents,' published in *Journal of Criminal Justice*.

There are four paragraphs that make up the introduction. In the first paragraph, second sentence, the authors write, 'Scholars have found that crime is generally a staple of news programming, comprising from 10 to 50 percent of all news stories [citations omitted]' (p. 262). Sentences like this summarize the state of the literature, so the code SPL ought to be written in the available margin. The first five sentences are written in a similar spirit, as a way of summarizing previous literature. Then in the last sentence of the first paragraph, the authors write, 'Despite such increased attention, an empirical void remains in the literature regarding the factors that contribute to the decision-making process …' (p. 262). Sentences like this critique the previous literature (CPL) and identify a GAP in the knowledge base. In one paragraph, the authors have summarized the literature and provided a critique of, and identified a gap in, the existing literature.

The first sentence of the second paragraph reads, 'To date, few studies [citations omitted] have seriously considered how the gender and race of homicide victims and offenders, and their interaction, affect news media selection and prominence decisions, and whether these interactions supersede incident characteristics in increasing the newsworthiness of a particular homicide' (p. 262). Again, the sentence points to a CPL and identifies a GAP in it: few studies have examined how gender and race affect the decision-making process in the news.

The rest of the sentences in the paragraph go on to provide other shortcomings in the literature (e.g., criteria used to assess newsworthiness; lack of Hispanics in previous study samples; lack of a specific examination of race and gender). Thus far, in the first paragraph, the authors have provided a broad summary of the literature, ending it with a critique. In the second paragraph, the authors have put forth more GAPs that exist in the literature. So what? Why should these GAPs matter?

The authors answer that, 'The scholarly understanding of newsworthiness criteria is important for several reasons' (Gruenewald et al., 2009, p. 262). They list three. The answers to the 'So what?' question constitute a rationale for the study (RAT): our proposed work is warranted and necessary because others have not addressed the GAPs. Every study and/or experiment has to be able to answer this question. After the three RATs are proffered, the WTD appears in the fourth paragraph: 'This study examined the relationship between homicide participant and incident characteristics and news media decision-making in the city of Newark, New Jersey' (p. 262). Again, WTD tells readers what will be done in the paper. In the rest of the article, the authors will remedy the GAPs they have identified. The general introduction, very much similar to an abstract, provides a taste of the full-course meal to emerge in the rest of the article. In the preceding introduction, that initial 'taste' is offered in the form of SPL→CPL→GAP→ RAT→WTD in four paragraphs.

Notice how this pattern is mirrored again in Gershenfeld's (2014) article 'A review of undergraduate mentoring programs,' published in *Review of Educational Research*. Similar to the Gruenewald et al.'s (2009) article, Gershenfeld's (2014) introduction is composed of four paragraphs. In the first two sentences of the first paragraph, Gershenfeld (2014, p. 365) writes,

> Research on mentoring has not kept pace with the proliferation of under-graduate mentoring programs (UMPs) on college campuses [citations omitted]. The purpose of establishing UMPs can vary, but they generally aim to strengthen student engagement and relationship building in order to improve academic performance and college retention, and/or assist with career planning [citation omitted].

The negation marker in the first sentence suggests that the sentence could be a CPL, but it could also function as an SPL. In such cases, it is best to move on and examine the next sentence; the second sentence definitely functions as an SPL so that code should be written in the right margin. The third sentence is a bit more explicit: 'However, without methodologically rigorous and valid research, it is unknown if mentoring programs are achieving their intended outcomes' (p. 365). The author is now critiquing the state of research on under-graduate mentoring programs; she is claiming that previous research has not assessed the merits of mentoring programs in methodologically valid ways.

Sentences like that illustrate a CPL, which logically points to a shortcoming in the literature (GAP).

What does Gershenfeld do after she has identified a GAP in the literature? Consider sentence #4: 'With universities heavily investing both financial and human resources in mentoring, it is prudent that research guide the development and continuous improvements in mentoring programs for undergraduate students' (p. 365). If we now ask the brutally simple 'So what?' question of Gershenfeld, how would she answer it? If readers asked of her why her topic, her paper, and her GAP are significant, how would she answer that question? Sentence #4 provides an answer to the 'So what?' question. Sentences like #4 would illustrate a RAT. Once this RAT is provided, notice the next sentence that follows: 'This article is the third review of studies that examine the impact of UMPs' (p. 365) – in other words a WTD.

Notice the recurring pattern here: in one paragraph, Susan Gershenfeld has broadly summarized the literature on undergraduate mentoring programs (SPL); critiqued the research by pointing out that it is unknown whether such programs are accomplishing what they purport to accomplish (CPL); stated why that shortcoming in the literature is important (RAT); and how she will remedy that shortcoming in the literature (WTD). The WTD logically appears after the SPL, CPL, and RAT. As a 'taste' of the full argument to emerge in the rest of the sections of her paper, the first paragraph takes readers from a broadly formulated SPL to a WTD in one sublime paragraph. Most introductions are not that structurally elegant.

In the next two paragraphs, the author SPLs prior research, summarizing and critiquing the previous literature in greater detail. Then in the fourth and final paragraph, Gershenfeld writes the following sentence: 'The value of this current review is fivefold' (p. 366). She then goes on to flesh out what those values are: (1) her paper extends the review of UMPs from 2008 to 2012, thus covering the period omitted in a previous researcher's period of study. (2) She assesses the methodological rigor of previous studies using evidence-based criteria. (3) She evaluates the role of the mentor in previous studies. (4) She incorporates social validity as a measure. (5) Finally, she identifies key features of mentoring programs from previous studies. In other words, Gershenfeld provides five separate and distinct answers to the 'So what?' question or five RATs for why her paper is necessary and warranted. Readers do not have to wonder why her paper and topic are important. She provides readers with five good reasons.

Shumaker and Prinz's (2000) review article 'Children who murder: A review,' published in *Clinical Child and Family Psychology Review*, has four paragraphs that make up the introduction. The first sentence of the first paragraph begins with, 'Though homicidal youth have received considerable attention in the media and in the social sciences, children under age 13 who committed homicide are understudied' (p. 97). That is, the authors provide a summary of the literature ('homicidal youth have received considerable attention in the media and in the social sciences'), and a critique of the previous literature (but 'children under age 13 who committed homicide are understudied'). Thus far, the sequence of the logic of ideas in the first paragraph of the introduction can be represented by the reading codes SPL→CPL→GAP.

If a GAP exists in the literature, so what? Why should that deficiency matter? Why should anyone care? Consider Shumaker and Prinz's (2000) answer to the 'So what?' question: 'Despite the low base rate, preteen offenders should be studied for several reasons' (p. 97). They list three reasons why the topic is important and should be studied: (1) young killers pose problems for the juvenile justice system; (2) juvenile homicide rates have doubled; (3) for prevention purposes. These are the RATs for why their work is important. RAT, again, follows the GAP in the logical sequence of how ideas in introductions are structurally organized. Since Shumaker and Prinz (2000) are writing a review article in a psychology journal, the third paragraph elaborates on how the authors selected the published studies to be included in their review paper.

In the last paragraph of the introduction, the authors write, 'The review examines classification schemes and typologies of youthful homicide, predictors of homicidal behavior in children, and how childhood behavioral characteristics of adult murderers, particularly adult serial killers, might bear on the study of preteen homicide' (p. 98). The occurrence of the first three words of the paragraph 'The review examines' ought to signal that the sentence and/or paragraph will be related to what the paper is about – WTD. In four paragraphs, the authors have summarized the literature (SPL), critiqued it (CPL), and by doing so they have identified a shortcoming (GAP), which has served as a rationale (RAT) for why their paper is warranted – why someone should care. The last paragraph tells readers what the authors will do in the paper (WTD).

As can be seen, introductions, like abstracts, are not formless; they have a logical form and structure. As appetizers before the main course – the literature review, data and methods, and results – they provide an outline and a map of what is to come in the rest of the article. When students are reading social science journal articles, they should follow the logic and form that is already inherent in them. As shown here, abstracts are organized in a way that is predictable and anticipatable. The reading codes ought to be used as boundary markers so that students know what they are reading, page by page, paragraph by paragraph, line by line. Thus, the ideas contained in the abstract should appear in the introduction, and the ideas in the introduction elaborated to a greater extent in the literature review. And by using the reading codes, students should be able to anticipate the next item to appear in the article; if the reading codes are used during the act of reading, students should never have to ask 'Where is this article going?' or 'What's the author trying to do?' The answers to those questions should emerge naturally and ineluctably from the way social science journal articles are structured and organized.

When students become adept at reading, they will begin asking themselves, 'Will this assertion that is fraught with tension be resolved in the subsequent sections?' (WIL). Such questions arise because the reader has already antici- pated several potential paths of the author's logic and her argument's possible itinerary. If the author fails to connect logically related points, the reader will note that she missed an obvious theoretical, conceptual, and analytical con- nection to earlier works (MOP). Sometimes, the reader may 'see' points that even the author did not intend or anticipate. Such omissions in the text that you are reading do not point out any limitations and gaps; rather, the stated point could be used as a Point of Critique (POC) in a future paper. That is, a Relevant Point to Pursue (RPP) and mine in another paper.

How to Read the Data and Methods Section

One of the primary objectives of the methods section parallels the hallmark of science – reproducibility. That is, those interested enough – for whatever reason – in a study ought to be able to recreate its conditions sufficiently so that the results could be challenged or confirmed. According to Jordan and Zanna (1999, p. 464), readers ought to pay attention to the following guide- lines while reading methods sections: (1) how the independent and dependent variables are measured, and (2) do the measures accurately reflect the intended concepts? This means if a student wants to critique the previous literature (CPL) on methodological grounds, then the deficiency in the cur- rent article or literature is a limitation and a GAP that the student could exploit as a way of remedying the gap in the literature (POC).

Consider how Piquero, Farrington, Nagin, and Moffitt (2010, p. 157) mea- sured 'life failure' of men at ages 32 and 48 based on history of employment, relationships, substance abuse, mental health, criminal justice involvement, and self-reported delinquency. If the men at those ages scored high they were considered failures in life; a low score indicated success in life. So what consti- tutes a high score? If the men kept an unclean apartment or home, or moved more than twice within the past five years, that would be counted as life fail- ure. Furthermore, if the men were not living with a female partner, or had been divorced within the past five years, or did not 'get along well with female partner,' the men would have been counted as a life failure. If the men had self-reported offenses in the past five years (excluding theft from work and tax fraud) they would have been counted as life failures. There are six other mea- sures of life success and failure. Although an established and accepted way of measuring psychopathy and antisocial personalities, I am sure that readers could find a way to critique those measures. An astute graduate student can find a way to argue that the purported measures do not accurately reflect the intended concepts. The grounds on which you – the student – could critique the measures used illustrates a Point of Critique (POC). Or one could find issue with the statistical tests that are used. If a previous study used a single measure, your POC could be that only one measure was used, and that you will remedy that GAP by using multiple measures.

Jordan and Zanna (1999) provide detailed instructions on how to read quantitatively designed social psychology journal articles. However, social science journal articles are not exclusively composed of quantitative studies. There are qualitative – non-statistical – approaches to data and analysis. Reading qualitative social science journal articles, however, is somewhat similar to reading quantitatively designed studies. Consider Stephen Lyng's (1990) article entitled, 'Edgework: A social psychological analysis of voluntary risk taking' that was published in the *American Journal of Sociology*. In this article, Stephen Lyng introduces a new concept to explain various forms of voluntary risk-taking activities (e.g. sky-diving, motorcycle racing); he does so by drawing on a rich theoretical tradition in sociology (e.g., Marx, Mead). So how did the author arrive at the new concept? What data did he use?

> As a jump pilot, I was able to observe the most intimate details of the group's activities. These observations were recorded in the form of field notes written up at the end of most weekends at the drop zone (an area approved by the FAA for parachute drops) and after many sky-diver social events. The accuracy of participant-observational data was also checked in intensive semistructured interviews with strategic respondents. In these interviews, which totaled scores of hours, respondents were asked to describe the experience of dealing with the various risks associated with the sport. (Lyng, 1990, p. 856)

Lyng conducted semistructured interviews with sky-divers. Based on the respondents' answers, the author identified recurring patterns in the data that led to three analytical categories: (1) various types of edgework activities; (2) specific individual capacities relevant to edgework; (3) sensations associated with edgework. Note that no independent and dependent variables were measured. That is because in qualitative research, hypotheses are not tested as much as they are generated. In qualitative research – whether the form of the data is ethnographic text, transcriptions of interviews, or historical documents – the data are collated and classified into distinct analytical categories based on the principle of induction (Strauss, 1987). Those analytical categories 'emerge' from the textual data.

To develop a POC from the analytical categories, readers can question the validity of the theoretical concept the author introduces: does the measure accurately reflect the intended concepts? That is, are the activities that Lyng lists as edgework sufficiently reflective of the concept of edgework? Moreover, readers can critique the fact that insufficient details were presented in the paper. Thus, how many participants did the ethnographer interview? How were the participants selected? How long did these interviews last? Were the respondents paid? And so on. These are all valid potential POCs that could be used to remedy methodological GAPs in the literature and as RATs for another study (RPP).

As shown here, the abstract provides a brief synopsis of the main ingredients of an article in less than 200 words. The general introduction (not psychology introductions) elaborates on the main components of the article (SPL, CPL, GAP) hinted at in the abstract in two to four paragraphs, but explicitly tells readers what it is the authors are going to do in the article (WTD). The literature review section (psychology introductions) will provide a much more extended SPL, CPL, GAP, and RAT (see Chapter 4). The methods section presents the materials, methods, and procedures used in the study. If a critique will be made on methodological grounds, it will revolve around the issue of measurement – measurement of independent and dependent variables and the accuracy and commensurability of measures intended to reflect a particular concept (Harris, 2014). During the act of reading, the code POC should be inserted whenever the reader finds either of the two issues questionable and debatable.

10

So What? How to Read the General Literature Review, Psychology Introductions, and Results Sections

Ho Shon, P. C.

There is consensus in previous how-to books that the literature review is the most important component of any research paper, from undergraduate theses to PhD dissertations. This point is true of journal articles as well, for it is here that authors review the work of others and make their proposed work relevant to previous works. Furthermore, the critique of the previous works provides a rationale for why our – your – proposed work is necessary and warranted. That is, before we can proffer our own 'knowledge claims' (Vipond, 1996), we must tell readers which authors carried out similar studies and examined similar topics – why our work is sufficiently different and contributes to the knowledge on a given topic.

If the literature is inadequately covered, then the ideas that we present in our papers – knowledge claims, arguments, findings, results – might be framed as being too one-of-a-kind, often ignoring – unwittingly – the work that preceded ours; by doing so, we fail to acknowledge that other scholars have had similar ideas long before. In plain language, undergraduate students and beginning graduate students often try to reinvent the wheel on a given topic. Academic writing, however, should not be conceptualized as wheel invention. Instead, it is more accurate to frame the proposed work as wheel modification. As Vipond (1996, p. 39) advises, do not 'expect to develop your own knowledge claim without first examining and understanding those of other scholars. Claims are seldom completely original; instead, they are connected to, and grow out of, the claims of others.'

One of the elementary mistakes that students make when writing undergraduate research papers and drafts of master's theses is the failure to connect to the work of previous researchers – the literature. Out of deference, a fledgling student might leave out the name of a prominent scholar for fear of contradicting and disagreeing with a 'big name' scholar; or, the omission arises from insufficient reading. Students need to understand that citations are acknowledgements – good or bad – and they are the currency of academic life and business; omitting a relevant name/theorist from the literature review constitutes a slight of the tallest order. Therefore, do not be afraid to critique and disagree. Disagreements are better than omissions, witting and unwitting.

Others who have written books on how to do a literature review have lamented the fact that students simply rehash the work of others in a literature review. We might call this practice making a 'laundry list.' Rudestam and Newton (2001, p. 56) write that:

> many students erroneously believe that the purpose of the literature review is to convince the reader that the writer is knowledgeable about the work of others. Based on this misunderstanding, the literature review may read like a laundry list of previous studies, with sentences or paragraphs beginning with the words "Smith found ... Johnson found ... Jones found ...'

I too made this mistake when I finished my dissertation and submitted a chapter from it to a journal. Both reviewers noted that the literature review read like a laundry list. A laundry list literature review is a simple compendium of facts from previous works, author by author, year by year; it is cumbersome and tedious to read; in a journal article it takes up too much space. Most importantly, a laundry list literature review fails to identity thematically parsimonious points of similarity across the literature. That is why creating a laundry list leads to the laundry list problem.

Previous literature must be organized in some logically connected way. Landrum (2008, p. 96) instructs students to 'group research studies and other types of literature according to common denominators such as qualitative versus quantitative, objectives, methodology, and so forth.' This advice simply means that the laundry list of authors has to be grouped in some principled way. Methodological distinctions are one way to group prior studies; conceptual distinctions are another. However, merely stating what others have said about a topic – author by author, year by year – constitutes only a quarter of a competent literature review. The other quarter entails a thematic and principled summary of previous works. The remaining half entails a thematically connected critique of the previous literature that identifies gaps in the knowledge base, which leads to the rationale for a study.

Summarizing the work of others – the first half of the literature review – is represented by the reading code Summary of Previous Literature (SPL). SPL refers to sentences, paragraphs, or pages that describe a summary of the results from prior studies and works. SPL requires a tremendous amount of condensation, taking complex ideas and reducing them into paragraphs, sentences, and if the author is brilliant enough, one word (see Chapter 8).

How to Read a Literature Review

The location of literature reviews in journal articles differs by discipline. In most psychology journals, the literature review is placed up front as part of the introduction; psychology journals therefore combine a general introduction, where the subcomponents of an article are briefly described, and an extensive literature review into one section. There is a separate section for literature reviews, usually under that very heading, in most sociology, criminology, communication, education, and health journals. No matter where literature reviews are located in a journal article, the work that is done in them is the same: summary of previous work, critique of previous work that highlights a gap in the knowledge, and a rationale of why the proposed – your – work is necessary. Consider how literature reviews are structurally organized.

There are 11 paragraphs in the introduction section of 'Distinguishing juvenile homicide from violent juvenile offending' in DiCataldo and Everett's (2008) article that was published in *International Journal of Offender Therapy and Comparative Criminology*. The first sentence of the first paragraph reads, 'Homicide, particularly by means of firearms, among contemporary American male adolescents has been the focus of intense media coverage, social science research, and moral commentary' (p. 158). This topic sentence provides a succinct yet broad overview of juvenile homicide as a topic. It introduces the reader to what the paper will be about. Moreover, it tells readers that the topic has been addressed by three different stakeholders as well. The rest of the sentences in that paragraph support and illustrate that first topic sentence. The first paragraph and first sentence would be an example of SPL. In the right margin next to this paragraph, the code SPL should be written after the paragraph is read.

The second paragraph begins with the following sentence: 'Juvenile murder is essentially a legal category defined within a state's criminal codes, statutes, and case law' (p. 159). Readers ought to expect that the rest of the sentences that follow this topic sentence will be related to the various definitions of juvenile murder. In fact, the very next sentence reads, 'It is not a diagnostic term, like schizophrenia, or personality disorder' (p. 159). The authors are introducing the distinction between a legal definition of murder and a clinical term used to diagnose offenders' psychological states. Notice that the second sentence supports and elaborates on the first sentence. The rest of the sentences in that second paragraph go on to differentiate between the two categories. So far what we have is SPL, and that code ought to be written in the right margin next to the paragraph. Then the following sentence appears as the last sentence of the second paragraph: 'It remains an empirical question as to whether juvenile murderers are a scientifically valid category apart from their existence as a legal one' (p. 159).

The last sentence clearly does not provide a summary of the previous literature. All of the preceding sentences, in one way or another, have provided support for the ways in which juvenile murder has been conceptualized, defined, and discussed (SPL). The last sentence, however, does not perform that summarizing function. It does suggest that there is a missing element in the existing literature on juvenile homicide: no one has yet to determine if juvenile killers is a 'scientifically valid category.' Another way of describing sentences like that would be to state that they are pointing out a critique

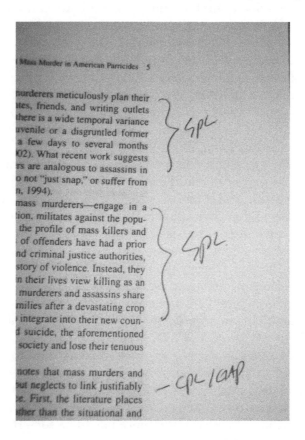

FIGURE 3

(CPL) and a gap (GAP) in the existing literature. There is a gap because no one has addressed that topic; we could also state that that sentence is a Critique of the Previous Literature (CPL) because, again, no one has addressed that question. Next to that sentence, the codes CPL/GAP should be written in the right margin next to that paragraph (Figure 3).

So far, we have examined two paragraphs in one journal article. In those two paragraphs, the authors of the article have summarized the literature into two themes: (1) significance of juvenile murder as a topic; and (2) definition of juvenile murder. In the last sentence of the second paragraph, the possible shortcomings or deficiencies (CPL/GAP) in the literature have been suggested. A CPL provides a critique and points out a limitation contained in previous scholarship. CPL highlights the deficiencies in the existing works on a theoretical, methodological, and analytical level; CPL is conceptually related to GAP since GAP specifically identifies the shortcomings in the literature as well. And notice how those codes, SPL, CPL, and GAP are structurally and logically connected. Before something can be critiqued, the content of that something has to be filled in first. In most, if not all, literature reviews, that is how a critique of the literature is done. The author(s) proffers a body of ideas, theories, and works of previous researchers; if this component is listed one by one, and presented that way in undergraduate research papers, master's theses, PhD dissertations, or journal articles, what we would have is a 'laundry list' – the cardinal sin of any literature review.

But DiCataldo and Everett (2008) do not discuss the literature author by author and year by year in a way that resembles a laundry list. They have synthesized their readings and identified a recurring theme, and structured their literature review along those recurring thematic lines. If you are instructed to synthesize your readings, by definition, you must combine all of your assigned readings and form something new. No one can do that for you. You, the reader and author, must create those thematic categories from the readings you have done. That is what makes the research and writing process – scholarship – creative acts. In addition to developing thematic categories, DiCataldo and Everett (2008) have also begun to subtly hint at the missing dimensions of the existing literature. That is, they have tacitly begun the critique of the previous literature and set up an expectation of the rationale (RAT) for their own work. Structurally, then, SPLs precede CPLs and GAPs. When reading journal articles, CPLs will follow SPLs. Remembering this order is one way to avoid unstructured reading. Readers should understand that ideas in journal articles are structurally and sequentially organized: summaries of literature introduce the reader to a topic in some thematic and principled way; critiques then follow. Again, one cannot begin a critique out of nothing; there has to be something to critique. Film critics cannot – do not – exist if there are no films.

There are other grammatical clues to look for that show CPLs and GAPs are emerging in the text. The third paragraph of 'Distinguishing juvenile homicide' begins with, 'The search for the clinical science behind adolescent murderers is more than a century old.' The sentences that follow clarify in greater detail how that topic has been relevant for at least 100 years, the main feature of previous research being limited sampling. Then the following two sentences appear at the paragraph's end: 'More recent studies have examined larger samples **but** often did not included [sic] control groups of nonhomicide offenders. Some more methodologically sophisticated studies use control groups for comparison purposes **but** elected to use questionable samples of nonviolent delinquents' (p. 159). Notice that phrases like 'more recent studies' and 'some more methodologically sophisticated studies' summarize previous works. In those types of sentences, the first clauses perform the work of SPL; the second clauses do the work of CPL which leads to a GAP. Coordinating the two contrasting ideas are disjunction markers. What do those do in a text?

Pretend for a minute that you are the recipient of the following words from someone you have a crush on: 'I like you; I think you're great. You're sweet; you're funny and really nice ...' Even before I finish the rest of the sentence, I know a lot of readers will know the word that will appear next: '... **BUT** ...' We know because some of us who have lost the parental lottery and have not received the cute gene have heard the painful phrases that follow. In fact, I suspect that when men and women hear a list like that – a series of complimentary assertions that appear independently and without any context or follow a strongly encouraged request for a dialogue ('we should talk') – their gut (not intellect) already senses the bad news to come; the word 'but' confirms the initial suspicion; the actual bad news – 'we should just be friends' – hammers the nail in the coffin.

That disjunction marker – 'but' – coordinates the rejection to come – about why it would be better to be 'just friends' than dating partners. In other words, words like 'but,' 'however,' 'while,' 'albeit,' and 'although' do the work of highlighting and contrasting the consequent from the antecedent. Hence, in the preceding sentences discussed, SPL comes first ('I like you'; 'more recent studies have examined larger samples'; 'some more methodologically sophisticated studies use control groups for comparison purposes'), followed by the CPL/GAP ('we should just be friends'; 'often did not included [sic] control groups of nonhomicide offenders'; 'elected to use questionable samples of nonviolent delinquents'). That a CPL/GAP is on the way is signaled by the appearance of the disjunction marker such as 'but.' In the context of literature reviews, again, SPLs, as a rule, precede CPLs. Grammatical disjunction markers such as 'but' and 'however' are good indicators that the ideas proffered in the first clause or paragraph will be critiqued and qualified in the second. In addition to the structural locations of texts, looking out for grammatical markers that contrast ideas is another way to structure reading so that readers can anticipate critiques.

Does this pattern hold true in other disciplines besides criminology? Does SPL precede CPL and can disjunction markers serve as signs of GAPs to emerge? Consider the following article that J.S. Kim (2001) wrote, 'Daughters-in-law in Korean caregiving families,' published in the *Journal of Advanced Nursing*. The literature review is composed of six paragraphs. The first sentence of the first paragraph of the literature review reads, 'The dynamic of family caregiving and its health consequences may differ by culture because caregiving behaviours may reflect a country's present culture' (p. 401). This sentence does not critique the literature in any way; nor does it declare the results of the author's own studies. Rather, it summarizes the literature on the topic the author has selected. Therefore, the code SPL should be written in the appropriate margin. The second sentence then reads, 'Family caregiving in Korea is influenced by multiple sociocultural factors' (p. 365). Again, the second sentence elaborates on the main topic hinted at in the first sentence. The first paragraph could be thematically coded as 'why DIL caregiver' to reflect what the entire paragraph is about. The remaining paragraphs go on to explain why daughters-in-law (DIL) in Korea have to be caregivers to elderly parents on their husband's side.

So why do daughters-in-law have to be caregivers in a Korean context? Kim (2001) explains in the literature review section that in Korean culture, heavily influenced by the Confucian principle of filial piety, the eldest son must assume responsibility for taking care of his elderly parents; the wife of the husband, by default, takes on the role of being a caregiver. Kim writes that normative expectations and social pressures compel daughters-in-law to accept their gendered role as caregivers. This background information on the social organization of families in Korea, as well as how industrial and social changes have altered the roles of women in society, and the context of caregiving are covered in the six paragraphs of the literature review. The previous literature on DILs as caregivers in a Western context suggests that they experience the highest level of negative health outcomes. But, as noted, it is not enough to simply summarize the literature; there must be shortcomings in the literature that warrant Kim's study of DIL as caregivers in Korea. What is Kim's CPL?

The first sentence of the last paragraph of the literature review states the following: 'In Korea, no study has been conducted to differentiate between blood-tied and affinal relationships' (p. 402). That is, while DILs as caregivers have been examined from a Western perspective, DILs as caregivers in a Korean context have been absent. That criticism is a valid one, for there may be cultural, social, and economic reasons why caregiving may be different in a Korean – or any other national and cultural – context. Now, notice how that CPL is rehearsed in the introduction. The following sentences appear in the second paragraph of the introduction:

> Previous Western studies have reported that DIL caregivers experience the greatest adverse health consequences of parent caregiving [citation omitted] and have found that in-law caregivers provide less help to their PILs (parents-in-law) than blood-tied caregivers [citations omitted] ... Although DIL caregivers have comprised a significant portion of caregivers and have an increased risk status in Korea, DILs as caregivers in Korea have not been studied extensively and systematically ... However, no study has been conducted of the health outcomes of DIL caregivers who care for impaired older people in the context of Korean culture. (p. 400)

Notice that the SPL precedes the CPL: previous research has found that DILs provide less help to parents-in-law (PIL) than those related by blood. From an evolutionary perspective, those findings would be logical and expected. However, that assumption cannot be extended to Korea for cultural reasons (i.e., Confucianism). That claim is the basis of Kim's CPL of the prior literature on caregiving. Again, SPLs precede CPLs. Furthermore, disjunction markers portend the contrastive point that follows the antecedent. While readers are not led to see how the CPL emerges from the SPL in the literature review, that pattern does occur in the introduction. What answer would Kim provide if we asked the 'So what?' question? Consider the next sentence: 'As little is known about this topic, a study which explores the health outcomes of DIL caregivers who care for impaired PIL (parents-in-law) in the sociocultural context of Korea is necessary' (p. 400). That sentence would constitute the RAT for her paper. Kim provides only one RAT, but there are several more RATs she could have provided that would bolster the significance of her work.

For example, as two non-blood-related family members, the potential for violence increases between DIL and mothers-in-law as the evolutionary rule of nepotism predicts. For DIL, living amidst husbands' family members as part of a patrilocal residence structure would place them at risk of violence, at least according to an evolutionary theory of violence. Second, as cohabitants within the same household, or as a result of prolonged contact as a result of caregiving, there is potential for domestic discord between mothers- and daughters-in-law, thereby increasing the risk of expressive violence. Third, DILs as caregivers have the potential to be parricide offenders, as ordinary caregiving tasks turn into elder abuse that turn fatal. From a criminological perspective, there are numerous reasons why a study of DILs and caregiving in a Korean context may be significant. From a nursing and health perspective, readers are proffered one. But the one RAT that is provided suffices to convince readers why a study of DILs as caregivers in Korea is necessary.

The literature review in Hu and Ma's (2010) article, 'Mentoring and student persistence in college: A study of the Washington State Achievers Program,' published in *Innovative Higher Education*, is five paragraphs long. The first two sentences of the first paragraph of the introduction read as follows: 'Policy makers, institutional administrators, and researchers have been interested in student persistence in college over decades [citations omitted]. One of the best-known models on college student persistence is the integration model proposed by Tinto' (p. 330). Both sentences introduce readers to a broad SPL. The first paragraph is spent reviewing the prior work that Tinto has done; Tinto's work constitutes the SPL in the first paragraph. The phrase 'integration model' would aptly summarize what this paragraph is about in a thematically concise way; 'Tinto model' would also work, for the first term originates from Tinto.

In the second paragraph, Hu and Ma (2010) discuss alternative models of student persistence, and their strengths and weaknesses; in the third paragraph, the authors go on to discuss the role that faculty mentoring plays in student persistence. In addition to the SPL codes that ought to be written in the right margin, the appropriate one- or two-word phrases should be written in the left margin as thematic codes. Then in the fourth paragraph, the following sentences appear:

> Several studies have examined the relationship between mentoring and student persistence, and overall results indicate that mentoring has a significant and positive impact on student persistence [citations omitted]. However, these studies have focused on the impact of a mentoring program without examining the specific aspects of mentoring. Consequently, they have not investigated how student background characteristics are related to different aspects of mentoring and, subsequently, how different aspects of mentoring influence student persistence. (p. 331)

Then, in the last two sentences of the last paragraph of the literature review, the following sentences appear:

> The mentoring aspects of the WSA [Washington State Achievers] Program reflect the domains or features identified by Freeman (1999) as well as Nora and Crisp (2007). However, it has been unclear how different mentoring elements of the WSA Program contributed to student persistence, which was the focus of this study. (pp. 331–2)

As can be seen here, SPL occurs before CPL, repeating the pattern noted in the literature reviews in other disciplines. Similarly, the disjunction marker 'however' again portends the CPL to follow the SPL. Although there may be other techniques that scholars have used to summarize and critique the literature, I have found that the structural organization of texts and the grammatical markers that indicate conceptual transitions are good heuristic devices to employ during the act of reading. Thus, without even elaborating on the content of the sentences, their structural location in the text, the grammatical clues proffered, and by examining only the form of the sentences, readers can discern that the second sentence critiques the first – pushes against the ideas contained in the first sentence. Understanding the work that sentences and paragraphs perform in a journal article is the first step in organizing the information that one reads in the literature. Thus, without even reading the content of the sentence, we know that the sentences in the literature review which begin with declarative assertions such as, 'Several studies have examined …' 'The mentoring aspects of the WSA …' 'According to Tinto …' will be a summary of previous works (SPL). The disjunction marker 'however' intimates that the rest of the words to follow will push against the preceding SPL. Similarly, sentences that begin with words such as 'although,' 'despite,' 'yet,' 'unfortunately,' 'regrettably,' and 'sadly' connect the SPL and CPL by putting the disjunction marker first, but still abide by the SPL→CPL format. That is why SPL, CPL, and GAP are logically connected. Although only heuristic, the reading codes represent simple guidelines to follow when reading social science journal articles.

Hu and Ma's (2010) critique of the student persistence literature (CPL) is that prior researchers have failed to delve into 'how student background characteristics are related to different aspects of mentoring,' and how that omission has led researchers to overlook other aspects of mentoring. Furthermore, Hu and Ma (2010) charge that previous researchers have neglected to examine how 'different mentoring elements of the WSA Program contributed to student persistence.' In other words, Hu and Ma reviewed the literature on student persistence and noticed that there were missing components in the literature. Those missing elements constitute the GAPs in the literature. The existence of those GAPs serves as a rationale for why Hu and Ma's work was necessary (RAT). That is why they carried out their study.

Some journals (and authors and disciplines) organize summaries and critiques into separate and distinct sections. For instance, Dixon and Linz (2000) organize the summary of the literature of their article on 'Race and the misrepresentation of victimization on local television news,' published in *Communication Research*, into the following thematic categories: (1) overemphasis on White victimization; (2) indices of victimization; (3) intergroup comparisons of victims; (4) interrole comparisons of victimization; (5) utility of intergroup and interrole measures; (6) interreality comparisons. Again, notice what the authors have not done. They have not listed the literature author by author and year by year in the manner of a laundry list. They have organized the voluminous literature on race, media, and crime into the afore-mentioned six categories, in a way that is meaningful for what they aim to do in their work. Dixon and Linz (2000, pp. 553–4) go on to provide a separate section for the limitations of previous literature section: 'This section attempts to overcome several of the limitations of prior works that examined race and victimization. In this section, we lay out three limitations of this prior research and how this addresses them.' One could even anticipate what the criticism might be based on the way the existing literature is organized and discussed. This type of a structural format makes reading and organizing voluminous amounts of information easier, for readers are spared from acting like textual detectives. Even this type of format, however, follows the general rule stipu-lated here: SPL, then CPL. Again, that is because, before we can critique a body of work, the reader has to know what that body of work is so the critique can be meaningful. The GAP emerges from this process.

GAPs are conceptually related to RATs. The deficiencies in the present state of knowledge justify and warrant a study that will remedy the missing gap in the knowledge base – that is the rationale for why a study is necessary. So if someone asks, 'So what? Why should anyone care about your work?', the answer ought to be a derivative of CPL and GAP. Thus, if someone asks you why any-one should care about your work (senior thesis, master's thesis, or dissertation), your hypothetical response should be something like the following:

> My study is worth doing because: (1) few have done it; (2) others who have done the type of work have used incorrect measures, used the wrong statis-tical tests, or incorrectly defined the problem; (3) they have made little progress beyond what the seminal theorists have done.

In journal articles, the answers to the 'So what?' question come in three to five carefully argued RATs.

Dixon and Linz (2000) list three answers to the 'So what?' question that is logically connected to CPL and GAP. (1) Previous studies have used one mea-sure. This sentence would be an example of CPL/GAP. So how will this gap be remedied? 'This study uses multiple indicators' (p. 554). The use of multiple indicators is RAT #1. (2) 'Very few studies have analyzed portrayals of Latinos on television news.' This sentence would be an example of CPL/GAP. So how will this gap be remedied? The current work analyzes Latinos. Analysis of Latinos on television is RAT #2. (3) No one has examined Los Angeles television news. This sentence would be an example of CPL/GAP. So how will this gap be remedied? Our current work examines Los Angeles television news where a lot of Latinos live. This answer is RAT #3. The three GAPs in the literature and their proposed remedies function as the RAT – the rationale for the study. In a proper literature review one must review and summarize the literature (SPL), critique the literature (CPL) by finding shortcomings and deficiencies in the literature (GAPs); and the remedy of those gaps constitutes the rationale for the proposed study (RAT): SPL→CPL→GAP→RAT. A competently done literature review – not a laundry list – generally follows the format outlined above.

Rudestam and Newton (2001) write that a literature review is more than a simple list of previous works. As argued here, that is only half of a literature review. A competently done literature review ought to transport the reader to the destination before arriving. In Rudestam and Newton's (2001, p. 58) words, 'by the end of the literature review, the reader should be able to conclude that "yes, of course, this is the exact study that needs to be done at this time to move knowledge in this field a little further along".' That 'yes' moment occurs because the SPL→RAT process unfolds in a logical, thematic, and anticipatable way; and advances in disciplines do not occur by leaps and bounds; they occur incrementally, one study at a time. Each study modifies the wheel little by little. When readers finish reading the SPL, CPL, and GAP, they should be able to anticipate the RAT, the hypothesis to be tested, or argument being made. When students are writing, the logical structure of their papers ought to follow along the preceding lines so that readers can expect and anticipate the next item from the previous one.

For example, White, Bates, and Buyske's (2001) article that examines the delinquent trajectories of adolescents into adulthood, published in the *Journal of Abnormal Psychology*, tests two hypotheses:

> On the basis of previous studies of childhood-to-adolescence persistence, we hypothesized that three different trajectories would be identified ... we also hypothesized that adolescence-limited and adolescence-to-adulthood-persistent delinquents would differ on selected measures of neuropsychological functioning, personality risk, and environmental risk. (p. 601)

How did the authors arrive at these two hypotheses? The key theorist in this area is Terrie Moffitt (1993a, 1993b), a developmental psychologist who claims that delinquency is temporary for most delinquents while for some it persists into adulthood (SPL). The authors organize the SPL into three themes: (1) neuropsychological dysfunction; (2) personality; (3) environmental adversity. White et al. (2001) go on to write,

> **Yet**, little is currently known about the utility of this typology for differentiating adolescence-limited from adolescence-to-adulthood-persistent delinquency ... **Although** neuropsychological functioning and personality characteristics have been found to differentiate early-onset from late-onset delinquents, few studies have examined their ability to differentiate those individuals who persist in delinquency beyond adolescence from those who do not. (p. 601; emphasis added)

White et al. summarize the literature (SPL), point out the limitations of previous works (CPL) and identify a deficiency in the literature (GAP); and by pointing out the shortcoming in the previous literature, the authors have provided an implicit RAT for why their work is necessary and warranted. If someone were to ask them, 'So what?' they could answer by stating that no one knows the 'utility of this typology' and that 'few studies are able to differentiate life-course-persistent offenders from adolescent-limited offenders.' Those answers to the 'So what?' question are their way of remedying the GAP in the literature. From this logical chain of reasoning, the hypothesis emerges. The emergence of the hypothesis is not an act of magic – out of the blue – for authors carefully set up the reader to anticipate the hypothesis, and to see the logic of their reasoning by introducing her to the literature (SPL), its limitations and criticisms (CPL), and shortcomings (GAP). The hypothesis follows naturally and inevitably from the way the authors have crafted and organized their ideas. That is why, by the end of a literature review, the reader is able to 'conclude that "yes, of course, this is the exact study that needs to be done at this time to move knowledge in this field a little further along"' (Rudestam & Newton, 2001, p. 58).

How to Read the Results Section

Results sections are probably the easiest to read, for authors simply lay out their main findings. In 'Urban black violence: The effect of male joblessness and family disruption,' Sampson (1987, p. 377) reports the following results, published in *American Journal of Sociology*: 'while male joblessness has little or no impact on crime, it has the strongest overall effect on family disruption, which in turn is the strongest predictor of black violence.' An assertion like the preceding one in the results section constitutes a 'knowledge claim' and should be treated as such by marking in the right margin ROF (Result of Findings). ROFs describe the primary results of the article being read. That particular finding is significant given the author's summary and critique of the previous literature – previous theories that have explained black criminality in the US as a function of a subculture that condones and promotes violence. Sampson is arguing against such views in this article.

The ROFs are the most significant, accessible, and visible pieces of information in social science journal articles for the simple reason that they are found in the abstract, results, and discussion and conclusion sections of most, if not all, social science journal articles. They tend to be repeated at least three times in the course of a journal article. The main ROFs are what need to be marked, highlighted, and noted, for they are the golden nuggets of journal articles; they are what the article is 'about'; the ROFs contain the central claims of authors – the citable points; ROFs will also become the SPLs of the papers that students write. So what are some of the notable ROFs from the articles we have examined thus far? DiCataldo and Everett (2008, p. 167) report in their results section (published in the *International Journal of Offender Therapy and Comparative Criminology*) that 'the non-homicide group had more significant delinquent histories than the homicide group on a number of the delinquency variables.' Such a ROF is significant because it is counterintuitive and also supports previous literature. Pritchard and Hughes (1997, pp. 58, 60) report in their results, published in *Journal of Communication*, that 'the race of a homicide victim accounted for almost all of the predictive power of race,' and that the 'most consistent predictor of newsworthiness was whether the victim was a child or a senior.' The ROFs are noteworthy because the authors are showing patterns in newspaper coverage that others have simply assumed.

J.S. Kim (2001) reports her findings, published in the *Journal of Advanced Nursing*, that relationship type was not an important predictor of caregivers' health, that daughters and DIL fared similarly to one another. Those findings are significant because one would expect non-consanguineous relatives to experience more health problems when caring for the family members by marriage. Hu and Ma (2010) report their findings, published in *Innovative Higher Education*, that the educational aspirations of college students are salient factors that explain the effectiveness of faculty mentors and student persistence. They also report that students who have at least one parent with a college degree are more likely to seek out mentors for support and encouragement. That finding is noteworthy because the very students who may need the most encouragement and support (first generation college students whose parents never attended college) may be the least likely ones to seek them out.

All of the significant and relevant – for your paper's aims – ROFs ought to be highlighted, underlined, or made salient in some way; the code ROF should be written in the right margin so that even if the reader wants to go back and look up the main findings several months later, she can look at the ROF code and know exactly what it is that she is looking at. Students should not have to re-read an article in order to figure out what the paper is 'about.' Instead, they should be able to look at the most important parts of journal articles – highlighted portions – and figure out exactly what claims are being made by the authors. The ROFs are also significant because they will need to be synthesized and integrated into the student's own literature review. The ROFs of the journal articles that students read will become the SPLs of their papers.

Transitioning from ROF to SPL: Making the Quarter Turn

As I have shown here, the reading codes are meant to facilitate critical reading by having students understand the work that sentences and paragraphs perform in a particular type of text, the social science journal article. By writing the pertinent reading codes in the right margins, the readers are actively reading by summarizing (SPL), critiquing (CPL), identifying short-comings (GAP), and cultivating points of critique (POC). Simply put, the general instructions that previous scholars have proffered to 'read critically' and 'think critically' have simply been condensed into operational codes that could be deployed during the act of reading. When it comes time for students to write their own literature reviews, for a research paper, thesis, or disser-tation, they have to reproduce in their papers what they have read others do in those social science journal articles. The reading codes are meant to help students in the writing process by actively and critically engaging with texts – precisely by summarizing, critiquing, identifying gaps, and cultivat-ing their own unique contributions to the literature during the act of reading. For example, let's say that an undergraduate senior is writing an honors thesis on personality and crime, and she has found 30 journal articles that have been published on that topic within the last 10 years. How should she organize her literature review?

First, the ROFs from the 30 articles she has read will become SPLs of her paper. That is because the 30 articles she found on personality and crime while searching Psychinfo or any other database constitutes – is – the previ-ous literature. The authors of those 30 articles will have read the seminal works of other researchers in the field, and the works they have read became the SPLs of their articles. The 30 authors identified CPLs and GAPs and proposed to remedy those GAPs in the literature (RAT) by conducting origi-nal studies. The results of those original studies constituted the ROFs of their papers – these ROFs become the SPLs of your (the student) paper. Therefore, the first step involves looking through the 30 articles and figuring out what common denominators exist in all of her ROFs because those ROFs will become her SPLs. Again, Landrum (2008) tells us to 'group research studies and other types of literature according to common denominators such as qualitative versus quantitative, objectives, methodology' and so on. Second, the said student will have to look for common patterns that could be collapsed into several themes. Once students read enough previous works, they will begin to 'see' thematic patterns in the literature. The left margin thematic codes, once entered into the Reading Code Organization Sheet (RCOS), will enable students to visually inspect those themes in the previous literature. What students cannot do is list the 30 authors one by one; then a laundry list problem is created. There is a way to mine the 30 articles you have read to assist you in your writing process.

Our hypothetical student who is writing her paper on personality and crime can begin by looking through the 30 articles and scanning the right margins and identifying all SPLs. She would then examine that sentence and/or paragraph and write a sufficiently broad theme or a word in the left margin of the printed articles. For example, in DiCataldo and Everett's (2008) article on juvenile murder there should be three words that summarize the three paragraphs we used as excerpts: (1) significance; (2) definition; (3) time – or something along those lines. For the Dixon and Linz (2000) article, there should be six words/phrases that thematically summarize the paragraphs and sentences: (1) White emphasis; (2) victimization indices; (3) comparisons; (4) intergroup/interrole; (5) interreality. Thematic code insertions can be done at the same time that reading codes are inserted, on the first act of reading, or saved for later. Doing both simultaneously, however, requires practice. Until the reader is familiar enough with the reading codes, and comfortable enough with the act of reading, the left margin insertions ought to be done after the first act of reading. When trying to come up with ways of organizing your own literature review, the thematic codes and summaries ought to serve as a guide in the preparation of your paper. Use the way previous SPLs are organized from your reading of the 30 articles as a way of framing and guiding your own SPL from the ROFs. Students will begin to see a pattern in the prior literature between articles number 12 and 15; once students have read between 12 and 15 journal articles, they will begin to understand the debate, notice the recurring themes in the literature, as well as important theorists in the area. The most frequently occurring thematic SPL codes are a hint that those themes should be included in the student's literature review. We might call this practice turning the SPL a quarter turn. Why reinvent the wheel?

The second step in the writing process involves coming up with a critique of the previous literature so that you can justify your paper on personality and crime. Your research question is shaped by the shortcomings in the literature; your paper is attempting to remedy those gaps that exist in the literature. You do not 'just' write a research paper or 'just' make a claim of your own. Your 'take' on a topic arises from what is missing in the literature. You need to be able to answer the 'So what?' question. How do you go about finding limitations and deficiencies in previous literature? Go through your 30 journal articles and identify all the GAPs. What patterns exist in your GAP collection? What POC can you develop based on those GAPs? POC is a deficiency in the articles you have read or the literature in general that you could use as a way of remedying a deficiency in the literature. POC is easily developed with experience; that is because POC is developed and refined over time – through years of continuous reading. First-time graduate students and upper-class undergraduates do not yet have the experience of cultivating POCs when they embark on their research papers. There is a way, however, for beginners to exploit their reading codes to cultivate their POC.

Students should consult books and articles on developing a critique of existing works. For example, Crasswell and Poore (2012) instruct students to follow their hunch as they read. Lipson (2005) advises undergraduates to pay attention to questions that have not been asked or pursued in readings; those shortcomings, he advises, should be explored in one's undergraduate thesis. A much more systematic and heuristic way of critiquing social science journal articles is to examine the following (see Harris, 2014): (1) definition – its lack of consensus and ambiguity; (2) measurement – its inconsistency, variable choice, and selection; (3) causal relationships between variables; (4) ethics; (5) policy implications. Harris's (2014) book provides an excellent introduction to the typical ways that social science journal articles can be critiqued. There is one more way that students can develop a critique for their own research purposes.

Go through the 30 articles again and scan for CPLs. As mentioned earlier, CPL is a critique of SPL. On what grounds did the previous authors – authors of the 30 articles you will have read – critique the SPL? That is, are there common denominators in the way that the authors of the 30 articles on personality and crime have CPLed the SPL? Usually, the answer is yes. Use those existing themes to cultivate your own POC. Moreover, look at the right margins again and identify all the Recommendations for Future Works (RFWs). RFWs are signposts to the GAPs in the literature. That is why the authors put them in their conclusions – because there is still a GAP in the literature that needs to be remedied. RFWs, along with patterns and trends in the way SPL is CPLed, are a good way to mine for one's own unique way of organizing a literature review. The RFWs are shortcuts to formulating your own GAPs. Using that existing pattern others have used as a way of framing your own paper might be called 'making a quarter turn.' Such turns do not invert or subvert the established ideas, theories, and critiques in paradigm-shifting ways; you are simply turning the SPL and CPL just enough to be different from previous studies while justifying the necessity of your own proposed study. That is why a careful reading of the discussion and conclusion sections is important.

11

Becoming a Part of the Scholarly Community: How to Read the Discussion and Conclusion

Ho Shon, P. C.

In previous chapters, I noted that one of the elementary mistakes students make when writing undergraduate research papers and drafts of graduate theses is the failure to connect to the works of previous researchers. Regrettably, this problem is not unique to students; freshly minted PhDs and even seasoned academics fail to connect their papers to the relevant literature. I am no exception. I too have made this error, and continue to make it because I have not read sufficiently or widely. In previous chapters, I also argued that connecting to the work of others in the literature review entails doing two things: (1) summarizing the work that others have done (SPL); and (2) identifying shortcomings in the current state of the literature as part of a critique (CPL, GAP). Once previous works are discussed and critiqued, students have set up a rationale (RAT) for why their proposed work (e.g., honors thesis, master's thesis, and PhD dissertation) is warranted and necessary. The proposed work will be necessary because it will remedy the knowledge gap that exists in the literature. Once you – the student – are able to defend why your proposed study is necessary, you can begin the data collection process, analyze the data, and present the results of your study as part of an undergraduate research paper, undergraduate honors thesis, master's thesis, and PhD dissertation. As I have argued in this book, social science journal articles that students have to read also follow the aforementioned general format (SPL→CPL→GAP→RAT). After authors have critiqued and provided a rationale for their studies, they have to provide a description of the data and methods used to analyze them. After the data and methods are introduced, authors present their findings in the results section. After the results are presented, then what? In most, if not all, social science journal articles, the authors provide readers with a discussion and/or conclusion section. This chapter teaches students how to read them.

In the discussion section, the Results of Findings (ROFs) are interpreted and explained in the context of the previous literature; ROFs from a study are significant given the author's summary and critique of the previous literature. In the results section, the findings are generally stated, without additional commentary or elaboration. If the literature review transports readers into the history of a discipline and a topic by bringing the past – previous scholars – to the present, the current study – then the discussion and conclusion take the findings from present research into the past and back to the future. In the literature review, the past is made relevant to the present by pointing out the limitations of previous works, which the current work attempts to overcome; in the discussion section, the present is made relevant to the past by interpreting current results in the context of past findings; moreover, the deficiencies in the current work are made relevant for other scholars who may want to remedy those gaps in the future. The discussion section thereby transports readers across three time periods – past, present, and future – by interpreting the present in the context of the past, and through self-reflexive criticism that sets up the RAT for future research.

For example, Glatthorn and Joyner (2005) instruct their writers (readers) to ask themselves what the study 'means' when writing discussion sections. To do so, they provide helpful questions to follow when writing – and I would argue reading – one's own discussion section: what is the 'relationship of the current study to prior research?' and what are the 'theoretical implications' of the study? Are there insights that the researcher could proffer? Are there unanticipated results that need to be reconciled and resolved? As Jordan and Zanna (1999) note, discussions can be 'particularly interesting when the results did not work out exactly as the researchers anticipated.' Furthermore, what are the limitations of the current research and what recommendations could be made for future and further research? If a competently executed literature review demonstrates its debt to the works of previous researchers and scholars by building upon their research, then the discussion and conclusion sections also perform a similar function by tethering the results of the current study to the past. That is why knowledge claims grow out of the claims of others: they are conceptually, methodologically, and temporally bound to the cyclical and historical character of academic scholarship. Knowledge claims do not – cannot – begin *ab initio*. Those types of questions that previous scholars have instructed writers to contemplate while writing discussion sections are also applicable to students who are reading journal articles. In this chapter, reading codes that are particularly related to discussions and conclusions (i.e., RCL, RTC, RFW, RPP) are taught and discussed.

How to Read the Discussion Section

If there are minute differences in where the literature reviews are located in social science journal articles, discussion and conclusion sections almost always appear toward the end of an article – for the same reason that introductions have to appear at the beginning of an article. In the section below, selected paragraphs from discussion sections are reproduced in order to teach students how to read the discussions and conclusions. To describe the function of the sentences in the discussion section, and for accessibility, clarity, and ease of reference, each sentence has been numbered consecutively. There are ten paragraphs in the discussion section of 'Distinguishing juvenile homicide from violent juvenile offending' in DiCataldo and Everett's (2008) article published in *International Journal of Offender Therapy and Comparative Criminology*. The first paragraph of the discussion begins the following way:

> (1) This study set out to determine if adolescent homicide offenders could indeed be distinguished from a sample of violent nonhomicide perpetrators. (2) The overall findings contradict the predominant portrayals of adolescent homicide perpetrators in popular media outlets as the clinically distinguishable super-predator or cold psychopath compared with violent nonhomicide perpetrators, many of whom had been charged or convicted of murder. (3) In this study, the nonhomicide participants proved more problematic on many of the variables of analysis. (4) They often began their delinquent careers earlier, had significantly greater numbers of total offenses, and had more violent offenses. (5) The nonhomicide participants often had less stable early childhood histories, with more frequent placements out of the home and more frequent sibling delinquency. (6) They also reported being more likely to use knives in crimes of violence than the homicide group.

The first sentence of the first paragraph of the discussion tells readers the main research question that the authors have asked and attempted to answer in their paper. Sentences like it describe What They (the authors) Did (WTDD).WTDD is a logical and historical cognate of WTD that appears in the past tense in discussions and conclusions. Thus, there is temporal symmetry between WTD and WTDD, for authors instruct readers what they will do in the introduction and what they have done in the discussion and conclusion. The reading code WTDD should be written in the right margin next to that sentence. The next sentence interprets and contextualizes the primary results of the findings (ROF) from their study to the broader literature and culture.

The word 'contradict' explicitly informs readers that DiCataldo and Everett's ROF was inconsistent with the popular notion of what it means to be a juvenile killer. Such sentences are best represented by the code RTC (Results To the Contrary), and that code ought to be written in the right margin. The rest of the sentences in that paragraph go on to elaborate on the ROFs from their

study: that nonhomicide offenders were more problematic on several measures; they started criminal careers earlier than the homicide offender group,
and had less stable lives at home. In the very next paragraph, DiCataldo and
Everett (2008) note that the nonhomicide group had anger control issues and
bad memories of their parents as well.

If the code RTC describes the way the ROFs contradict the findings from the
literature, Results that are Consistent with the Literature (RCL) describe
findings that corroborate and support results from previous studies. Thus,
sentences like:

> The homicide perpetrators' more frequent reports that they were intoxi-
> cated at the time of their deadly violent acts are consistent with recent
> research by Dolan and Smith (2001), who also reported that their sample of
> juvenile homicide offenders were more likely to report that they had abused
> alcohol at the time of their offenses than the nonhomicide offenders.

and:

> The homicide participants' greater exposure to guns at home within their
> personal histories as a predisposing factor to their later homicidal acts is
> consistent with a recent report by Bingenheimer, Brennan and Earls (2005),
> who concluded that being exposed to firearm violence nearly doubled the
> probability that an adolescent would commit a serious violent act in the
> subsequent 2 years. (DiCataldo & Everett, 2008, p. 170)

in these third and fourth paragraphs nestle their findings in the context and
work of previous researchers. That is, rather than simply presenting their
findings as new knowledge claims, they bind their ROFs within the context of
work that others have already done. By doing so, DiCataldo and Everett
(2008) join the community of researchers whose work corroborates a particular finding; they participate in the construction and reproduction of knowledge
in the scholarly community – their claims become tied to the claims of others.
Although their primary findings are RTC, other facets of their findings are
consistent with the literature (RCL) on the topic, and next to those types of
sentences, the code RCL should be written in the right margin (Figure 4).

So far, the authors have described how the findings from their research
contradict and support the work that others have done. By linking their work
to those of others, they are executing the very advice that writers like
Glatthorn and Joyner (2005) have provided: answering questions like, 'What
is the relationship of the current study to prior research?', and what are the
'theoretical implications' of the study? The codes RCL and RTC describe two
interpretive possibilities for ROFs of a study, and by elaborating on the relationship of the current ROFs to past ROFs the current findings are made

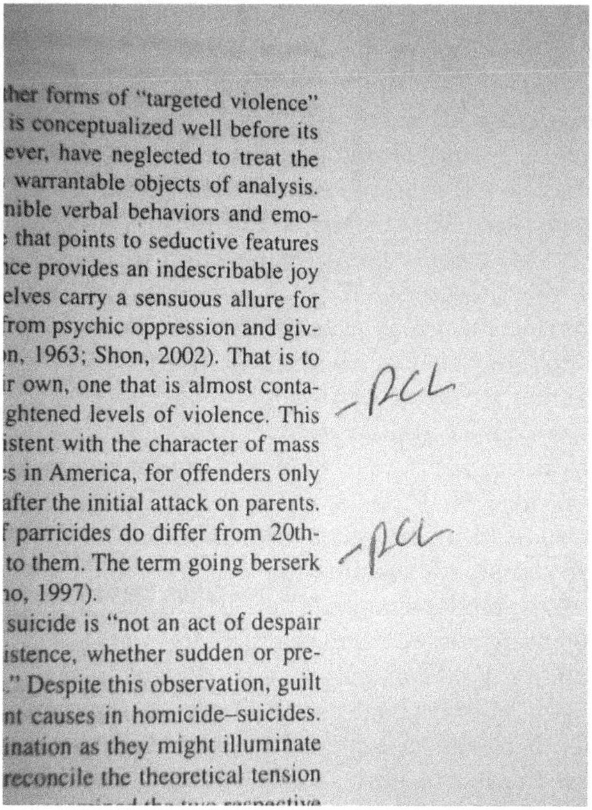

ther forms of "targeted violence"
is conceptualized well before its
ever, have neglected to treat the
warrantable objects of analysis.
nible verbal behaviors and emo-
: that points to seductive features
ice provides an indescribable joy
elves carry a sensuous allure for
from psychic oppression and giv-
n, 1963; Shon, 2002). That is to
r own, one that is almost conta-   *-PCL*
ghtened levels of violence. This
istent with the character of mass
:s in America, for offenders only
after the initial attack on parents.
f parricides do differ from 20th-   *-PCL*
to them. The term going berserk
io, 1997).
suicide is "not an act of despair
istence, whether sudden or pre-
." Despite this observation, guilt
nt causes in homicide–suicides.
ination as they might illuminate
reconcile the theoretical tension

FIGURE 4

meaningful and situated in the community of scholars who have carried out similar and related works. Although DiCataldo and Everett (2008) do not discuss the theoretical implications of their work, they do address the policy implications of their findings. They go on to critique the legislative changes that have occurred in the US, which seek to treat adolescent killers like adults in the criminal justice system; such policies, they argue, are aimed at the wrong population, for their ROFs would indicate that nonhomicide offenders are much more psycho-socially problematic than homicide offenders. Again, by teasing out the implications of their research and findings for public policy, the authors make their research meaningful in the larger social context: they are able to contextualize their findings and make them relevant in the ongoing debate about crime and punishment; they are able to critique a social policy that may be targeting the wrong group and causing undue harm; more importantly, they can substantiate such criticisms based on empirical research. Those types of implications – theoretical, conceptual, methodological, policy – are teased out and pursued in the discussion section.

Their work, however, is not complete. In the first sentence of paragraph five of the discussion, the authors write 'There exist a number of selection biases within this study that may account for the findings' (p. 170). They point out that 'a differential processing of cases within the juvenile justice system may be operating that may alternatively explain the differences identified within this study' (p. 170). In other words, the authors are pointing out shortcomings – GAPs – in their own work. That means, in future works, someone could address those shortcomings of juvenile homicide research to overcome a GAP in the current state of the literature. Those types of sentences would illustrate Recommendations for Future Works (RFW) and Relevant Point to Pursue (RPP). RFWs highlight the fact that the current paper is incomplete; the authors are providing a map of what is still missing (GAP) in the literature. Such POCs could be mined in a future paper by someone who is interested in the topic, and has the capacity to overcome those limitations. In the first sentence of the last paragraph of the discussion, a similar sentence appears: 'This study did not attempt to investigate the motivations or circumstances of the homicides for this sample of juveniles' (p. 172). This sentence again is a POC, for the authors tell the reader what was not done in the current paper; logically, the authors are pointing out a GAP in the literature. Those GAPs could be used as POCs in another paper and represent RPPs and RFWs. Next to relevant sentences, the pertinent codes ought to be written in the right margin.

The last sentence of the last paragraph of the discussion is even more explicit about how the shortcomings of the current paper can be remedied:

> Future research with this sample will progress toward a finer-grained, within-group analysis of the homicide perpetrators, coding the multidimensional contextual features of their acts of homicide by looking at the physical setting of the homicide, the interactional and historical relationships with the victims, the means and methods of homicide, the posthomicide behavior of the perpetrators, and the legal outcomes' (p. 172)

In other words, the RFWs just mentioned illustrate the missing elements in the literature on juvenile homicide (GAPs) – they need to be addressed in the future. The code RFW should be written in the right margin of paper. That is five POCs and GAPs the authors have provided in one sentence alone. That such GAPs and POCs are already contained in the articles being read is the reason why reading should not be treated as a secondary activity. The components of a future paper – most importantly GAPs – are already embedded in the current work. Writers do not necessarily have to come up with 'new ideas' because they are already buried in the readings. Future writers just have to know how to find them during the act of reading. RFWs represent POCs and CPLs/GAPs that are already embedded in the discussion and conclusion sections that should be used as a resource for students who are reading social science journal articles.

There are seven paragraphs that make up the discussion section, in addition to the two paragraphs on limitations and suggestions for future research, and one conclusion paragraph in E.H. Kim et al.'s (2014) article on 'Hwa-byung among middle-aged Korean women: Family relationships, gender-role attitudes, and self-esteem' published in *Health Care for Women International*. In all, ten paragraphs are spent on the discussion and conclusion. The notable sentences that we want to examine in greater detail from the discussion section begin the following way:

(1) Our main purposes for this study were twofold: (a) to examine how family relationship problems, attitudes toward women's roles, and self-esteem were related to HB [hwa-byung, Korean anger syndrome], and (b) to test gender-role attitudes as a moderator for the relationship between family relationship problems and HB. (2) Our study was one of the first attempts to empirically examine these variables in a nonclinical sample of Korean women. (3) Only three demographic variables, including single/never married status, education status, and hours husband worked were found to be positively associated with HB ... (6) In terms of hours that husbands worked, we speculated that the more the husband worked, the less he is available for emotional support and help. (7) This result is similar to Kim and Kim's (1994) findings that emotional support of the husband was positively related to married women's mental well-being. (p. 505)

Sentences #1 and #2, again, describe what the authors did in their study. Consequently, the reading code WTDD is most appropriate and should be written in the right margin next to those sentences. Sentence #3 reports the significant results of their study, so the reading code ROF should be written in the right margin next to that sentence. Sentence #6 reports a significant ROF from their study, and speculates as to its causes. In sentence #7, Kim et al. again interpret their ROF and contextualize it against the broader literature. They note that their results are 'similar to Kim and Kim's (1994) findings.' The phrase 'similar to' means that their results are consistent with Kim and Kim's (1994) findings. Therefore, the reading code RCL should be written in the right margin. Throughout the rest of the discussion and conclusion section, Kim et al. go on to interpret and contextualize their ROF against the literature.

Consider the following sentences in the fourth paragraph of Kim et al.'s discussion:

(1) We found that as women endorsed egalitarian and profeminist attitudes, HB symptoms increased. (2) This result is consistent with that of Choi and colleagues (2009), in which individualistic and less traditional family values were positively associated with HB. (3) It differs from other studies, however,

> where HB patients in psychiatry and primary care settings noted strong com-
> mitments to traditional feminine roles. (p. 506)

Notice the repeating pattern in the discussion again. The authors repeat their main ROF, and then go on to contextualize their findings relative to previous research. For example, sentence #2 interprets sentence #1 (ROF) against the findings of Choi et al., which indicates that Kim et al.'s findings are consistent with Choi et al.'s (RCL). That is to say that HB in Korean women increases as more Western values permeate the social infrastructure of Korean society, according to the two findings. Kim et al.'s findings also differ from those of others – Results to the Contrary (RTC) – in that HB women in clinical samples held more traditional (non-Western) values. One's results either support or refute work already done; or each finding can do both throughout the course of a discussion section. Where relevant and appropriate, the codes RTC and RCL should be written in the right margin.

Throughout the first seven paragraphs of Kim et al.'s (2014) discussion, the authors repeat this process – ROF→RCL, ROF→RTC – always tying their primary findings to the larger literature, noting how their work supports or refutes the work that others have done. And, just as we saw in DiCataldo and Everett's (2008) discussion, Kim et al. are not finished. They must now critique their own article by pointing out the limitations of their work, as well as making recommendations for future research. Their first self-critique is that their sample was drawn from metropolitan areas where Western influence is prevalent; hence, they caution that their findings may not be generalizable to rural areas (Kim et al., 2014, p. 507). Finally, they point out that GAPs exist in the literature in the form of RFWs. Again, RFWs are made because the current state of the knowledge is necessarily incomplete. Consider the RFWs that Kim et al. proclaim:

> (1) First, the IFR [Index of Family Relations Scale] used in our study mea-
> sures the respondents' feelings about their family relationship as a whole,
> rather than their feelings about any specific relationships … (3) Researchers
> should conduct future research to examine how women's feelings about dif-
> ferent relationships with family members (e.g., husbands, in-laws, and
> children) might be related to HB symptoms. (4) Second, our finding of a
> significant relationship between profeminist gender beliefs and HB stimu-
> lates further questioning. (5) In particular, how are Korean women's
> egalitarian, feminist attitudes perceived in the family? Do family members
> support or accept the Korean women's perspective, and how does that con-
> tribute to more or fewer HB symptoms? (p. 507)

The preceding RFWs, which by default become GAPs, logically follow and emerge from the authors' current findings. That is, if current measures only reflect women's attitudes toward the family as a whole rather than specific relationships within the family, then it makes sense for future works to disentangle those measurement choices. Should any undergraduate student in health sciences, counseling, social work, or women's studies need ideas for an honors thesis or a senior-level capstone project; should any master's student in the aforementioned disciplines need a topic for his or her thesis; should a doctoral student need a topic to pursue as part of his or her PhD dissertation, all they need to do is find, and then use those RFWs as GAPs of their own. In other words, the potential new ideas for future works are buried in the text being read, again illustrating the importance of learning to read critically through the use of the reading codes. The first one to initiate and complete the project and publish the results gets dibs on the claims.

Eight paragraphs make up the discussion in Oliver and Armstrong's (1995) article on 'Predictors of viewing and enjoyment of reality-based and fictional crime shows,' published in *Journalism & Mass Communication Quarterly*. The first paragraph of the discussion begins the following way:

> (1) The purpose of this study was to explore predictors of exposure to and enjoyment of reality-based crime programs. (2) Consistent with Zillmann's Disposition Theory, the results of this telephone survey suggest that these types of programs may be most appealing to viewers predicted to be particularly likely to enjoy the capture and punishment of criminal suspects who are often members of racial minorities. (3) Namely, this study found that reality-based programs were most enjoyed by viewers who evidenced higher levels of authoritarianism, reported greater punitiveness about crime, and reported higher levels of racial prejudice.

The first sentence repeats the main research question examined in the study; the code WTDD ought to be written in the right margin. The second sentence informs readers that the results of the study support the work of a previous researcher; hence, the code RCL ought to be written in the right margin. The third sentence provides the readers with the primary findings from the study: people who tend to be authoritarian, people who report greater punitiveness about crime, and those who tend to be racially prejudiced enjoy reality-based crime shows. The code ROF ought to be written in the right margin. The first paragraph is consistent with the form and structure of discussions that we have examined thus far: WTDD, ROF, RCL, RTC. Discussion sections are sites where the initial research question is repeated in the past tense, the primary results echoed, and then evaluated against the literature. Whether the reported results are consistent with the existing state of the knowledge or contradict it is played out in the discussion. Oliver and Armstrong (1995) do not explicitly tease out the social or policy implications of their work.

Simply noting if results support or contradict previous literature, as we have seen, is not enough. In the articles discussed thus far, the authors took time to bring to our attention the limitations and deficiencies that exist in their own works. For example, Oliver and Armstrong (1995, p. 565) write:

> While the present investigation did not attempt to directly assess the relative beneficial or harmful functions of reality-based programs, the idea that these shows appeal to viewers with punitive, authoritarian, and prejudiced attitudes is worthy of further investigation.

Put another way, the present study did not assess the benefits or harms of reality-based programs; however, that such shows appeal to those who tend to be conservative in their political orientation should be pursued further. This statement means that there is a GAP somewhere in the literature. Again, the authors do not simply end there. They specifically provide four Recommendations for Future Works (RFWs) that are based on the presence of GAPs in their own works (pp. 565–6): RFW #1 'future research may consider exploring reactions to these types of shows among a wider variety of respondents.' RFW #2: 'Further research may consider exploring the specific portrayals within this genre that appeal to viewers.' RFW #3: 'research could examine how long-term exposure may affect estimates of the prevalence of crime or the percentage of people of color who are involved in crime-related activities.' RFW #4: 'future studies may consider exploring how exposure to reality-based crime shows relates to perceptions and judgments about crimes witnessed or reported in other contexts.' Next to these sentences, the code RFW should be written in the right margin so that they are easily identifiable and retrievable. There are always GAPs in social science journal articles that could be used as POCs and serve as RATs in a future paper.

Nine paragraphs make up the discussion section of Hu and Ma's (2010) article on 'Mentoring and student persistence in college: A study of the Washington State Achievers Program,' published in *Innovative Higher Education*. The first paragraph begins in the following way:

> (1) This study showed that the assignment of college mentors varies by institutional types; (2) and public, four-year institutions seem to have done a better job in this regard. (3) Hispanic students and 'other' students are more likely than White students to seek support and encouragement from their mentors. (4) In addition, Hispanic students are more likely than their White counterparts to perceive their overall experiences with mentoring as more important. (5) Previous research has suggested that ethnic minority students report lower coping efficacy and expect to confront more educational and career-related barriers than White students [citation omitted].

(6) Thus, the findings of this study offer support for the hypothesis that mentoring experiences vary by race and ethnicity (Barker 2007; Nora and Crisp 2007). (p. 337)

The first four sentences repeat the ROFs of Hu and Ma's study. They do not repeat what they did in their study (WTDD); they simply inform the readers about the significant results of their study. These ROFs should be high-lighted, and the code ROF written in the right margin. Notice how the ROFs in sentences #1–4 are interpreted against the broader literature in sentence #5. Sentence #5 provides the background or the previous literature (SPL) against which the current ROFs are interpreted, that minority students expect to face more difficulty than White students. It is this SPL that sentence #6 pushes against; it turns out that one of Hu and Ma's ROFs is consistent with (RCL) what Barker (2007) and Nora and Crisp (2007) have reported in prior works. The code RCL should be written in the right margin. Such interpretive moves are played out again in later paragraphs.

In the first paragraph, then, Hu and Ma (2010) do what scholars in other disciplines have done: repeat their main findings (ROFs) and interpret their findings relative to the work that others have done. Primarily, those interpretive possibilities exist in two forms: results that support previous research (RCL) or results that contradict established findings (RTC). It is this contextualization and interpretation of one's findings and arguments that are accomplished in discussion sections. Without such linkages to the broader literature, one's findings and arguments become orphans in a community of scholars and knowledge claims, unconnected to the genealogy of their ideas. There are times, however, when ROFs require a bit more extended discussion and elaboration, especially when unexpected results of a study are encountered. Consider the following fifth paragraph of Hu and Ma's (2010) discussion section:

(1) Considering that the frequency of contact has been identified as an important aspect of the student–mentor relationship [citation omitted] and that it is reported to be positively related to students' adjustment to college [citation omitted] and persistence [citation omitted], it is somewhat surprising to find that the number of meetings with college mentors is not significantly related to the probability of persisting by the WSA recipient in this study. (2) It is uncertain whether this result arises from the combination of the nature of the college mentoring programs affiliated with the WSA program and the distinct feature of the sample used in the study. (3) In addition, all the mentees in this study are high-achieving, low-income students. (4) They are different from the 'at-risk' mentees in many mentoring programs sponsored by individual institutions. (5) This should be taken into consideration in understanding the findings of this study. (p. 338)

In the first half of sentence #1, Hu and Ma (2010) reiterate findings from previous research (SPL); in the second half, they report their ROF and interpret it against the literature. The phrase 'it is somewhat surprising' suggests that their ROF is not consistent with the literature as well as their expectations. Therefore, the code RTC, Results to the Contrary, would be the most appropriate code to write in the right margin. Notice, however, that the unexpected nature of Hu and Ma's finding leads to speculation and further elaboration. They are almost compelled to explain this unexpected outcome and sentences #2–5 do exactly that: they qualify and offer educated conjectures about why the unexpected results may have been found: maybe the current sample was different from prior studies; the WSA sample was composed of high-achieving but low-income students: 'This should be taken into consideration in understanding the findings of this study' (p. 338). Hu and Ma (2010) are offering their readers ways to understand the unexpected findings of their work.

What Hu and Ma (2010) do not do is provide a roadmap of what is still missing in the literature and the work that future researchers ought to do. In other words, they do not make recommendations for future works (RFWs). That absence should not mean GAPs do not exist. The study that Hu and Ma conducted can be critiqued on some points (POC): they may have missed an obvious connection to a previous claim (MOP) or future scholars can cultivate a POC and pursue it further in their own paper (RPP). Discussion sections, whether in sociology, psychology, criminology, nursing, or education, generally end with RFWs due to the tentative state of the knowledge in the social sciences, and as a way of moving the literature forward. More work could always be done to improve the state of the literature. Consider how those RFWs occur in the discussion section of the article by Thapa, Cohen, Guffey, and Higgins-D'Alessandro (2013), published in *Review of Educational Research*:

> (1) As this review makes clear, the majority of studies do not examine the effects of climate within multilevel/hierarchical frameworks, and very few examine school change over time, a key to understanding school improvement processes and efforts. (2) Building on the important school improvement research that Bryk and his colleagues (2002, 2010) have conducted in Chicago, we suggest that more studies examine school climate from multiple perspectives, including experimental, quasi-experimental, and correlational, as well as case studies and qualitative analyses, and as much as possible integrate process and outcome concepts into time-sensitive analyses. (p. 371)

The preceding paragraph is the second to the last paragraph of the entire article entitled 'A review of school climate research,' and in the article, the phrase 'we suggest that more studies examine ...' appears in the discussion section and would be aptly coded as an RFW, for that is what the authors are doing. Thapa et al. (2013) are suggesting that future scholars conduct the type of work that they recommend. Why would they make such a recommendation? After reviewing numerous previous studies in their article on school climate, they are pointing out the shortcomings that still exist in the literature on school climate. RFWs are shortcomings that exist in the literature, and should be treated as such: they should be faithfully written in the right margins when they are spotted.

How to Read the Conclusion Section

Robert Entman's (1990) article entitled 'Modern racism and the images of blacks in local television news,' published in *Critical Studies in Mass Communication*, examines how local news challenges conventional views of racism and facilitates it at the same time. There is no discussion section; three paragraphs, however, make up the conclusion section of the article. In the first paragraph, the author summarizes the ROFs from the current study: showing blacks as offenders and victims makes them look ominous, thereby perpetuating a negative stereotype, while showing positive images of blacks in the news leads to the false impression that racial discrimination is no longer a significant problem. In the second paragraph, Entman goes on to explain the paradox of news as it relates particularly to blacks. He states that the constraints and market-driven and standard operating practices of TV journalism, rather than malicious intention, may account for the paradoxical outcome that local news produces. He ends the second paragraph by stating that, 'The implication of this research, then, is that local news is likely to continue the practices hypothesized here' (p. 343). In the third and final paragraph, Entman (1990) writes the following:

(1) To be sure, images of blacks in the local news are complicated and replete with multiple potential meanings. (2) And audiences bring to the news a variety of predispositions. (3) Social scientists have no more than a rudimentary understanding of how audiences perceive and process media messages [citations omitted]. (4) Nonetheless, the exploratory study provides ample support for a hypothesis that local television's images of blacks feed racial anxiety and antagonism at least among that portion of the white population most predisposed to those feelings. (5) Quantitative research on the impact of exposure to local TV news seems in order, as does extensive content analysis of large samples of local and network news. (6) Such work would also illuminate the ways that television helps to alter and preserve dominant cultural values and structures of power. (p. 343)

The main thrust of the conclusion is that local news carries several meanings; as the last sentence suggests, TV – local news – shapes and maintains culture and power. The paradoxical way that local news creates and debunks racism is again reflected in a much broader context in the conclusion. Moreover, the author's work is consistent with his initial hypothesis. His work, however, is not complete. He proffers two RFWs: (1) additional quantitative research of exposure impact, and (2) more content analysis using larger samples of local and network news. The code RFW should be written in the right margin. Although no discussion section is present, readers can see that certain components are essential elements of the conclusion. The larger meaning of the current study is teased out; limitations of current research and recommendations for future works are stated in the conclusion, despite the absence of a discussion.

In the discussion and conclusion sections we have read through, we have seen how the authors have made their ROFs relevant and meaningful by linking their works with past research; furthermore, we have seen how the authors have teased out the policy implications of their work – doing in their papers what numerous how-to books have instructed students to do. That does not mean POCs do not exist. In fact, the authors themselves might have Missed an Obvious Point (MOP) and this MOP can be used as a POC to be RPPed in a future paper. MOP should be written in the right margin. For instance, one of the implications that Sampson (1987) teases out in his article is that black men face economic deprivation and labor-market marginality, which can then lead to family disruption and crime. One of the scholars that Sampson cited, William Wilson, argues that black men face and have faced structural impediments to employment by being segregated in inner cities, black men display characteristics that make them less attractive to potential employers, black men have been the first to lose their jobs in the deindustrialization that took place in rustbelt cities. That is, black men face cumulative disadvantage of sorts. So, if an astute reader asks why black men have faced economic deprivation and labor-market marginality, how might Sampson answer this question? To find a cogent and comprehensive answer, that reader will have to go outside of sociology and criminology; the answer to that question lies in disciplines such as history and communication. Even the most influential articles published in the highest-tier journals, written by a highly influential scholar teaching at one of the most prestigious institutions, can be critiqued; even such scholarship can be CPLed and used as a POC and RPP in a future paper. That process begins during the act of reading.

As argued throughout this book, the reading codes serve several purposes. First, they slow down the act of reading so that readers do not gloss over words and phrases; by enacting the role of a textual detective during the act of reading, readers are trying to figure out the function of a particular text in addition to processing its contents. Reading therefore occurs on two levels. Second, reading with codes leads to critical thinking during the act of reading. Rather than reflecting on the merits or limitations of an article after the reading is completed, the use of reading codes engages the reader with the text in real time, while the reading is taking place. Problems of recall and memory are thus minimized since observations and notes about the readings are made on the text itself. The use of reading codes structures the mind toward a purposive task with realizable objectives that can be accomplished, thereby avoiding unstructured – unproductive – reading. The use of reading codes leads to questions such as 'What function does this sentence/paragraph serve in the article?' rather than 'What did I just read for the last 15 minutes?'

By identifying sentences and paragraphs that perform a particular function (RCL, RTC, RPP, RFW, MOP) within a social science article, students are not only thinking critically and evaluating the paper's strengths and weaknesses, but they are also implicitly structuring their own papers to write in the future. That is, readers are identifying the relevance of current research to the past literature, and spotting deficiencies and gaps in the literature for their own exigent (e.g., end-of-semester literature review paper) and future-oriented tasks (e.g., thesis, dissertation). That is why reading cannot be treated as a secondary activity. Before a writer can even think about constructing an outline, the contents of that outline have to be filled in somehow. The left margin thematic codes along with the themes in the SPLs in the right margins proffer a starting point for an outline. As argued in this book, trying to recall the contents of 50-plus articles and trying to organize them in some cogent way are daunting tasks: the reading codes facilitate the organization and management of information necessary for academic writing.

Critical analysis, perspective and argument

Greasley, P.

If you can't say anything nice, don't say anything at all.

(Old English proverb)

Good advice for social occasions, perhaps, but potentially disastrous for your assignments.

In this chapter we'll be discussing the importance of adopting a critical perspective, developing an argument, and making a case for the position you have decided to adopt. To help you appreciate the significance of this when writing your assignments, we'll be looking at:

- a model of learning and teaching that probably forms the basis for how your course is taught and how your assignments are assessed
- some questions you might ask when presented with a theory, a model, or the findings from a research study
- a crucial difference between what you think is important when writing your assignments and what tutors think is important when marking your assignments
- the importance of adopting a perspective on the issues you are discussing (and making a case for your position)

You'll also learn that there are no 'right' answers, and that you should trust no one.

Tip 43: **Stop describing, start critiquing**

One of the most significant outcomes from the survey is that it highlights the importance of critical thinking and argument as the feature that tutors value highest when marking assignments. The message is that you need to step up a gear: from simply describing and reporting to being analytical, critical and evaluative. In this respect, there's something you should know about. It's called Bloom's taxonomy (Figure 8.1) and it probably forms the basis for how your course is taught and assessed.

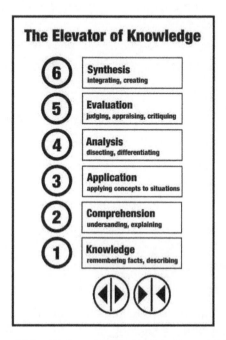

Figure 8.1   Illustration of Bloom's taxonomy of educational objectives

Bloom's taxonomy (Bloom et al., 1956) outlines six levels of thinking, from the simple to the complex. Pay particular attention to what lies at the bottom in Figure 8.1: description, recalling facts, and simply reporting what others have said. If you want high marks, particularly as you progress through the years at university, you will need to climb this ladder by applying, analysing and critically evaluating concepts.

So you start by building up your knowledge about a concept, theory, model, etc. until you are able to understand it, describe it, give examples and then apply it, but then you progress beyond this level of understanding (merely knowing about and accepting something because it's in a book or a manual) to a more critical, analytical perspective.

Generally speaking, then, description won't get you many marks; it certainly won't get you high marks. So, if the question asks you to 'analyse', 'critically appraise' or 'evaluate' and you spend most of the essay describing things, reporting lots of facts and figures and covering as much ground as possible, you're heading for disappointment. This emphasis on critical analysis rather than description is highlighted in the comments from the survey of tutors:

What tutors dislike

- Description rather than analysis (particularly from second year upwards)

- Presenting lots of bullet points instead of discussion

- Long bits of description which could be condensed into a sentence or two

- Not providing some sort of critique of, or reflection on, the work they've read (i.e. assuming because it's in print it must be 'right')

What tutors like

- Students who attempt to look critically at models/theories

- Analysis of reading rather than description

- Concise critical appraisal (with citations in support, where appropriate)

- Ability to see more than one side of an argument

- Being aware that just because something is in print it doesn't make it a for-all-time, concrete, unassailable fact!

- A good mixture of discussion and argument

- Comparison of sources and analysis

- Critical comment on the literature (author A takes this view in contrast to author B - what they both fail to account for fully is...; or an alternative interpretation can be offered by...; or this does not account for the problematic nature of [this concept], etc.)

Tip 44: When presented with a theory, a model, or the findings from a research study, there are certain questions you should ask

If you are going to adopt a more critical perspective, it's useful to have some questions at the ready to get you started (Neville, 2009a; G. Taylor, 2009). I've listed a few below along with some examples of how they might be applied.

Where does the theory/model/statistic come from? Who says? How do they know? What's the evidence? What's the sample?

Did you know, for example, that women talk more than men? Of course you did: an average 20,000 words per day compared to 7,000 for men. When these statistics were featured in *The Female Brain*, a bestselling book by Louann Brizendine

(2006),they were circulated throughout the media (e.g. 'Women talk three times as much as men, says study' was the headline in the *Daily Mail* newspaper; Macrae, 28 November 2006). However, on closer inspection it was discovered that these figures were derived from a self-help book and other second-hand sources – not research – and they were removed from a later edition of the book (Lilienfeld et al., 2010). A more reliable primary source based on a study by Mehl et al. (2007), reported in the journal *Science*, found that men and women both use around 16,000 words per day, though with 'very large individual differences'.

Does it make sense based on your own experience?

Your own experience may lead you to question the conclusions from the Mehl et al. (2007) study. There were, after all, 'very large individual differences', and the study was based on a particular sample: 396 university students (210 were female).

Does it apply across different contexts and cultures?

We should also question whether these results apply across different contexts and cultures since the study was limited to a sample of university students from the USA.

Does it apply in the real world?

When Newstead and Dennis (1994) asked 14 experienced examiners to mark six essays some of the marks were so inconsistent that they ranged from a 2:2 to a first – for the same essay. Does this mean that the mark you are awarded for your assignment depends to a large extent on the tutor who is marking it? Not necessarily, because this was an experiment rather than real-life marking with real consequences for the student. Furthermore, the marking was conducted by tutors not involved on the course, it was a 'rather abstract and obscure topic that examiners might have great difficulty in marking' (Newstead, 2002: 73), and they weren't using marking schemes with clear criteria. In research terms, this is known as lacking 'ecological validity', because the study didn't really reflect the real-life situation.

Is it plausible?

The problem with research is that it can be contradictory. Think about health advice: one minute we are advised to eat fewer eggs and the next minute we are told we can eat as many as we like (within reason of course). In my own area of interest, complementary and alternative therapies, there have been decades of research providing conflicting evidence on whether treatments like homeopathy or acupuncture work or not. While it's important to be selective about the evidence you choose to believe (the more robust studies), it's also important to look at the *plausibility* of the treatments: what's the rationale – the underlying mechanism of action? Is it plausible that acupuncture works because it claims to release a mysterious 'energy' called 'qi' through equally mysterious channels referred to as meridians? At this point you might want to consider carefully the underlying rationale for a particular therapy. We would apply the same criteria to pseudosciences like astrology.

Are there exceptions which challenge the theory/model?

Most students in the social sciences will at one time or another come across Abraham Maslow's (1987) famous model outlining the 'hierarchy of human

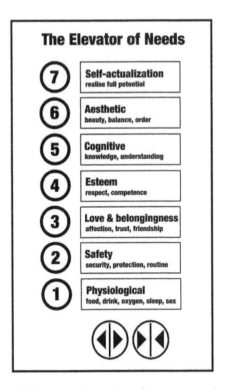

The Elevator of Needs

Figure 8.2 Illustration of Maslow's hierarchy of human needs

needs'. I've represented it as an 'elevator of needs' in Figure 8.2. The model has been used to account for why most people are never satisfied: having satisfied one set of needs, our priorities move on to the next. For example, once you've achieved safety and security (job, house, etc.), you might then start to focus on 'love and belongingness' (personal and social relationships); and once that's sorted out, you might start to think about your esteem needs (e.g. promotion at work); and so on. The problem is, of course, that there are many exceptions. For example, many people in affluent countries are satisfied with a house, car, family, etc., and don't crave a higher level of 'self-actualisation' epitomised by the famous few upon which Maslow's concept of 'self-actualisation' was based (e.g. Albert Einstein, Abraham Lincoln). They may be happy with their lot. Another problem is the idea that we have to satisfy needs at one level before moving on to the next. For example, must we satisfy the more basic physiological needs before dealing with the higher needs? (Dear Tutor, I won't be attending your lecture today because I have some needs lower down the hierarchy that I have to satisfy...).

There is an important issue to be aware of here: beware of simplified secondary accounts of a theory. For example, in many textbooks Maslow's hierarchy is criticised for stating that we must satisfy the lower needs before moving up to the higher needs. But Maslow didn't actually say this in such simplistic terms. He took a more realistic approach, pointing out that we move up the hierarchy when lower levels are partially satisfied. New motivations *emerge* as lower needs are becoming fulfilled. He was also well aware of exceptions (e.g. the starving artist who forgoes the more basic needs in favour of aesthetic needs).

This illustrates an important point: be careful that you don't simplify or mis-interpret the theory/model. This highlights the importance of comparing a few sources of information and, preferably, going back to the original source.

Tip 45: Appreciate the good as well as the bad

It's important to remember that being critical is not just about being negative. Rather, it's about demonstrating that you appreciate the *pros and cons* – discerning the good and the bad – of something. In academic studies this usually means evaluating a theory, model, research study, etc., but in real life we do it all the time when we make judgements about the quality of a movie, music, fashion, cars, etc. In assignments, though, you just need to be a bit more rigorous:

- What's good about it (and why; with references to support your case)
- What's problematic about it (and why; with references...)

Critically appraising research articles in academic journals is a common assign-ment topic for students in the health and social sciences. It requires them to appraise the various parts of an article, including the title (is it clear and inform-ative?), the abstract (is it a good summary of the article, providing details about the sample, methods, results?), the methodology (was it appropriate to the aims of the study? Was it clearly explained? Was it well designed?), and so on. It's sup-posed to be a detailed critical examination of the research, but sometimes this isn't quite achieved, as the following extract from one assignment illustrates:

> **Critically appraising a research article (extract from student assignment)**
>
> The title is easy to read as it has big font and it's bold so it stands out ... The abstract is not as clear to read from as it has small font which makes it difficult to read because the words are so close together ... The good thing about the abstract is that it's placed in the middle so therefore it differentiates itself from the rest of the literature...

There are lots of books (and many websites) providing guidelines to help you critically appraise the quality and reliability of research studies. In the health sciences, for example, Trisha Greenhalgh's (2006) book, *How to Read a Paper*, is a classic text providing guidance on critically appraising a range of research designs (e.g. randomised controlled trials, systematic reviews, qualitative research).

Tip 46: You think it's all about content and coverage, but tutors value argument and understanding

Studies have highlighted a 'mismatch' between what students and tutors think is most important when writing essays (Norton, 1990; Defeyter and

McPartlin, 2007). While both students and tutors agree that the top rank goes to 'answering the question', a mismatch appears between the importance of content and argument:

- Students rank content and coverage of relevant information higher than argument

- Tutors rank argument and understanding higher than content

Another way of putting this is that tutors place greater emphasis on the importance of a deep approach – displaying *understanding* – whereas students tend to focus on a surface approach – covering lots of information. (Remember Tip 25: you should be writing 'a lot about a little, rather than a little about a lot'.)

Tip 47: Try using the 'therefore test' to check for arguments

If you're not totally clear about what an argument is, and whether your assignment includes any, there's a simple test you can use: see if you can insert the word 'therefore' at the end of a series of statements. Here's a simple example from Richard van de Lagemaat (2007: 10) which illustrates the difference between (1) merely listing a series of unsubstantiated statements and (2) constructing an argument:

1. Astrology is the belief that the position of the stars at the time of your birth affects your destiny. There are ten times more astrologers than astronomers in the United States. Despite its popularity, astrology cannot be classified as a science.

2. One of the hallmarks of a genuine science is that it makes testable predictions. Admittedly, astrologers do make predictions, but they are so vague that they cannot be verified or falsified. So, unlike astronomy, astrology cannot be classified as a science.

Whereas (1) lists a series of unrelated statements, (2) constructs an argument – and we could use 'therefore' to replace 'so' before the final sentence. (Other words like 'so', 'consequently', 'thus', and 'hence' may also be used to indicate the conclusion to an argument.) Out of interest, I decided to go through the excellent student assignment that I referred to in Chapter 6 to see if I could use the 'therefore' test to highlight arguments in the text, and I was pleased to find two opportunities in the opening paragraph of the introduction:

Introduction

According to the National Asthma Campaign, there are 5.4 million people in the UK currently receiving treatment for asthma and the cost to the NHS is over £996 million per year. In 2007, Killingham's Primary Care Trust had the 4th highest hospital admissions rate for asthma in the whole of the UK, which suggests [**therefore**] that the management, treatment and education of asthma is not effective in the Killingham area. [**Therefore**] New strategies to help reduce strain on emergency departments, respiratory clinics and local

GP surgeries need to be brought into play to ensure that asthma sufferers are receiving the treatment they require, when they need it.

Here we can see that the 'therefore test' makes the underlying argument in this introductory passage explicit. If we break it down into premises (statements which lead to a claim), it looks like this:

- Premise 1: Asthma affects millions of people in the UK

- Premise 2: Treatments for asthma costs millions each year

- Premise 3: Killingham Care Trust has one of the highest hospital admission rates in the UK

- Conclusion: Therefore new strategies to treat asthma might be considered: the argument provides a justification for examining the use of acupuncture as an alternative or complementary treatment for asthma

It is this logical reasoning, made explicit by the 'therefore' test, which makes this introduction so effective.

Here's one more illustration of an argument from this excellent assignment:

The review [of research studies] drew limited conclusions regarding the effectiveness of acupuncture in treating asthma. Out of all the trials, only two of them reported the participants to have an improvement in overall well-being and this could not be distinguished between needle or sham acupuncture. Patients who received the acupuncture or believed they were having acupuncture (a placebo) did improve in general health, but not specifically in their asthma symptoms. [**Therefore**] This suggests the placebo effect of acupuncture may play a part in the therapeutic role of the treatment.

If we turn the main argument here into premise and conclusion, it might look like this:

- Premise: Patients who received real acupuncture showed some improvement in general health, but so did those who received sham acupuncture

- Conclusion: This suggests [therefore] that the placebo effect plays a part in the therapeutic role of the treatment

But did you also notice another (related) argument in this passage? Sometimes the conclusion is stated prior to the premise, so if we reverse the first two sentences this reveals another premise and conclusion:

- Premise: Only two of the trials in the review of research studies reported an improvement in well-being

- Conclusion: [Therefore] There is limited evidence regarding the effectiveness of acupuncture in treating asthma

I would suggest (therefore) that this might be a useful test to apply in your assignments to see if they contain any arguments. Though it's important to note, of course, that some arguments are better than others:

> There is a strong correlation between ice-cream sales and crime rates: as ice-cream sales rise, so does the crime rate. Therefore ice-cream causes crime ...

Incidentally, and perhaps unsurprisingly, since writing this book I've witnessed many assignments that are superficially peppered with the word 'therefore'. Remember that the extracts in the excellent complementary therapies assignment that I used to illustrate the presence of arguments didn't actually include the word 'therefore' – I inserted it to make the argument explicit. The point I'm making is: don't overdo it. A student who is comfortable arguing doesn't make it look like a special effort (or a cheap trick). Argument should be implicit in your discussion of the topic, not something that's superficially tagged on at the end of paragraphs with sentences beginning with 'Therefore'.

Tip 48: What do you think? Adopt a perspective - have a point of view

What tutors like

- Balanced argument but own opinion included within the arguments
- Ability to see more than one side of an argument
- The student's own conclusion
- A student not afraid to express an opinion (where relevant)
- A presence of voice - a sense that the author has a 'political' stance, or indeed conviction. The better essays are usually written by those students.

In the study by Defeyter and McPartlin (2007) referred to above, it was also noted that some students felt they shouldn't be presenting a particular view. Rather they should be presenting a balanced evaluation. Well, this is partly true – you should consider different perspectives, both sides of the argument, but as we saw in Chapter 4 (Tips 4 and 5), you should come to some position yourself before you start writing the assignment. What do you think? What will you be ultimately arguing for?

Tip 49: How to make the jump from a B to an A: act like you're a lawyer making a case

I have just spent a couple of hours comparing a batch of assignments which were awarded a B with those that were awarded an A. What was the difference?

Well, while the Bs were generally well written, structured and presented, covered all the key issues and included key references, they didn't make a clear and focused case. Most of the relevant information was there – it just wasn't organised, structured and focused like a first-class essay. This is usually apparent from the start, with a good introduction presaging a clear and focused argument – and everything in the assignment, every section, every paragraph is a building block towards a clear conclusion.

In a good essay you should take a position, take 'a line' on the subject matter, and argue for one or other position – as if you're a lawyer making a case. This will help you to structure the essay, for example, by presenting the case against your argument first, but then presenting the (better) case for your argument afterwards. So any information you are discussing is only relevant to the extent that you are using it to support your case – your argument.

A word of warning, however. I have seen students reduced to a crumbling bag of nerves because they've been told they must include more critical analysis in their assignments. Their ability to write a clear and simple descriptive account goes to pieces in their quest to embark on deep, impenetrable critical discussion. It's about finding a balance: yes, you do need to adopt a critical perspective, but this will include descriptive writing to provide essential background information so that the writing makes sense to the reader.

Tip 50: **Support your argument with evidence**

Now obviously you'll need to support your arguments with evidence – the best and most reliable and robust evidence – but you already knew that from Chapter 5.

> ### What tutors like
> - Statements substantiated
> - Backing up of ideas
> - Use of good evidence to support assertions, including research findings
> - Use and critique of appropriate reference resources that demonstrate a thorough literature search
> - Reading widely and using the literature to develop a critical argument
> - Critical debate supported with appropriate literature

So when you're advised to say what you think, this doesn't mean, well, just saying what you think – off the top of your head, as it were. It needs to be backed up with evidence or other support.

Tip 51: **Illustrate and apply ideas to specific contexts**

The survey also highlighted the importance of 'illustrating and applying ideas to specific contexts', grounding the discussion in actual examples, rather than remaining vague about the issues under discussion. In the ranking of themes, this actually came third in the list of what most impresses tutors.

What tutors like

- Relating discussion to actual examples
- Linking theory and practice through the explicit use of examples
- Linking literature to practice
- Reflections on practice that indicate taking the assignment seriously
- Using a case study/example to illustrate their comments/analysis
- Application of the reading and student learning to the context they are discussing/analysing

For example, if you're doing an assignment on some psychological issue, let's say positive and negative reinforcement of behaviour, don't just focus on the experimental studies, relate it to real life – gambling, punishment, learning. How does it work in the real world? So if the theories say 'this' and the research says 'that', think: how does this apply to the real world?

The student assignment that I have been discussing did a very good job of illustrating and applying ideas in the 'real world', particularly in the recommendations section where the *practicalities* of introducing acupuncture as a treatment for asthma are discussed. I've extracted the key passage for illustration in Box 8.1.

box 8.1

Applying the results of research to the real world

The following extract from an example assignment critically reflects on the systematic review of research examining the use of acupuncture for asthma. It highlights the difference between research and practice, and the extent to which results are generalisable and apply in real life (actual practice).

(Continued)

(Continued)

> This systematic review has several limitations. Acupuncture trials are highly complex to carry out simply due to the variation in methods. For example, the review did not specifically list the type of needle, needle depth, duration and location of needle insertion for each study, introducing potential bias. This review describes the positive outcome measures of acupuncture but does not mention any adverse effects. This does not give a fair representation of acupuncture as a whole. Another limitation is that it focuses only on mild to moderate asthma, so the findings cannot be generalised for all classifications. Finally, the accuracy of acupuncture used in the trials compared to actual acupuncture practice could be questionable. Acupuncture often comes in a complementary and alternative medicine 'package' which involves lifestyle changes and/or herbal medicines to promote physical – as well as emotional – well-being and is tailored to each person individually. This would not have been achieved in the clinical trials.

Tip 52: There are no 'right' answers – only positions you can adopt and cases you can make

It's often the case that the more you think about an issue, the more difficult it is to provide a simple, straightforward answer. So if you think you have a simple answer to an assignment question, beware. It probably means you've not looked into it deeply enough. As the saying goes: 'The more you know, the less you know.'

When William Perry (1968) studied the intellectual development of students at Harvard University, he discovered a similar progression from certainty to uncertainty. He identified three main stages or 'positions', as he referred to them:

> Position 1: Student's view of knowledge is dualistic: there's 'right' and 'wrong', and 'good' and 'bad'. Knowledge consists of objective facts, and authority figures (tutors) and textbooks provide the answers. All you need to do is listen out for the right answers and reproduce them in assignments.

> Position 2: Student realises that there is more than one viewpoint – there is diversity of opinion – but the right answers are out there if we can find them. From this perspective, the lecture is like a guessing game in which the student has to figure out which theory is correct but discover the answer themselves.

> Position 3: Student sees all knowledge and values as contextual and relative: some solutions are better than others depending on the context – we have to assess and choose. There are no 'right' answers, only positions you can adopt and cases you can make (with supporting evidence and arguments).

Remember that we were talking about 'cue-seekers' in Chapter 3? Well, the researchers, Miller and Partlett (1974), suggest that the cue-seekers (most of whom got a first) have reached this final stage: they are aware that, for many topics, particularly in the social sciences and humanities, there are no 'right' answers – only 'positions' you can adopt and cases you can make (with pros and cons), that are supported by argument and evidence. Think about it.

This sentiment is reflected in a statement by the Higher Education Council of Australia:

> Perhaps the most important 'generic' skill that a graduate can possess is the ability to recognise that knowledge is provisional, and that no answer is final, and that there is always a potential for a better way of doing things. (Cited in Naylor, 2007: 87)

Tip 53: **Dare to know**

This is the motto of the Enlightenment, a period in the eighteenth century when philosophers questioned the received ideas derived from authorities, traditions and faith. For the philosopher Immanuel Kant (1724–1804), it was about having the courage to use your own understanding; for the philosopher Diderot (1713–1784), it was about questioning everything: 'All things must be examined, debated, investigated without exception and without regard for anyone's feelings … We must ride roughshod over all ancient puerilities, overturn the barriers that reason never erected' (Diderot, *Encyclopédie*, 1775, cited in Smith, 1998).

This is the attitude you should adopt when you're writing your assignments. The Royal Society, which is the world's oldest scientific academy (founded in 1660) bears a similar motto, *Nullius in verba* – roughly translated as 'Take nobody's word for it' (where's the evidence?).

Tip 54: **Trust no one**

This is a more contemporary take on the Enlightenment motto, which recognises the fact that, human nature being what it is, people tend to operate with their own interests at heart, and this can lead to all kinds of bias. For example, studies have shown that research funded by pharmaceutical companies is four times more likely to give results that are favourable to the companies than independent studies (Bausell, 2007; Goldacre, 2009). Box 8.2 provides another example of how bias can subtly influence the results of research, illustrating the point that you should trust no one – not even yourself.

---

box   8.2

Does water remember? (Or 'the devil is in the detail')

In 1988 a paper appeared in the highly prestigious journal *Nature* claiming that an allergen triggered a chemical reaction in cells even after it had been diluted to such an extent that it had long since ceased to contain a single molecule of the original ingredient (after the fifteenth

(Continued)

(Continued)

dilution it would be essentially just water, but they used 120 successive dilutions). One explanation proposed by the director of the research, Jacques Benveniste, was that the water may have retained a memory of the original ingredient. As such, the experiment would provide support for homeopathy, one of the key principles of which is that remedies (mainly herbal) become more powerful the more they are diluted.

Since this was such a remarkable finding, contradicting the laws of physics, *Nature* agreed to publish the paper (Davenas et al., 1988), but with the proviso that they could visit the laboratory to observe how the experiments were being conducted. After observing several repeated experiments, the investigators became concerned that the people recording the changes in the cells knew which ones were being treated with the highly diluted allergen: judging whether a change had occurred was quite subjective and therefore prone to interpretation and bias. So they asked them to repeat the experiment but this time they were 'blinded' to ensure there could be no bias in their observations of changes in the cells: this time there was no effect.

One of the investigators from *Nature* was very relieved: James Randi, a well-known sceptic and magician had staked $1 million on the outcome of the experiment – or any experiment which contradicts the laws of science, including the existence of psychic, supernatural, or paranormal phenomena. The money has been available since 1964 and is still there, unclaimed, to this day (despite over 1000 attempts, and a few famous refusals to accept the challenge).

This shows the importance of 'blinding' in order to avoid unconscious (or deliberate) bias in interpreting data. It also, however, raises some other issues of potential bias. The research was initiated by a young homeopathic doctor, Bernard Poitevin, and the experiments were largely conducted by Elisabeth Davenas who also believed in homeopathy. The laboratory was part funded by a French homeopathic company – the Laboratories Homéopathiques de France.

The investigation by the team from *Nature* was filmed for a BBC *Horizon* programme (26 November 2002). Further details can be found at www.bbc.co.uk/science/horizon/2002/homeopathy.shtml (accessed March 2016).

Tip 55: Ask the question, 'Whose interests are being served here?' (follow the money)

Jeremy Paxman, the presenter of BBC's *Newsnight* for over 20 years, famously said of his approach to interviewing that he starts by asking himself the question, 'Why is this lying bastard lying to me?' Perhaps it's not appropriate for every interview, but when it comes to politicians and people with a vested interest, Paxman advocates a degree of scepticism, asking yourself, 'why are they saying this?' and 'is it likely to be true?' (Wells, 2005).

Continuing on the theme of bias, then, these are important questions to pose when a particular viewpoint may be being promoted. As the example below illustrates, there may be a degree of self-interest, especially where money is involved:

> New research claims ten squares of dark chocolate a day for two weeks can cure stress ... 'The study shows that a daily consumption of 40 grams over two weeks can modify the metabolism', said Nestlé researcher Sunil Kochhar. (*Metro* newspaper, 13 November 2009)

If you want more details about how self-interest, money and the media can bias the results of research, there are a number of books and internet sources to get your critical juices flowing and develop your 'critical consciousness'. For example, Ben Goldacre has written extensively on these issues in two books (*Bad Science*, 2008, and *Bad Pharma*, 2012) and has a website at http://www.bad science.net/about-dr-ben-goldacre/. On the subject of mental health, James Davies exposes the interests of pharmaceutical companies in his book *Cracked: Why Psychiatry Is Doing More Harm Than Good* (2013). And for a more general exposé on self-interest, politicians and the media, Owen Jones's book *The Establishment: And How They Get Away With It* (2014) examines the extent to which self-interest, power and corruption may be ruling our society, and our lives.

Being critical: Strategies to detect bullshit

In this final part of the chapter I've highlighted three useful strategies for the detection of dubious claims. I've also included a few websites devoted to critical thinking and sceptical inquiry for those of you who don't like being duped.

He used to be happy, but since going to university he never stops moaning...

Illustration 8.1

Tip 56: **Apply Occam's razor**

Yorkshireman wakes up from a coma speaking fluent Japanese – despite never having been to Japan!

I once overheard a conversation in which this newspaper story (or something similar) was recounted with bewildering interest: a man who'd received a bang on the head fell unconscious, and woke up speaking a different language. In the ensuing discussion it was argued that memories must have been revived from a past life or that there must have been some genes containing Japanese language, handed down from past generations, which had suddenly been released after the bang on the head. Well, that's two possible explanations, but in such circumstances we might do well to apply Occam's razor, which recommends that when two or more theories are competing to explain a phenomenon we should choose the simplest – or the one that makes the fewest assumptions.

So, returning to our proposed explanations for the mysterious case of waking up speaking a foreign language, the assumptions include:

1. We have past lives.
2. We retain memories and skills (like language) from these past lives that can suddenly spring into action.
3. Memories can be passed down through generations, through genes, which contain a whole language.
4. A bang on the head, for some reason, can ignite these memories.

Alternatively, we might opt for the slightly more prosaic and simpler explanation that it's a largely fabricated report by a newspaper based on a grain of truth (he did wake up speaking gibberish which sounded a bit like Japanese), noting the familiar newspaper motto: never let the facts get in the way of a good story.

In a more concrete example, R. Barker Bausell (2007: 109) uses Occam's razor to compare two possible explanations for why patients report reductions in knee pain after receiving acupuncture:

Explanation 1: The reduction in pain following the insertion of tiny needles in the body is due to those needles modulating the flow of a type of energy (qi) through meridians that are specifically designed for this purpose (somewhat similar to the role of arteries in blood flow) thereby reducing the subject's pain.

Explanation 2: It's the placebo effect.

In making our decision, Bausell invites us to adopt Occam's razor and count up the number of unsupported assumptions. For the first explanation we must assume:

(a) the existence of an unmeasured energy form called qi
(b) an as yet undetected system of meridians through which this qi flows

   (c) that the acupuncture needles are in fact capable of affecting this flow

   (d) that this altered flow is capable of reducing pain

The second explanation requires us to assume:

   (a) that a ceremony (of inserting tiny needles into the body accompanied by promises that such practices have reduced pain for thousands of years) can engender psychological explanations of benefit

   (b) that these psychological explanations (or suggestions) can influence our perceptions of the pain we experience (or cause us to imagine that we were experiencing less pain than we really were)

Using Occam's razor, then, combined with a large body of evidence for the analgesic placebo effect, we would be guided towards the second explanation.

Applying Occam's Razor to pretentious art descriptions

Illustration 8.2

Tip 57: **Beware of 'meaningless' statements**

In February 1968, the Beatles went to study transcendental meditation with the Indian guru Maharishi Mahesh in India. A journalist present at the time recounts:

> They used to get together in a big hall in the evening and sing songs, and the Maharishi would give them a lecture which would proceed on the following lines: 'When we're delving into the meaning of the Raga you come up with those nether regions which are beyond the stellar spaces,

which are so transcendental...' And the more incomprehensible he became the greater was the ecstasy and the rapture on the faces of the audience – including the Beatles.

(Bombay's Beatle, BBC Radio 4, 9 August 2009,
available at www.bbc.co.uk/programmes/b00hv1dt)

In the 1930s there was a movement in philosophy called 'logical positivism'. Its target was so-called metaphysical statements like those attributed to the Maharishi above. For a statement to be meaningful, the logical positivists argued, it should be possible to show that it's true or false. If we can't, then it should be dismissed as 'meaningless'. Here's an example from the philosopher Alfred Ayer (1936):

- 'To say that "God exists" is to make a metaphysical utterance which cannot be either true or false.'
  - o   it is wrong to say that 'God exists' is true
  - o   wrong to say that it is false
  - o   wrong to say, along with the agnostic, that one does not know if it is true or false
  - o   what one should say is that it is meaningless

This approach to language provides an interesting form of attack on woolly, obscure statements which often feature in the more fringe-like subjects of parapsychology and alternative medicine, as, for example, when someone offers to 'balance', 'cleanse' or 'energise' your chakras.

Tip 58: **Watch out for Barnum statements**

If you look at the palm of your hand, you'll see a line that begins between your thumb and index finger and curves down towards the centre of your wrist. It's called the 'life line' and, according to chiromancers, it can tell you lots of interesting things about your fate. For example, if you notice a break or a fork in the line this indicates a change in your life – perhaps a career break or some other change in lifestyle. You may also see a few lines that cross your lifeline, which signify obstacles in your path, perhaps an accident or an episode of ill health. Take note of where these forks and crosses occur on the lifeline, because that indicates the time in your life when these significant events will happen.

And when you get to the age of 30 or 40 or 50 – wherever the forks or crosses in the line seem to occur – and you do find yourself changing career, moving house, meeting someone (or meeting someone else), you can gaze back into the palm of your hand and it will say 'I told you so'.

Unless, that is, you are a critically aware sceptic. Then you'll say 'Hold on a minute – don't these things happen to everyone throughout their life? Don't we all change jobs, move houses, have relationship problems, go through periods of poor health during our life?' If you did say this, then you'd recognise these as 'Barnum statements', named after the circus promoter P. T. Barnum, who aimed to provide 'something for everyone'.

Imagine that I've conducted a detailed assessment of your personality, using questionnaires and other assessment techniques, such as handwriting analysis, and having analysed all the data, I can now present you with your own detailed personality profile. Here's *your* profile:

> Some of your aspirations tend to be pretty unrealistic. At times you are extroverted, affable, sociable, while at other times you are introverted, wary and reserved. You have found it unwise to be too frank in revealing yourself to others. You pride yourself on being an independent thinker and do not accept others' opinions without satisfactory proof. You prefer a certain amount of change and variety, and become dissatisfied when hemmed in by restrictions and limitations. At times you have serious doubts as to whether you have made the right decision or done the right thing. Disciplined and controlled on the outside, you tend to be worried and insecure on the inside. While you have some personality weaknesses, you are generally able to compensate for them. You have a great deal of unused capacity which you have not turned to your advantage. You have a tendency to be critical of yourself. You have a strong need for other people to like you and for them to admire you.

What do you think – pretty accurate? Most people think so. And that's the problem. This profile, which consists mainly of statements taken from an astrology book, was given to a class of students who each believed that it had been produced for them individually as a result of completing a personality assessment. When asked how accurate it was on a scale of 0 (poor) to 5 (perfect), it received an average rating of 4.26. Sixteen of the 39 students gave it a perfect rating and only five gave it a rating less than 4 (Forer, 1949). I've tried it myself with students and I'm amazed how effective it is. As the psychologist Gordon Allport puts it:

> When the analyst says, 'You have a need for other people to like and admire you,' the subject is likely to say, 'How true! How accurate you are!'. He should of course say, 'Who hasn't?' Similarly glittering and worthless are such diagnoses as, 'You like change and variety and become dissatisfied when hemmed in by restrictions'; 'Security is one of your major goals in life.' Not only do such statements catch all mortals, they are likely to be interpreted in an individual way by each subject to fit his [*sic*] unique pattern of life, and he therefore credits the diagnostician with an acumen he does not have. (Allport, 1969: 452)

The banalities of these so-called 'Barnum statements' are present in all disciplines, from politics to psychology, but they're particularly prevalent in the pseudosciences, such as astrology, palmistry and graphology, and among spiritualist mediums, especially when conveying messages from 'the dead' (Greasley, 2000a, 2000b).

Tip 59: Have a look at some websites devoted to critical thinking and sceptical inquiry

There are a number of useful websites devoted to critical thinking and sceptical inquiry. I've listed a selection below:

The James Randi Educational Foundation (www.randi.org)

James Randi is a magician famous for investigating people who claim to have psychic or paranormal abilities, e.g. Uri Geller. The Foundation offers a $1 million prize to anyone who can demonstrate psychic, supernatural or paranormal ability of any kind under mutually agreed upon scientific conditions.

The Skeptics dictionary (www.skepdic.com)

This website has lots of articles covering most supernatural, paranormal and pseudoscientific topics (from acupuncture to zombies).

Science-based Medicine (www.sciencebasedmedicine.org)

Science-based Medicine is run by a group of physicians who subject 'unscientific and pseudoscientific health care' practices to critical examination. This is an excellent resource for those studying health-related topics.

Quackwatch (www.quackwatch.com)

This is another excellent resource for students in the health sciences. It includes articles on health-related frauds, myths, fads, fallacies and misconduct. There's also a link to 'the quackometer' where you can type in the name of someone (e.g. Prince Charles) and it will provide you with a quack rating.

summary

In this chapter we've seen the importance of reaching beyond the lower levels of description that we saw in Bloom's taxonomy towards a more analytical, critical, evaluative perspective, through which an argument is developed and a particular position adopted.

There are some philosophers and psychologists who argue that we are born with a predisposition to believe what we are told, and that we wander around in a kind of hypnotic state with blind belief and uncritical obedience (Schumaker, 1990). As an influential leader once remarked: 'What good fortune for those in power that people do not think' (Adolf Hitler, cited in Macedo, 1994: 36).

One of the primary aims of a university education is to teach students to think critically about what they are told. Perhaps this is what the psychologist B. F. Skinner meant when he said: 'Education is what survives when what has been learned has been forgotten' (Skinner, 1964: 484). So when the 'facts' you learned about your subject at university have been long forgotten, you should hopefully retain the intellectual skills and abilities that encourage you to adopt a critical perspective rather than just accept what you are told. This is important because, as the Princeton philosopher Professor Harry G. Frankfurt (2005: 1 and 63) points out:

> One of the most salient features of our culture is that there is so much bullshit. Everyone knows this. Each of us contributes his share. But we tend to take the situation for granted ...

> Bullshit is unavoidable whenever circumstances require someone to talk without knowing what he is talking about. Thus the production of bullshit is stimulated whenever a person's obligations or opportunities to speak about some topic exceed his knowledge of the facts that are relevant to that topic. This discrepancy is common in public life, where people are frequently impelled – whether by their own propensities or by the demands of others – to speak extensively about matters of which they are to some degree ignorant.

Introductions, conclusions and structure

Greasley, P.

Introductions

As we all know, essays should have a beginning (introduction), a middle (main section) and an end (conclusion). Basically, you tell the reader what you are going to say, say it, and then tell the reader what you've said. In this chapter we'll look at each of these elements, along with more general issues about structuring assignments.

And that was the sum total of my original introduction to this chapter – the problem being that it's too short, which is a common problem in assignments. The trouble is that most people, me included, don't like wasting time (and words) going over what we are going to say; it's tedious – we'd rather just get on with it. But as we'll see in this chapter, a good introduction may be more important than you think when it comes to writing assignments. So let's have another go.

Introductions (second attempt) ...

As we all know, essays should have a beginning (introduction), a middle (main section) and an end (conclusion). Basically, you tell the reader what you are going to say, say it, and then tell the reader what you've said. What could be simpler? Well, if it is that simple, why did issues relating to structure, introductions and conclusions feature so highly on the list of things that frustrate and impress tutors? In this chapter we'll be discussing each of these elements: introductions, conclusions, and then more general issues about structuring assignments.

First, we'll see that a good introduction is crucial for an assignment – providing an outline and overview of the contents, and signposting the route you've taken to address the question (a planned itinerary rather than a mystery tour). We'll also look at *five key criteria* for an effective introduction, proposed by Townsend et al. (1993), which were shown to improve the grade of an assignment.

Next we'll look at three key criteria for a good conclusion, along with an interesting tip about when to write it (not at the end). And finally, we'll examine some tips for maintaining a clear, logical structure to your assignment, using headings and subheadings along with signposting throughout to help the marker on their journey.

It is concluded that paying attention to your introductions and conclusions may be especially important in assignments due to the psychological impact of first and last impressions – which may have a significant influence on markers.

There, so much better, don't you think? I've provided a clearer outline of the contents, added a couple of sentences in the first paragraph justifying the discussion of introductions, conclusions and structure (because they featured as common problems in the survey of tutors) and I've also added a few details about the conclusion.

Tip 23: **Use signposting**

When markers pick up an assignment they often have very little idea of what's in store for them. A good introduction can resolve this problem in a few lines by stating the aims of the assignment and providing a brief outline of the content and argument. It gives the reader a map of where they are going to be taken on the essay journey. In contrast, an essay without an introduction is a bit like a mystery tour – no one has a clue where they are going. So a good introduction shows that you've thought about the itinerary and planned the route.

Not surprisingly, then, the main source of marker distress in the survey of tutors was failing to provide a simple outline or overview of the essay.

What tutors dislike

- Failing to provide a simple introduction and outline of the subject (what is this essay about?)
- Poor introductions which give little overview of the assignment and what to expect
- Not introducing to the reader the content of the assignment or the context
- Not stating the aim of the essay

If you want to impress the marker you should provide a clear introduction that outlines the content, as the following comments illustrate:

What tutors like

- A clear introduction that presages a clear structure
- Good introduction summarising the assignment
- Identifying clearly in the introduction what issues the student is going to investigate

Clearly, it is a good strategy to summarise what you are going to say, with some signposting indicating the route and the directions you will be taking. This is what the introduction to this chapter did – at the second attempt.

Five key criteria for a good introduction: how to move up a grade

A study by Townsend et al. (1993), published in the *Journal of Educational Psychology*, examined a range of essay-writing guides and arrived at five key criteria for an effective introduction. A good introduction for an essay should:

1. Discuss the importance or timeliness of the topic
2. State the problem to be addressed
3. Indicate the scope of the essay
4. Define the terms to be used
5. Delineate the argument to be presented

What makes this study more interesting is that the researchers used these criteria to alter the introductions in some students' essays and found that the marks awarded rose by one grade (see Box 6.1).

box   6.1

An introduction proven to increase your grade

When Townsend et al. (1993) removed the original introductions from student essays, and substituted the following introduction constructed using the five key criteria, the grade increased on average from a B to a B+.

(Continued)

(Continued)

Essay Question: Discuss the role of genetic and environmental factors in IQ scores.

'Geniuses are born not made!' Is it really that simple? The 'nature vs nurture' dispute, in relation to intelligence, remains unresolved. In an attempt to separate the influence of genetic and environmental factors, two kinds of investigation have been important – twin studies and adoption studies. This research has shown that both genetic and environmental factors interact with each other to determine an individual's IQ score. The evidence presented in this essay indicates that IQ is shaped by many influences. In the context of current concerns about the validity of intelligence testing, an understanding of these influences is essential.

This is a good introduction because it:

1   Opens with a common belief about the subject which sets up the debate to be examined and questioned
2   Points out that this is an issue which remains unresolved (the problem to be addressed)
3   Delineates the scope/content to be discussed – evidence from twin and adoption studies
4   Indicates the outcomes of this research and the argument/ conclusion in the essay (that IQ is shaped by an interaction between genetic and environmental factors)
5   Concludes by putting the debate into a context – concerns about the validity of intelligence testing (importance/timeliness of the topic)

Why might a good introduction like the one in Box 6.1 make such a positive impact on the grade? Because when you provide an overview of the assignment in this way it helps the marker to understand the relevance of what follows; it contextualises and frames the assignment, and facilitates comprehension.

Bearing this point in mind, try to work out what the following passage is about:

The procedure is actually quite simple. First, you arrange things into two different groups. Of course, one pile may be sufficient depending on how much there is to do. If you have to go somewhere else due to lack of facilities, that is the next step; otherwise you are pretty well set. It is important not to overdo things. That is, it is better to do fewer things at once than too many. In the short run this might not seem important, but complications can easily arise. A mistake can be expensive as well. At first the whole procedure will seem complicated. Soon, however, it will become just another facet of life. It is difficult to foresee an end to the necessity for this task in the immediate future, but then one can never tell. After the procedure is completed, one arranges the material into different groups again. Then they can be put into their appropriate places. Eventually they will be used once more, and the whole cycle will have to be repeated. However, that is part of life.

Did it make sense? Struggling? What about the next passage:

A newspaper is better than a magazine. A seashore is a better place than the street. At first it is better to run than to walk. You may have to try several times. It takes some skill, but it is easy to learn. Even young children can enjoy it. Once successful, complications are minimal. Birds seldom get too close. Rain, however, soaks in very fast. Too many people doing the same thing can also cause problems. One needs lots of room. If there are no complications, it can be very peaceful. A rock will serve as an anchor. If things break loose from it, however, you will not get a second chance.

Just as bad? Just as frustrating? Well, perhaps it would make sense if you knew that the first passage was about washing clothes and the second was about making a kite. And that was the point of John Bransford and Marcia Johnson's experiment from 1972 when they presented these passages to people with or without this contextual information: readers required some knowledge of the topic in order to facilitate comprehension.

While these are quite extreme examples, I think they illustrate the point quite well: you need to signpost and guide the reader/marker through the relevance of what you are saying. This will help them to read it and mark it.

The 'halo effect' and 'confirmation bias'

It is important to note, in this respect, the famous 'halo effect', where our judgements about a person are influenced by a favourable or unfavourable first impression (e.g. Nisbett and Wilson, 1977). A good first impression, at a job interview, for example (smart, friendly), might create a positive feeling towards the candidate, minimising the impact of any subsequent gaffes. A poor first impression, on the other hand, can have the opposite effect – finding fault, etc. – which is known as 'reverse halo effect' (or 'devil effect'). In terms of assignments, then, it may be that a well-written introduction creates a 'halo effect', favourably disposing the marker to the assignment; a poor introduction, on the other hand, may have the opposite effect. Although it could also be that the quality of the introduction simply reflects the quality of the rest of the assignment. In the words of an old Japanese saying, 'One instance shows the rest'.

Studies have also shown that we tend to seek out information that confirms our views and beliefs. This is known as 'confirmation bias' (Nickerson, 1998; Shermer, 2002). For example, if you believe in astrology, and you know the supposed personality traits associated with the different star signs, then you'll tend to look for confirmation in the people you know. Your Taurean friend actually is quite stubborn and bullish. But isn't everyone at times? Aren't they also quite indecisive at times, like Librans, or inquisitive, like Geminis? Confirmation bias means you'll tend to find what you're looking for.

One instance shows the rest...?

Illustration 6.1

How might this apply to the marking of an assignment? Well, if it starts with a good first impression from the opening introduction, then the marker might be predisposed towards focusing on those aspects that confirm this initial positive impression. Conversely, a poor first impression might bias them towards focusing on any errors and inadequacies. As the philosopher Francis Bacon (1561–1626) recognised many years ago:

> The human understanding when it has once adopted an opinion ... draws all things else to support and agree with it. And though there be a greater number and weight of instances to be found on the other side, yet these it either neglects and despises, or else by some distinction sets aside and rejects. (Cited in Shermer, 2002: 296)

A good introduction and a less good introduction: two examples

Bearing all this advice in mind, Box 6.2 provides an example of a very good introduction. It is taken from an assignment written by a second-year student, which received a very high mark. As the comments after each paragraph show, this introduction meets most of the criteria suggested for a good introduction:

1. **Importance and timeliness of the topic (criterion 1) along with the problem to be addressed (criterion 2).** National statistics are provided, stating the scale of the problem, and local statistics indicate relevance for the

local context – also justifying the need to consider new treatments (like acupuncture).

2. **The scope of the essay (criterion 3) and the argument to be presented (criterion 5).** The second paragraph outlines the aim of the report (looking at the possibility of introducing an alternative treatment) and refers to a systematic review that will (presumably) be discussed. Finally, there is an overview of the contents, reflecting the assignment brief: the report will discuss the history, rationale and evidence – leading to an informed decision about using acupuncture to treat chronic asthma.

---

box   **6.2**

Example of a good introduction

The following introduction is taken from a student assignment, which asked students to evaluate a complementary therapy:

> Assignment question/brief: Having been employed in a local health clinic, your manager has asked you to write a 2,000 word report outlining your views and specific recommendations about using a complementary therapy. The report should discuss the history, underlying principles and research for the therapy. You should justify your choice of therapy as being relevant to the clinic where you are working.

> **Essay title: A review of acupuncture as an alternative treatment for chronic asthma**

> ### 1. Introduction

> According to the National Asthma Campaign, there are 5.4 million people in the UK currently receiving treatment for asthma and the cost to the NHS is over £996 million per year[1]. In 2007, Killingham's Primary Care Trust had the 4th highest hospital admissions rate for asthma[2] in the whole of the UK, which suggests that the management, treatment and education of asthma are not effective in the Killingham area. New strategies to help reduce strain on emergency departments, respiratory clinics and local GP surgeries need to be brought into play to ensure that asthma sufferers are receiving the treatment they require, when they need it.

> ✓

This introductory paragraph states the scale of the problem, providing general statistics *and* local statistics – making an interesting argument for looking at acupuncture, justifying and contextualising the issue for the assignment.

> This report will focus on the possibility of introducing a complementary and alternative medicine as a treatment option for chronic

(Continued)

(Continued)

asthma at the Killingham Royal Infirmary (KRI) Respiratory Clinic[3]. In 2003, McCarney et al. carried out a systematic review on investigating the effects of acupuncture[20] in treating chronic asthma. This review has recently been updated, sparking new interest in the treatment. The history, rationale and evidence of the alternative therapy will be critically reviewed in this report, leading to an informed consideration of whether acupuncture has a potential role in treating chronic asthma, and essentially in the health care system.

✓

This second paragraph focuses on a particular clinic addressing the assignment question, and provides an overview of contents - history, rationale and evidence 'critically reviewed', as requested in assignment brief.

It is worth noting that this introduction is 200 words in length – which is 10% of the assignment. Given the importance of a clear introduction which summarises the contents of an assignment, I would recommend that an introduction is at least this length. Indeed, my only slight criticism is that the introduction might also have given an indication of what the assignment concludes – is the recommendation in favour or against the use of acupuncture as a treatment for asthma? For example, the writer might have added:

It is concluded, based on this review of the evidence, that acupuncture may have a role to play in the treatment of asthma, but further research is needed in case of possible adverse effects.

Box 6.3 provides an example of a poor introduction – a second-rate version of the one provided in Box 6.2. In comparison, it is short, vague, cursory and tokenistic.

box 6.3

Example of a poor introduction

Essay title: Acupuncture as a treatment for pain

Introduction

This assignment will provide a discussion of the principles and practices of acupuncture. The assignment will provide a brief background to acupuncture, look at the practice, and discuss the evidence from research. Some types of health problems it might be used for, and risks, are also discussed. Finally, the conclusion will end with a discussion of my recommendations about using acupuncture.

x ☹

While this introduction does provide an overview of the contents, it's very tokenistic. Compared to the very good introduction in Box 6.2, this is just a vague regurgitation of the assignment brief. It needed to be longer, more specific and detailed.

Tip 24: Complete the writing of your introduction after you've written your assignment

If the introduction is going to provide an overview of what is in your assignment (the topics, issues and argument), it is better to write it up properly after you've completed the assignment. So it's pointless agonising over it too much before you start. A rough outline should suffice until the assignment is completed.

Tip 25: Write 'a lot about a little' rather than 'a little about a lot'

Chris Mounsey (2002: 30) makes an interesting observation about the transition from school to university:

> An important difference in essay writing between undergraduate level and school ... is that at the higher level you are graded more on your ability to make a coherent argument, and less on the amount of information presented. The way to think about it is to remember that in all the essays you have written so far, you have had to say a little about a lot of information. In an undergraduate essay, you need to say a lot about a little bit of information.

In other words, you need to focus. However, this does not mean, for example, providing every minute detail of a research study. Rather, it's about focusing on a few things in depth rather than many things superficially (depth rather than breadth).

Why is this relevant to introductions? Well, because the introduction needs to set the parameters, the scope and the focus of the assignment. In a typical 2,000-word assignment you can only cover so much about a topic, so you have to be selective. If you acknowledge this in your introduction, it shows that you are aware of the broader issues, but that you have set your parameters. As we shall see later, this strategy is also important to avoid covering too much ground (superficially) at the cost of more detailed argument and analysis.

Conclusions

Conclusions are *very* important. Remember, this is the last thing a marker will read before they turn to the marking sheet.

Tip 26: **Provide a good conclusion summarising your answer to the question**

What tutors like

- An ability to sum up
- A concise conclusion that reflects the introduction and the student's own conclusion
- A good conclusion, summarising the answer to the question
- A conclusion that really does conclude what has been presented

A good conclusion should be arrived at: if you've written your assignment well, your conclusion should be obvious, since it should summarise the arguments made throughout the body of the essay.

The study by Townsend et al. (1993), referred to earlier, examined a range of essay-writing guides and arrived at three criteria for an effective conclusion. A good conclusion should:

1. Summarise the main ideas of the essay
2. Provide an answer to the question posed
3. Discuss the broader implications of the topic

Using these criteria, they constructed a conclusion for the essay 'Discuss the role of genetic and environmental factors in IQ scores' and came up with the example provided in Box 6.4.

box   6.4

A model conclusion

This is the 'model' conclusion constructed by Townsend et al. (1993), using key criteria from essay writing guides, for the essay title 'Discuss the role of genetic and environmental factors in IQ scores':

> In conclusion, statements such as 'Geniuses are born not made' are too simplistic. The evidence from studies of twins and adopted children demonstrates the importance of both

genetic and environmental factors in the development of intelligence. While the genotype may set the upper and lower limits for development, a range of environmental factors determine the extent to which that potential will be realized. Rather than attempting to answer the 'nature vs nurture' question, researchers should investigate ways to enhance the cognitive potential of all individuals.

Notice how this conclusion:

- starts by referring back to the opening quote
- summarises the outcomes from the evidence discussed
- discusses broader implications by making recommendations about further research

In Box 6.5 I have also provided the conclusion from the student assignment discussed earlier, which does a fairly good job of meeting these criteria within the context of a 2,000-word assignment.

box   6.5

Example of a good conclusion

The conclusion below is taken from the student assignment discussed earlier, in which the student evaluated the use of acupuncture for chronic asthma.

Conclusion

In conclusion, the McCarney et al. systematic review has been critically analysed to allow consideration of whether acupuncture would be useful treating asthma at the KRI Respiratory Clinic. The background, rationale and efficacy of the alternative treatment have been reviewed and it has been suggested as a treatment option at the Clinic. Further research is needed into the area along with analysis of the treatment's adverse effects in relation to chronic asthma. Acupuncture may have a role in the health care system as there were some positive findings in the review. Whether these are purely placebo-based may have to be further researched, so more funding will be needed.

This provides a good conclusion to the assignment, with recommendations:

(Continued)

(Continued)

1   It provides a summary - the assignment has critically analysed the evidence (from a systematic review) as well as reviewing the background, rationale and efficacy of the treatment (all as requested in the assignment question and guidelines).

2   It provides an answer to the question posed - based on this review the conclusion says that acupuncture is recommended as a treatment option for the clinic.

3   It also refers to broader implications by identifying limitations of the report and further areas of research - the issue of possible adverse effects and placebo effects, which may require further research or monitoring if acupuncture is used as a treatment in the clinic.

Tip 27: **Do not introduce new information in your conclusion**

And remember, a conclusion should summarise what has been discussed – it should not introduce new information:

What tutors dislike

- New information in the conclusion

- Things talked about in conclusion that were not discussed in the body of the text leaving me to go back to see if I missed it!

Tip 28: **Write your conclusion before you start and your introduction after you've finished (eh?)**

We already know (Tip 24) that you should complete the writing of your introduction after you've finished your assignment, so you can provide an overview of the contents – what you've actually discussed. By the same token, you might like to formulate your conclusion before you start, remembering that 'clever people work backwards' (Tip 5). To use our analogy of a journey again, it's no good charting the route before the destination has been decided.

General structure and organisation

In the survey of tutors, issues relating to structure came seventh in the list of common problems and fourth on the list of things that impress markers.

Problems relating to structure

Problems included:

- hopping from one theme to another – and back again
- lack of signposting
- lack of headings
- use of appendices

The following tips address each of these issues.

Tip 29: Don't hop about: keep all the information on one issue / theme / topic in one place

One of the main causes of marker distress was essays that lack a logical development and seem to flit back and forth from one theme to the next:

What tutors dislike

- Essays that lack structure and seem to hop from one theme to the next at random; no sense of flow, very little (if any) signposting
- Poor structure, which means going back and forth through pages
- Poor structure, which means that you comment on the absence of detail when the relevant detail appears later on

These last two comments certainly hit a nerve, especially when you've made notes on the script about the need for further details only to find said details turning up later in the essay. The key point here, then, is to keep all the information on one issue, theme or topic together.

Tip 30: Use signposting to summarise and make your essay flow

What tutors like

- Clear signposting of ideas that enables the work to flow in a logical manner to a conclusion

- A clear structure, especially when signposted

- Logical structure so the marker is not required to keep going over parts that have already been read in order to keep a grasp of how the parts of the assignment/ essay interrelate

- That the points made clearly link into each other

We've already talked about signposting in the context of introductions, but signposting is also an important strategy throughout the assignment. At certain points/junctures it is useful to provide a brief reflective review of your argument and look towards the next section of the assignment. For example, you might make the transition from one section to another like this:

> Having critically appraised the underlying rationale for acupuncture, we will now examine the evidence from research studies.

> There have been hundreds of studies over the years, but I will be focusing on two recent systematic reviews as the best source of evidence …

This helps you *and your tutor* to monitor your argument and the points you are making.

Tip 31: Use headings (and subheadings) to structure your work

Personally, I like headings. You know where you are with headings. Literally – as a writer or as a reader/marker – you can see what's where.

What tutors like

- Good use of headings and subheadings

- Use of subtitles – as long as the discussion then matches the subtitle!

Headings and subheadings are useful because they help to structure an assignment into manageable chunks. They can also help to show that you've addressed the relevant areas in the right proportions. In the complementary therapies assignment, for example, students often used the following headings:

- Introduction
- Historical Background
- Rationale of Therapy
- Principles of Practice
- Research Evidence
- Conclusion

These headings are useful to ensure that the relevant issues are covered in the assignment.

However, if you are using headings/subheadings to help structure and organise your assignment, don't overdo it. Too many headings may be disruptive; they should only be used to delineate major sections of a report. So if you end up with 40 headings in your 2,000-word assignment, something is not right.

Tip 32: Check with your tutor about the use of headings

The use of headings may depend on the type of assignment. Strictly speaking, using headings in an essay may not be recommended by some tutors, especially if it's a very short essay, but for research reports or projects they are extremely important and, indeed, essential to ensure that all relevant aspects of the project are clearly reported. Since these are a special case, I've provided a brief outline of the typical sections used in a research report in Chapter 15 (which also includes some common problems).

Note: if your tutor is an essay purist and does not want you to insert headings, you can always write it with headings to help you structure the assignment, and then remove them when you actually submit the assignment. But don't forget to check the flow after you've removed the headings; you may need to add some linking sentences.

Tip 33: Don't use appendices as a dumping ground

Problems with appendices were noted by quite a few tutors and, in fact, came eighth on the list of common problems.

What tutors dislike

- Appendices that are not referred to or discussed in an assignment or have little point for being there

- Putting lots of information in appendices and expecting me to sift through it for the relevant bits

- Poor use (almost any use) of appendices, usually an attempt to gain more words

Appendices are used to provide further information that is relevant but not essential to the main body of a report (if it is essential information, it should be included in the body of the assignment). They are more typically used in reports, such as research proposals, or portfolios of work, to include additional materials that would otherwise clutter up the main body of the text, for example a copy of a questionnaire referred to in the main text, or tables of raw data which, importantly, should have been summarised in the main text. They should not be used as an attempt to gain more words since they are not usually included in the word count of an assignment. If the information is important and necessary to address the assignment question/brief, it should be integrated into the body of the text. Appendices should be treated as additional information which may be consulted by the interested reader.

If you do need to include appendices make sure you refer to them in the text (they should be numbered of course) and also guide the reader through the information. Do not use it as a dumping ground and expect your tutor to sift through it for relevant information. On a practical note, it can sometimes be difficult for the marker to locate the relevant appendix in larger documents (such as dissertations, which may include quite a few appendices), so it's helpful if you can include the page number to help the marker locate it, for example '(see Appendix 10 on p. 79)'.

summary

In this chapter we've seen the crucial importance of:

- providing a good introduction which outlines the content of your assignment (along with five key criteria that could raise your grade)
- concluding your assignment with a summary of what you said and how you've answered the question
- using 'signposting' (in the introduction and throughout the assignment) to help the reader navigate through the assignment

- using headings to structure your assignment
- focusing the scope of your assignment (by writing a lot about a little, rather than a little about a lot)

We've also seen the importance of first impressions – how the 'halo effect' and 'confirmation bias' may influence the marker in subtle ways. There's an interesting phenomenon in psychology which shows that our memory is influenced by what are known as 'primacy' and 'recency' effects (Murdock, 1962; Jones et al., 1968). For example, we tend to remember the first words and the last words in a list more than those in the middle. You might like to think about this when writing your assignment. It would suggest that the introduction and the conclusion are disproportionately prevalent in a tutor's thoughts when it comes to completing the mark sheet. In other words, it's back to making a good first impression and a good last impression.

The literature review

Thomas, G.

INTRODUCTION

LITERATURE REVIEW

You are here in your project

METHODOLOGY

FIELDWORK AND FINDINGS

ANALYSIS AND DISCUSSION

CONCLUSION

You are not an island. Your work must occur in the context of what is already known. What have other people thought about this or similar questions? In doing the literature review you find out, and in finding out you can focus and sharpen up your original research ideas.

This chapter considers:

- that the literature is not all the same quality – there are different kinds of sources, each with strengths and weaknesses;

- keeping records of your searches;

- telling a coherent story – not writing a list;

- using the library (remembering that it's the twenty-first century!) – find out on the web through online databases, Google Scholar, Web of Knowledge, Amazon and others;

- beginning a storyboard;

- being critically aware.

Once you have outlined the problem or issue that you wish to examine and you are happy with the expression of this in the form of an initial question or questions, you will need to find out about what other people have accomplished in researching this topic. Assuming that you have done your work properly in making sure that your research question is precise and doable, this review of the literature should lead you down some paths that will help you to define more exactly what you wish to do. Ultimately, you will be able to refine your research questions.

In thinking about a literature review, you first need to establish what's meant by 'literature'. Literature can be almost anything that represents the results of research or scholarship on a subject. It is written material that may appear in books, articles, conference proceedings, dissertations, websites, and so on. The shorthand for these kinds of information is *sources*.

Just running through these sources, you will see, even at first glance, that they are of different kinds, and they will be viewed differently by your tutors. Some have more credibility than others, and you must be careful not to be taken in by something just because it is in print. Just because it is in written form doesn't mean that it is of unimpeachable quality as a piece of information. You will need to be clear about the status of the evidence that you are drawing on when you cite literature. You should ask yourself what kind of literature it is. Let's look at a few sources as shown in Table 3.1.

Primary and secondary sources

In Table 3.1, you'll notice that mention is made of primary and secondary sources, and I note that secondary sources are not usually as highly thought of as primary sources. It is worth spending some time looking at this distinction between primary and secondary, since tutors may place stress on using one

(usually primary) rather than the other. Most of the sources mentioned in Table 3.1 will usually be primary (though textbooks are always secondary). Let's look at some others.

Examples of primary sources:

- autobiographies
- diaries
- government documents and statistics
- letters and correspondence (including electronic kinds such as email)
- original documents (such as birth certificates)
- photographs and audio or video recordings
- reports from commercially produced surveys or other research (e.g. using focus groups)
- speeches
- technical reports.

Examples of secondary sources:

- biographies
- dictionaries and encyclopaedias
- review articles
- textbooks.

> A primary source is 'straight from the horse's mouth' – in other words, no other person has subsequently analysed or summarised it. A secondary source is a reworking of usually many primary sources, either in analysis or summary. Textbooks are the most common form of secondary source.

The main difference between a primary source and a secondary source is in the directness of the data or evidence being presented. Think of the primary source representing a first presentation or first analysis of the data, and the secondary source representing a second look, usually by someone other than the author of the primary source. In practice, it is difficult sometimes to distinguish between a primary and a secondary source, so you should not get too worried about strict demarcations between them. And one thing that Table 3.1 highlights is that there is no automatic **correlation** between the quality of a source and its 'primary-ness' or 'secondary-ness'.

NOTES

Some primary sources may be very suspect, while some secondary sources may be excellent.

You'll notice that I include *review articles* in secondary sources, and these are worth a special mention since they are taken to be rather more authoritative reviews of the literature than those that exist in encyclopaedias and textbooks. There are two kinds of review article: the *systematic* review and the *narrative* review. The systematic review uses particular methods to search for research on a topic in a wide range of **peer review** sources. Only studies of a predetermined type and/or quality are included in the ultimate review. A narrative review, by contrast, discusses and summarises the literature on a particular topic without conforming to a particular search formula. Narrative reviews often do not report on how they searched for literature or how they decided which studies were relevant to include. There are also **meta-analyses**. These are studies which use particular techniques for selecting and summarising the findings of many pieces of research.

Review articles and meta-analyses can be very valuable as sources, if you can find up-to-date ones which are relevant to your topic. While they appear in general academic journals, you can look especially for journal titles that contain 'Review' such as the *Review of Educational Research* or *Educational Review.*

A relatively new and increasingly important resource is the 'collaboration' that brings together high-quality evidence and then synthesises and summarises it for the reader. The most important of these for the social sciences is the Campbell Collaboration (www.campbell collaboration.org/). This gives as its general purpose 'Improving decision-making through systematic reviews on the effects of interventions within the areas of education, crime and justice, and social welfare'. This is an example of one of its summaries on the impact of street lighting in the reduction of crime:

This review of 13 studies of street lighting interventions in the United Kingdom and United States, spanning four decades, finds that crime decreased by 21% in areas that experienced street lighting improvements compared to similar areas that did not. The review also notes that street lighting appears more effective at reducing crime

Table 3.1   Sources of written information

Kind of source	What is it?	☺ Good things about this source	☹ Not-so-good things about this source
Article in a peer review journal (usually primary)	This has been offered by the author to the journal to be judged. The peer reviewers (i.e. other academics in the same field) will ask themselves if it is good enough for publication. Only the best articles will be accepted, and for this reason the peer review journal is seen as the 'gold standard' for quality.	Only the best articles get published. You can therefore be sure of quality (in theory).	This material is published for the author's peers in the academic community, and may be difficult for anyone else to understand. Also, it will usually be on esoteric or cutting-edge matters and not necessarily straightforward issues. It may give little attention to explaining the wider context, or explaining in simple terms.
Article in a professional journal (usually primary)	A professional journal is similar to a peer review journal, and may be reviewed by peers. However, criteria for judgement will be rather different. It will be judged principally on its practical usefulness to the professional, rather than on the satisfactoriness of the design of the study or the methods used.	Likely to be of practical relevance.	May be simply the view of the author. The work will not have been subject to such stringent scrutiny of research design, method, analysis, etc. It is difficult to assess the difference between a professional journal and a peer review journal, since both have elements of peer review. If in doubt, try to make an assessment of the article itself. Does it just seem to be a personal view? Is it well referenced? How thoroughly does it seem to have been done?
Authored book (usually primary)	Books vary in their 'scholarliness'. They will usually have been written as a major presentation of the author's work – research work or academic study – but they may be explanations of other people's work (see 'Textbook').	Books written by a single author represent an extended academic treatment of a particular topic. Because they are by one person they have integrity: they tend to 'hang together'.	Tend to be personal representations of a topic, unmoderated by the comments or views of others. So be cautious: this may be a very particular 'take' on a subject, or a personal view.
Chapter in an edited book (primary or secondary)	Edited compilations are books all on one theme brought together by an editor. These are like journals, but without the same degree of peer review.	Edited books are a good way of gathering related material on a topic. The editor will be an expert in the field, often taking an interesting slant.	Can be 'bitty', with some very weak chapters interspersed with good ones. The multiple authorial 'voice' may be confusing.

Kind of source	What is it?	☺ Good things about this source	☹ Not-so-good things about this source
Textbook (secondary)	A textbook is a bringing-together of much work on one theme. This is not original work by the author, but work that she or he has summarised for the particular purpose of meeting students' course needs.	Saves a lot of time searching sources. It may, if the textbook is good, provide a very effective summary.	Because an author is reporting on others' work it is susceptible to distortion or misunderstanding (think of 'Chinese whispers'). It is referred to as a 'secondary source' for this reason. When other people's work is brought together in this way by a textbook author it is summarised, perhaps not very well. It can become out of date quickly. For all these reasons a textbook is not valued highly as a source.
Conference paper (usually primary)	A paper that has been presented at an academic conference and that has then been printed in a collection of papers (called the 'proceedings' of the conference).	Usually right up to date, and often reporting on work that is still in progress.	Conferences vary in their status, and papers are often subject to only a minor form of peer review, if they are peer reviewed at all. Conference proceedings are therefore of very variable quality.
Thesis or dissertation (usually primary)	The theses and dissertations that you will be able to gain access to are written by students who have written master's degrees or PhDs.	May be on a topic very similar to your own. May be very good (but may not – see the next column).	May be very weak. Do not use one as a model for your own. It may only have scraped a pass.
Research or technical report (usually primary)	A report written by researchers and addressed directly to the people who funded the research.	Direct, to the point and well focused on the issue being researched.	Not peer reviewed, so no quality control. Also, since paid for by the funder ('contract research'), conclusions may have been influenced by those funders.
Magazine or newspaper article (usually secondary)	Like other forms of publication, newspapers and magazines (periodicals) take various forms, though the differences are more marked. Some periodicals and newspapers are as 'respectable' as some journals. Others are not.	Right up to date, and can be used as a starting point which leads you to a more reliable source.	Most of these publications depend on good sales and may be willing, even the 'high-quality' ones, to distort material to make it more interesting. Reporters are subject to none of the peer review checking used in academic journals. It is not unheard of for reporters simply to make up stories.
Website (usually secondary)	These are as varied as the sources of information above. A website is really just a medium for carrying a range of sources and has no inherent strengths or weaknesses. It's up to you to judge.	Most websites carry reliable information, some for example taking you directly to a publisher's site, where you can download peer-reviewed articles.	Some websites, even quite well-known ones, carry misleading information. Be particularly wary of those offering off-the-shelf answers to essay questions. Wikipedia can be helpful for giving you an impression of the breadth of the area, but is unreliable. Always verify from another source.

in the United Kingdom compared to the United States – a 38% reduction compared to 7%. In general, the American studies were older and several reported just nighttime crime, rather than both nighttime and daytime crime.

A similar resource is the Evidence for Policy and Practice Information and Co-ordinating Centre (EPPI-Centre) at http://eppi.ioe.ac.uk/cms/.

Another of these banks of summaries is at the Cochrane Collaboration (www.cochrane.org/). This is a library of systematic reviews in healthcare. Also see the Educational Evidence Portal (www.eep.ac.uk/DNN2) and digests such as the Social Policy Digest Online (http://journals.cambridge.org/spd/action/home). This provides an easily accessible listing of new developments across the whole social policy field.

I'll finish this section on the quality of sources with a warning story. In 2007 BBC News, the *Guardian*, the *Independent*, *The Times* and Reuters all wrote obituaries of the composer Ronnie Hazlehurst. Unfortunately, they all contained an error that revealed that the obituary writers had simply cut and pasted a phoney fact from Wikipedia. A joker had maliciously edited the Wikipedia entry for Hazlehurst to say that the composer had emerged from retirement to write a song called 'Reach' for the pop group S Club 7, and this strange and interesting 'fact' was duplicated by the journalists without bothering to check its veracity. Result: red faces all round.

However, the moral is about more than just Wikipedia, which can be (and usually is) an excellent resource. It's about all published material. Try to avoid using only one source, and wherever possible corroborate and verify from others. Use primary sources if you can. It's not just facts that can be wrong. Perhaps more of a problem is the impression that you can get from one source where matters of opinion are involved and varied interests at play. If interpretations of data or analysis are involved, be aware that these can take many shapes and hues. By reading from a variety of sources you will get an overview and a more rounded picture of the topic.

Quality of sources

Aside from your judgement about the source that is being used, make a more general assessment of the work that you are referencing. Ask the following questions of it:

- Is this literature written following a piece of research? If so, what kind of research was being undertaken? Was it a large-scale or small-scale study? What was being claimed of the research? Usually research authors are 'up-front' about the limitations and weaknesses of their research, and work that is published in a good journal should not have been accepted if it makes unrealistic claims. This is not to say that small-scale research is in any way inferior to large-scale research: each has its strengths and weaknesses. The main thing is to be aware of these and to show that you understand the limitations of any kind of research – to show that you are critically aware (see 'Critical awareness' below).
- Or, if it is not a piece of research appearing in a journal, is it, by contrast, someone's opinion? Who is the person? What authority do they have? Do they have any vested interests that may have caused them to give the opinion or advice that they have given?

> Not all sources are equal. Think about the quality of the source. Is it primary or secondary? Is it based on research evidence? Has there been a peer review process?

Your literature review should tell a story – it should not be a list

Your aim is to examine the literature for material that is relevant to your research topic. What have other people done that is relevant to your research question? You don't, after all, want to be reinventing the wheel. Your search will take you up against some disparate ideas and some interesting information, but your principal aim here isn't simply to make a list of everything that has been written on a topic. Such *summarising* and listing is necessary but is by no means enough. To conduct a good literature review, you also need to *synthesise* and *analyse*.

Summary is not too difficult, and this is perhaps why it tends to dominate student literature reviews. Analysis and synthesis are more difficult.

When you *analyse*, you see what is going on; you see how one part relates to another; you see the wood for the trees. For example, political journalists don't simply write down everything that is said in Parliament: they analyse how one statement relates to another; they remember what was said last month and note whether it is consistent with this; they look for the vested interests that might be held by those making a statement.

 Your literature review should be a story with a beginning, a middle and an end. It is a synthesis that links ideas or finds differences. It is not a list.

When you *synthesise*, you bring things together, relating one to another to form something new. When chemists synthesise a new molecule from two existing molecules, they don't simply glue one molecule to the next one. Rather, they put the molecules through some process that creates something entirely new and different, with different qualities from the two original molecules. This is what happens in the best literature reviews: there is an intelligent appraisal of a range of sources that in some way extracts the key messages and accounts for them in the context of an overarching statement or idea.

In the end, your literature review should make sense as a story with a beginning, a middle and an end, with lots of connections between one part and another. You outline the issues at the beginning; you provide the analysis and synthesis in the middle (always linking one bit with another: 'Sikes found more fluff in men's trouser pockets, while Cratchett discovered more in women's. The reasons for this may be found in …'); and you tie it up at the end by summarising the issues, differences, paradoxes, dilemmas and questions yet to be resolved.

Making it a story

I have stressed that your literature review should be more like a story than a list. The aim is to find themes – or, by contrast, discontinuities, breaks, disagreements – that run through the literature. When you have done a reasonable amount of searching you will be able to see these emerging, and it is useful at this stage to draw a storyboard – a plan that sums up and brings together the ideas that are emerging from your literature review.

Let's look at the storyboard in Figure 3.1. The original question that has been posed is 'How do head teachers cope with difficult people?' This might be the sort of question posed by a head teacher or deputy head teacher undertaking a master's degree in education. To draw your storyboard you will need to have done some reading already, and it will help if you have thought about or brainstormed on this reading.

Think of this process of combining summary, analysis and synthesis as telling a story or a series of stories. A story makes sense: it is not simply a list. A story has a beginning, a middle and an end, and you can make your literature review take this structure.

Try to build an interest in the area, rather like a novelist does. Start by establishing what the great educator Jerome Bruner (1997: 142) calls the 'trouble' in the story – not literally 'trouble', of course, but rather the issue, question or uncertainty. A good novelist begins a story by capturing the reader's interest with this 'trouble', and this is what you should do when you begin your literature review. You could begin by saying, for example, that although your area of interest is clearly a matter of national concern, researchers have tended not to focus on it, or have focused on an aspect of it that is not relevant to the practising professional. Or you could establish some 'trouble' by pointing out a major area of controversy, which still exists even after decades of research. You then need the 'middle' of the story – the establishment of what people are actually saying, and how they are disagreeing or agreeing. The end will come with a summing-up and a moving-on to the reasons for doing your own thesis.

Do authors concentrate on a particular theme? Do they disagree? Are there areas of controversy? Are there surprising areas of agreement or similar findings? Are there gaps that no one seems to be looking at?

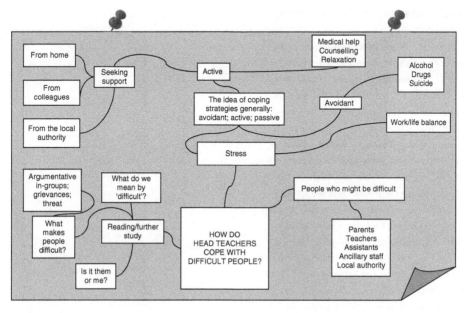

Figure 3.1 Storyboard

Use your words cleverly to tell the story

When writing your literature review, try to make links between different areas of work and make those links explicit with the words that you use at the beginning of sentences or paragraphs. For example, if Smith has found something different from Brown, don't simply list one after the other. Instead, show that you recognise the difference in their opinions by simply inserting a 'however', and relating one with the other: 'Smith (2006) found that boys in Year 9 were significantly below the level of girls in reading ability. However, Brown (2007) found no such difference.' Useful linking words are given in Table 3.2.

Figure 3.2 shows a few paragraphs from the literature review of my own PhD thesis, which was about additional adults in the classroom – people such as classroom assistants and parents. In this particular bit, I was looking at how difficult it seems to be for adults to work together there and I was making connections with similar kinds of situations that had occurred earlier, during the 1960s and 1970s, in team teaching. This excerpt is useful, I think, since it shows how different ideas can be linked.

In this excerpt you can see that I was trying to do two things as far as telling a story is concerned. I was trying to *link* the work of the researchers (Geen and Cohen) that I had located, and I did this by using words and phrases such as 'similar' and 'like Geen'. I was also linking the ideas that seemed to be coming through from the literature – ideas that were linked with the kinds of observations I had made myself and which had made this an area I wanted to research. I had noticed that working together in classrooms seemed to be difficult, and here were researchers saying exactly the same, and proffering reasons for the difficulties. So those difficulties were a thread I could pull out of the review. It wasn't simply a question of summarising what was found by the researchers, but rather a question of finding a theme or themes. For me, the theme was about teams being much more difficult to operate in classrooms than anybody seemed to be assuming.

Table 3.2 Useful linking words

When there is a difference	When there is agreement	When one idea leads to another
however; but; notwithstanding this; although; yet; conversely; in spite of this; nevertheless; on the other hand; despite; then again; besides	moreover; indeed; further; furthermore; additionally; likewise; also; similarly; equally; and; what is more; again	hence; because of this; thus; for example; as a result; consequently; therefore; accordingly; so; for this reason; this is why; otherwise; then; finally

And this is where your own research fits into the review. Would you be aiming to add some weight to one view or another? It is here that your research will begin to take shape, since you may now see the original research question you posed in a different light as you start to uncover what other people have already discovered.

Joining the pieces

Being in a research area is a bit like being told to go into a room in which pieces of a jigsaw puzzle have been scattered around the furniture, with half of the pieces missing: not only do you have to find the pieces you have been given and how they fit together; you also have to understand what is missing. Doing the literature review is like being at that first stage; doing your own research is the second – filling in the bits that are missing. In the first stage you have to discover what is already there and how one bit of the puzzle relates (or doesn't relate) to another. But when you embark on a literature review you are not only

looking for pieces, you are also seeing how they fit together and interrelate. Does this piece go here, or there? What can we tell from these several pieces that seem to fit together? What do they tell us about the gaps that are in the area that is missing?

Speed reading and taking notes

You will not find a stock of books and articles that cover the precise subject of your project. You will, however, find literature that is related and you must do what you can to see the relevance of this.

When you are reading, try to develop the skill of speed reading – 'gutting' an article or book for the material that you need. Keep an eye out for key words or phrases and ignore what is irrelevant. You cannot read an academic book in the same way that you read a novel or even a newspaper. Academics write in strange prose that is sometimes meaningful only to the limited group of people who work professionally in that area, and if you spend your time trying to decipher it all you will go mad. For a particularly important book or article that you need to study in detail (maybe it is a key reference for your research), you may wish to try the SQ2R method. (Francis Pleasant Robinson developed what is called the SQ3R method – see the 'Further reading' section at the end of this chapter – but I suggest a variant which deletes the last 'R', so it becomes SQ2R.) It's a good method, because it avoids the feeling that you have to plod through, interpreting or remembering every word. It reminds you that you are reading for a

...

In team teaching, relationships are found which raise many of
the issues already outlined: there may be clashes in educational
ideology among participants, and/or interpersonal tensions.
However, there will also be managerial issues in determining
where sets of responsibilities begin and end, and who defines
them, as well as practical issues concerning time for negotiation
and planning.

*Synthesis, analysis
and the drawing
of a narrative*

Geen (1985), in tracing the history of team teaching in England
and Wales, found that there are serious difficulties encountered
when teachers are expected to work together in one class. He
found, from sending letters to Chief Education Officers in the 104
LEAs of England and Wales, that despite the enthusiasm for team
teaching in the sixties and seventies, 'it has failed to establish itself
as a permanent strategy in many schools'. Out of 49 schools who
pioneered team teaching in the 1960s only 7 retained it by 1984.

*Reporting directly
on specific findings
from the literature
and relating these
to other findings.*

Among the reasons Geen identifies for schools abandoning
team teaching are: the time and energy consumed in planning;
the reluctance of some teachers to teach before colleagues;
and differences between team members. These relate to the
constructs already identified: time and energy in planning is a
practical issue; reluctance before colleagues an interpersonal
one; differences between team members may be due to clashes
in ideology or personality.

*The opening of
this sentence links
the previous
and present
paragraphs.*

Interestingly, very similar results are found in the US. Cohen (1976)
longitudinally analysed questionnaire data from 469 teachers. The
data are taken at two points: in 1968 and 1975. She notes, like Geen,
that the amount of teaming has dropped substantially over the
period; in 1968, teams of five or six teachers were common but
by 1975 the most common team size was only two (45% of all
teamed teachers were in teams of two; 35% were in teams of
three and only 8.5% were in teams of 5 or more). Suggested
reasons for the decline were to do with the amount of coordination
and communication needed for the effective functioning of the
larger group; teachers do not have the time for it. Associated
with successful teaming are attention to team dynamics and the
support of school management; teaming was 'not unconditionally
associated with teacher satisfaction'. Satisfaction rested in part
on the balance achieved in the teaming process with balance
in turn being determined by the enabling of participation in all
team members. Analysis of respondents' replies led to a growing
understanding of the fact that when team participation was good
it was very good, and when it was bad it was awful (p 58). Cohen
concludes that team arrangements are extremely fragile: 'Teaming
appears to be an organisational innovation trying to survive without
effective preparation or support' (p 61).

*These two
words, 'like
Geen', link the
ideas of Cohen
and Geen.*

*Drawing links
between two
particular findings
and drawing out
themes.*

Figure 3.2   Telling a story

purpose, summarised by the questions that you set yourself as part of the process.

- *Survey* or skim the whole piece, remembering that key nuggets of information occur at the beginning and end of a chapter or article, and at the beginning and end of paragraphs.
- *Q* – now ask yourself *questions*, related especially to what you intend to find out. Don't worry too much about stuff that is irrelevant: stick to questions that are important to you.
- *Read* the whole piece, again fairly quickly, don't get hung up on difficult bits – and, if the book is yours, mark it with a highlighter or a pencil for key words or phrases, especially those that are relevant to your questions.
- *Recall* what was in the piece (having shut the book first). Jot down notes. If you aren't able to remember anything, start again with *survey*.

Whether or not you are using the SQ2R method for your speed reading, keep a Word file of notes from your reading. Call it 'My project notes' (or something more imaginative). To this file you can add downloaded material from online copy or from websites. Internet material is easy to copy by cutting and pasting, so paste straight into your file. Then create a new folder into which you can put this file. If you don't know how to create a folder, click on 'Start' (at the bottom left of your screen), then 'My Documents', 'File', 'New, Folder' and a new box will appear in your Documents called 'New Folder'. You can now type in your name in the place of 'New Folder'. So type in 'Lucy's project folder' (only if your name is Lucy, obviously), and your folder is made – and it didn't cost you a penny. Now drag 'My project notes' into 'Lucy's project folder'. Now, into this folder you can add all of the files that you download. Your main file in this folder will be 'My project notes', but it will also comprise all of the files of articles and webpages that you have downloaded. It's worth noting that when you download a file from the internet, it will be directed straight to 'My Documents' (or possibly 'Downloads'), so drag all of these downloads from 'My Documents' (or 'Downloads') into 'Lucy's project folder'. A quick tip: if, like me, you tend to lose files on your computer (and, like me, you find the new Windows search facility incomprehensible) download a free program called Agent Ransack, which ferrets around wonderfully to find all your lost stuff.

Critical awareness: be your own Jeremy Paxman

Critical awareness is a key phrase that will come up again and again in your university work, and despite the efforts of tutors to instil it in their students, it remains a rare commodity. You will get good marks for having it, and you will be marked down for not demonstrating it.

What, then, is critical awareness? The key thing about study in higher education is your *attitude* to knowledge rather than the *amount* of knowledge that you can show you possess. While at school the key thing seems to be to learn as many facts as possible and then reproduce them in a more or less logical form for an assignment, the attitude at university is rather different. Certainly there may be issues and knowledge with which you will be expected to be familiar, but it is your attitude to such knowledge that is more important than your familiarity: your approach should always be of scepticism – of suspicion and doubt. You will be expected to be aware that there will always be different ways of interpreting some observation, different ways of arguing a case, different interests at play in any argument. In short, you'll be expected to recognise, and to demonstrate that you recognise, that truth is hard to come by.

Why is this lying bastard lying to me?

You will usually be marked more for your *approach* to facts than for your knowledge of them. You should understand how someone comes to a decision, judgement or conclusion, and understand that there will always be other kinds of decision, judgement or conclusion that could have been drawn from data that have been gathered. As the great biologist J.B.S. Haldane put it, this is really about 'the duty of doubt'. Or as René Descartes (1647/1996) said: 'Doubt is the origin of wisdom.'

Or as Jeremy Paxman put it, less elegantly though perhaps more straightforwardly: 'Why is this lying bastard lying to me?' Actually, Jeremy Paxman claims that he never said this. He says of his reported use of this phrase:

Do I think that everybody you talk to is lying? No I do not. Only a moron would think that. But do I think you should approach any spokesman for a vested interest with a degree of scepticism, asking 'why are they saying this' and 'is it likely to be true'? Yes of course I do. (Wells, 2005)

What Jeremy Paxman says is just about the best way of summing up critical awareness, and it applies not just to politicians and spokespersons. It applies to anyone who reports a finding or expresses an opinion, because everyone reports those findings and expresses those opinions in the context of their own experience. And this experience may be more or less valid, more or less loaded, more or less interested (where 'interested' means 'having a stake in'). You have to put out of your mind the idea that all researchers, indeed all people who write anything anywhere, are fair-minded, neutral observers. There may be any one of a thousand reasons why someone takes a particular slant on a research question, so they will go out and look for data in a particular way or analyse those data in particular ways to suit their purposes and end up with the sort of findings that they expect. They may simply start off with an involvement or personal investment in a particular area, or they could be sponsored by a particular company or government department which may have an interest in a particular finding being made. So, start with Paxman's question (paraphrased), 'Why are they saying this?'

Critical awareness, however, is not just about spotting bias or personal involvement of this kind. It is about an awareness that knowledge is frail, not fixed, and that you should approach everything you read and hear with a questioning mind, always asking yourself whether something could have been done differently.

So, however respectable the source, be questioning, be critical. Also, be tentative about any conclusions that you yourself feel you are able to make: avoid phrases such as 'this proves' and 'this shows' and instead use words such as 'this indicates' or 'the evidence suggests' or 'points towards' or 'implies'. Try to use moderating phrases such as 'tends to' or 'one might conclude that'

instead of bolder ones. Academic writing is an area where it pays to be tentative: no one will give you high marks for making unwarranted claims about your own research, or for gullibly believing the reports of others. Doubt everyone's findings, even your own. Remember again 'the duty of doubt'.

That duty of doubt, of *critical thinking*, has a long and illustrious intellectual tradition. Socrates started the ball rolling 2,500 years ago. He emphasised that you cannot rely on the views and declarations of those in authority. Authorities – that is to say, people in positions of power and influence – may sound impressive but may in fact be irrational and confused. He said that we should always subject any claim to knowledge to rigorous questioning as to its validity. His system of questioning has become known as the 'Socratic method'. All our beliefs, all our knowledge, should be subjected to such questioning, so that we can separate reasonable beliefs from those which lack rational grounding or adequate evidence.

> Demonstrating critical awareness, critical thinking and reflective thought is as important as anything else in your work. It's about being instinctively sceptical about claims to knowledge and truth.

You can employ critical thinking about sources that you encounter – any piece of research or any scholarly argument – in your literature review by asking yourself these questions:

- Are there any vested interests at play?
- Might the writers' objectives in undertaking the research sway their reasoning in some way?
- Would different methods have yielded different findings?
- What sources of information are being drawn upon – is there evidence of balance, or are sources being 'cherry picked'?
- What is the quality of the data being drawn upon – are they from good primary sources?
- Is the writer's reasoning sound? So, if you were arguing with them, what would you say? (But ask yourself also how much validity your own criticisms would have, and whether you yourself are likely to be swayed by tradition, sentiment or vested interest.)

Click on 'Search': finding information

Finding information is one of the areas that has changed most dramatically over the past few years. Before the mid-1990s, researchers had to rely on printed articles in paper journals and on abstracts and indexes catalogued on paper, microfiches and cards. They had to go to the library to find these resources. Then at the end of the 1990s came the widespread use of the internet, and researchers came to depend on big library databases, using key words to search them.

But then came Google. I'll say this very quietly so not too many of my colleagues hear (and I'm hoping you won't tell them), but when I am doing my own research I rarely use any other means of starting my searches. There is no point in being snobbish about Google. It works. Not only does it work, but it works better than all of the posh library databases. Somehow (and it remains a total mystery to me how it does it) it seems to know what I am thinking and what I am wanting. It is free, reliable and quick. Not only is there Google, but there are also Google Scholar and Google Books. If you don't already know how they work, here's how …

Google

Unless you have been residing on Mars for the last 20 years you will know how to use Google. Just a few hints:

- Type as much or as little as you wish into Google's search box. For example, if you are interested in whether the Head Start programme produces beneficial consequences for primary school children, you could either type in the whole sentence (that is to say, just like this: *Does the Head Start programme produce beneficial consequences for primary school children?*) and click on 'Search', or you can pick out the key words (*primary Head Start benefits*). Try it in different ways and see what emerges.

- Google searches for the words in your query in any order; it doesn't keep the words you type in as phrases. If you want to keep the words in the same order – as phrases – then put them in double quotation marks. So, for example, if you wanted Google to search for the phrase 'Head Start' among the other words, you would type in *primary "Head Start" benefits*. It will then search just for the phrase 'head start', leaving out all other occurrences of 'head' and 'start'.
- If you want to search for something and you want the search to become narrower, so that it leaves out references to certain subjects or areas, you can put in a minus sign before a word or term that you wish to omit. So, if I wanted to find out about primary Head Start benefits, but I wanted only to look at children above reception age, I could type in *primary "Head Start" benefits -reception*. It's good to practise with many different ways of phrasing a Google query.

Google Scholar

Google Scholar works in much the same way as Google, but it is more targeted at the kinds of reading material you will be looking for in university life. You can access it from http://scholar.google.com/. Once you have accessed the Google Scholar main page you use it in the same way that you would have used Google. That is to say, you can type in a question or a more targeted inquiry based on a particular article that you have already identified.

For example, try typing in the same question that I used above for testing Google: *Does the Head Start programme produce beneficial consequences for primary school children?* When you do this and click on 'Search' you will get many thousands of responses, as you do on ordinary Google. However, these responses, rather than being general, will only be to books and articles. The 'best' ones will usually be at the beginning, but you will also find good ones lower down (though they will become progressively less relevant as you proceed downwards).

Figure 3.3 shows the first 'answer' I got when I typed that question into Google Scholar. The figure shows the various elements of the Google Scholar 'answer' page. As with all forms of electronic resource, the key is to keep playing with it: click on links to see what happens.

Google

Does the Head Start programme produce beneficial consequences for prima ▾

🔍

✎ My Citations

Scholar   About 67,100 results (0.05 sec)

Articles

Case law

My library

Any time
Since 2017
Since 2016
Since 2013
Custom range…

Sort by relevance
Sort by date

Does Head Start make a difference?
J Currie, D Thomas - 1993 - nber.org
… participation in **Head Start** is a significant predictor of the **child's** participation (Mott and Quinlan,
1992), it **does** not explain … Nelson and Startz (1990) report then in these circumstances, IV estimates
can be very misleading. … About half of all **children** in the sample **did** not attend any …
Cited by 1061   Related articles   All 25 versions   Cite   Save   More

[PDF] ucla.edu

Long-term effects of early childhood **programs** on cognitive and **school** outcomes
WS Barnett - The future of **children**, 1995 - JSTOR
… regardless of the age at which a **child** begins out-of- home care.-6 It **does**, however, indicate …
Programs designed for disadvantaged **children can produce** immediate boosts in … All but two
studies **did** not select par- ticipants on the basis of IQ: the Perry Preschool study selected …
Cited by 1599   Related articles   All 14 versions   Cite   Save

[PDF] princeton.edu

Socioeconomic disadvantage and child development.
VC McLoyd - American psychologist, 1998 - psycnet.apa.org
School social systems and student achievement: **Schools can make** a difference. New York:

[PDF] academia.edu

This tells you how much the work has
been cited, which is a good indication
of how well regarded the work is in
the academic community. It's
certainly not a watertight indication of
quality, and is not an indicator that
you would want to quote in your own
dissertation or thesis, but it is a pretty
reasonable indicator of how much it is
used and relied on by academic peers.
*If you click on this it will take you to all
the works that have cited (referred to)
this work,* enabling you to 'jump
forward' in time from the work itself.

Underneath the main answer are the
report's authors, and then some text from
the report itself. This is usually the first
words of the article/book/report. Usually
they give a rough indication of what
might be in the document.

On the right, here, are publicly available
versions of the document. These can be
very useful for quick access or if your
library doesn't stock the journal or
report in question.

Figure 3.3   Google Scholar – the important bits

I am reliably informed by librarians that Google Scholar will not pick up all relevant references because the information released to it is sometimes restricted by publishers. Although this may change with time, do be aware that you will also need to use the subject-specific databases I mention later in this chapter. You can start off with a Google Scholar search and then supplement it with the targeted databases.

Google Books

As if Google Scholar weren't miraculous enough, there is also Google Books, which will find relevant books, point you to the page(s) relevant to your search inquiry, and even show you the page(s) themselves. From the Google main page, just type 'Google books' directly into the search box.

Typing a general inquiry is less likely to be successful with Google Books than with a general Google search. So you may have to begin your search by using fewer words and making a more general enquiry. Remember that when you are asking Google just to look for books it is searching a far narrower range of resources, so keep your options open by reducing the number of words in your search.

Getting access to journals via your library

Some of the sources that you access using Google will be journal articles. You will emerge from the Google Scholar page with a publisher's journal page which provides an abstract and an invitation to buy a full download of the article. Don't be tempted to buy it, because you will probably have access to the journal through your university library. Most, if not all, university libraries nowadays enable you to access, without paying, a huge array of journals via a central jumping-off point. That jumping-off point at my university is called FindIt@ Bham; the one at yours will be called something similar, such as iDiscover or SOLO. When you click on the right page, you'll come up with a screen something like the one in Figure 3.4.

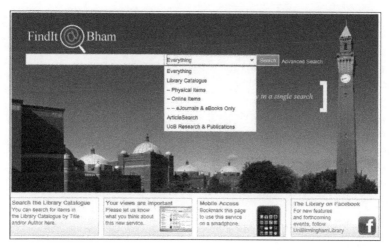

Figure 3.4   Finding resources in your university library

In the empty box near the top left, you type the name of the resource that you want (e.g. *Harvard Educational Review*), and from the drop-down menu to the right of it you click on the appropriate option. I advise avoiding the 'Everything' choice since it seems to check everything in the world, which – maybe it's just a personal thing – leaves me confused by the sheer multiplicity of offerings; if you want the online version of the journal, click on 'Online Items' but remember that while most *journals* are online, not many *books* are.

University libraries get access to packages of journals (for which they pay large amounts of money) via something called 'Shibboleth', which should take you automatically to a set of resources. (You don't actually need to know about Shibboleth, since your search should take you robotically through the system; I'm only mentioning it in case 'Shibboleth' flashes up momentarily on the screen, as it sometimes does, and you think 'What the plonking hell is Shibboleth?') If, on your introductory tour of the library, you haven't been told about how to get access to journals in this way, go along to one of the librarians and ask about it. Don't be frightened to do this: in an information age this is what librarians are expected to do – to help you gain access to all kinds of information sources. It's what they get paid for.

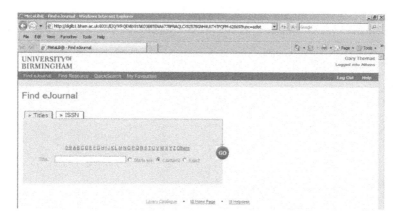

Figure 3.5   Searching for an e-journal

Remind them of this. (That's a joke, by the way.) Actually, most librarians I know don't conform to the frosty stereotype at all; they are friendly and helpful. And the new information finding systems are easy to use: just be prepared to invest an hour or two playing with whichever system your library uses and seeing what it can do for you.

You will be given a username and a password for your library system. Usually these will be the same ones as for your university. Once you have entered your username and password details you will have access to an array of databases that carry the journal. Figure 3.5 shows the sort of page that emerges when you have done this. It is from my own university library, and yours will be similar.

Type in the name of the journal that came up from your Google inquiry and press 'Go' (or the equivalent in your library's system) and you will come up with a page like the one in Figure 3.6. My library's system gives information about which databases have access to the journal, and when I press 'Find It!' at the bottom of the page it gives me the choice of locating the article I want in one of several databases. It doesn't matter which one you use, but just check that the particular database (such as SwetsWise) carries the journal for the *year* that you want.

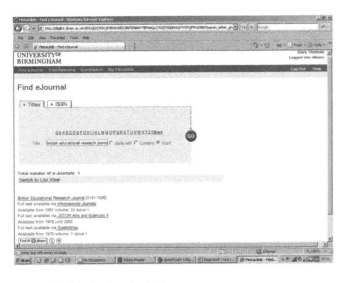

Figure 3.6 *Selecting from the databases*

Because every university's system is different, giving you more exact information from this point on in the process will not be of much use to you. So the next step is to make that library visit. Before you start asking librarians lots of questions, though, ask for the library's various leaflets and sheets on electronic access and try to make sense of them. Play around for a while on the computer, and find what you can and can't do – what you can and can't access. Make a list of what will hopefully be more targeted questions and then go and see the librarian.

The Web of Science

The Web of Science provides the fullest and most authoritative resource on citation information. In other words, it gives you 'leads' to all of the articles published on a particular subject (or by a particular author) in reputable peer review journals over a certain timespan; and, like Google Scholar, it will also tell you lots of other information about those articles, such as the other articles that have referenced it.

You will be able to log in to the Web of Science only if your university subscribes (and nearly all do), so you will need to log in via your university library system. Type 'Web of Science' into the library search box and look for the answer that comes up with 'Thomson Scientific'. Once you are at the Web of Science home page and you are asked which databases you want to search (under the dropdown box labelled 'All Databases'), click the option labelled 'Web of Science™ Core Collection'. You'll be able to search for a range of years, by topic and/or by author.

It's big. Because of its size it has a bit of a reputation for being clunky to use. However, it has recently been

Citation: A reference to a particular piece of work, usually by using the Harvard system (e.g. 'Smith, 2002').

redesigned and is now much more user-friendly. Because of its size, though, it's easy to miss out on many of its features, and I would recommend taking a look at the official Thomson Scientific tutorial on how to use it. To find this, type 'Web of Science quick tour' into your search engine.

Zetoc

Your university library will provide a way for you to use Zetoc, which gives access to the British Library's 30,000 journals and 16,000 conference proceedings, published every year. Type http://zetoc.jisc.ac.uk/ and fill in your university's details. Zetoc is particularly useful as it includes an email alerting service to help you keep up to date with relevant new articles and papers – in other words, Zetoc will automatically send you an email when a new article appears that 'hits the spot' as far as certain criteria that you specify are concerned. You could, for example, tell it to send you all articles by a certain author, or all articles with certain key words in the title, or all articles in each new issue of a certain journal.

Zetoc will give you:

- a *search* facility, for citations of journal articles and conference proceedings – a bit like Google Scholar.
- the *alert* facility, to send you email alerts of new articles that may be of interest to you.
- *facilitated access* to full texts of articles and papers. Zetoc itself provides access to the table of contents rather than the full text. However, once you have found an article of interest, the full record page provides links to help you access the full text.
- *feeds* (also called RSS feeds – RSS stands for Really Simple Syndication), which help you to keep automatically up to date with what is happening in a journal. Click on 'Zetoc RSS – Access' in Zetoc, and then click on the feed you want to see. In the example in Figure 3.7, I've clicked on the feed for the *American Educational Research Journal*. When you subscribe to the feed, it will be added to your 'Favorites Center' in your browser, which will automatically check the website and download new content so you can see what is new since you last visited the feed.

Finding books

As with journals, your first port of call in finding books will be your university library site. Here, the usual course of action is to use your university's library catalogue, which will normally have some kind of search box. You can then use key words (any combination

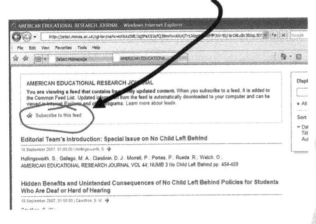

Figure 3.7   Subscribing to a feed

of subject key words, words in the title or authors' surnames) to find what you are looking for.

There are other resources for hunting down books which may not be in your university library's stock:

- *WorldCat* is a catalogue of major libraries throughout the world which can show the location of specific titles in the libraries nearest to you.
- *The Library of Congress* catalogue is a major catalogue which is often used to check bibliographic details of hard-to-find books.
- *Bookdata Online* is a database of books in print available from UK and some US publishers. It can search for chapters or sections within books as well as by title, author and publisher, and it also keeps details of books which have gone out of print.
- *Amazon* is also a good resource for finding books (but not articles). Type www.amazon.co.uk (or www.amazon.com for the US version). It's not as good as Google Book Search but it does have some useful features such as 'Look Inside!' which allows you to look at the contents pages and to read the first chapter, the index and some other information about the book. Also, it gives you information about what other customers who have bought the book have also bought – surprisingly useful, since many will, inexplicably, seem to be on much the same train of thought as you. There will be a publisher's synopsis of the book too and, if you are lucky, some reasonably informative reviews (but often also some spectacularly uninformative ones). Clearly, this is not information disinterestedly given by Amazon out of the love of knowledge – they want to sell you books, so be wary.

Something that the Amazon website is particularly useful for is when you are compiling your reference list. Unless you are absolutely perfect, you will have lost certain references, or you will have somehow missed off a key bit of the reference when making your notes. The Amazon website has co-authors, the publisher, the date of publication and dates of various editions, and this is often all you need to enable you to plug the holes.

EThOS

EThOS is the British Library's digital repository of all doctoral theses completed at UK institutions. Such work can provide invaluable help on precisely targeted subjects, though I should re-state the point I made earlier – don't use other people's theses as a model for your own, since they are of highly variable quality.

EThOS is part of the British Library's programme of digitisation of research theses in the UK. A lot of theses are already digitised, in which case you can download them straight away as PDFs, but those that are not you can ask to have digitised (amazing!).

To search further afield for relevant theses, you can try:

- Networked Digital Library of Theses and Dissertations: Electronic open-access theses, available at http://search.ndltd.org/
- DART-Europe e-Theses Portal: Electronic open-access theses from Europe, available at www.dart-europe.eu.

Find these via your favourite search engine if they are not immediately available via your library.

Inter-library loan

I've been at pains to point out that you should be very wary about clicking on any link that asks you to part with money for an article download. This is partly because there is an excellent chance that you will be able to access the article or book completely free through your university library account. Or you will be able to see enough of it to gain a sufficient impression of what it is about. If the worst comes to

the worst, though, and you decide that you simply must have a copy of the article and you are not able to access it by one of the means already explained here, you can get the article via inter-library loan, either electronically or as a photocopy. Ask your librarian about this. There will probably be a charge, but it won't be nearly as much as it would be from a publisher's website.

Specific subject databases

Aside from the generic databases I have just mentioned, there are also specific databases for particular subjects.

ERIC

ERIC stands for the *Education Resources Information Center*, which is an online digital library of education research and other information. (I'm not actually sure how an 'online digital library' is different from a database, but never mind, I'll give it its Sunday-best name since that's what its publishers call it.) ERIC is paid for by the United States Department of Education, and, as you would guess given these credentials, it is a pretty hefty piece of kit. It provides access to over one million records, including the 'grey literature' of, for example, fact sheets, information briefs, research syntheses, conference papers and policy reports. The latter are difficult to get hold of from any other source, and ERIC is worth consulting for this alone. It is updated continuously. With a move to open-access publishing of scientific findings now, many of the records are available in full text.

To search on ERIC, Google 'ERIC basic search', and try their Thesaurus for key terms that will take you to the area in which you are interested. Also try 'My ERIC', which enables you to join a community of people interested in the same subject as you, and lets you save searches, get alerts and even submit your own material for inclusion in the database.

BEI

The BEI is the British Education Index, which is the British equivalent of ERIC. It is rather smaller than ERIC, with, at the time of writing, 175,000 references to journal articles. The database grows by over 8,000 records per year. One particularly interesting feature of the BEI is the access it gives to Education-*line*, which offers a collection of over 6,000 full-length texts, most of them conference papers.

PubMed

If you work in healthcare, including medicine, you will almost certainly want access to PubMed, which is the repository for biomedical literature. It is truly enormous, containing 26 million citations for biomedical literature from life science journals and online books.

CINAHL

For students of nursing, CINAHL offers, as the producers put it, 'the definitive research tool for nursing and allied health professionals'. It indexes more than 5,400 journals, with full text for more than 1,400. The topics included cover nursing, biomedicine, health-sciences librarianship, alternative/complementary medicine, consumer health and 17 allied health disciplines. It also gives access to healthcare books, nursing dissertations, conference proceedings, educational software, audiovisuals and book chapters.

PsycINFO

Primarily for psychologists, PsycINFO is run by the American Psychological Association and contains 4.2 million records in the behavioural sciences and mental health. It ranges over the literature in psychology and allied disciplines such as education, linguistics, medicine, nursing, pharmacology, physiology, psychiatry and sociology.

Other databases

There are dozens of other subject-specific databases. To review these to see which would be useful for you, go to your appropriate library webpage. As I have already noted, most university libraries nowadays will provide a page that is a bit like Google, which lets you search the vast expanse of the whole library. My library's (open to everyone) is at http://findit.bham. ac.uk/. From here, you go to the top right of the page and click on 'Find Databases', then click on 'Search by Subject', then choose a category such as 'Healthcare', and then a subcategory (if you wish) such as nursing, and the webpage will list all relevant subject-specific databases.

It's worth finishing this section on the world of subject-specific databases and other online resources by saying that some of them offer remarkable resources, while others don't seem to last very long. In fact, I wonder how some of them last even as long as they do, given the power of the competition in big search engines such as Google Scholar. How should you judge which to look into? I think that you should look to see if these resources offer some added value over Google, such as the ability to connect with other like-minded people or the facility to export citations or help you to organise and format those that you export. These latter features can be really useful.

Reference managers

One of the advantages of using databases such as ERIC, PubMed and Web of Science is that they enable you to export citations directly into reference management programs such as *EndNote, Reference Manager* or *ProCite*. Your university library will have a webpage which explains how to use these. The reference management software will organise all of your references for you and even format them appropriately. For undergraduates, I think that probably the easiest to use is a web-based system called *RefWorks*, to which you will have free access if your university subscribes. (If it doesn't, you have to pay, but 1,200 universities across the world do subscribe so there's a fair chance yours will.) It enables you to gather, manage, store and share all types of information, as well

as generate citations and bibliographies. Once you have been a member, you stay a member, even when you leave your university.

Similar to RefWorks are WorldCat, which finds books and articles in the collections of 10,000 libraries worldwide and lets you export the citations that you find into your own **bibliography** or **references** list, and CiteULike, which offers reference to 8.4 million articles and enables you to receive automated article recommendations and to share references with your fellow students.

> ***Think Digital* working with other students and researchers** Research can be isolating. It's surprising how often I feel that I know all I think it is possible to know about a subject, having done a thorough literature search, and then I talk to a colleague or to one of my students and I'm off on an entirely new line of inquiry that I hadn't even considered before I spoke to them. It might be a tangential topic that turns out to be not so tangential, or the name of a researcher who happens to be at the centre of the field of inquiry, but for some reason had eluded my gaze. For this reason, it's good always to try to connect with others, and there are now some easy ways of doing this via special social networking services:
>
> - MethodSpace (www.methodspace.com) is a social networking service for social scientists run by the publisher SAGE. As well as networking, it offers video clips and advice.
> - ResearchGate (www.researchgate.net) offers networking with other researchers (mostly professional researchers) and a search engine that browses academic databases.
> - Graduate Junction (www.graduatejunction.net) is a social networking service aimed at postgraduates and postdoctoral researchers.
> - Academia.edu enables you to connect with professional researchers and to keep updated with their latest publications.

Hints on searching – separating the wheat from the chaff

When you begin to search the literature, it's a good idea, first of all, to draw up a *search strategy* in which you assemble key words and phrases, together with

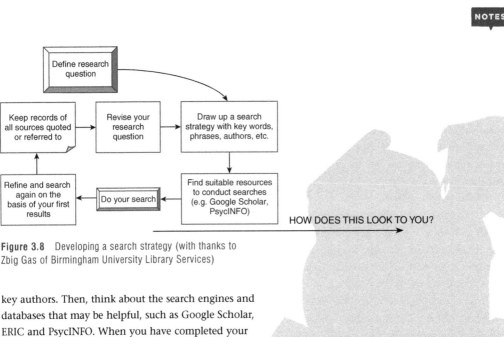

Figure 3.8 Developing a search strategy (with thanks to Zbig Gas of Birmingham University Library Services)

key authors. Then, think about the search engines and databases that may be helpful, such as Google Scholar, ERIC and PsycINFO. When you have completed your searches, refine the first search by perhaps adding a new key name that you have found in your first search, or making one of your research terms more tightly defined. And don't forget: keep records of where sources have emerged from (particularly page numbers, if you quote), together with the internet reference (the URL) if the material is only available from an internet source. If you record all of this information at this stage, you'll save yourself a lot of time later on. The process is summarised in Figure 3.8. Note that the process is cyclical: it may be the case that you need to redefine your research question after you have done your first search, for you may discover that there is already a lot of research on the topic you wanted to address, or you may find that there is a particular area that is clearly crying out for further research.

Two common problems that students come up with on doing a literature review are (1) that they can find no information, and (2) that there is just too much information.

Let's look at the first one: you can find absolutely no information at all on your topic of interest. The thing is, it is most unlikely to be the case in reality that there is no information to find on your topic, so if you are finding nothing in your various searches you should

The literature review 229

examine where you may be going wrong. It may be the case that you are not using enough search facilities, or, more likely, that you are making your search too narrow. You are pinpointing your search terms too finely, or throwing away related information that is not on the precise subject of your interest, but is connected and therefore useful. Remember that your literature review ultimately will not be on the exact topic of your research, but rather it will be on the more general subject *surrounding* your research. So, if you wanted to look, for example, at how head teachers cope with difficult people and you are coming up with nothing, it may be that you are searching too specifically. Your searches may need to concentrate on something broader, such as teacher stress, and you may wish to think about what 'difficult people' means. This will in turn suggest that you think about the 'people' with whom head teachers come into contact: there are the other teachers in the school, other head teachers in the area, parents, pupils, teaching assistants, administrators, support staff, etc. Were you thinking of all of these when you posed your question, or just certain categories? So, think about the broader ways that your question may be framed. Think about alternative search terms.

 Think like a search engine. Find alternative ways of formulating ideas connected to your research question.

You'll see in Figure 3.9 that the original question about how head teachers cope with difficult people has been reformulated into a range of terms that you might not have thought of originally; you might, for example, ask why 'drugs' and 'suicide' are included as alternatives to 'coping'. The key is to try to think like a search engine. The search engine is sorting through words and phrases in an unimaginably large set of websites, a tiny fraction of which will contain, in some sense or other, 'stories' about head teachers and difficult people. But these 'stories' are hardly likely to be framed in these exact terms. They are more likely to contain words that are associated with the words you have identified. What are difficult people likely to do to a head teacher? To cause stress. What does stress lead to? Possibly drinking excess alcohol, taking drugs or even suicide. These may not be the coping strategies you were thinking of, but they will lead into stories that address the topic, perhaps comparing these routes out of stress with more positive ones. So the key is – if you don't at first succeed, try thinking like the search engine and formulating your question in a number of different ways using a range of related words.

Remember also that your literature review is a general contextualisation. So stress in *teachers* as a *general* group is likely to be of relevance when you are thinking about stress in *head* teachers. Don't limit your search by a very precise word when you may find some very interesting information that relates to broader issues.

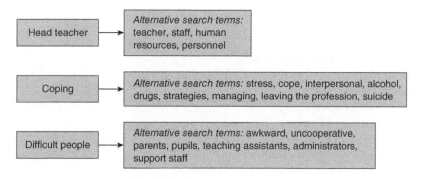

Figure 3.9   Turning your question into alternative search terms

Now the second common problem: you are swamped with information on the topic. Suppose you are interested in the attainment of black boys and you enter *black boys attainment*. The search emerges with nearly four million 'answers'. If you now put in a term that is related to your interests (say *14–19*) it will reduce the number dramatically. Or you can put in the name of a key academic or a key commentator to delimit the search. Ask your tutor for key names. For example, if I put in the name of someone who I know is an expert here – *'Gus John'* (in double quote marks because I want Google to find *only* references to Gus John, not to all the Johns and all the Guses in the world) – it reduces the four million to 3,280.

So, the key is to imagine that in your literature review the process is like sieving: with too coarse a mesh you let through too much; with too fine a mesh you don't get enough. Or imagine that you are trying to separate the wheat from the chaff. If you blow too hard you get rid of the wheat as well as the chaff. If you don't blow hard enough you don't get rid of the chaff.

Understanding how sources are cited – the Harvard referencing system

You need to understand the Harvard referencing system for two reasons. First, when you are reading, you need to understand the way that sources are referenced by authors in books and journal articles. Second, when you are writing, you need to know how to provide references yourself when you write up your literature review – in other words, how to give the full details of books and articles you refer to so that others can find them. There are various ways in which referencing can be done, but the overwhelmingly preferred method in the social sciences is the Harvard system. (It has several variants, and you will find that the Harvard system may be called one of these variants, notably 'APA', which stands for American Psychological Association. Don't worry too much about the variations unless you want to submit something for publication: just go for bog-standard Harvard.)

This is how it works. You find a source – let's say an article written by Jane Brown. If you then want to refer to the article in the literature review of your project you do so by using the author's surname, followed by the year of the publication in brackets – for example, by saying 'In a large study, Brown (2004) discovered that little bits of fluff accumulate in people's pockets.' You will then give the full details of Brown's publication in a list headed 'References' at the end of your report (not 'Bibliography', incidentally, which has the meaning of 'here are some interesting books that are related to my thesis' – by contrast, 'References' applies only to the works you have actually referred to in your text). We'll come on to how to compile the list in a moment, but first let's look at how you make reference to various kinds of sources in the text, since these will take a variety of forms.

How you make reference *in the text*:

- For a single author of a book or a journal article, use the author's surname (without first name or initial) followed by the date of the publication in brackets, e.g. 'Sweedlepipe (2005) found that the fluff referred to by Brown (2004) is composed mainly of cotton fibre and dead skin.'
- Where a work is by two authors, use both authors' names followed by the date in brackets: 'Sweedlepipe and Sikes (2007), in later work, showed that the ratio of cotton fibre to dead skin (by weight) is between 3:1 and 5:1.'
- For more authors, use the first author's name, followed just by 'et al.' (which means 'and others'), e.g. 'Sweedlepipe et al. (2008) illustrated the mechanism by which cotton fibre bonds to dead skin.'
- If you actually quote from the author, you must give the page number from which the quotation comes, putting the page number after a colon after the publication date: 'Sweedlepipe (2005: 134) sums up the importance of the topic this way: "The precise mechanism involved in the accumulation of fluff in the pockets is one of the greatest mysteries remaining for science to solve."'
- In the unlikely case of an author having two outputs in 2005 that you are referencing in the text, this is indicated by 'a', 'b', 'c', etc. after the date: 'Sikes (2005a) found that trouser pockets of male students contained significantly more fluff than those of female students, and in later work (2005b) hypothesised that the lower amounts of fluff in

female pockets were due to a higher frequency of personal hygiene measures (principally by washing and clothes laundering) among females.'
- A book that has been republished long after the original publication may be cited with the author's name as usual, but followed by both the first publication and republication dates, e.g. Ryle (1949/1990).

Then, at the end of your dissertation, you will have a *reference section*, headed 'References', which contains the full details of all the material to which you have referred. This is how you set out your 'References' section:

- For a book: name(s) and initial(s) of author(s) followed by year in brackets, followed by book title in italics, followed by place of publication and publisher. For example:

  Sweedlepipe, P. (2005) *The Fluff in People's Pockets*. London: Sage.

- For a journal article: name and initial(s) of author(s) followed by year in brackets, followed by article title, followed by name of journal in italics, followed by volume number, issue number and page numbers. For example:

  Sweedlepipe, P. and Sikes, B. (2007) Ratios of cotton fibres to exfoliated skin in trouser pockets of US males. *International Journal of Fluff and Allied Detritus*, 31 (1), 252–7.

- For a downloadable internet source: name and initial(s) of author(s) followed by year in brackets, followed by article title, followed by the words 'Available at' and the internet source, followed by the date you accessed it in brackets. For example:

  Wells, M. (2005) Paxman answers the questions. *Guardian Unlimited*. Available at: https://www.theguardian.com/media/2005/jan/31/mondaymediasection.politicsandthemedia (accessed 15 January 2017).

When formatting the reference list, it looks good if each reference has a hanging indent – in other words, the first line is formatted to the left, as normal, and the subsequent lines are indented. You can produce the hanging indent in Word by putting the cursor anywhere in the reference and pressing Ctrl+T. Or do the whole lot together by selecting all the references (with your mouse, left-click at the beginning and drag down to the end) and then pressing Ctrl+T.

The list should be in alphabetical order. To alphabetise a list automatically in Word (pre-2007),

select the whole list with your mouse, then click on 'Table', then click on 'Sort', and click on 'OK'. In Word 2007 (and after) look for the 'Sort' button. You will find this under the 'Home' tab, in the 'Paragraph' group: there's a little box that looks like this: [⇅]. Click on it. The list will miraculously appear in order. (If it doesn't, the settings on your copy of Word may have been changed and you will need to look at the particular instructions under 'Sort' more carefully.)

As I mentioned in relation to subject-specific databases, there are now several software systems for organising your references automatically, such as EndNote, Reference Manager and RefWorks, and your library will almost certainly offer support in using these through leaflets, courses and email query and will provide a web link on this and related issues. My own library's (open to everybody), which also offers detailed advice on the use of the Harvard method, is at www.i-cite.bham.ac.uk/. This excellent website provides all you need to know and more. Click on 'How to reference correctly' and on the next page click 'Harvard (author-date)'. It's most likely that you will be asked by your tutors to use Harvard referencing, but it may be the case in some subjects that you will be asked to use Numbering (Vancouver) or Footnotes or OSCOLA (for law students). The website also gives guidance on all of these.

Taking notes and quotes

There used to be a time when people had to take careful notes on small cards of every source they consulted, which would be filed alphabetically. (For people like me, who suffer from a mild variant of Asperger's syndrome, this was enormously satisfying.) Researchers had to be meticulous about everything they did, punctiliously keeping records of references – because if you lost one or forgot to record it, it would take hours or even days to track it down again. Things aren't like that any more: you can now find a lost reference on the internet in seconds. And note-taking is different too: you can now be a lot more creative and idiosyncratic in the way that you keep notes on your word-processor. The problem with the old card index file systems was that they almost encouraged you to think of the literature review as a collection of names and notes. Now, though, if you take notes more fluidly – as I suggest in the next section – you can add observations, make connections and link one source with another through the notes that you take as you are reading.

A notes file in Word

The software packages I have just mentioned (End-Note, etc.) seem to work for some people. However, I find a simpler system is just to paste everything that would conceivably be of interest into a Word file which I can then search for the key words that I want. When I say 'key words' I don't mean anything very technical. I just mean that I use Word's search facility (Ctrl+F) to look for a word or part of a word that will find the topic I am looking for. So, for example, if I were interested in finding anything mentioning *science* or *scientists* I would ask the program to find 'scie'.

As I am reading, I copy quotations (and, importantly, the references from which they come) willy-nilly into the file. I always make a point of recording the reference as exactly as possible, and then the notes as I see fit at the time. I make it clear with the use of quotation marks which are my own words and which are the author's. This may not have the satisfying tidiness of the old card index, but the question arises how far that alphabetical imperative is still necessary. When you can now simply find what you need to find in a file, why does it need to be in alphabetical order? You simply need to type a search word or phrase into the 'Find' box and the machine will do the rest. When you can easily fillet and sort a list alphabetically (see pp. 84–5), why bother putting them in alphabetical order at the outset?

Many of the notes I take are copied directly from the internet by cutting and pasting. This is particularly useful in copying reference details. However, you should always be very clear in your recording which are the author's words and which are your

own. Whenever you quote someone else's words you must always *make full and clear attribution to the author in question.*

Plagiarism

Occasionally students are tempted to try to pass off the work and the words of others as their own. Your university will almost certainly have a policy on plagiarism, how it is defined, why you should not do it, how you can avoid it and the penalties for doing it. My own university defines plagiarism as:

the submission for formal assessment of an assignment that incorporates, without proper citation or acknowledgement by means of an accepted referencing standard, the intellectual property or work of a third party.

Its policy, which is fairly typical of all, is given at https://intranet.birmingham.ac.uk/as/studentservices/conduct/misconduct/plagiarism/index.aspx.

> **What your supervisor wants for your literature review** You'll probably have to produce a draft of your literature review, which your supervisor will usually comment on and edit, probably using 'Track Changes' in Word. (Find out how to use 'Track Changes' in Chapter 2.)

Having had the sense to read my book, you are not of course the sort of person who plagiarises. However, just speaking generally for a moment, plagiarism is a pity for a number of reasons.

- First, it is against the spirit of the thing: the aim is to learn, develop and improve – not just to get a certificate. So why pretend?
- Second, there is a real risk of being caught, as the likelihood of being found out is increasing as plagiarism software improves, and the penalties at any university are serious for those who are found plagiarising. Indeed, most universities are now demanding that all work must pass through plagiarism software such as Turnitin at submission, and students may be deducted marks, made to resubmit or even failed if they are deemed to have plagiarised.

- Third, there is no penalty for drawing from others or using their ideas and words, as long as these are acknowledged. In fact, your marker will be pleased to see evidence of wide reading and the intelligent synthesis of this.

Although, having said this, you should avoid overdoing quotations. Generally, one short quotation per page would be the maximum I would want to see, with perhaps the occasional extended quotation. The aim in a literature review is to outline and demonstrate interconnections, not to present a list of other people's verbatim words. The key is analysis and synthesis, and quotations do not really play a role in either, unless you are using them to provide an excellent illustration of a point that an authority is making.

Overview

Your literature review is not an add-on: it should be a major contributor to the development of your project. It should help you to shape your questions by enabling you to find out what has already been done. The literature exists in many shapes and forms and you should be discriminating in what you choose to include – even seemingly unimpeachable sources can be wrong. This is where critical awareness begins: show that you understand that there is always room for interpretation in the reading of any piece of work. Interpret and understand what others have done, and weave their contributions into a narrative. The literature review should be a narrative – a story – not a list.

Further reading

Arksey, H. and O'Malley, L. (2005) Scoping studies: towards a methodological framework. *International Journal of Social Research Methodology*, 8 (1), 19–32. Available at: http://eprints. whiterose.ac.uk/1618/1/Scopingstudies.pdf. Defines, describes and discusses the use of detailed literature reviews, which are sometimes called 'scoping studies'.

Campbell Collaboration. Available at: http://www.campbellcollaboration.org/. This contains systematic reviews in education, crime and justice, and social welfare. Useful not just for the analysis and synthesis of studies, but also for examples of the way that evidence is balanced.

Cochrane Collaboration. Available at: http://www.cochrane.org/. This is a library of systematic reviews in healthcare.

Evidence for Policy and Practice Information and Co-ordinating Centre (EPPI-Centre). Available at: http://eppi.ioe.ac.uk/cms/. This is similar to Campbell, but tends to focus more on education.

Fink, A. (2013) *Conducting Research Literature Reviews: From the Internet to Paper* (4th edn.). London: Sage. Systematic, with good examples on searching in health, education and business domains. Not just the process, but also good on evaluating the articles you select to review.

Hart, C. (2018) *Doing a Literature Review: Releasing the Social Science Research Imagination* (2nd edn.). London: Sage. This detailed book goes far beyond the mechanics of the literature review to discuss the organisation of ideas, the development of argument and the liberation of what the author calls 'the research imagination'. Oriented towards the postgraduate rather than the undergraduate.

Pears, R. and Shields, G. (2016) *Cite them Right: The Essential Referencing Guide* (10th edn). Basingstoke: Palgrave Macmillan. Very helpful on the intricacies of sorting out your Harvard from your APA, and especially good on the problems of referencing internet sources.

Research Information Network (2011) *Social Media: A Guide for Researchers*. Leicester: RIN. Available at: http://www.rin.ac.uk/system/files/attachments/social_media_guide_for_screen_0. pdf (accessed 14 October 2016). This is an excellent guide on the value of social networking and social media generally, with some good advice on how to connect with others.

Ridley, D. (2012) *The Literature Review: A Step-by-Step Guide for Students* (2nd edn.). London: Sage. Practical and easy to read with lots of examples, and a good section on 'voice'.

Robinson, F.P. (1970) *Effective Study* (4th edn). New York: Harper & Row. Good for advice on speed reading.

Williams, K. and Carroll, J. (2009) *Referencing and Understanding Plagiarism*. London: Palgrave. A useful little book that tells you all you need to know about the subjects of the title.

 Still have questions? Check out my supporting website for more advice and activities at: https://study.sagepub.com/thomasrp3e

CHAPTER 3 CHECKLIST

You may find it helpful to copy this table and write down the answers to the questions. Have you …

	Notes	
1 … used the main databases in your field of applied social science to locate relevant literature?		✓
2 … secured some relevant and high-quality sources from which to draw?	What are the main themes, agreements and disagreements? Write them down here.	✓
3 … mapped out the main issues?		✓
4 … drawn a storyboard?	What are the 'stories' that emerge? Which will you follow?	✓
5 … understood how the Harvard referencing system works?		✓

Reading and researching the literature

Greasley, P.

Most of the learning that happens at university is achieved by you – the student. We're just there to facilitate learning – and provide some feedback. Unfortunately, for some students at least, this means researching and reading the literature. And that doesn't mean a quick look at Wikipedia.

In this chapter we'll look at the importance of exploring the literature and taking account of different perspectives (being aware that just because something is in print doesn't necessarily mean it's true), along with some advice about the kinds of references you should be citing in your assignment.

Tip 14: **One thing leads to another**

This is not a tip about amorous liaisons; rather it's about the process of reading and researching for an assignment. If you're doing it right, one thing should lead to another. That is, you might start with (heaven forbid) Wikipedia, or perhaps a general textbook, and then follow the references to other sources of literature. It's called research and it's like conducting an investigation, digging deeper and deeper into the literature.

When I used to write assignments I would often spend the day on a tangent: having read one article, the references would lead me to another, and then that would lead to another, and so on, until I found myself in another place completely. As the following comments from the survey (see Chapter 2) show, this is a good thing (if you have the time). It shows that you're adopting the role of the explorer (Chapter 1), venturing beyond the set texts (and in doing so you may be able to impress the tutor by telling them something they didn't know – Tip 21).

What tutors like

- Reading widely and using the literature to develop a critical argument

- A good, broad range of quality references that are appropriately employed and correctly cited

- Demonstrating wide, detailed reading around the subject

- Evidence of a good range of reading (including texts taking a different perspective)

- Reading over and above the set texts

- Use and critique of appropriate reference resources that demonstrate a thorough literature search

- Well-referenced points

- Good use of references to support discussion such as when students cite several authors for one 'statement', showing they have read around and integrated what they have read

What tutors dislike

- Failing to engage with literature

- Not reading widely enough to give a basis for the arguments (or assertions)

- Reliance on only one or two reference sources

- Poor reading round the subject and not using up-to-date references

Tip 15: **Use up-to-date references**

Obtaining up-to-date references can be crucial for a good mark. I recall marking one assignment discussing the evidence for homeopathy (an 'alternative therapy') and it failed to discuss or reference the most recent review of the evidence, which I had, incidentally, highlighted in the lectures. This oversight significantly reduced my impression of the assignment, and the mark, which was largely justified: here was a key reference that had been ignored. This also highlights the importance of conducting a literature search (see Tip 22).

The most up-to-date articles will be in journals, and it's worth checking whether such articles are available in a preprint electronic version, since journal articles can actually take a while before they become available in print. For example, it took over two years to publish the results of the survey upon which this book is based (Greasley and Cassidy, 2010). Now obviously, this depends on the article and the journal. If the title is 'A cheap and simple cure for all known diseases' or 'Cold fusion repeatedly demonstrated', it may only take a few months for it to appear in print. But if it's 'Injuries due to falling coconuts', or 'Pigeons' discrimination of paintings by Monet and Picasso', you could be waiting a while. (These are actual articles – the former appeared in the *Journal of Trauma* and the latter appeared in the *Journal of the Experimental Analysis of Behavior.*)

Tip 16: **Avoid dodgy sources**

The source of your references may be crucial to the reliability of the information you are providing in your assignment. For example, I remember reading an essay evaluating the evidence for acupuncture in which the main reference was from *Acupuncture Today* (a 'trade' magazine) – which is not necessarily the most objective and unbiased source of information. It's a bit like citing *Flying Saucer Review* for evidence of UFOs.

It's not surprising, then, that 'poor-quality references' was an issue raised in the survey of tutors.

> **What tutors dislike**
>
> - Using weak references, e.g. Reader's Digest, 9 o'clock news
> - Not using original sources, e.g. Doctor on the video shown in the lecture talking about his research [rather than a published source of information]
> - Citing the *Sun* newspaper as the main source of evidence for whether a therapy works!

Imagine if the assignment preceding yours has been citing original articles from the *Lancet*, the *British Medical Journal*, the *Quarterly Journal of Experimental Psychology* and the *Harvard Law Review*, and all you've got to offer is the *Sun*, *Wikipedia* and 'the video shown in the lecture'. It's not going to look good, is it?

Tip 17: **www.usesparingly.com**

The increasing use and reliance on references from the Web was another source of marker distress. Here are a few comments.

> ### What tutors dislike
>
> - Using too many internet references
>
> - Internet reference sources – a small number may be OK, particularly when they come from reputable sources, however copious unrecognised sources will not do
>
> - Non-existent web addresses on the references list [markers do sometimes check the web references – especially if they look dodgy]

Perhaps the key word in the above comments is 'reputable': synonyms include 'of good reputation', 'highly regarded', 'trustworthy'; antonyms might include 'dubious', 'biased' or 'dodgy'. The problem is one of quality assurance. Unlike articles in journals, there is no peer-review process (where other academics review the quality of the article prior to acceptance).

There is no doubt that the internet is a wonderful tool – information at your finger tips – but you need to be selective. Aside from dubious websites promoting their own agendas (e.g. alternative remedies that will cure all ills), some people purposely enter false information, on Wikipedia, for example.

Tip 18: Wikipedia: cite it at your peril?

Wikipedia, the online encyclopaedia, is one of the most popular sites on the web – the seventh most visited site, according to web information service Alexa. And no wonder, it contains over 10 million articles, nearly 3 million in English, covering virtually everything you would ever need to know as a student. But you already know this. Surveys suggest that most students consult Wikipedia when writing assignments. For example, a survey of Cambridge University students reported that over 75% 'had used Wikipedia for researching essays'. But you are probably also aware that most tutors discourage the use of Wikipedia – especially citing it as a primary source.

So what's wrong with using Wikipedia? Why do tutors have such a problem with it? Well, aside from the fact that Wikipedia is a secondary source of information (a second-hand summary of original research reported elsewhere), the primary concern is the reliability of the information, since anyone with access to the internet can contribute and edit the contents. So there are justifiable concerns about the quality of the information contained on the site – its accuracy, validity and objectivity, all of which are key criteria in assignments.

It is for this reason that one academic department proposed a 'wiki ban' on students. In 2007, tutors in the history department at Middlebury College in the USA voted to bar students from citing Wikipedia in their assignments. While a ban was not enforced (or enforceable), the head of the department warned that Wikipedia is not an appropriate source for citations: 'The important point that we wish to communicate to all students taking courses and submitting work in our department in the future is that they cite Wikipedia at their peril' (Jaschik, 2007).

How unreliable is Wikipedia? In 2005 the highly respected British journal *Nature* asked expert reviewers to check the accuracy of information in a range of scientific articles on Wikipedia and compare this to articles in the *Encyclopaedia Britannica* (a more established source of information). They reviewed 42 entries and reported:

> Only eight serious errors, such as misinterpretations of important concepts, were detected in the pairs of articles reviewed, four from each encyclopedia. But reviewers also found many factual errors, omissions or misleading statements: 162 and 123 in Wikipedia and Britannica, respectively. (Giles, 2005: 901)

So, in terms of accuracy, it would appear that Wikipedia is nearly as reliable as the well established and generally respected *Encyclopaedia Britannica* (although the reviewers did report concerns about the 'readability' of some articles which were poorly structured and confusing). But that's still, on average, four errors per article (162 errors in 42 articles).

Perhaps the sensible advice would be to consult Wikipedia as a convenient initial source of information and use the links provided, but not to cite it. The same advice would be given for citing any encyclopaedia. Use it as an initial source of information but try to consult and reference original sources or reputable textbooks.

Tip 19: **Make the move to journals as soon as you can**

What should you be reading and what should you be citing in your assignment? Well, you might start with general textbooks in your first year and then begin to include more specialised sources like journals in your second and third years, but this does depend to some extent on the academic discipline. For more classical subjects in the arts and humanities, the relevant literature may be more book-based, but for scientific subjects where the evidence is constantly updated, you will need to consult the academic journals which contain the most up-to-date literature.

So while a good textbook is excellent for general information, providing an overview of the subject, as you progress through the years you should be consulting and referencing journal articles more and more, as the following reflection from a student illustrates:

> I think it was learning the research skills. I didn't know how to research really and you pick that up as you go along using the libraries and journals. In the

first year I tended to get a lot of the information from books and also searching other areas like the internet. I was getting Cs. In the second and third year
I started to go beyond that and started to use journals. [And then her grades
started to improve.] (Norton et al., 2009: 28)

We've already noted that the information from journals should be more up to
date than that found in books (which can take a few years to write). It may also
be more reliable due to the peer-review process.

When an article is submitted to a journal it will be sent out to (typically)
three academics with some expertise in the area to 'referee' or 'review' it, that
is, to appraise the design of the study, note any errors, suggest improvements,
etc. Once the article has been reviewed, the journal editor will write to the
author(s) with recommendations about what needs changing for the article to
be accepted in the journal (or not accepted, as the case may be). Most recommendations are along the following lines:

- Accept without changes (rare - especially if you've got three academics picking at every word)

- Accept with minor revisions (corrections, clarifications, etc.)

- Reject but invite resubmission with major revisions (e.g. rewrite, collect more
  data)

- Reject outright (fundamentally flawed, or it could be that the article is not
  appropriate for that particular journal)

So the peer-review process helps to ensure a level of 'quality control'.

Tip 20: **You can get any rubbish published**

Articles in journals may have been through the 'peer review' process, but you
should still remember that 'peer review' only means that the paper has been
critically evaluated by two or three other academics. The review process is
usually anonymous and quite a good means of quality control, but it certainly
doesn't mean that the content of the article is 'the truth'. It just means that the
article has been through a process to try to maintain standards.

You should also be aware that standards vary across journals. The 'top'
journals, such as *Nature* and the *British Medical Journal*, only publish about
5% of submitted articles. The acceptance rate for many other journals, however, can be much higher. So you need to be mindful of the hierarchy of
quality across different journals. As the former editor of the *British Medical
Journal* once commented: 'You can get any rubbish published, just go down
and down and down and down the food chain [of medical journals]' (Fister,
2004: 923).

Although this quote refers particularly to medical journals, the same principle applies in most academic subjects: the top journals in your subject area will
usually contain the most important and more rigorously conducted studies,

but there will be journals where the standards are less rigorous. As the deputy editor of the *Journal of the American Medical Association*, Drummond Rennie, once commented:

> There seems to be no study too fragmented, no hypothesis too trivial, no literature too biased or too egotistical, no design too warped, no methodology too bungled, no presentation of results too inaccurate, too obscure, and too contradictory, no analysis too self-serving, no argument too circular, no conclusions too trifling or too unjustified, and no grammar and syntax too offensive for a paper to end up in print. (Cited in Smith, 2009)

This is a very important message to remember: journals may be a good source of information, but that doesn't mean you should accept what they say without question, even if they are subject to peer-review:

> Editors and scientists alike insist on the pivotal importance of peer review. We portray peer review to the public as a quasi-sacred process that helps to make science our most objective truth teller. But we know that the system of peer review is biased, unjust, unaccountable, incomplete, easily fixed, often insulting, usually ignorant, occasionally foolish, and frequently wrong. (Richard Horton, editor of the *Lancet*, cited in Horton, 2000: 148)

Remember, no study is perfect, and the authors will usually be requested to present their own list of limitations at the end of the study, all of which reinforces the importance of appraisal skills when reading journal articles. (We will be discussing critical appraisal in Chapter 8.) As an interesting aside, Box 5.1 provides an example of 'the rubbish' that can actually appear in a journal.

box   5.1

Sokal's hoax journal article

In 1996, Alan Sokal, a professor of physics at New York University, sent an article to the American cultural studies journal *Social Text*. The article, entitled 'Transgressing the boundaries: toward a transformative hermeneutics of quantum gravity', was submitted as an 'experiment' to see if a leading North American journal of cultural studies would 'publish an article liberally salted with nonsense if (a) it sounded good and (b) it flattered the editors' ideological preconceptions' (Sokal, 1996b: 62).

When the article duly appeared in the spring/summer 1996 issue of *Social Text* (Sokal, 1996a), Sokal announced that it was intended as a hoax, full of meaningless sentences and nonsensical quotations about physics and mathematics produced by prominent French and American intellectuals. For example:

In the second paragraph I declare, without the slightest evidence or argument, that 'physical reality' [note the scare quotes] ... is at bottom a social and linguistic construct. Not our *theories* of physical reality, mind you, but the reality itself. Fair enough: anyone who believes that the laws of physics are mere social conventions is invited to try transgressing those conventions from the windows of my apartment. (I live on the twenty-first floor.) (Sokal, 1996b: 62)

For a detailed account of the hoax see Sokal and Bricmont (1998) or Sokal's webpage: http://www.physics.nyu.edu/sokal/ (accessed September 2010).

Tip 21: 'Tell me something I don't know'

Some students are not very adventurous – they don't stray beyond the confines of what is covered in the lectures. Perhaps this reflects lack of time, but an assignment which simply regurgitates what was covered in the lectures is not flattering, it's disappointing. The lectures should be seen as the start of your reading and investigation, not the end. Obviously you will need to do the essential reading that has been recommended for your assignment, but as the comments from the survey illustrate, if you really want to impress your tutor, try going beyond the set texts and 'thinking out of the box'.

How to impress tutors

- Telling me something I didn't know by going beyond the reading/lectures

- When I actually learn something from what I've read

- Students who tackle the question in a new/original way

- Thinking out of the box ... occasionally you do get a very well written, meticulously researched and highly polished piece of work that either subverts the question or deals with it in an unusual, but pertinent way. Nice when that happens. Especially if you've got a bunch of 150 scripts to mark!

So try to tell the tutor something they don't know and tackle the question in a different or original way (though make sure you follow the guidelines and meet the learning outcomes, of course).

Tip 22: **Do a literature search**

Although you should be provided with a list of essential and recommended reading, a further search of the literature identifying other good sources of information will usually impress tutors. As we've noted, students who receive the higher marks will usually delve further into the literature, exhibiting the 'deeper' approach to learning.

You might start with a search on the internet. Google Scholar, for example, will provide you with an indication of what's been published in academic journals, along with links to relevant citations, but if you want reliable academic sources use your library's online subject databases. In Table 5.1, I've listed some of the common databases in my own subject area, the social and health sciences.

Table 5.1   Some common literature review databases

Subject	Database
Health	**AMED** (Allied and Complementary Medicine Database)
	Includes: physiotherapy, occupational therapy, rehabilitation, palliative care and complementary medicine
	CINAHL (Cumulative Index to Nursing & Allied Health)
	Nursing and allied health
	Cochrane
	Database of systematic reviews for health interventions
	PubMed
	PubMed comprises more than 24 million citations for biomedical literature from MEDLINE, life science journals, and online books. Citations may include links to full-text content from PubMed Central and publisher websites
Social sciences	**ASSIA** (Applied Social Sciences Index and Abstracts)
	Health, social services, economics, politics, race relations and education
Psychology	**Psychinfo**
	Psychology (journals from 1887 to the present)
Business and Management	**Proquest**
	Business and management

Techniques for searching the literature within these databases vary, so you will need to consult the relevant guides provided by your university library (which may also offer training in the use of electronic resources), but they generally share the following principles:

1. **Select the appropriate database** for your search, e.g. Medline for medical topics, Psychinfo for psychological topics. (Note: it may be possible to search across several databases at the same time, avoiding the need to repeat your search strategy across individual databases.)

2. **Identify the key words/terms** for your search, e.g. 'acupuncture' and 'pain'.

3. **Use 'filters' to restrict and focus** the literature retrieved, e.g. dates, context. You can also ask it just to search for literature reviews on some databases. This can be a good start if you find one that's recent.

4. **Keep a record** of your literature search by saving the search. Aside from saving you repeating the search at another time, this might be useful to put in an appendix if your assignment warrants it (e.g. if it's a research proposal).

For example, a search of the literature on 'acupuncture' and 'pain' might proceed as shown in Table 5.2. The aim is to reduce the number of 'hits' to a manageable amount. At step 4, I could have filtered by a more recent year of publication to reduce the 'hits' to a manageable amount (publications since 2006), but instead I chose to have a look for any recent literature reviews – which is usually a good start.

Table 5.2   Narrowing down a literature search

Step	Search	Results
1	Search term: 'acupuncture'	= 2,000 hits
2	Search term: 'pain'	= 4,000 hits
3	Combine 'acupuncture' and 'pain'	= 400 hits
4	Filter by year of publication (studies published since 2000)	= 200 hits
5	Restrict to literature reviews only	= 10 hits

For larger assignments, like dissertations or postgraduate research projects, you may be required to conduct a more thorough review of the literature. Indeed, conducting a literature review may be the assignment itself. Chapter 16 provides more detailed guidelines about how to conduct a systematic literature review.

summary

In this chapter we've seen the importance of:

- using up-to-date references – especially for subjects where the knowledge base is updated regularly through new research (e.g. health interventions)
- citing reputable sources (e.g. peer-reviewed articles in good journals)
- being aware that just because something has been published in a book or a journal doesn't mean it's 'the truth' (reliable, beyond criticism, etc.)

(Continued)

(Continued)

- obtaining different perspectives from different sources
- going beyond the recommended reading and perhaps tackling the assignment in a different or original way (telling the marker something they don't already know)
- doing a literature search

So, you've read the relevant literature and identified some interesting information. Now you just need to start working backwards ...

How to deliver excellent presentations

Burns, T. and Sinfield, S.

Okay – we're all terrified of public speaking! This chapter is designed to crack the code of the academic presentation. This chapter is supported by a Presentations Pack downloadable from the Sage website (https://study.sagepub.com/burnsandsinfield4e/).

Introduction

I really hated the thought of presentations, but once they were over I felt so good about myself. In the end I wanted more of them.

Presentations are meant to exploit the fact that most of us are much better at speaking than we are at writing. Of course, what this glosses over is that students, like every other normal human being on the planet, tend to be terrified of public speaking, of presentations. In this chapter we are going to explore the what, why and how of presentations. We cannot make all the fear go away, but we can help you to realise that you can get really good at presentations – you might even get to enjoy them.

What is a presentation?

There are several 'whats' to a presentation that we are going to cover here – they are all true. The trick for you, as always, is to think, 'How will knowing this help me to give better presentations?'

It's a talk

I remember this presentation, it was on breast cancer, a really frightening topic, and the students had left all the funny noises on their PowerPoint. So there they were giving life and death statistics and scaring everyone silly, and all the while there are explosions, whistles, flying noises and breaking glass!

A presentation is a formal talk of a set length on a set topic given to a set audience. When preparing your presentation you have to think about all these factors: time, topic, audience. That is, you have to fit the topic into the time you have been given – and no longer. Check with the tutor if there are penalties for going over time.

You also have to pitch the topic at your actual audience. Again, as with the report, think about real people with real knowledge, thoughts and feelings. You have to make sure that your language, style and tone are just right for the real people that you are going to address. Finally, you have to make sure that any audiovisual aids (AVA) – your supporting material, handouts, PowerPoint, websites, photographs, posters – are appropriate and will connect with your actual audience. There are two main purposes of using AVAs:

- to help the audience follow and make sense of your presentation, e.g. an outline of the whole presentation, a poster or pattern note of the whole presentation
- to illustrate, emphasise or underline key points, e.g. a quote, a picture, an example, a physical object.

─TIP─

Use posters to support your presentation – even if not asked to – they help your audience follow and understand your talk. Prepare a creative visual collage – or go for the more formal academic poster: www.fobit.biz/?p=1605.

It's an act

No matter what anyone else tells you, remember that a presentation is a *performance*. You are standing in front of people and talking to them: they are looking at and listening to you – this is a performance. Therefore you are a performer. Use this knowledge – and *act*. To make presentations work for you, act happy, confident and interested – even if you are bored silly or scared witless. If you are happy, your audience can be happy, if you are not, they cannot. If you are bored – your audience will be too … So act your socks off.

─TIPS─

Positive body language

- Do face the audience.
- Do not only look at the wall or whiteboard behind you.
- Do stand or sit straight.
- Do not hold anything in front of your face.
- Do smile.
- Do not tap your foot or make chopping motions with your hands.
- Do draw people calmly into your presentation with brief welcoming gestures.
- Do not hold your arms defensively in front of your body.
- Do stand in a relaxed manner.
- Do not stand there with clenched fists or looking as if you want to be somewhere else.
- Do dress for success.
- (In a group presentation) do not act as if you hate everybody else on the team.
- Do *act* calm, confident and in control.

It's interactive

As a performer, you will have to build a rapport with your audience and create a relationship with them: you *interact* with them. This means that you will need to *look at them*. You will have to make eye contact with your audience.

So ignore those who advise you to look at the ceiling at the back of the room. That may be okay if you have an audience of 1,000 or more people, but in a small group it looks weird, and not in a good way. You will need to look at people to draw them into your talk and take them with you. You will need to check that they are following and understanding what you say – to check if you need to repeat or explain something. You will never discover this if you do not look at your audience.

Finally, for it to be a successful interactive performance, just like an actor on the stage, *you must never, ever speak from a script.* You must not read a presentation. You must learn your presentation and then deliver it fresh, as though for the first time. Reading a presentation is the quickest way to lose your audience and lose marks.

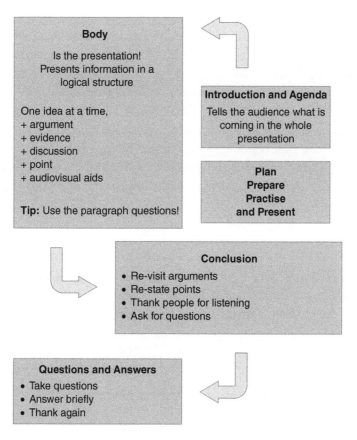

FIGURE 12.3.1 Structure of a presentation

It's a formal convention

The presentation has the same shape as the essay – and it has the same need to address real audiences as the report. Therefore, you should have a sense of the presentation already from what you now know about essays and reports.

A beginner's guide to presentations

Introduction

The introduction should include a clear agenda:

- Introduce yourself.
- Give the topic title.
- Hook your audience.
- Give the agenda.

The introduction is where you acknowledge the question and help the audience understand how you are going to tackle it. Think hook and agenda: the *hook* tells them *why* they should be listening to you: are you going to be interesting, useful or funny? Will it help them pass an exam or get better grades? Will it save them time or effort? Think of something. The *agenda* is where you tell the audience exactly *what* is coming in your presentation. Without an agenda the audience does not know where the talk is going. This is unsettling – and confusing. A confused audience is not a happy audience. Tell them what is coming … and this simple technique will dramatically improve the presentation itself – and your marks.

Presentation body

This is the presentation. This is where you answer the question that you were set, making a logical case. As with the five paragraph essay, think: three big ideas – introduction – conclusion. For each idea, think: argument – evidence – AVA.

TIPS

Use the paragraph questions to structure *each section* of your presentation:

- **What is this section about?**
- **What exactly is that?**

- Tell me more?
- What is your evidence? What does it mean?
- How does this relate back to the question as a whole?

Conclusion

As with the essay conclusion, this is where you draw the whole presentation together. Re-visit your main arguments, re-emphasise your main points – and use all the words from the question to prove that you have answered the whole question.

─**TIPS**─────────────────────────────

- Write introductions and conclusions last.
- Accept this is a repetitive structure: tell them what is coming; tell them; tell them what you told them. This can feel silly, obvious or uncomfortable, especially in a short presentation. But this is what is required, so bite the bullet and do it!

The question and answer session

It's over – you want to rush out screaming! Don't. You now have to thank the audience for listening and ask them for questions.

─**TIPS**─────────────────────────────

- Do re-phrase difficult questions – check that you have understood.
- Do keep answers short.
- Do keep answers good-natured.
- Do notice when people put their hands up – take questions in order.
- Do not fight with your audience.
- Do not try to make everyone agree with you.
- Do not think that you have to know everything (unless it is a job interview or an oral exam).
- If you cannot answer why not try: 'That is a very good question – what does everyone else think?' If no one else knows, 'Well, that has given us all something to think about. Thank you again for listening!'
- Do bring the question and answer session to a firm end. The audience likes to know when it is all over safely.

Why do we set presentations?

As with planning and preparing any assignment, the process of preparing a presentation is designed to be an active learning process. As you plan, prepare, practise and perform your presentation you are really getting to grips with and learning the material. As you think about how to *communicate* a topic effectively to your audience you are synthesising and using information.

It's an opportunity

> I did everything you said and practised again and again. The tutor said I was a natural – if only she knew.

And, yes, presentations really are an opportunity to shine. Before you have successfully delivered and survived your first presentation you may find this hard to believe, but once you have done this, you may find that given the choice between an essay and a presentation, you would choose the presentation every time. Once you have cracked how to do presentations well, you will realise that it is easier to get good grades for a presentation than for a piece of writing.

It's a job skill

Further, good oral communication skills are definitely required by employers – some even require a formal presentation as part of the interview. Developing good presentation skills whilst at university can make the difference between getting that job you want – or not.

TIP

Make notes on what you did well in all your presentations and put these in your CV folder (see Chapter 13.1).

It's self-confidence

Finally, once you can do presentations, your self-esteem really improves. From the very first one that you plan, prepare, practise and present, you start to feel better about yourself as a student and this enhances all your studies. This is not just something that we are telling you here to make you feel better – this is something that all our students have told us: succeeding in presentations is the best confidence booster they have ever had.

TIP

Think positive thoughts to drown out your negative ones: *I can do this; This is a great presentation.* Check out Chapter 3.

How to succeed in presentations: the four Ps

Here we will be looking at the four presentation Ps: plan, prepare, practise and present.

Plan

Think about your time limit, your topic and your audience:

- *Time limit:* how can you fit the topic in the time you have been allowed? What will you have to put in – what will you have to leave out?

TIP

Be interesting!

- *Topic and audience:* remember – an audience is made up of real people with real knowledge and expectations of their own. They will not want to be patronised – they will want to learn something.

PLANNING TIPS

 I knew a postgraduate student who went all the way to Japan to deliver a presentation based on a video. The technologies were incompatible, they couldn't show the video. The whole thing was a huge and expensive disaster!

When you start planning your presentation, consider the following:

- What can I expect my audience to know about this topic before I start?
- What will I want them to know when I have finished (= the aim of your presentation)?

- How will I get them from where they are to where I want them to be (= a logical structure to your presentation)?
- What language, tone and style will be right for this audience?
- What arguments and evidence will they understand – and relate to?
- What audiovisual aids will help – and will work with this audience?

  ○ think of visual aids to *illustrate the topic* – photographs, charts, diagrams, key quotes, posters
  ○ think of visual aids that will help people *follow your presentation* – have the agenda on a handout or write it on the board, make a large pattern note of your presentation, and display it, make a poster.

- How will my audience react to this topic? Will they be resistant, happy, frightened, interested? What will I have to do to get them to respond positively?
- What questions might they ask me? What answers will I give?

Action plan: now that you have considered all these things: what will you do, read, find and make to get your presentation ready?

Prepare

I must stress the research and preparation!! When I've participated in presentations, either on my own or in groups, confidence came from how well we had worked together and how much research we had done.

Preparing a presentation requires the same research and hard work that an essay does, and then you have to make audiovisual aids as well.

Some preparation guidelines

- *Remember the ten steps* (Chapter 11.3): brainstorm the topic, link to the learning outcomes ...
- *Read actively and interactively:* gather all the information you need to answer the question.
- *Plan the presentation:* give it the shape that will take your audience from where they are to where you want them to be.
- *Be interesting!* Never tell the audience everything from A to B to C. This is boring. Choose an interesting aspect of the topic – focus on, elaborate and illustrate that.
- *Remember to make your AVA*: with backups (e.g. handouts of PowerPoint slides).
- *Convince yourself first:* if you can act as though you believe it, it will help the audience to believe you.
- *Prepare a script*: once you have collected all your data and understood and shaped it, you may wish to prepare a script for the presentation. A script can give you a sense that you have

taken control of your presentation and organised your material to your satisfaction. That is okay – if you remember that you must not read from your script. So at some point you *should destroy your script.*

- *Prepare your prompts*: make cue cards or prompt sheets to guide you through the presentation itself. This could include:

  ○ key words or pictures instead of words
  ○ key examples and quotes
  ○ key names and dates.

- *Number your cue cards and your points.*
- *You must destroy your script* – no really!

–TIPS–

- **You must not read from a script – you will be boring and dull and you will lose your audience.**
- **Re-create your presentation from the key words on your cue cards.**
- **It does not matter if you forget something – the audience won't know. Better to be lively and miss a bit – than say everything and be dull and boring.**

Practise, practise, practise

 The success of the group presentation relied very heavily on how well we had got on before the day and the solo presentation relied very heavily on how much effort I had put into the preparation and research. There were very few students who could 'wing' it and often those that tried fell short when questions were put to them.

Once you have a shape to your presentation, with your prompts prepared, you are now ready to review, revise, edit and learn your presentation – and this comes through practising or rehearsing your presentation. You must not say the presentation for the first time in front of an audience – the words will sound extremely strange to you. You will confuse and upset yourself. This is not a good thing. You must learn and be comfortable with your presentation.

There are several key stages to your rehearsal:

- *Tidy it*: your first rehearsal allows you to review, refine and finish your presentation – and turn it from a written thing to an oral thing. When speaking we have to get to the point – quickly.
- *Learn it*: rehearse your actual presentation – in front of a critical friend. Keep making it shorter – more direct – more effective. Walk around your home delivering the presentation to your cat or a chair. Make yourself feel comfortable speaking those words out loud.

TIP

Do not rehearse in front of your children. Our mature students always say that their children tend to say 'it's boring, it's silly'.

- *Refresh it*: once you are comfortable with speaking out loud and you know your presentation by heart, then you need to practise until you can say it every time as though you are saying it for the first time. This will keep your presentation fresh and alive and it will appeal to and grip your audience.

Perform: tips and tricks

 I think one of the pitfalls of doing the presentation is not approaching it in the same way as any other assessment … and forgetting the extra element of practising beforehand.

Okay – you are going to be nervous. Do not focus on that. Think positive thoughts and get on with it. Here are some positive things to do.

Before your presentation

- *Be positive*: read 'Believe in yourself' in Chapter 3. Practise your positive thinking. Keep saying: 'I am prepared', 'This is a great presentation'.
- *Be mindful*: when travelling to your presentation, run through your main points with and without your cue cards. Reassure yourself that you do know it.
- *Be early*: get to the room early so you will be as cool, calm and collected as you can be. Rushing in late will increase your stress levels.
- *Be organised*: take control of the environment. Organise the seating. Where will you want people to sit so that you feel good and they can all hear you? Do you want them in rows, in a semi-circle, sitting on the floor?

TIP

Arrange to stand behind a desk or a lectern. This small barrier between you and your audience will help you feel safe and in control.

- *Be in control*: check that the equipment is working.

─TIP───

Have a back-up system in place – have print-outs of your PowerPoint slides to circulate as handouts if the computer does not work.

- *Be alert*: use your adrenalin – it will help you think on your feet.
- *Be positive again*: say, 'I am prepared' and, 'I can handle this'.
- *Be physiological*: stress has a biofeedback effect where the things our bodies do when we are stressed actually increases our stress. We have to learn to de-stress our bodies. If too stressed before or during your presentation:
  - stop
  - sigh
  - drop your shoulders (we hold our shoulders up when tense and this increases tension)
  - wriggle your toes (we clench our feet when stressed and this increases our blood pressure and hence our stress levels)
  - unclench your fists – this is a typical anger/fear reaction – let it go
  - take a few deep, slow breaths (deep quick ones and you will pass out)
  - start again more slowly (stopping and refocusing never counts against you, it can even impress your tutor).
- *Be on the ball*: write your agenda on the board, on a handout, on an overhead transparency (OHT) or on the flip chart.

During your presentation

- Introduce yourself and your topic.
- Give a brief introduction and say your agenda even if it is written up.
- Speak slowly and clearly. Let people hear and follow you.
- If you get lost – don't panic! Pause, look at your prompts, and carry on.
- Remember to use linguistic markers: 'We have looked at ...', 'Now we are going to cover ...', 'Moving on to ...'
- Make good eye contact – look at everyone in the room.
- Do stand so that you can see everyone and everyone can see you. Don't stare fixedly at one person so that they want to get up and leave.
- Use your AVA with confidence. Make sure everyone can see your AVA. Allow people to notice what is there – then take it away.

─TIP───

Do not write an essay on your slides: key words or pictures only.

- Remember your conclusion – re-visit and re-state your main points … no matter how silly it seems. Your audience does not know the topic as well as you do – they will need to be reminded of what you have talked about and what it means.
- Thank people for listening – ask for questions.
- Chair the Q&A session fairly – keep those answers short and sweet. Bring the Q&A to a firm conclusion. Thank people again.
- After your presentation, review your performance.

After your presentation – be a SWOT

As with the essay and the report, it is useful for you to be able to review and evaluate your own presentations. However, because of the especially emotional dimension of presentations, we recommend that you undertake this in two stages:

1. Immediately after your presentation, tell yourself what a wonderful presentation it was and how brave you were for giving it. Do not dwell on anything that went wrong; this just makes it harder to do a presentation next time. So make this first review a very positive one.
2. After some time has elapsed undertake a more detailed SWOT analysis of your presentation.

   - What were your strengths? What did you do very well? What sections of the presentation were you particularly pleased with? Why? Sometimes we are so busy correcting our faults that we forget to repeat our strengths. Make notes so that you remember.
   - What were your weaknesses? What did not go so well? Why was this? Was it *form* – perhaps it was not structured or presented properly? Was it *content* – was it a poor argument unsupported by evidence? Did you forget to discuss your evidence? Did you forget to refer back to the question? Make notes.
   - Opportunities: now, go on, try to think of just how good you can become at presentations and of all the opportunities this gives you, both as a student and in future employment. Make notes.
   - Threats: if you are still feeling threatened by presentations, what are you going to do next? Will you practise more? Do you need more support with your positive thinking? Do you need to find a study partner? Do you need to seek out Learning Development or Academic Support and get some more help? Make notes.

TIPS

- **Make notes of your strengths – repeat them.**
- **Make notes of your weaknesses – repair them.**
- **Use your tutor feedback.**
- **Use video play-back to refine your performance.**

Get creative

One presentation that really impressed me was one on Fibonacci numbers in maths. The group used sunflowers and pineapples to illustrate the numbers in nature. One played the flute to illustrate the link between maths and music. There were wonderful drawings illustrating numbers and rabbits (don't ask!) … I thought it was excellent.

The presentation can be more flexible than the essay. Whilst it is not usually a good idea to write a poem when you have been asked to write an essay, it can be a good idea to be creative with a presentation. If your tutor is the sort of person who will appreciate a little creativity, then play with how you will communicate with and involve your audience. We have seen tutors really impressed when students have performed a mini-play instead of giving a straight presentation. So when thinking about your presentation – do all the good planning and preparation discussed above – but also think whether a different sort of performance would actually get you a higher mark – and go for it.

Presentations: essential things to do

I feel that you need to really emphasise group presentations, as they can differ greatly and rely heavily on the success or failure of the group. My group presentations worked because we got on – we worked together well – and we rehearsed together.

- *The three-minute presentation*: before delivering an assessed presentation for your coursework, practise by preparing and delivering a three-minute presentation to a friend, study partner or study group. Choose a simple topic like a hobby or a holiday – but something that really interests and engages you. Use your energy and enthusiasm for the topic. With this presentation get the form right: introduction, agenda; body = logical structure + AVA; conclusion; Q&A. This will build your confidence for your assignment.
- *Rehearse, rehearse, rehearse*: for an assessed presentation, practise with a critical friend. Use their feedback.

TIP

Use the presentation checklist to evaluate yourself and ask your friend to complete one for you, too.

- *Team work*: if asked to prepare and deliver a group presentation – plan together, get together, make the AVA together, rehearse together:

  - Have a *team leader* and a *note taker* – help people play to their strengths. Encourage everybody – hate no one!
  - Do *look like a group* – have badges, dress in similar colours.
  - Do *act* as though you were a good group that worked really well together – even if you all now dislike each other!
  - Do *listen to each other* when presenting – do not chat whilst someone is speaking – look fascinated.
  - Do *learn each other's sections* – be ready to carry on if someone disappears.

- *Role-play*: build some element of dramatic performance into your presentation, especially with a group. When students act out a scenario or role-play a point to illustrate it, tutors are usually really impressed and give higher marks.
- *Poster presentations*: even if not asked to prepare a poster for your presentation, make one anyway. Research indicates that audiences find it easier to follow, understand and enjoy a presentation that has been backed up by a well-designed and beautifully illustrated poster.

Summary

We have looked in some detail at the academic presentation, emphasising the opportunity for developing your communications skills, your self-confidence and your employability. As with all assignments, presentations are heuristic, they bring about active learning – and the presence of an audience is an excellent incentive to ensure that you communicate well what you have learned. Try to enjoy your presentations – and use the four Ps of the presentation: plan, prepare, practise and present – and the 'fifth P' – positive thinking.

Activity

Use the presentation checklist

Photocopy this checklist and use it to review your own presentations.

- ☐ My introduction: tells the audience what I am talking about and why.
- ☐ It has a 'hook' telling the audience why they should listen – it is …
- ☐ I have a clear agenda telling people the 'order' of my talk.
- ☐ I will write my agenda – and speak it.
- ☐ I have a logical structure – it does answer the question set.
- ☐ I have thought about my audience – in terms of language, tone, style and interesting AVA.
- ☐ I prepared a script – made my cue cards – then destroyed my script.

☐ I have illustrated my main points in my AVA.

☐ I have made a poster to support my presentation – and will display that as I speak.

☐ I have made a PowerPoint or Prezi presentation and embedded all my resources on that.

☐ I will not pass anything around because that disrupts a presentation.

☐ My slides and handouts are simple and clear – I have used mainly pictures – and few words.

☐ Each part of my presentation follows the paragraph questions.

☐ I discuss my evidence.

☐ When I want people to make notes, I will pause and let them do so.

☐ I have concluded each section by making a point that relates back to the overall question.

☐ I have remembered my signposts and my discourse markers.

☐ I have a conclusion that revisits my main arguments and re-states my main points.

☐ I am prepared for the question and answer session.

☐ I have checked my mannerisms or gestures (I won't fiddle with a pen or scratch my nose).

☐ I have practised my positive thinking.

Access the companion website to this book and find helpful resources for this chapter topic:
https://study.sagepub.com/burnsandsinfield4e

Structuring the literature review

Ridley, D.

Chapter summary

This chapter considers:

- the cyclical nature of all the activities involved in the creation of a literature review;
- the close relationship between the processes of reading and writing;
- ways of structuring the review;
- the complementary relationship between the introduction and the literature review;
- some examples from theses and dissertations which illustrate how different researchers organise their use of the literature.

The processes involved in the creation of a literature review

Searching for the literature, reading the source material and writing the review are all interconnected and cyclical processes. There is no clear cut-off point when one activity ends and another begins. Indeed, although there may be an intensive focus on the literature review in the earlier weeks and months of a research project, the processes connected with the review continue to be interwoven throughout the research project. In particular, Wellington et al. (2005) emphasise the significance of continually revisiting the research questions or research focus to help you determine and adapt more precisely what and how much you read in relation to your research topic. Figure 6.1 illustrates the continuous, cyclical and interconnected processes which all contribute to the literature review. The literature searching, reading and writing feed into each other constantly; and all the other activities, such as formulating research questions and justifying the research problem, influence and are influenced by the literature searching and reading, providing inspiration for the writing. Your writing in turn helps you discover and clarify your ideas and can result in the refinement of the focus of your research and the content of your review.

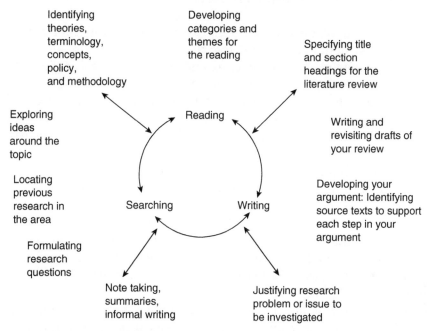

FIGURE 6.1   The literature review process

Beginning to write

It is a good idea to begin writing about the literature as early as possible and it definitely is not necessary to wait until you have a finalised plan or outline. Indeed, starting to write about the literature before the overall organisational structure of your review is clear in your mind is a means of helping you to understand the literature, and discover and clarify how you want to use it (see the sections on note taking and summarising in Chapter 4). In this vein, Murray (2011: 110) suggests various techniques to guide informal writing about the literature before moving on to more formal structured writing. She recommends regular writing to prompt questions, such as: 'What do I know about my research topic?'; 'What I am looking for in the literature is … '; 'What are the schools of thought in the literature?'; 'The "great debates" in my area are … '.

This type of regular writing is a means of establishing what you already know, identifying what further reading you need to do, clarifying how your research links with that of others, and developing your own understanding and interpretation of the literature. Some of your informal writing may form the basis of drafts for your actual literature review which will appear in your dissertation or thesis.

The structure of the literature review

Gradually, as your reading, note taking, summarising and informal writing progresses, you should try to pull together the various threads and move towards an arrangement with headings and subheadings to provide a framework for your review. The categories that you develop to organise your reading material can often provide the basis for the outline of your written review. You will have your own preference for the stage at which you devise an outline for your literature review; some researchers like to do this very early on in the process whereas others prefer to spend longer exploring the literature in a more free-ranging way. But at whatever point you decide on an outline, it will almost certainly change and evolve through a series of drafts.

Because every piece of research is different, it is difficult to suggest a common organisational structure but some suggestions are given below to help you think about the possibilities. The important point to remember is that in your review you should present a logical argument that leads smoothly into your own research, justifying both the need for work and the methodology that is going to be used.

Even if the review is not presented in a single chapter and you integrate your citations fairly evenly throughout the thesis, it is still helpful to make it clear to your reader how and where you address the various issues which have come from your reading. If integrating the literature in this continuous way, an overview of your approach in the introduction of the dissertation or thesis as well as appropriate headings and subheadings in the different chapters throughout the text is recommended.

For the more conventional and still more common practice of writing your literature review in one or more distinct chapters, it is strongly recommended that you include the following:

- an introduction which explains how your review is organised;
- headings and subheadings that provide a map to show the various strands of your argument;
- a summary where the key arguments are reiterated in a concise way.

If the review is long, as is likely for a PhD thesis, summaries interspersed throughout the chapter are helpful; these explain what you have argued so far and how this connects with what follows. An example of a 'transition statement' between sections is given in Example 6.1. The researcher refers to what she has discussed and makes a link with the relevant literature that she is going to address next. The italics indicate the signalling language which informs the reader about how the text is organised.

Example 6.1 The transition between sections

eg → *Having defined* comfortable intelligibility as a target in pronunciation for learners, *the next question to be addressed is* how we can help learners to achieve this. The teaching profession believes that instruction does help; however an intuitive belief is not reason enough to plan a course of instruction. *The next section will look briefly at* research on the effects of second language instruction in general *and then turn to* the area of pronunciation instruction in particular.

Source: Moore, 2001: 5

Although it is impossible to prescribe a uniform structure for a literature review, there are some organisational principles which are followed by many research writers. You may draw on a combination of the different approaches mentioned below depending on which is most suitable for each particular part of your review.

Weissberg and Buker (1990: 45–6) propose three ways for ordering citations:

1 Distant to close
   Most distantly related to your work→Most closely related to your work
2 Chronological
   Earliest related work→Most recent related work
3 Comparison and contrast of different approaches or particular features or characteristics of relevant theories and research
   One approach→An alternative approach→Another approach

In relation to the first of these approaches, Rudestam and Newton (2007) talk about long shots, medium shots and close-ups to describe the different degrees of depth that you may go into when referring to source texts according to their closeness and relevance to your research. Long shots describe the references that provide the background context to the research. These references tend to be quite general, acknowledging that research has been done on the topic without going into detail. Medium shots are the references which have more bearing on the current research and although not critiqued in detail, enough information is given to show how they impact on the proposed research. The close-ups are the references that are particularly pertinent for the proposed research and include a critical examination of the work cited. For example, it might be that a limitation in a study cited provides the basis for your research question in which case you would have to do a detailed critique of the study to show how your work connects to it.

I often advise research students who are uncertain about the best way to structure their literature review to think of it as having two distinct but related parts: one which presents the current state of knowledge in the field where your research is situated (including differing perspectives of pertinent theories and concepts) and the other which reviews and critiques relevant empirical research studies and shows how these provide a niche and lead into your own work. For example, if conducting research into how children learn to read, in the first part of the review, one would review and critique the competing theories on children's literacy acquisition and learning and in the second part, empirical research studies which have investigated the topic would be discussed, focusing on the different methodologies and findings. You would then be able to show how your own research relates to and extends this work.

It may be helpful to visualise the structure of your review as a picture or diagram. Wellington et al. (2005: 82) use some diagrams to illustrate the possible ways of organising your use of the related literature (see Figure 6.2).

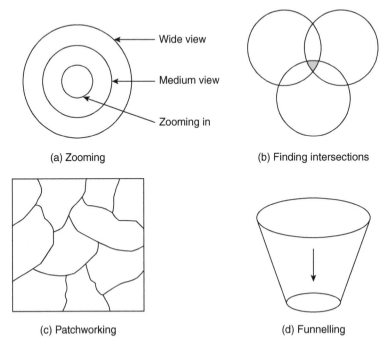

FIGURE 6.2   Organisational patterns for the literature review

Source: Wellington et al., 2005: 82

Based on these ideas, you may find it useful to devise your own picture or pictures to represent how you structure your review. You might draw a patchwork for the whole review, labelling each patch according to the different strands of your review, and devise other diagrams for each section. For example, for one theme in your review, you might choose to adopt a general to specific pattern moving from long shots to close-ups, in which case the funnelling or zooming diagrams would be suitable.

Example 6.2 Sample structure of a literature review from International Business and Management

The following example is from an MSc dissertation in the field of International Business and Management and provides an illustration of Weissberg and Buker's (1990) third approach to organising a review. The research consists of a case study which investigates the process of internationalisation and expansion for a company when entering an overseas market. The literature review explored the theory behind this process, breaking it down into four phases: pre-entry (2.2.–2.4), entry (2.5), growth and repositioning (2.6). Thus, from the contents page of the dissertation, we can see the following structure.

2.0 Literature Review

2.1 Literature Synopsis

2.2 Motives behind Internationalization

2.3 Choosing the Right Market

2.4 Deciding on When to Enter the Potential Market(s)

2.5 Entry Modes

    2.5.1 Establishing Wholly Owned Subsidiaries (WOS)

    2.5.2 Joint Venture (JV) as an Entry Mode

    2.5.3 Franchising as an Entry Mode

    2.5.4 High Control vs. Low Control

2.6 Expansion within the Market

    2.6.1 Growth Strategies – Corporate Level Strategy

2.7 Research Contribution

Source: Ovcina, 2010:7

In this chapter, the researcher explores chronologically the phases of a company's entry into a new international market from pre-entry to growth and repositioning. Within each phase he compares, contrasts and critiques different authors' theories and models. This review serves as the theoretical underpinning and framework for the case study analysis of a US retail company's entry into Latin American markets.

In the literature review example above, Dino provided a theoretical overview of a process which was then used to provide a basis for exploring a case study. As explained above, it is often relevant to also include a section or sections in your review which report on related empirical studies in your field. Findings are compared and contrasted, limitations in previous studies may be highlighted and a niche for your own work is identified (See Chapter 2, Example 2.13; Example 6.6 below, section 2.2.1; Example 6.7 below, section 1.3; Chapter 8, Example 8.2a). The tabular presentation of related empirical studies shown in Chapter 4 can provide a stepping stone for this part of the review. Thus, it is helpful to think about how the different purposes of the review will be realised in different sections and how the information and arguments in each may be presented in different ways.

Developing the structure of your review

Having considered the structure or organisational pattern of your literature review, it is important to consider the process which will help you achieve this. Swales and Feak (2000: 118–24) provide a practical reading and writing task which demonstrates, first, the importance of 'creating an architecture' for the literature review and, second, a means for creating this architecture. The underpinning principle to this process is that you put together an argument and draw on your source texts to provide support for your assertions. By developing your own argument, you show that you are using the literature for your own purposes rather than being controlled by the authors whose work you have read and are citing in your own writing.

The process involves devising an outline of your argument steps which then form the basis of the architecture of your review. For each step of your argument, group together the sources that contribute to or provide support for your assertions. If you number each of your references in EndNote or the filing system that you are using for your references, you can insert the relevant numbers beside each argument step at the planning stage. You may also wish to write down the page numbers from particular references that contain the information which is relevant for supporting your argument. Table 6.1 provides a scaffold for this planning.

TABLE 6.1 The literature review architecture

Argument steps	Relevant references and page numbers

From the argument steps that you devise, you can then develop the headings and subheadings that become the framework for your review. Using tables such as the one offered in 6.1, it is recommended that you create an overall architecture for the whole review and then more detailed ones for each section. Some researchers prefer to develop a plan like this before they start writing, whereas others write first and gradually extricate a framework from their writing.

The note card system described in Chapter 4 is a useful technique for grouping together ideas from different authors which support the particular points that you wish to make. You can physically move around the significant pieces of information from your source texts that you have recorded on your note cards according to where they best fit into your argument steps. The arrangements you make with your cards can then be recorded in an 'architecture table' such as the one shown in Table 6.1 (for a worked example, see Table 6.2).

 Example 6.3 Planning your literature review

This example shows how a researcher planned and developed his argument for one section of the literature review, and is from a psychology PhD thesis first cited in in Chapter 1, Example 1.6. In the extract from the contents page of this thesis shown in Chapter 1, we saw how the literature review was introduced in the first chapter and was then revisited in different places throughout the thesis, appearing before relevant research studies. The plan reproduced in Table 6.2 was created for a section of the literature review on goal-achievement which appeared at the beginning of Webb's chapter 3, before two studies investigating the influence of personal goals on goal-attainment. The literature review discusses the wide variety of goal theories which influenced the focus of the empirical studies.

(Continued)

(Continued)

TABLE 6.2   An example of the architecture of a literature review

Section title: Models of goal-achievement

Argument steps	Relevant references
Limited previous research on comparison of goal theories	Bagozzi and Kimmel, 1995; Fredricks and Dossett, 1983; Valois et al., 1988; Cacioppo and Berntson, 1995; Weinstein, 1993
Introduce 'Rubicon model': action phases (as a means of categorising goal theories): predecisional; preactional; actional	Heckhausen, 1987; Heckhausen and Gollwitzer, 1986, 1987
Predecisional action phase: theory of planned behaviour; models of goal setting	Ajzen, 1985, 1991; Sheeran, 2002; Bandura, 1977 Locke and Latham, 1990; Carver and Scheier, 1981; Hyland, 1988; Baumeister, Heatherton and Tice, 1994; Emmons and King, 1988; Hook and Higgins, 1988
Preactional phase: theory of self-regulation; implementation intentions	Bagozzi, 1992; Abelson, 1988; Latham and Locke, 1991 Gollwitzer, 1990
Actional phase: self-regulatory strength; emotion; social influences; performance feedback.	Baumeister et al., 1994; Luminet et al., 2000; Muraven and Baumeister, 2000; Baumeister et al., 1998; Webb and Sheeran, 2003 Martin and Tesser, 1988, 1996; Keltner and Gross, 1999; Lazarus, 1991; Levenson, 1994; Kuhl, 1996, 2000 Povey et al., 2000; Rutter et al., 1993; Deci and Ryan, 1985; Tauer and Harackiewicz, 1999

Source: Adapted from Webb, 2003: 50–1

In terms of a structural pattern for this section of the review, it involved a comparison of different approaches. The diagram of a patchwork from Figure 6.2 depicts it well, with each patch representing a different goal theory.

    Task 6.1 Structuring your own literature review

Try the activities below in relation to your whole literature review or one or two sections of it.

1   Draw a picture which represents the structure of your own literature review.
2   Fill in a table outlining the steps of the argument that you intend to follow in your review. Give the supporting references and specific page numbers for each argument step. You will add to these references gradually and over time as your reading progresses.

The relationship between the introduction and the literature review

Another important aspect of the integration of the literature into your dissertation or thesis to consider is the relationship between the references cited in the introduction and those cited in the literature review. In some fields, such as medicine, the introduction is a long chapter which includes the literature review. However, in many other disciplines, you are likely to have a separate introduction followed by the literature review. If uncertain about the best approach to adopt, you can clarify the conventions and expectations in your field by consultation with your supervisor and by looking at previous dissertations or theses in your field.

Some of the multiple purposes of the literature review which were referred to in Chapter 2 of this book may be partially or fully realised in the introduction. These purposes are repeated here as a reminder of the variety of reasons for which we include references to the work of others in research writing.

- to provide a historical background for your research;
- to give an overview of the current context in which your research is situated by referring to contemporary debates, issues and questions in the field;
- to discuss relevant theories and concepts which underpin your research;
- to introduce relevant terminology and provide definitions to clarify how terms are being used in the context of your own work;
- to describe related research in the field and show how your work extends or challenges this, or addresses a gap in previous work in the field;
- to provide supporting evidence for a practical problem or issue which your research is addressing thereby underlining its significance.

If adopting a conventional structure for your thesis or dissertation, where in the final version of the paper you have an introduction that is followed by one or more chapters which constitute the literature review, there will be references to sources of information and related research in both these parts. As suggested above, it can sometimes be difficult to decide which references to include in the introduction and which ones to refer to in the literature review. Researchers make individual decisions about how to organise the information in these two parts of the dissertation or thesis. Nevertheless, there are some general principles regarding which purposes are likely to be fulfilled in the different chapters. The discussion below offers suggestions which will help you decide how to differentiate between the content you decide to include in these initial chapters.

The introduction is usually relatively brief compared with the literature review. An approximate guideline to bear in mind is that the introduction should be about 10 per cent of the whole dissertation or thesis and the literature review 20 per cent (Barnes, 1995 cited in Blaxter et al., 2010).

In the introduction, it is common practice to provide:

- a brief historical and/or contemporary context for the research;
- a concise reference to research already carried out in the field;
- an outline of the research problem that needs to be explored as a result of a gap left by previous research or an issue that needs resolving;
- a justification for the proposed research;
- an outline of the contents of the different chapters in the dissertation or thesis.

Some of these purposes will be revisited more comprehensively in the literature review. For example, you may expand on the historical and contemporary context in which your work is situated. You are also likely to identify and discuss the key theories, concepts and terminology which are relevant to your research topic and explore these in sufficient depth for the type and level of research that you are undertaking. Additionally, you will probably *explore* in more detail related empirical research studies in the field and once again highlight how your work extends that of others or fills a gap. Examples 6.4–6.7 included below show how different researchers have developed an organisational structure for their literature review. They illustrate how the categories for the reading led into argument steps and section headings in the literature reviews. The extracts also show how each of the researchers gives an overview of the structure of the literature review in the introduction of the chapter to signal to the reader how the argument will be presented.

Example 6.4 Reading, planning and signposting the structure of the review

For her masters dissertation in town and regional planning, Emma conducted research into the range of influences on planning decisions in urban settings. She was interested in the role universal values have in planning decisions, in particular those decisions which are concerned with conservation and regeneration issues. Her research focus was on how the various stakeholders in the process are conditioned by different values. She analysed this in the context of two case studies.

eg → To make the reading manageable, she broke it down under the following headings.

1 The role of 'values' in planning research
2 Stakeholders in planning decisions
3 Universal values in relation to planning

4 Particularity of place in planning decisions
5 Participatory planning
6 Conservation in urban settings
7 Regeneration in urban settings

This resulted in the following framework or 'architecture' for her literature review which appears as Chapter 2 after the introduction of her dissertation. The headings which appear on the contents page are shown below.

2.0 Literature Review: introduction
2.1 The importance of value
2.3 The public interest and stakeholder relations
2.4 The universal and the particular
2.5 The value of conservation and regeneration in historic urban quarters
2.6 Implications for conservation/regeneration initiatives: the case studies

Source: Adapted from Coveney, 2003: i

The connections can be seen again with the introductory paragraph of her review which outlines how she is going to discuss the literature which underpins her research.

eg → As stated in the introduction, this study is about values in planning and uses the relationship between conservation and regeneration in historic urban quarters as an illustration. This chapter introduces the 'values approach' to planning, looking firstly at why questions of value are so important. It then considers three notions fundamental to the approach in more depth: those of the public interest and stakeholder relations, the relationship between the universal and the particular, and finally the implications for participatory planning. The final part of this chapter considers the relationship between the practices of conservation and regeneration and the values surrounding them and explains the choice of the case studies.

Source: Adapted from Coveney, 2003: 5

Example 6.5 Signposting and structuring the review

In her PhD thesis on Education for sustainable development, Ling outlines the organisational structure of her literature review in two different places: in the Introduction, Section 1.4,

(Continued)

(Continued)

'Outline of the thesis', and in Section 2.1, which is the introduction of her literature review (see Table of contents of full thesis in Chapter 1, Example 1.4). I include the paragraph from the beginning of her literature review (Section 2.1) below.

eg → The main body of this review consists of five sections. To set the scene for and to provide contextualising information about the research topic, I critically review the notion of SD (section 2.2), and the history of sustainability education (section 2.3). I move on to discuss four key curriculum perspectives – technical, socially-critical, liberal-progressive and postmodern perspectives – and their relevance to sustainability education (section 2.4). Amongst the four perspectives, I focus on the last three as the theoretical framework of the research. Finally, I introduce English and Chinese HE and their respective responses to sustainability education, their differences and similarities (section 2.5) as well as issues involved in learning across national and cultural boundaries (section 2.6).

Source: Feng, 2010: 14–15

To focus more specifically on one part of the literature review chapter, we shall now turn to Section 2.2. In preparation for this part, where the concept of sustainable development is explored and critiqued, Ling organised her reading into the following areas. These themes later led to her choice of the subheadings for the Section.

Sustainable development: origins and ongoing issues (2.2)

Interpretations of 'sustainable' (2.2.1)

Interpretations of 'development' (2.2.1)

Sustainable development and capitalism (2.2.2)

Intragenerational equity: developing countries and climate change (2.2.3)

Anthropocentrism and ecocentrism (2.2.4)

Overall complexity and uncertainty of the concept of sustainable development (2.2.5)

Positive and encouraging examples which support the potential of sustainable development (2.2.6 and 2.2.7)

The subheadings below show how Ling organised her critique in the thesis. Sections 2.2.1—2.2.5 raise a number of challenges to the concept of sustainable development and then in Sections 2.2.6 and 2.2.7 she argues how specific international conferences, documents and events offer hope for overcoming some of these and thus support sustainable development.

2.2 The notion of sustainable development (SD)

    2.2.1 Oxymoron?

    2.2.2 Business as usual

2.2.3 Intragenerational equity

2.2.4 Anthropocentrism versus ecocentrism

2.2.5 Complexity and uncertainty

2.2.6 A way forward

2.2.7 Changes occurring

Source: Feng, 2010: i

Examples 6.6 and 6.7 below illustrate the choices different researchers have made with regard to way they have used the related literature in the introduction and the literature review. No hard and fast rules exist with regard to what is covered in each part of the dissertation or thesis, but from these two examples we can see how two more researchers have organised their content to fulfil all the necessary purposes of using the literature for their particular piece of research.

Example 6.6 The introduction and the literature review

This example is taken from doctoral research which investigated information management among health visitors in the UK. Extracts in Example 6.6 are adapted from Bacigalupo (2000).

The title

The Information Management of Health Visitors: with particular reference to their public health and community development activities

The research questions

How can the way that health visitors deal with information in public health and community development settings be understood in relation to the health service context and current information management concepts and processes?

What are the implications of that understanding in terms of developing recommendations and guidelines for practice?

(Continued)

(Continued)

Reading categories

The researcher developed the following categories for her reading:

Information management

History

Concepts

Processes

Previous research

User studies

Information needs

Information seeking behaviour

Information audit (methodology for assessing needs)

Information management in the NHS

Strategies

Problems

Achievements

Needs and resources

Public health

Health visiting

Community development work

Government policy and legislation in public health

This led into the following structure for the first three chapters of the PhD thesis.

The contents page

Chapter 1 Introduction (pp. 3–9)

1.1 The motive for the research

1.2 The research questions

1.3 The current context

    1.3.1 Changes in the UK National Health Service

    1.3.2 Changes in UK government policy: a focus on the community

    1.3.3 NHS policy: maximizing the potential of IT

Source: Bacigalupo, 2000: i

In terms of the purposes served by the references to the literature, the different chapters cover the following. The introduction outlines the current context in relation to the National Health Service, information management, and government policy; states the research questions and research focus; justifies the research; and provides a definition of information management. At the end of this chapter, an outline of the content of each of the chapters of the thesis is given.

Chapter 2 outlines the historical context of information management and information management in the NHS; introduces concepts and terminology relevant for the field; and shows how the current research addresses a gap in existing research. Chapter 3 gives more detail of the historical and current context within the field of public health.

(Continued)

(Continued)

The conclusion to Chapter 2 is included below. The phrases used give an example of how the researcher signals what she is doing in relation to the literature in the different chapters of her thesis.

Summary of chapter 2

 This chapter has discussed information management concepts in general and recent developments with regard to information management in the NHS. The need for information management research into how health visitors deal with information has been highlighted. The next chapter reviews the literature regarding the public health and community development activities of health visitors in order to show that this area is particularly relevant for research.

Source: Bacigalupo, 2000: 39

Example 6.7 The introduction and the literature review

The study here was for a masters dissertation and looked at the effect of instruction on two aspects of EFL (English as a foreign language) learners' pronunciation: the production of specific features of pronunciation and general intelligibility. Extracts in example 6.5 are adapted from Moore (2001), referred to in earlier chapters.

The title

The Effects of Formal Instruction on EFL Pronunciation Acquisition: A Case Study from Germany

The hypotheses

H0 = a course of pronunciation instruction does not improve a learner's production of specific features of pronunciation.

H1 = a course of pronunciation instruction improves a learner's production of specific features of pronunciation.

H0 = a course of pronunciation instruction does not improve a learner's general intelligibility.

H1 = a course of pronunciation instruction improves a learner's general intelligibility.

Categories for reading

Features of pronunciation and 'intelligibility'

Second language learning and acquisition

Second language instruction

Pronunciation instruction

Other factors that influence effective pronunciation

The architecture of the first three chapters of the dissertation, which was developed from the reading, is shown in the following extract from the contents page.

The contents page

Introduction

Justification for the research

The context: the English Language Teaching Institution and the learners

Outline of the dissertation

Chapter 1 Literature review

1.1 Historical Background

1.2 Target Pronunciation and Intelligibility

1.3 Research into the Effects of Instruction

      1.3.1 Second Language Research

      1.3.2 Pronunciation Research

1.4 Specific Features of Pronunciation

      1.4.1 Strong and Weak Forms of words

      1.4.2 Contractions and Elision

      1.4.3 Assimilation

      1.4.4 Liaison

      1.4.5 Stress

      1.4.6 Intonation

1.5 Summary

Chapter 2 The experiment

2.1 Aims and rationale of the experiment: the hypotheses

Source: Moore, 2001: iii

(Continued)

(Continued)

In terms of the purposes served by the references to the literature, the different chapters cover the following. The introduction introduces the topic of pronunciation; provides a justification for the research; outlines the current context of the research; and gives an outline of the content of each chapter in the dissertation.

The literature review (Chapter 1) provides a historical context, describes related research which shows how current research is filling a gap and extending work that has been done before; and defines relevant terms for the field of research. The hypotheses are given at the beginning of Chapter 2.

The final paragraph of the introduction is included below to show the way in which the researcher signals how the literature is integrated into the dissertation.

eg → Having briefly outlined the rationale behind the study, the first chapter will review the pertinent literature on the effects of instruction both on second language learning in general and also specifically on pronunciation. Other factors involved in the learning process will also be considered since second language acquisition is a highly complex process. By considering the research in the field, a general framework will be provided for this study and the discussion presented in the second chapter. Finally, the first chapter will present an outline of the specific features of pronunciation under consideration in this study. The second chapter will describe the experiment that was conducted to investigate the effects of instruction on pronunciation and present the data analysis and a discussion of the results. In the final chapter, the constraints of this study will be discussed, followed by implications for further research.

Source: Moore, 2001: 2

Task 6.2 Reflecting on your own research field

Ask your supervisor to recommend a thesis or dissertation in your field. Look carefully at the contents page and identify whether a distinct chapter or chapters constitute the literature review. Read the introduction and the literature review chapter/s. Identify the purposes for which the researcher is using the related literature. Note, in particular, the way the various purposes are realised in either the introduction and/or the literature review.

Summary

To summarise, this chapter has considered:

- the cyclical, continuous, and interconnected nature of the various processes involved in the literature review;
- techniques for starting to write about the relevant literature of your field;
- the various structures that might be adopted for the literature review or for different parts of it;
- the relationship between the introduction and the literature review;
- some examples from dissertations and theses which show how different researchers have organised their use of the literature.

The continuing process

Ridley, D.

Chapter summary

In this chapter, we discuss:

- the continuous process involved in the creation of the literature review;
- the integration of the literature when discussing the findings of your research.

The literature review process

As emphasised in both Chapters 1 and 6, the literature review process is a continuous one which begins when you first start to develop an idea for your research and does not end until the final draft of the dissertation or thesis is complete. Throughout the book, we have highlighted that the ongoing nature of the literature review is an integral part of the research process, because your work is always interconnected with that of others. For this reason, it is important that you are continually exploring the related developments in your field and that you keep reading as new publications appear which may be relevant to your research. As time goes by, it is possible that you will come across different theories, methodologies and ideas which cause you to see your own research in a different light. These references will then need to be integrated into your writing in later drafts of your literature review.

You may also wish to revise your literature review in the light of your own research findings. It may be that your research generates certain results which cause you to change the focus of your literature review or even to introduce and discuss an area of reading that you had not included previously. Finally, it is important to mention again that it is through the redrafting of your literature review that you are able to fine-tune your arguments, and clarify and articulate the focus of your research and the research questions.

The following quotes are from the writers of some of the dissertations and theses from which extracts have appeared throughout this book. They describe what the literature review process means to them.

My reading gradually broadened out from a narrow base, as I looked up references in articles/books I read. Sometimes I returned to original sources for more in-depth information. The more I read, the better it all fitted together, and it linked back to undergraduate research on other topics so gradually, it became part of my 'overall world view'. In terms of writing the dissertation, the lit review took longer than anything else! As I read more, I could edit out bits no longer necessary/relevant. This took a long time, and I found it quite challenging. However, the benefits of having done all the reading paid off in my dissertation, as well as in my working life. I feel I have a serious understanding of the subject, and it has built my confidence enormously. My research was based on educational e-learning projects, so I had the 'working knowledge' of the subject before I had the literature 'underpinning'. It helped validate what I had learned in practice.

Claire Allam, MEd Education

Given the primarily practical nature of my dissertation, the original focus of the literature review did not change greatly during the writing process. At the onset, I focused on three main areas: a general background to the position of pronunciation in English Language teaching, the effects of instruction on learning and the specific features of pronunciation under consideration in the study.

The most obvious change in focus came from the fairly general reading which accompanies early research to the more specific reading which becomes necessary as ideas and focus are refined. For example, while reading about the position of pronunciation within language teaching, it quickly became apparent that I needed more information on what kind of pronunciation model was desirable for students. This in turn led to needing information on the notion of 'comfortable intelligibility' and accepted definitions of the concept.

With respect to the effects of instruction on learning, I began by reading easily available books about general theories of Second Language Acquisition (SLA). This helped me to provide evidence that instruction appears to facilitate learning. The majority of research, however, focused on general learning rather than the specific learning of pronunciation. Through some of the reading I did, I found references to articles about other studies which were of interest. In addition I used ERIC and ATHENS extensively to search for relevant articles which were ordered from the British Library (I was working in Germany at the time and had limited access to libraries).

Analeen Moore, Education and Applied Linguistics

Writing a PhD dissertation is like swimming in an ocean-size pool full with a variety of different marine life. You need to sort out them in accordance with the differences and similarities. Most of all, it is important to find a niche habitat for your own PhD or restructure the whole ecosystem of the pool, if you can. Since a student starts from scratch, it is normal to revise the original literature review in the course of doing research. In many cases, the aims and objectives are shifting over time, a development which makes the student change the focus of his or her literature review. At the end of the day, it is just a process of building a solid and coherent foundation prior to making the main arguments in the next chapters.

Key-young Son, PhD East Asian Studies

I must confess that my literature review was written in the final few months of my PhD. My PhD was done before the requirement that students write a literature review in the first year. Thus, I focused my time on writing papers (with specific literature reviews to complement the data being presented) and then wrote the overall literature review for the thesis by drawing from these.

Having said this, I agree with the argument that the literature review is often revised in the light of data collection. In fact, so much so that I have given up trying to write an introduction to a paper before I have the data. I usually start with the method and results sections, then write the introduction, then the discussion.

Tom Webb, PhD Psychology

Referring to the literature in your discussion chapter

When reaching the 'Discussion' sections or chapter/s of your dissertation or thesis where you interpret your research findings, it is important to revisit the literature to contextualise your work again within the wider field of study. At both the beginning and end of your thesis or dissertation, your reader must be able to see how your research is rooted in and contributes to the ongoing development of knowledge in your field.

At this point in your thesis or dissertation, it is helpful to remind your reader about the content of your literature review. This could entail a summary of the main points or you could refer back to the literature discussed in earlier sections and chapters, providing cross-references for your readers.

When interpreting your own research findings, citations can be integrated to compare and contrast your findings with those of previous studies. It is important to point out how your work either supports or contradicts related previous work in your field. The literature may also provide a way for you to interpret your findings. A particular theory might provide a framework for your data analysis and interpretation. Alternatively, your data analysis may enable you to propose an amendment or development of a theory in your field.

Examples 10.1 to 10.7 illustrate these purposes for including references to the work of others in the discussion chapter/s of the dissertation or thesis. The italicised parts of the texts indicate how and where the writers make connections and show relationships between their research findings and the related literature.

Findings support an existing theory

In Example 10.1, taken from the masters dissertation on the relationship between pronunciation instruction and learning of pronunciation among English as a Foreign Language students, Analeen discusses the extent to which her results support Krashen's hypotheses on language learning and acquisition. Note the first sentence of the section, which reminds the reader about the purpose of the study.

Example 10.1 Findings support an existing theory

Discussion

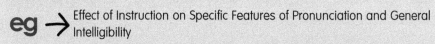

eg → Effect of Instruction on Specific Features of Pronunciation and General Intelligibility

This study was designed to investigate the effect of instruction on pronunciation performance for learners at an elementary level of English. Given the time restrictions on the study, an elementary level was chosen so that there was not too much phonological fossilisation present in the sample and greater improvement could be expected from each learner than with a more advanced level sample where phonological fossilisation may have been greater.

It is interesting to note that both groups displayed improved pronunciation skills at the end of the study. Given that the control group received no instruction, this suggests that pronunciation skills are improved by exposure to the target language in the classroom. The control group appears to have noticed features of the phonological system and this has produced improvement. *This would seem to support* Krashen's theory (1982) of exposure to TL at a level of (i + 1) producing acquisition because in the classroom a teacher monitors their use of language and new items introduced. Therefore it would be hoped that a large amount of input is provided at a level suitable for the students to acquire it. The findings of the t-tests on the post-test results indicate that there was a positive relationship between instruction and the production of specific features of pronunciation but not between instruction and overall general intelligibility. *This would seem to confirm* Krashen's hypothesis that instruction produces learning but not acquisition since the learners were able to use what they had learnt when focusing on form, but they did not transfer it to their spontaneous speech when the focus was on meaning.

It is important to consider the listener-raters in relation to the results here. Despite the fact that the correlations between raters were very high indicating reliability, it may be the case that rating sentences is easier than assessing general intelligibility. When rating a sentence the rater is looking for a particular feature and the number of possible errors is limited. Spontaneous speech, in contrast, may contain many errors in areas such as grammar, phonology, fluency and discourse. The rater may be affected by a combination of these errors when making a judgment and thus not fairly represent just the subject's phonological intelligibility. A further complication may have arisen due to the fact that all raters are used to German learners' pronunciation of English, which may have influenced their perception of pronunciation performance. The raters may have penalised the subjects for making typical German pronunciation errors which did not impede intelligibility, or they may have not penalised the subjects for errors which could cause problems with intelligibility for those not used to German learners pronunciation of English. It might have been better to include some non-specialist raters so that any possible influence could have been controlled for. *For these reasons, it is not possible from this study to provide clear evidence* supporting Krashen's hypotheses of instruction only producing learning and not acquisition.

Source: Moore, 2001: 31–2

Comparing a new model and an existing theory

In Example 10.2, taken from a discussion section of a Psychology PhD thesis, Tom describes a theory (the factor model) which he has developed from his data analysis and compares it with a theory (model of action phases) previously discussed in his literature review. As in Example 10.1, observe the way the introductory sentence in the section reminds the reader of the focus of the research studies.

Example 10.2 A comparison between a new model and existing theory

General Discussion

eg → Studies 2 and 3 provide an important analysis of both the conceptual structure of constructs from goal theories and their relative importance in predicting goal attainment. Both retrospective (Study 2) and prospective (Study 3) designs provided evidence that five factors – motivation, task focus, implementation intentions, social support, and subjective norm – distinguish when people succeed in achieving personal goals from when they fail. This discussion will consider the implications of the factor model for the distinction between motivational and volitional processes and then the predictive effects.

The factor structure supports the model of action phases (Heckhausen, 1987; Heckhausen & Gollwitzer, 1986; 1987, see Section 1.2). The first factor – motivation – embraced concepts relating to goal selection; intention, commitment, and attitude toward the goal (perceived utility). *Thus, the first factor neatly parallels* the predecisional phase of action, which consists of deliberating wishes and setting preferences (Gollwitzer, 1990). *The factor structure also supports* the distinction between the predecisional (goal setting) and preactional (planning) phases of action – variables measuring implementation intentions were distinct from motivational constructs. Notably, in Study 3 items measuring acquiescence negatively loaded on the implementation intentions factor which suggests that the opposite of forming a plan is 'letting things slide' and 'not making things happen'. The model of action phases *also acknowledges* that achieving a personal goal is not simply about initiation of the relevant behaviour, but also requires maintenance of the behaviour over time. Thus, the actional phase refers to ideas of goal striving that *parallel* the present conception of task focus. For example, goal striving requires that one 'puts energy into the task' and 'does not allow thoughts to wander.' *In sum, the identified factor structure discriminates between constructs that influence behaviour at different phases in the course of action.*

Source: Webb, 2003: 84–5

Explaining a finding using the literature

In Example 10.3, which comes from the same section of the psychology thesis as the previous example, Tom uses the literature to support his explanations as to why a particular factor (self-efficacy) was not a distinguishing one between successful or failed attempts to achieve a goal. Note how Tom, in the first two sentences, makes a connection between the material that has been previously discussed and the discussion that is going to follow. This is an example of a smooth and effective transition in the text.

**Example 10.3 Using the literature
to help explain a finding**

eg → The discussion thus far has focused on the five factors that discriminated successful from failed attempts to achieve personal goals. However, findings pertaining to factors that failed to distinguish the groups also merit discussion. It is notable that self-efficacy did not discriminate between participants who failed and participants who succeeded. *One explanation for this finding* is that self-efficacy may influence performance through the selection of personal goals, rather than influencing goal striving itself (Locke & Latham, 1990). For example, people are unlikely to try to achieve behavioural targets over which they feel they have little control (Bandura & Wood, 1989; Earley & Lituchy, 1991; Gibbons & Weingart, 2001). *Alternatively,* self-efficacy could have influenced goal achievement indirectly through task focus. For example, there is evidence to suggest that high self-efficacy leads to greater focus on the task whereas low self-efficacy directs attention to self-evaluation and increases self-doubt (Gibbons & Weingart, 2001). *In sum, self-efficacy may not have affected performance directly because* its effects were mediated by the selection of personal goals and/or task focus.

Source: Webb, 2003: 87–8

Contribution of current research to existing theory

In Example 10.4, from East Asian Studies, Key-young discusses the contribution of his research to the theoretical debates in the field of international relations. After reiterating the limitations of realism and liberalism, he explains how his research has extended the role of constructivism in the field by using it to analyse the specific context on the Korean Peninsula between 1998 and 2003.

Example 10.4 The current research contributes to existing theory

Contributions to theory

International Relations (IR) is rich in terms of the amount of literature on diverse features of international life. The works of theorists in this field, however, deal with similar subjects, war and peace, or conflicts and cooperation, but come up with diametrically opposed positions and interpretations. In spite of the abundance in terms of quantity, IR theories suffer from poverty mainly because of their incommensurability (Wight 1996). Realism witnessed its heyday for half a century between 1939 and 1989, a period marked by World War II, the Cold War and localized conflicts. Nevertheless, realism has somewhat lost its predictive and descriptive power with the end of the Cold War and the Soviet Union's voluntary retreat from its Cold War status (Kegley 1995: 7). As part of efforts to overcome the discipline's polarization and incommensurability, the neo-realists and neo-liberals formed the so-called 'neo-neo partnership', but fell short of formulating a grand theory, which can be called a paradigm.

Against this backdrop of inter-paradigm debates, constructivism emerged, seemingly invalidating decades of debates between the established theoretical schools. Constructivists claimed that another round of debate had begun between positivism and post-positivism, dismissing all past dialogues between realists, liberals and Marxists as positivist ones (Wight 1996). Constructivism imbued IR students with new ideas and tools that showed the potential for explaining the complex world of international politics. The new tools of constructivists, comprising such ideational factors as identities and norms, were potent weapons to explain the underlying forces of continuities and transformations. Nevertheless, constructivism 'remains more of a philosophically and theoretically informed perspective on and approach to the empirical study of international relations' than a full-fledged theory (Ruggie 1998: 856).

Therefore, this dissertation aimed to sharpen the constructivist approach to international relations and *formulate a testable hypothesis* in the field of strategies of engagement. *In particular, this dissertation discovered* the necessary conditions and social settings for the shift of a state's identity vis-à-vis an enemy state *and explained* what kinds of tools an activist government could mobilize in engaging an enemy state to implement strategies of comprehensive engagement. *Having analyzed a set of case studies, this research demonstrated that* a constructivist approach is able to play a significant role in supplementing 'problem-solving theories' in times of momentous change. *By formulating* the identity norm life cycle, which is an historically grounded conceptual framework, *this dissertation demonstrated that* a given government, in this case South Korea, which finds itself somewhere on the friendship–enmity continuum, is able to act as a norm entrepreneur in order to successfully resolve the conflicts of interests with an enemy state, a dimension that was not addressed by the theories of realism and liberalism.

Source: Son, 2004: 359–60

Interpreting the data using the literature

In the first paragraph of Example 10.5, Ei leen Lee refers back to a theory discussed in the literature review and explains how it has influenced her data analysis of the shift in language use of the Creole being studied. In the latter paragraph included in the extract, she introduces the concept of 'negotiation' to assist in the interpretation of her data.

Example 10.5 Using the theory to interpret the data

From the Findings and Conclusions (Chapter 8)

In Chapter 2, three main approaches to the study of language shift (LS) in minority communities were discussed, namely investigating LS through domains, through

(Continued)

(Continued)

behaviour and through bilingualism. The theoretical constructs underlying the approaches are drawn from sociology, social psychology, and bilingualism respectively. *The review of these approaches demonstrates that* the LS of [the Creole] needs to be studied, analysed and understood through an eclectic approach drawing from an interdisciplinary perspective as the language behaviour of the speakers which is directing the LS of [the Creole] is brought about not by one but [by] an interdependence of these factors.

…

Most studies of negotiation apply to the field of corporate conflict resolution and the term describes a problem-solving encounter between parties who each have their own agenda and goals. According to Firth (1995: 10), in many cases, 'negotiation is used metaphorically to stress that the essential nature of a phenomenon is not stasis or fixity but its contingent mutability, its situated emergence, and its intersubjective interpretation … '. As human interactions are not predetermined or fixed entities, the concept of negotiation has been applied to the interactional and pragmatic use of language such as the studies on context (e.g. Kendon, 1999), turn-taking (e.g. Fairclough, 1992) and topics (e.g. Gumperz, 1982), to name a few. In most of these studies the concept of negotiation applies to how the parties concerned make an ongoing assessment of the situation to make the appropriate 'move'. In the case of LS and revitalisation of [the Creole], *I would like to extend the concept of negotiation to refer to* [the Creole] speakers' ongoing assessment of what is most important to their situation and how these priorities are manifested in their language choice, language use, attitude and response to the shift and revitalisation of [the Creole].

Source: Lee, 2003: 325–7

Application of theory to the findings

In her literature review, Ling discussed three curriculum perspectives (socially critical, liberal progressive and postmodern), which she used to provide the theoretical framework for her research. She conducted three HE case studies in China and the UK, focusing on the curricula for education for sustainable development. In the first part of her discussion chapter, she compares how the three case study HE institutions engaged with each of the curriculum perspectives, thereby linking back to the literature cited earlier in the thesis. In the extract below, she begins to discuss socially-critical education for sustainable development and how it is realised in the three case study curricula. In this extract, she provides explicit cross-references back to the literature review chapter.

Example 10.6 Connecting the theory with the findings

 Socially-critical sustainability education and the three curricula

With regards to how the three curricula applied aspects of socially-critical sustainability education (Saha 2002; Thomas 2005; Plant 2001), the research findings show that only Course A was generally committed to and applied socially-critical sustainability education; two out of three Course B staff interviewees explicitly expressed their disagreement with socially-critical sustainability education, but one aspect of socially-critical sustainability education – critical thinking – was adopted by Course B in a pragmatic fashion; Course C adopted one aspect of socially-critical sustainability education – 'action-orientation' without explicitly linking this with socially-critical sustainability education.

TABLE 7 Key characteristics of the three curricula that reflected socially-critical sustainability education

	Course A	Course B	Course C
Socially-critical sustainability education: key characteristics	explicitness of values and positions, transformative learning and action-orientation	critical thinking	action-orientation

Firstly, both Courses A and C contained a key curriculum characteristic I called 'action-orientation'; however, 'action' meant different things in the two curricula: through transformative learning, Course A encouraged students to identify political and social actions that could contribute to social change towards SD with a focus on social justice and democratisation whereas Course C encouraged students to plan and implement feasible and practical actions mainly in the context of Chinese schools. Both types of 'action-orientation' were commented on favourably by students on both courses.

Before asking the question what the courses can learn from each other in the socially-critical sustainability education framework, it is important to analyse the social and political backgrounds of 'action-orientation' in England and China. The politically radical curriculum of Course A was enabled by the relative institutional autonomy and academic freedom of English HEIs (Department for Education and

(Continued)

(Continued)

Skills, 2003) (see Section 2.5.1) … On the other hand, Course C was operating in the more restrictive intellectual environment of Chinese HE, as I have discussed in section 2.5.2.

Source: Feng, 2010:179–80

Highlighting an unexpected result

In Example 10.7, extracted from the discussion of results in an engineering thesis, the writer presents an unexpected result in relation to previous work in the field. He then draws an overall conclusion beginning with the phrase, 'It appears'.

Example 10.7 A surprising finding in relation to previous research

eg → Several important ideas resulting from the microcosm work have now been considered at the field scale. Transferring the microcosm model to field scale has resulted in a new fully-kinetic, two-step syntrophic biodegradation model for plumes. This model has generally reproduced observed detailed MLS (multi-level sampler) profiles at a field site, and the pattern of concomitant TEAPs (Terminal electron accepting processes) in the plume core. In examining the similarities and differences between the laboratory and field case, it has been important to have a consistent conceptual framework, yet with flexibility to include differing parameter values as required by the different cases, and the fully kinetic model has met these needs. It was found that while the microcosm conceptual reaction model was transferable to the field scale, the value of the rate parameters were not, since the reactions are much slower in the field.

In both field and laboratory cases, the microbial activities of both fermenters and TEAPs change with time, and space, due to processes such as growth, bioavailability, acclimatisation, and toxic effects. An important result of considering acclimatisation, and consequent increase of rates with exposure time, is that the core reactions turned over more contaminant mass than the fringe reactions, *which was not expected from former studies of the plume* (Mayer et al. 2001; Thornton et al. 2001). It appears, in general, that reactive transport models used for NA (natural attenuation) assessment should consider such temporal and spatial changes.

Source: Watson, 2004: 69

Task 10.1 Reflecting on making the connections in your own research

When interpreting the findings from your own research, for example in the discussion chapter of your dissertation or thesis, consider how you make connections with the related literature from your field. Have you done any or all of the following?

1   Have you referred back to a literature review chapter presented earlier in the dissertation or thesis by, for example:
    • summarising the main points from your literature review?
    • reminding your reader of the content of your literature review with a cross-reference (e.g. 'In Chapter two, there was an overview of local authority policies on recycling')?

2   Have you compared your findings with those of similar research projects in your field?

3   Have you drawn on a particular theory or theories in your field through which to interpret your findings?

4   Have you shown how your findings have shed new light on professional practice or theory in your field?

Summary

To summarise, this chapter has considered:

• the ongoing process of a literature review;
• the significance of revisiting the literature when discussing the research findings.

19

Contextual qualitative methods

Haslam, S. A. and McGarty, C.

RESEARCH BITE 13.1
(Re)populating psychological research

One of the key themes in the work of the British psychologist Mick Billig has been a concern with the 'depopulated' nature of psychology texts. In particular, he questions writing practices that treat participants as interchangeable voiceless entities. These, he argues, strip participants of agency and encourage researchers to imagine that the people who take part in their studies are merely passive consumers of research materials, rather than engaged contributors trying to make sense of their experience and to communicate nuanced points through their various responses. He also argues that this treatment – and the associated use of jargon – can reduce scientific understanding and precision rather than increase it.

Reference: Billig, M. (2011). Writing social psychology: Fictional things and unpopulated texts. *British Journal of Social Psychology, 50,* 4–20.

to move away from considering love as a variable and start thinking about the ways in which 'the idea of love' is used in everyday interaction.

Developing these arguments further, a third and final point on which the radical critique argues against quantitative approaches is its explicit recognition of the researcher's *involvement* in the research process and the interpretation of its outcomes, together with an associated belief that the products of scientific enquiry may only have *subjective*, not objective, validity. Such objections are targeted at a range of practices commonly associated with quantitative methods, but are most clearly expressed in an opposition to the standard practices for writing up research findings. If, for example, one reads the sample research report in Appendix A (entitled 'The Role of Children's Perceived Sex in Judgements of Their Emotions'), it is clear that it is written in a very detached style and tells the story of what was done and what was found in a dispassionate way. As a result, the facts appear to emerge as the consequence of a cold scientific process from which the wishes, beliefs and values of the researcher have been totally expunged. In fact, though, it seems reasonable to assume that these wishes, beliefs and values had a considerable role to play in the research and that, as aspects of the scientific process, they are just as important as the ones we conventionally report (and may be even more important; see Spears & Smith, 2001). For example, the fact that we chose to test a particular theory in a particular way might have depended upon our relationship with the proponents of that theory (do we see them as allies or opponents?), our personal ambitions (will doing this research help us to become famous or to receive more research funding?), and our political views (do we object to the theory on ideological grounds?). However, none of these issues is addressed in the report and a reader who was familiar with conventions in psychology would not expect them to be.

In important ways such factors mean that the outcomes of research *are* contingent upon researchers' own perspectives and objectives, and the apparent denial of this is something that many qualitative researchers object to. Among other things, this means that they are motivated to discover new ways of reporting psychological research that clearly identify their own role in the research process and which explicitly present their conclusions as *an* interpretation of the data, not *the only* interpretation. These points of divergence between quantitative and contextual qualitative research are summarized in Table 13.1.

Table 13.1   Distinguishing features of quantitative (and classical qualitative) and contextual qualitative research

	Quantitative (and classical qualitative)	**Contextual qualitative**
Distinguishing features		
Underlying philosophy	Positivist, realist	Relativist, constructionist
Goals of analysis	Nomothetic (oriented to discovery of universal causal laws)	Idiographic (oriented to understanding behaviour in its local context)
Products of analysis	Reliable, stable relationships between variables	Potentially variable meanings and rules
Application of findings	General	Particular
Stance assumed by researchers	Detached	Involved
Assumed status of analytical products	Objective	Potentially subjective

As presented in Table 13.1, the radical differences between quantitative (and classical qualitative) and qualitative research appear to be rather stark. However, it is important to note that in practice the distinction between the two is not so black and white. This is for at least three reasons. First, not all those researchers who use contextualist qualitative methods endorse a radical critique (or, if they do, they only embrace certain parts of it). Second, many quantitative (and classical qualitative) researchers are sympathetic to the issues that this critique raises and try to display sensitivity to it in their research practice and theorizing (e.g., see Spears & Smith, 2001; Research Bite 13.4 below). And finally, as we discuss in the next sections, while contextualist qualitative methods are definitely different from both quantitative research and classical qualitative research, these differences are not always as marked as one might expect.

constructionism/constructivism Philosophies that suggest that meaning and reality do not exist in a fixed form external to the perceiver, but rather are actively constructed by members of a particular community in order to achieve particular objectives. Although very similar, these two philosophies have slightly different nuances. In particular, constructivism can refer to an analytic approach that is based on examination of the way in which different realities are created.

idealism A philosophy that suggests that features of the world are created through the subjective act of perceiving the world and hence are not amenable to measurement or definitive characterization.

idiographic approach An approach to research that attempts to develop person-specific analyses of phenomena in the particular context in which they arise. This is not oriented to the discovery of universal causal laws (of the form 'A always leads to B').

nomothetic approach An approach to research that attempts to develop class-wide analyses of phenomena that apply generally to members of a given group or population. This is oriented to the discovery of universal causal laws (of the form 'A always leads to B').

positivism An approach to science that assumes that scientific activity produces (and should aim to produce) knowledge about objectively present and knowable features of the world.

postmodernism In popular (and rather loose) usage, a philosophy that embraces the tenets of idealism, relativism and constructivism in arguing that the constructs of value and worth are entirely dependent on the perspective of the judge and therefore that they are impossible to establish objectively.

relativism A philosophy which asserts that there is no such thing as universal objective truth. Instead it is asserted that different interpretative frameworks and perspectives create their own truths and that no absolute criteria exist for differentiating between these in order to establish their validity.

Examples of contextual qualitative research methods

A common feature of **contextual qualitative methods** is that in attending to the meanings that participants give to their own behaviour they are generally sceptical about the prospects of using *pre-existing tools* (e.g., those associated with the qualitative methods that we discussed in Chapter 12) to uncover that meaning. Instead, as a result of the idealistic philosophy they embrace, both approaches suggest that research methodology needs to be flexible and *participant driven*, rather than be informed by a prescribed formula or set of rules. At the same time, they also typically encourage researchers to display **reflexivity** by reflecting on their own role in the research process and the way in which they may contribute to the production of the particular patterns of behaviour that participants display (Henwood & Pidgeon, 1992; Wetherell, 2008).

Nevertheless, there are important differences between different contextual methods. Most particularly, following Henwood and Pidgeon (1994), one can differentiate between contextualist methods, which assume that theoretical understanding can be imposed upon, and abstracted from, the various contexts in which research is conducted, and **constructionist/constructivist methods**, which argue that meaning is contained within the context itself, and needs to be retained through attention to that context rather than abstraction from it.

> **constructionist/constructivist methods** Approaches to psychological research that embrace a philosophy of constructionism/constructivism. Among other things, they (a) reject the scientific method as a means of developing psychological knowledge and (b) involve research and theorizing that attempt to understand, but not go beyond, the perspective and experience of participants.
>
> **contextualist qualitative methods** Approaches to psychological research in which reliance on scientific method is tempered by an emphasis on developing theory that is sensitive to the perspective and experience of both participants and researchers as well as to the context in which research takes place.
>
> **reflexivity** The process through which a researcher reflects on his or her own role in producing particular research outcomes.

Grounded theory

One of the ways in which constructionist approaches differ from conventional quantitative methods is in taking seriously the perspective of participants and focusing on their understandings of the world rather than seeking to impose the (often different) understandings of the experimenter on the data that those participants provide. Contextualist approaches share an emphasis on the perspective and interests of participants, but seek to *reconcile* this with the scientific goals of the researcher rather than to see the scientific process of theory development as inherently flawed or restrictive.

One of the clearest examples of this is provided by **grounded theory**. In this (as the name suggests) researchers attempt to develop analyses of psychological topics that are *grounded* in participants' localized experiences of relevant phenomena. A particular concern of researchers who use this method is to attempt to lay bare the various processes through which psychological theory is developed. They attempt, in particular, to identify any biases, prejudices, predispositions or hunches that they bring into the research and to document how these are supported or challenged by particular findings. In this way, analysis of a particular phenomenon is presented as it emerges through what Pidgeon and Henwood (1997, p. 255) describe as the dynamic 'flip flop' between ideas and research experience.

It is worth noting that there are a number of different ways of working with grounded theory. These range from those that are more realist in treating participants' input as relatively unproblematic (and that are therefore very similar to thematic analysis, as discussed in the previous chapter) to those that are more constructionist in being sensitive to the multiple meanings and purposes that participants' input can have. In all cases, though, the research involves discrete phases of (a) data gathering, (b) data coding, (c) data organization and (d) data analysis. The last of these phases focuses on refinement, manipulation and management of the data.

To provide a concrete example of the method and the steps that involves, we can look at some pertinent aspects of a study conducted by Pidgeon and Henwood in which they explored engineers' assessment and management of risk during a project that involved handling hazardous waste (for more detail, see Pidgeon & Henwood, 1997).

Step 1: Data gathering

Data gathering focuses on attempts to gather a rich and varied set of materials that relate to the issue in question. The core materials that Pidgeon and Henwood focused on took the form of semi-structured interviews with various people working on the hazardous waste project, which were subsequently transcribed in detail. An example of a paragraph from one such transcript is as follows:

A. Paragraph from an interview relating to Hazardous Waste case study interviews, 27 April

Paragraph 8

I don't think there is any doubt that on this job I readily accepted the advice of the civil engineering consultant, L, and didn't have the experience to question that advice adequately. I was not aware of the appropriate site investigation procedure, and was more than willing to be seduced by the idea that we could cut corners to save money.

Step 2: Development of coding system

Having gathered data in this form, the researcher's next task is to develop an appropriate **coding system** for it. This involves identifying key concepts in the text that are perceived (a) to be relevant to the issue at hand and (b) to be useful for the purpose of cross-referencing ideas and ultimately abstracting key themes and ideas. In the above example such indexing might take the following form:

B. Significant concepts identified within paragraphs

Interview S

Paragraph 8

ACCEPTING PROFESSIONAL ADVICE

CRITICIZING OTHERS' WORK

CUTTING CORNERS

EXPERIENCE

The most important feature of such concepts is that they should **fit** the data by providing an appropriate representation of it. Again, as with thematic analysis, this issue of fit can be seen to hinge in largė part on abstracting concepts that have an appropriate amount of *meta-contrast* – being neither too specific nor too general. For this reason the concepts should not be predetermined, but be devised through a process of **open coding** as the research progresses.

Step 3: Development of concept cards

After multiple pieces of data have been indexed in this way, the researcher is then able to examine the different ways in which concepts (e.g., 'cutting corners') are used across the data set as a whole. This can be done on a **concept card** that lists *variants* of concept use across the data set as a whole. For this to occur, though, the concepts have to have been defined at an appropriate level of abstraction (not too specific, not too general), and, where necessary, the researcher has to go back to refine the coding system he or she has employed. In this case, a coding card (that need not be a card at all but could be a computer record) might have the following form:

CARD 22 CUTTING CORNERS

S Para 8   S said he was not aware of the appropriate site investigation procedures, and was willing to be seduced by the idea of cutting corners to save money.

T Para 12   G said he couldn't be bothered taking the time to do a neat job with the labels as nobody appreciated it anyway.

W Para 29   W's recollection of an instruction from a manager that he should save time by not checking whether concrete was permeable.

Precisely because this process of refining data handling is a subjective one (i.e., one that is based on the researcher's own interpretations of the data), and this subjectivity will clearly have a role to play in the conclusions that the researcher eventually draws, grounded theorists recommend that records be kept of the processes that guide data management and interpretation. These can take the form of memos, or a **reflexive journal** that explains why particular decisions were made and allows these to be retrieved at a later date. An example of such a memo might be as follows:

MEMO

18 July 2002 by A. Researcher on Splitting CUTTING CORNERS

I decided to split the concept Cutting Corners into two concepts: Cutting corners due to external pressure (Card 232), and Cutting corners as a personal choice (Card 233) because the original concept was too cumbersome and broad. It also appeared that this distinction could be useful analytically because cutting corners due to external pressure seemed to be associated with decisions that related to core aspects of the project (e.g., chemical tests of concrete) whereas cutting corners due to personal choice seemed to relate to more superficial decisions (e.g., putting labels on neatly). This is seen in a comparison of T para 12 with T para 32 and W para 22 with W para 29.

A concept card is typically completed when adding more entries no longer adds any richness to the information it contains. At this point the category it describes is said to have reached **saturation**. Having reached this, the researcher then attempts to develop the analysis further by identifying the particular features that give a particular card its coherence. This can be done by attempting to define the coding concept itself, again in the form of a memo. In our engineering example, this might take the following form:

DEFINITION FOR CARD 232

CUTTING CORNERS DUE TO EXTERNAL PRESSURE

Many participants (particularly junior ones) refer to a perceived need to cut corners on vital parts of the project due to external pressure. This generally occurred in order to save either time or money. Pressure is usually implicit and only rarely explicit. Implicit pressure is seen to be part of a general culture of economy that the project managers reinforce in various ways (e.g., through timesheets, costings, budget meetings). It is also reflected in references to fear of being ridiculed (e.g., for being slow or fussy). External pressures are thus subtle, and hard to pin down but easy for managers to deny.

Step 4: Rationalization and analysis of concepts

Having attempted to summarize the data on one card (possibly by defining the concept that it relates to), advanced stages of analysis then involve the researcher attempting to draw links between cards and to integrate the emergent concepts at a higher level.

This can involve at least three things: (a) the identification of general themes that unite and distinguish between multiple concepts (as in thematic analysis; see Chapter 12); (b) the development of analytic **taxonomies** (i.e., classification schemes that help to organize concepts); or (c) the clarification of relationships among concepts. Again, a key goal here is to maximize *fit* by ensuring that any analysis retains its fidelity by imposing structure on it that on the one hand is not so general that it loses contact with the specifics of the data that the

RESEARCH BITE 13.2
Saturation matters more than size

In qualitative research there are generally no hard-and-fast rules about how large a sample size should be, and no agreed methods for making this decision. This contrasts from quantitative research where power analysis is routinely used for this purpose. However, a key principle to which researchers often appeal when reporting their findings is that of *saturation*. The idea here is that one should continue to collect or analyse data up to the point that nothing new is being learned. As Patricia Fusch and Lawrence Ness (2015) note, it is important that researchers do not terminate data collection and analysis before reaching this saturation point, as to do so will undermine the validity of their analysis. They note, however, that this point will always be specific to the research question that is being investigated.

Reference: Fusch, P. I., & Ness, L. R. (2015). Are we there yet? Data saturation in qualitative research. *The Qualitative Report, 20,* 1408–1416.

researcher has gone to great pains to explore in detail, and on the other hand is not so specific that opportunities to abstract important generalities are overlooked.

Step 5: Report production

Having gone through this process, the final task is to produce a research report that allows others to benefit from the insights that the above steps have provided. In many ways this will resemble the procedures for reporting the results of thematic analysis that were described in the previous chapter. However, in the case of grounded theory, two specific goals remain paramount: (a) *documentation* of decisions relating to the analysis that allow the research process to be interrogated and audited; and (b) sensitivity to issues of *reflexivity* that demonstrate awareness of the role that the researcher's subjective decisions played in the analysis. In other words, the report needs to remain faithful to the *grounded* nature of the method itself.

In relation to all of these activities and goals, a residual question that you may be asking yourself is 'How will I know when any analysis is good enough?'. In other words, when does any analysis contain enough documentation, enough reflexivity and enough fit? Partly because it incorporates some of the idealist philosophy of constructionists, these questions are hard to answer in the abstract (in the way that we could when performing a *t*-test, say). Nonetheless, grounded theorists do assert that the method has the potential to take researchers' understanding of psychological processes forward, and that whether or not it does can be established with reference to a number of criteria. Among other things, these can include assessment of whether the research (a) leads to the development of *novel* understanding of relevant issues, (b) helps develop understanding that is (to some extent) *transferable* from one content domain to another, and (c) is validated, and perceived to be useful, by the research participants themselves. For example, the study of risk management in engineering projects might be perceived to have been worthwhile if it suggests that a particular type of organizational culture is a major contributor to accidents, and this is perceived to be useful by engineers themselves and helps them to eliminate accidents across a range of industries in future.

Whether or not grounded theory achieves these various aims also depends in part on the degree to which one engages fully with its idealist philosophy. As Braun and Clarke (2006) note, in practice, many researchers use 'grounded theory lite' as a method for organizing data and abstracting its key themes – so that, in effect, they are really conducting a fancy form of thematic analysis (and potentially not that fancy). This is all well and good, but it needs to be recognized that 'full-cream' grounded theory research involves being wary of researchers' attempts to impose meaning on reality without a full interrogation of the processes this involves and of the damage it can do to participants' localized understandings of their world.

> **coding system** In qualitative analysis, the categories used to summarize key features of a data set.
>
> **concept card** A card that lists the various ways in which a concept (or theme) has been used within a given data set.

Test Yourself 13.2**

What is the role of a reflexive journal in grounded theory?

a. To record data that are collected in the field, but that need to be analysed at a later stage, once the researcher has had an opportunity to reflect on them.

b. To allow participants to record their own thoughts and feelings about the research process – in particular, aspects of it that they are uncomfortable with and that they can discuss with the researcher later.

c. To allow researchers to record their thoughts about the research process, so that the rationale for their decisions is recoverable at some later stage.

d. To allow researchers and participants to reflect upon each others' activity so that differences in their perspective can be reconciled by a third party.

e. To record specific features of the physical environment that reflect on the research process as a whole, but that might be omitted from quantitative analysis.

The correct answer is (c). Reflexive journals are used by researchers so that the processes that lead them to collect and interpret data in particular ways are available for examination at a later stage. This is intended to ensure that decisions and activities that have a bearing on research outcomes (and which can help to explain why data have a particular form) are recoverable after data have been collected. Although they all sound plausible, each of the other answers is wrong: (a) is wrong because reflexive journals are not used to record data; (b) and (d) are wrong because they are not used by participants (though other forms of research journals or diaries may be); and (e) is wrong because, while it might discuss features of the environment that bear upon a researcher's decisions, those features are not its primary focus.

fit In *grounded theory*, the degree to which any aspect of analysis is an appropriate and recognizable description of the phenomena under investigation.

grounded theory A qualitative research practice in which understanding of a phenomenon is inductively derived from studying that phenomenon from the perspective of those to whom it is relevant. In this way, the researcher does not begin with a theory and then test it; instead, theory is discovered, developed and provisionally verified as it emerges from systematic examination of data.

open coding In *grounded theory*, the process of developing coding concepts and categories that fit the data as closely as possible. For this reason, such concepts are not predetermined but evolve over the course of the coding process.

reflexive journal A researcher's record of thoughts and activities that relate to the research process. Among other things, this is intended to provide insight into the decisions that guide data management.

saturation The point at which no more is discovered about a particular analytical construct through the collection of more data. In qualitative research this is often a key criterion for deciding how much data to collect and analyse (akin to power analysis in quantitative research).

taxonomy A classification scheme used to summarize and organize information.

Interpretative phenomenological analysis (IPA)

We noted in the previous chapter that qualitative researchers often adopt a hermeneutic approach, in which they seek to explore particular psychological phenomena by understanding the meaning that those phenomena have for people who encounter them. Another way of saying this is to observe that qualitative researchers are often interested in the **phenomenology** of psychological experience. What does it mean to be in love? What does it feel like to be depressed? Yet having asked such questions, concerns with issues of reflexivity might also lead to a secondary question – that is, how are researchers' understandings of the meaning that given phenomena have for people affected by the meaning that those phenomena have for the researchers themselves?

To return to one of the examples that has run throughout this book, as researchers, we may be interested in what 'love' means to you. And to investigate this question we may ask you lots of questions seeking to explore your thoughts about love – questions such as 'How does the way you love your mother differ from the way you love your partner?'. However, when one looks at this question, it is clear that there are a number of assumptions bound up within it that have led us to ask it in this way and which will therefore have consequences for the answers we get. Among other things, the logic of the question implies that there is a difference between these two forms of love (Grice, 1975), and in most contexts you would probably assume that we are not seeking to explore issues of incest. Clearly, though, this might depend on whether or not we were interested in Freudian processes of psychodynamic attraction (e.g., the Oedipus complex; Kulish & Holtzman, 2010), and whether or not you thought we were. Furthermore, the type of answer that you would give to such a question is likely to vary considerably depending on whether we asked it in a psychology class, in a counselling session, or on a bus where one of us just happened to be sitting next to you. In particular, in the first situation you might give us a relatively 'straight' answer, but in the last case you might tell us to mind our own business – or worse. Indeed, sensitivity to this fact would mean that in practice very few researchers would actually be prepared to ask the question in this context (even if they were able to obtain ethical approval to do so, which itself would not be straightforward; see Chapter 14).

The critical point to note here, then, is that the type of response you would give to the question (and your behaviour more generally) is bound up in both the meaning of the situation for you and the meaning of the situation for the researcher. This is what researchers refer to as a **double hermeneutic**, and a core goal of **interpretative phenomenological analysis** (which from now on we will refer as **IPA**) is to try to explore the ways in which these are involved in the meaning that experiences assume for research participants in the world at large. In this regard, the method is intimately concerned with people's sense-making activities as they seek to understand the world around them and to act meaningfully within it.

As with all the other methods that we have discussed in this and the previous chapter, the process of performing IPA can be formalized in terms of a series of discrete steps, and we can illustrate these with reference to a particular research example. In this case, we will look at work by Clare (2003) that examined the way in which people who have been diagnosed with dementia experience changes in their sense of self as the disease advances and their memory starts to deteriorate.

Step 1: Definition of research question and sample

The process of conducting IPA focuses on the process of conducting in-depth interviews with a small number of research participants whose experiences are directly relevant to the topic that you want to research. The key goal is then to use these interviews as a means of trying to discover and understand how people make sense of a particular set of experiences within their social world. In this regard, the researcher is meant to try to approach the interviews – and the topic as a whole – with questions that are broad and open. Indeed, the method is perhaps best seen as a tool of hypothesis generation rather than hypothesis testing, and that is best suited to early phases of theory development in which relatively little is known about the issues under investigation.

Because, as we will see, the process of conducting IPA is intensive and time-consuming, the method places an emphasis on interview quality rather than quantity. Also, rather than trying to find a broad, diverse or random population to study, the goal is to identify a small homogeneous sample that has direct experience of the topic in question. Indeed, some analyses take the form of single case studies, and very few involve more than a dozen. Building on the insights of Kelly's (1955) personal construct theory, Smith and Osborn (2015) have argued that three is an ideal sample size, since this allows researchers to explore similarities and differences within interviews in a manner akin to the process of examining sets of three elements in repertory grid analysis (see Chapter 12).

Clare's study in fact involved a relatively large sample of 12 Alzheimer's patients who were attending a memory clinic in the south of England. All were living at home with a partner or spouse, and all performed poorly on a standard test of cognitive functioning commonly used to inform dementia diagnosis.

Step 2: Data collection and transcription

The preferred method for collecting data upon which to perform IPA is the **semi-structured interview**. A **structured interview** is one in which a predetermined set of questions is asked in a predetermined sequence, and researchers endeavour to stay as close as possible to a given **interview schedule** in order to maintain consistency and hence increase the integrity and reliability of data. In effect, this involves taking a person through a survey like those that we discussed in Chapter 5, rather than having them complete it by themselves. In contrast, a semi-structured interview is considerably more flexible and should take the form of a conversation rather than an inquisition. Questions should thus be (a) open rather than closed (e.g., 'How are you feeling?' is preferable to 'Are you feeling sick?'); (b) asked one at a time rather than be double-barrelled (e.g., 'Has your memory changed?' followed, if the answer is 'yes', by 'How does this make you feel?', is preferable to 'Has your memory deteriorated and made you angry?'); (c) neutral rather than value laden (e.g., 'How has your personality changed?' is preferable to 'Have you become aggressive?'); and (d) couched in lay terms rather than jargon (e.g., 'Is the doctor giving you any drugs?' is better than 'Are you taking NMDA receptor antagonists?').

A key goal of early questions is to develop **rapport** with interviewees so that they feel comfortable and free to explore the topic in ways that they see fit. Rather than positioning themselves as the authority on the topic in question, then, researchers are encouraged to see and treat the interviewee as the expert.

Establishing rapport is especially important when working with communities who may be marginalized or vulnerable, and in every case when working with communities to which the researcher does not belong. This is true for all methods, not just those employing IPA, but, in general, rapport is most likely to be established when participants are treated with authentic respect (itself a complex matter; see Research Bite 14.1).

In preparing for the interview, the researcher needs to identify a number of key issues that he or she wants to explore and to organize these in some logical fashion. Typically this will start with relatively general and non-threatening questions that allow the interviewee to ease into the topic, but then delves deeper as the interview progresses. In this regard, the structure of the interview can be seen to resemble a funnel in which questions start at a relatively abstract level (e.g., 'How are you feeling?') but become increasingly specific ('Do you feel that your ability to remember things is changing?', 'Does this affect your relationship with your partner?', 'Does it affect your sense of who you are?').

At every stage the goal is to probe the topic gently rather than to fixate on an explicit agenda. If the participant finds questions hard to answer, it is also useful to have thought about a series of prompts that might reframe the question and make it easier to answer. There is also no requirement for interviews to proceed in a linear fashion, and when digressions are initiated by the interviewee it can be useful to explore these and then return to prepared questions later, if necessary. Interviews need to be recorded, so it is important to get the interviewee's permission to do this, and to ensure that he or she is comfortable about this and all other aspects of the interview process.

Once interviews have been conducted they then need to be transcribed. As we noted at the end of the previous chapter, this is a time-consuming and painstaking process, as it involves recording not only what the interviewee and interviewer said, but also any other significant features of the interaction – such things as pauses, laughs or external interruptions.

For example, part of the transcript in Linda Clare's research might have looked like this (where L = Linda and I = Interviewee; based on Clare, 2003, p. 1022):

L: Do you feel that your ability to remember things is changing?

I: Yes. Definitely. (looks away).

L: How do you think it is changing?

I: It's just getting a whole lot worse … I mean sometimes I forget really stupid things. Daft things. Things I never used to forget. (pause)

L: How do these changes affect you?

I: The changes … I think you're half aware of them and not quite sure what was going on, if anything was going on, maybe like when you're getting older that's well, so what? Um but then as it speeded up … I'd think, I wish I wasn't like this … and then my wife began to notice things as well and I thought, well there's something wrong even if she's not always right … and that was the business where we said, OK, let's try and get down to it and see the doctor.

Step 3: Identification of themes in the first case

The process of data analysis involves trying to identify units and patterns of meaning in respondents' accounts of phenomena within their psychological world (that accounts for the P in IPA). However, this is an engaged interpretative act on the part of the researcher rather than a passive mechanical one (that accounts for the I), and there are many ways of setting about this task.

However, Smith and Osborn (2015) recommend that researchers start by working with one of their interviews and familiarizing themselves fully with what it contains through a process of careful reading and rereading. In the process of doing this, you should start to make notes on the text by remarking on things within it that seem to be worthy of comment. Again, there are no rules about what these notes should refer to: they might be comments on the use of language, on the way in which a person talks about themselves, or on internal consistencies and inconsistencies. Having done this, you should then work through the text again and try to identify themes that start to tie together some of these various comments, and to organize them in meaningful ways and at a higher level of abstraction – always bearing in mind that it is the participants' meanings you are trying to capture, not your own.

In the example below, one can see how a range of initial notes on the left have been transformed into concise phrases on the right that capture what appear to be key themes within the text. As with both grounded theory and thematic analysis, the skill here centres on identifying themes that have sufficient *meta-contrast*: being abstract enough to allow you to identify similarities across different parts of the text, but specific enough to remain faithful to the meaningful differences within it.

Shame	L:	Do you feel that your ability to remember things is changing?
	I:	Yes. Definitely. (looks away).
	L:	How do you think it is changing?
Anger?	I:	It's just getting a whole lot worse … I mean sometimes I forget really stupid things. Daft things. Things I never used to forget. (pause)
Starts to notice	L:	How do these changes affect you?

I: The changes … I think you're half aware of them and not quite sure what was going on, if anything was going on, maybe like when you're getting older that's well, so what? Um but then as it   *REGISTERING*

Validation by close other triggers action   speeded up … I'd think, I wish I wasn't like this … and then my wife began to notice things as well and I thought, well there's   *REACTING* something wrong even if she's not always right … and that was the business where we said, OK, let's try and get down to it and see the doctor.

Step 4: Organization of themes

Once key themes have been identified within the first interview, the next step involves trying to organize these in ways that do justice to what participants had to say about the topic in question, but which also impose structure and order upon their accounts. This will typically involve three distinct phases. The first involves *clustering* themes that appear to go together and, if it appears appropriate, combining them. The second involves *ordering* themes in ways that meaningfully communicate the logic of participants' experiences – for example, as these unfolded over time or across different settings. Finally, the themes should be presented in a table that presents the themes in a coherent fashion, and in a way that is amenable to interpretation by others.

In Clare's study she identified five key processes that older adults with Alzheimer's discussed in their accounts of their difficulties: registering, reacting, explaining, experiencing and adjusting. However, she also noted that the way respondents engaged with these varied, so that sometimes they tried to protect themselves from the threat that memory changes caused and at others they tried to engage with that threat. In this case, Table 13.2 shows how the themes were ultimately organized.

Step 5: Examination of themes in subsequent cases

As noted above, it is possible to conduct IPA on a single case, in the event of which one could wrap up the analysis at this point. It is more common, though, to continue by working through subsequent cases (e.g., the second and third interviews in cases where you have conducted

Table 13.2

Process	Self-maintaining theme	Self-adjusting theme
Registering	Uncertainty	Acknowledging
Reacting	Minimizing	Disintegrating
Explaining	Normalizing	Switching the wires
Experiencing	Putting on a protective coating	Spending time in the depths
Adjusting	Holding on, compensating	Fighting, accepting

three) in order to both validate and refine one's initial analysis. Smith and Osborn (2015) recommend that researchers do this by starting from scratch with each interview and repeating Steps 3 and 4 with each. When this is complete, researchers should then look for patterns of convergence and divergence across the cases as a whole, again with a view to organizing the themes that have been identified in meaningful ways. This can involve either reconciling the themes across the different cases (as Clare, 2003, did – so that the above table was seen to capture the experiences of all her participants), or else presenting an analysis that exposes variations in the themes and their structure across those cases.

Step 6: Report production

As with all the other methods we have discussed, the final step of IPA involves the production of a research report. In basic terms, this needs to document the process that the researcher has gone through, to describe what has been found, and to discuss the significance of the findings for the topic in question. However, with IPA, as with grounded theory, special attention needs to be paid to the role of the researcher in the research process as a whole and to the process through which participants' experiences have been interpreted.

This sensitivity can be seen in the Discussion of the paper in which Clare (2003, p. 1025) reported her findings, where she concludes:

> The participants' accounts demonstrate the complex processes involved in the expression of awareness of memory problems and other changes in early stage AD. All participants acknowledged having problems with memory, and some were able to describe the gradual process of becoming aware of these; thus, none of the participants could be said to be entirely unaware. Participants made varying judgements, however, about the meaning or impact of their memory problems, expressed a range of emotional responses, and engaged in different strategies as they attempted to cope and adjust. ... There were, in addition, indications of the way in which the interview context sometimes influenced responses. Contact with professionals had important implications, too; both a lack of information and a very blunt presentation of the diagnosis could result in self-maintaining strategies

and thus apparent unawareness. Awareness was evident or not in participants' accounts of five multi-faceted processes …

However, as with grounded theory, one nagging question that you may be left with concerns the degree to which the method can ever live up to its aspirations. Can researchers ever really come to a question with an open mind? Can this analysis (or any other) ever really disentangle the phenomenology of participants from the phenomenology of researchers? Is this really what they are trying to do when they write up their reports?

Regardless of how one answers such questions, an important contribution of IPA (and of grounded theory) is to bring these interpretative issues into play and make them a legitimate focus for psychological enquiry. Nevertheless, for many commentators – particularly those who embrace a hard-line constructionist philosophy – the approach simply does not go far enough. To really come to grips with the constructed nature of psychological reality, they argue, one needs to engage much more closely with the construction process itself.

double hermeneutic A feature of the research process that reflects the fact that attempts to discover the meaning of phenomena for participants is necessarily bound up with the meaning that they have for researchers.

interpretative phenomenological analysis (IPA) A research method that attempts to discover the meaning of phenomena for participants, but that also recognizes – and

RESEARCH BITE 13.3
Double hermeneutic or half hermeneutic?

IPA has become increasingly popular in recent years, especially in the fields of clinical and health psychology. In a review of this work, Joanna Brocki and Alison Wearden (2006) identify 52 papers that have used IPA to explore the phenomenology of various medical conditions and other health-related issues. They note that an attraction of the method is that it allows researchers to delve into patients' experience of illness rather than to fixate on issues of cause and effect. Nevertheless, they also note that most research papers pay scant attention to the researchers' own interpretative role in the research process. In this, sensitivity to the double hermeneutic appears to be more an ideal than a reality.

Reference: Brocki, J. M., & Wearden, A. J. (2006). A critical evaluation of the use of interpretative phenomenological analysis (IPA) in health psychology. *Psychology and Health, 21,* 87–108.

Test Yourself 13.3*

In devising an interview schedule for a study that will involve interpretative phenomenological analysis (IPA), which of the following should one try to include?

 a. Double-barrelled questions.
 b. Jargon.
 c. Open questions.
 d. Value-laden questions.
 e. Offensive questions.

The correct answer is (c). A goal of the semi-structured interviews that are used as a basis for IPA is to explore the respondents' experience of a relevant phenomenon in a broad and open fashion. This is done by letting them take the lead and go where they want to – something that open (rather than closed) questions (of the form used in structured interviews) allow for. Answer (a) is wrong because double-barrelled questions should be avoided in all interviews (and surveys) because they make answers hard to interpret. Answer (b) is wrong because jargon will often create a sense of distance between interviewer and interviewee, and this is something that IPA seeks to reduce. Answer (d) is wrong because value-laden questions can induce reactivity and lead the interviewee to answer in particular ways (e.g., to say what they think the interviewer wants to hear). If the interviewee does not share the interviewer's values this may also undermine rapport. Finally, (e) is incorrect because all interviews (and surveys) should avoid offensive questions. Apart from anything else, this is because interviews need to conform to ethical principles and show respect for participants (a point we will discuss in more depth in Chapter 14).

attempts to do justice to the fact – that this is necessarily bound up with the meaning that those phenomena have for researchers.

interview schedule The plan for an interview that provides details of the issues that a researcher wants to explore and the questions that the researcher wants to ask. It may also include details of prompts to be used in the event that a question proves difficult for an interviewee to answer.

phenomenology The meaning that a given phenomenon has for the people who experience it.

rapport The process through which an interviewer seeks to establish a positive relationship and build trust with an interviewee. This is often important for the interview to flow smoothly and for it to yield useful data.

semi-structured interview An interview in which a researcher has a predetermined set of questions to ask, but where the interviewer does not necessarily stick to these or ask them in a particular sequence. Instead, the interview itself is conducted in a naturalistic and conversational manner that puts the interviewee at ease and facilitates rapport between interviewer and interviewee.

structured interview An interview in which a predetermined set of questions is asked in a predetermined sequence. The goal is to maximize consistency across interviews and ensure that all participants have a similar experience.

Discourse analysis

As suggested above, constructionist approaches are among the most controversial in psychology for the simple reason that they are founded upon a rejection of the scientific method as it is typically understood and applied in research. Indeed, rather than developing (or trying to develop) hypotheses about psychological states and processes and seeking to test these in empirical studies, constructionists see the empirical method itself as a medium for constructing particular meanings in order to achieve particular objectives – for example, to be seen as a scientist and to be seen to be 'doing science'. In this way, where another psychologist might seek to abstract meaning from quantitative or qualitative data in order to test and develop theory (so that the data are essentially a theoretical *resource*), constructionists see the process of abstracting meaning as a *topic* in itself. For this reason, constructionist methods focus very much on the fine-grained qualities of language itself, rather than seeking to abstract other forms of data from it.

Discourse analysis is possibly the clearest example of this practice. Among other things, it is commonly used to inspect the character of naturally occurring discourse in order to discover subtle (and typically undetected) features of it that allow people to achieve particular ends. Almost any form of language can be used for this purpose: conversations, discussions, speeches, advertising campaigns, the text of a dog licence, the instructions for using a food processor.

Where the analytical material takes the form of spoken language, this is usually reported using a standardized transcription system. Aspects of this system are illustrated by the following text reported by Potter (1997, p. 151) and transcribed from a famous BBC interview of Princess Diana by Martin Bashir:

Bashir:	Did you (.) allow your ↑friends, >your close friends,<
	to speak to °Andrew Morton°?
Princess:	Yes I did. [Yes I did.
Bashir:	[°Why°?
Princess:	I was (.) at the end of my tether (.)
	I was (.) desperate (.)
	>I think I was so fed up with being< (.)
	seen as someone who was a bas:ket case (.)

because I am a very strong person (.)

and I know (.) that causes complications, (.)

in the system (.) that I live in.

(1.0) ((smiles and purses lips))

Bashir: How would a book change that?

Princess: → I ↑dunno. ((raises eyebrows, looks away))

Maybe people have a better understanding (.)

maybe there's a lot of women out there

who suffer (.) on the same level

but in a different environment (.)

who are unable to: (.) stand up for themselves (.)

because their esteem is (.) cut into two.

→ I dunno ((shakes head))

In this text (.) refers to a pause of less than 0.2 seconds, (1.0) refers to a pause of 1 second, ↑ indicates raised pitch, > and < surround talk that is noticeably faster, °s surround talk that is noticeably lower in volume, : indicates a lengthening of the preceding sound, [indicates where talk starts to overlap, underlining indicates stress or emphasis, (( )) surround transcriber's comments, and → points to lines that are referred to in the researcher's commentary on the text.

We can see that the transcription system makes the text relatively hard to read. At the same time, though, once the reader is familiar with transcription conventions, the system makes it possible to recover precise features of dialogue (e.g., intonation, pitch, speed) that would otherwise be unavailable for scrutiny. And in this particular case, the method allows the researcher (Potter) to make a detailed examination of the role that the two instances of 'I dunno' play for the person who uttered them.

Two points are relevant here. First, it is clear that the utterance 'I dunno' could easily pass without note if it had not been subjected to detailed transcription of this form. This would be particularly true if the researcher who was recording the dialogue was concerned only to note its substantive content, as an 'I dunno' could easily be seen as trivial and irrelevant. Second, though, even if the researcher did note the presence of 'I dunno', from a realist perspective it is likely that it would be interpreted as a *literal* representation of the speaker's cognitions. In effect, then, it could be treated in the same way as a response of '1' on a five-point scale which asked the question 'Do you know why this book would help your cause?' and 1 represented a response of 'not at all' and 5 a response of 'very definitely'.

Against such literal interpretations of data (whether qualitative or quantitative), discourse analysts note that any single response can have a range of potential meanings. For example, when asked the question 'Did you enjoy yourself?', the response 'Oh, absolutely!' (a '5' on a five-point scale perhaps) could be meant to be taken literally, but it could also be intended to be ironic, sarcastic, witty or half-hearted. How can quantitative (or empiricist qualitative) methods differentiate between these various meanings? Constructionists argue that they cannot, and therefore insist that attempts at interpreting language and behaviour need to be tied firmly to the contexts of production. Their methods therefore focus on identifying those various features that ensure that responses and interaction have the particular meanings that they do.

Here, too, any hypotheses are intended to emerge *from* the data rather than to be *taken into* the data-gathering exercise. For example, in the case of 'I dunno', Potter suggests that this serves as a form of 'stake inoculation' in which the speaker expresses ignorance in order to deflect potential accusations that she engaged in particular behaviour (telling her friends to contribute to a book that was critical of the royal family) for self-serving or malicious reasons. Having made this assertion, the researcher can then examine other transcripts to find evidence (a) of the same construction ('I dunno') being used for the same purposes, (b) of the same construction being used for different purposes, or (c) of different constructions being used for the same purposes. Other aspects of the same or different transcripts – especially those that are contradictory or inconsistent – can also be used to shed light on the meaning and function of such a construction. For example, were Diana to indicate in some other discourse that she knew exactly why Andrew Morton's book would help her cause, this might suggest that her use of 'I dunno' in the interview transcribed above was not a reflection of genuine ignorance (although it is worth noting in passing that this logic in fact embodies some realist assumptions – specifically that ignorance, or anything else for that matter, can be authenticated as 'genuine').

The broad function of such analysis is to show how language is used actively and creatively by participants to achieve complex social goals (e.g., representing oneself positively and other people negatively), and, as a corollary, to show that an understanding of how those goals are achieved is impossible without detailed analysis of discourse. At a theoretical level it also serves to critique psychological (and other) research that treats language as a uniform, neutral and literal conduit for the transmission of information.

There is no finite set of ways in which discourse analysis can be performed and no prescribed set of methods by which means it should be conducted. For this reason it would be a foolhardy exercise to try to identify discrete steps that one should go through in order to conduct the analysis, in the way that we have with preceding methods. Indeed, some (but not all) of its proponents suggest that providing such prescriptions may lead them into the positivist trap of privileging one interpretation of a text or an interaction when many are usually possible and valid. For this reason, discourse analysts describe the method as a 'craft skill' akin to riding a bicycle: hard to learn and hard to describe (e.g., Potter, 1997, pp. 147–148). Nonetheless, like riding a bicycle, discourse analysis is seen as something that one can do badly or do well, and it is very definitely not a method where 'anything goes'. The question of whether this fact is incompatible with the idealist philosophy that often informs the approach is one we will return to later in the context of a broader philosophical reflection on the range of complex analytical issues that this chapter has brought to the fore.

> **discourse analysis** A constructionist practice that involves the fine-grained analysis of language. By this means researchers focus on how language does more than merely describe the world or relay information, but is used instead to achieve complex social objectives in particular contexts.

Test Yourself 13.4**

Which of the following activities might be carried out as part of discourse analysis?

    a.   Transcription of a conversation between two people at a breakfast table.
    b.   Identification of changes in pitch when a person is speaking.
    c.   Interpretation of linguistic features in the context of their production.
    d.   Both (b) and (c).
    e.   All of the above.

The correct answer is (e). All of the practices here are ones that discourse analysts might engage in. In particular, they are concerned with naturally occurring language (so (a) is correct), with recording detailed features of that language (so (b) is correct), and with tying the analysis of language to the context of its production (so (c) is correct).

Critiques of contextual qualitative methods

In the previous chapter we discussed three key criticisms that are often levelled against classical qualitative methods: first, that they are unscientific; second, that they focus on the particular rather than the general; third, that they are an easy option. These same three criticisms are often made in relation to contextual qualitative methods. For example, a critic may ask how we know that Princess Diana's use of 'I dunno' represents a stake inoculator rather than a statement of genuine ignorance, an habitual response to a difficult question, or a verbal tic. And he or she may also ask on what grounds we would use this finding as a basis for generalization to other contexts. Likewise, he or she might object that fine-grained attention to something like the Diana interview risks losing sight of general truths by attending only to those that are very specific. And, finally, he or she may say that because such data can be collected while watching television, this research is far too easy to conduct to be considered serious science.

It is possible to respond to all three of these criticisms in much the same way as we did in the previous chapter. First, one could make the point that, if one so desired, one could use contextualist qualitative methods in much the same way as other quantitative methods. Such analysis might, for example, show that Princess Diana used the phrase 'I dunno' much more commonly after a question in which her personal motives were questioned than when other types of difficult question were posed – and indeed such logic is often implicit in the sorts of research that discourse analysis and other contextual qualitative researchers conduct. Second, issues of generalization could also be addressed through the development of appropriate theory (as argued in Chapter 4), while at the same time observing that many phenomena of interest to psychologists are quite unique. After all, there will only ever be one Diana interview. Third, it is again a colossal mistake to imagine that the methods and techniques we have examined in this chapter are easy to apply and master. They are not. More generally, too, one should also recognize that the model of science against which contextual qualitative methods are routinely contrasted is itself very limited – and indeed this is a point that the methods themselves have been used, with powerful effect, to demonstrate (e.g., see Gilbert & Mulkay, 1984; Woolgar, 1988, 1996).

There are, however, two additional criticisms of contextual qualitative methods that do not apply to the classical methods we considered in the previous chapter. The first of these is that *they do not tell us much about psychology*, but are really only useful as tools of philosophical, sociological or linguistic analysis. This criticism is targeted mainly at constructionist approaches such as discourse analysis, and it is one that many researchers in this tradition would themselves accept. However, as with debate about the scientific credentials of qualitative research, such researchers would also question whether quantitative and classical qualitative approaches are really exploring underlying psychological processes in the unproblematic way that their proponents suggest. Rather, because almost all windows onto psychological states and processes involve the use of language of some form (either in participants' responses or researchers' interpretations), constructionists would argue that psychological research is essentially a social activity that serves merely to favour and formalize particular *accounts* of psychological processes. For this reason, constructionists would argue that it makes a lot more sense to draw on ideas from other fields that are concerned with understanding language (e.g., sociology, linguistics, philosophy) than to focus on psychology as if it were a self-contained island of knowledge and wisdom.

A second particular criticism of contextual qualitative methods is that *they fall foul of their own logic*. Again, this criticism is focused mainly on constructionist methods, with critics here observing that, although they are not always perfect, quantitative methods at least lay down specific criteria by which research procedures and outcomes can be judged. In the case of the three methods we have discussed in this chapter, how would we know whether the method had been performed well or badly, successfully or unsuccessfully – especially if one contends that all understandings of psychological processes are equally valid? And to which guidelines could we appeal if we disagreed with another researcher's assessment of our work? We alluded to this point above when noting that discourse analysts sometimes compare the method with riding a bicycle – something for which the instructions cannot be spelled out but which nevertheless people clearly succeed or fail at (Potter, 1997). The problem here, though, is that this response appears to rely on a level of realism that the approach itself rejects. Certainly, in suggesting that meaning and validity are relative constructions that can be gauged only from the perspective of the participant, but that research products can (and should) be recognized as successful or unsuccessful, constructionists have been accused of wanting to have their cake and eat it.

How to reference and avoid plagiarism

Burns, T. and Sinfield, S.

'Many students I met did not understand referencing straight away. They wanted to write something that showed what *they* thought, not what someone else had said. We didn't understand that using someone else's argument is a tool to support our own. Students are very keen for you to "see" them, to hear their voice. In many ways we are puppies wanting to please. We need to know why referencing does not detract from our own voice being heard.'

Introduction

> To my mind there is a solution. We need to chill out. First year students should be given time and freedom to learn. During this time plagiarism should not result in punishment for the student, but should be seen as a weakness of the teaching. Students should be free to make mistakes, and every university should be teaching referencing positively with the same rigour you would expect for any subject. After all, if it is that important, then we should be willing to give students time to learn how to reference correctly.

The English university system is based on research and independent learning: you are not *taught* your degree, but are expected *to read for it*: in the process you are acquiring ideas, arguments and evidence from other people. This may feel frustrating – you want to tell us what you think; but it is the academic way – you are expected to learn from and use the ideas of others. The reading that you do to prepare for your assignments helps you to engage with the thinkers in your subject – and it provides you with more ideas, knowledge-claims, arguments and evidence to develop your thinking and your writing. Yes, you are not 'empty', you do already have ideas and thoughts of your own, but you are supposed to do this reading to deepen your understanding and engage with the key people, ideas, concepts and theories that make up the subject you are studying.

Much is made in university of plagiarism and plagiarism offences – even first year students may be punished for not correctly showing their sources even if they stumble into plagiarism by accident. The aim of this chapter is to briefly discuss the what, why and how of referencing – and to explore some common reasons for accidental plagiarism – and how to avoid them. Meanwhile, keep this image in your mind: if studying is exploration, your *references are your maps* – recording your footsteps through the subject as it already exists.

TIP

When you read, record your sources immediately. Use online apps or index cards to keep a record of everything that you read – as you read it. Read Chapter 4 on how to survive academic reading.

Should I reference?

> Soon after the end of my first semester at university I heard about a course friend who had been accused of plagiarising. I never saw him again as he left soon after,

his confidence having been taken away by the experience. His 'crime' was simply that he had been educated in a different country that looks upon these things in a different way, and he had not fully understood the consequences of not properly referencing. To me though, the real crime was that education had lost a bright and inquisitive mind.

When you write, when you deliver a presentation, you must reference every time you 'refer to' or quote other people. This includes when you paraphrase their ideas – it even includes when you agree with them. For example, if you believe that we learn best when we learn actively, you might write:

Burns and Sinfield (2012) argue that we learn best when we learn actively and interactively.

Acknowledging a source does not weaken your own opinion – it demonstrates that you have ideas – and that you are prepared to do the reading to support your ideas. Your references show what a good student you are. Check out the flow chart in Figure 11.4.1.

TIPS

- Use Manchester University's Academic Phrasebank for examples of *how to write about your sources.* This link takes you straight to that section: www.phrase bank.manchester.ac.uk/referring-to-sources/.
- This easy to use resource from Nottingham shows how to reference: www.notting ham.ac.uk/nmp/sonet/rlos/studyskills/harvard/.
- If you want to follow this further, feel free to use both our Preventing Plagiarism and our Heroes & Villains websites:
  - http://learning.londonmet.ac.uk/TLTC/learnhigher/Plagiarism/ – if the link breaks, search online for LearnHigher + preventing plagiarism.
  - http://learning.londonmet.ac.uk/epacks/heroes-&-villains/ – if the link breaks, do an online search for Londonmet + Heroes and Villains.

Some reasons for plagiarising

Here are some reasons other students have given for plagiarising. As you read, think about how you could avoid making the mistakes that they made:

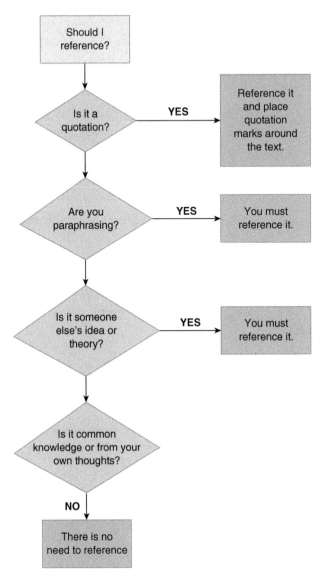

FIGURE 11.4.1 Should I reference?

We were working on the assignment together. It was a group project – but we were supposed to write individual reports. Somehow, I couldn't write a different report to my mate – so I copied her version and handed it in as my own. I was punished for plagiarism and got zero for that module.

I had done the reading for that assignment ages ago. When I finally wrote it up, I couldn't remember what was my work and what I'd read. I really didn't know that this was plagiarism ...

I found an essay on the web that was exactly on my topic. I did write my own intro-duction and conclusion – but it was still plagiarism. I'm lucky I didn't get suspended.

Well I did read that stuff – but it was what I was thinking anyway – so I didn't think I had to give any sources. Turns out I was wrong …

I just thought I had to write a bibliography at the end. No! You have to mention your reading as you write. You have to give the name and date of the source *where* you refer to it – and you have to give the page number as well if you actually quote it. Then you have to give the full author, date, title, town, publisher in the bibliography as well.

I thought I was doing well. I put all the good quotes down on the page – and just wrote little bits of essay around them. But that didn't work. You have to put it in your own words – still giving a reference – and discuss it. The tutor said I'd just handed in my notes rather than an essay. She said I was lucky not to be accused of plagiarism – and to digest my reading first next time. It's quite hard getting this bit right – harder than I thought it would be.

What advice would you have given these people? What advice would you give yourself if you find yourself doing these things? One big piece of advice would be to give yourself *time* to read, write and understand.

Further, these students did the reading but obviously did not record enough *source* information. Develop the habit of recording your sources every time you make notes. You save time – and you have your index cards to use again in future assignments. Remember to record the page numbers too in case you want to quote. Read Chapter 4 on how to survive academic reading.

A third issue seems to be about not understanding the referencing tradition in academic life. You are supposed to note where ideas come from. Even when you agree with what you are reading – or where the author agrees with you – you still have to acknowledge that those ideas also emerged from somebody in your subject. Your subject has not just been born – the ideas are out there – they exist in the his-tory and practice of your subject. You are showing off what a good student you are when you reference these ideas – when you acknowledge those debates – especially when you do so correctly.

Summary

So, what do I think? Well, I feel all this stuff on plagiarism comes from the wrong angle and I would turn this topic on its head. It isn't about plagiarism and in many ways it isn't about referencing, it's about being honest and having integrity. It is also about community. I reference every single day through sharing on Facebook, re-blogging and re-tweeting on Twitter. I want to acknowledge (and associate myself) when someone has said something I agree with or with something that supports my argument or beliefs. It is positive – and in social media it is inclusive and empowering for the person you're sharing.

We hope that you can see that giving references reveals that you are an engaged, thinking, focused student – yes, you have opinions of your own – but you have also done the reading. When you write with reference to your reading, you are showing that you have understood your subject, you can use sources well and you are joining your academic community – you are joining the conversation.

In our experience, many students plagiarise because they do not understand the convention of referencing – or because they agree with what they are reading … Do not plagiarise by mistake! Give yourself time to read and digest information. Keep good records of your sources and make sure you understand how to reference correctly – both in your writing and in your bibliographies. Plagiarism is treated as a serious academic offence – even when you do it in ignorance or by mistake. If in doubt, explore our Heroes & Villains website – or use the Preventing Plagiarism tutorial (search online). In the learning resources section of that resource, there are small animations that show you how to reference correctly – from a range of sources. Look at these animations and make sure you see and understand what is going on.

Activity

Use your index cards

Every time you read, keep a record – author (date) *title*, place of publication: publisher:

Author(s):

Date:

Title:

Place published:

Publisher:

Key quotes (and page numbers):

Always note these essential details so you can cite them correctly in assignments – and in your bibliographies:

- Record details of your reading on your index cards. Note the information above on one side of the card.
- Experiment: you could note what essay you used the book for; you could note the chapter or paragraph headings – so that you have an outline of the book; you can note a couple of good quotes … The trick is to make this process as useful to you as possible.
- There is software, extensions to browsers and apps for phones, tablets and computers which can also be used.

Preparation for Research Methods and Statistics

Wheeler-Mundy, R. & Bedwell, S. R.

You have come to the end of your journey on Psychology Research Skills. We hope you have enjoyed the module and have mastered the techniques needed to aid your access as a researcher.

By now you should have an understanding of core academic abilities as varied as critical literature reviewing, writing in appropriate academic style, ethical research design and APA style referencing.

This isn't the end of your research journey. The information you have covered so far will provide the foundation for understanding and implementing statistical analyses. This will help you as you are introduced to research methods and statistics in the second half of level 4 and beyond – right up to your dissertation project.

The skills you have developed will also help you in your future careers, even if you don't go into research directly. Look back over the topics you have covered in this text: you now have expertise in working effectively in groups, giving engaging presentations, critically analysing a variety of sources and constructing a persuasive argument.

We wish you luck as you take your next steps as a developing researcher! The next chapter will help you prepare for level 4 Introduction to Research Methods and Statistics.

Rebecca Wheeler-Mundy and Stacey Bedwell

22

Why is my evil lecturer forcing me to learn statistics?

Field, A.

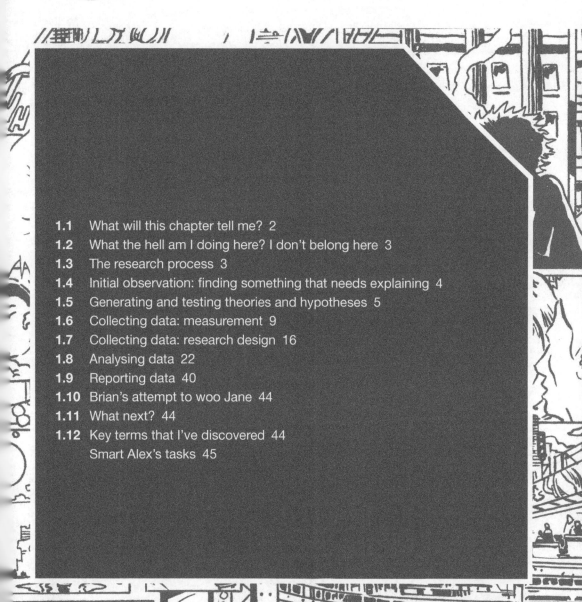

1.1 What will this chapter tell me?

I was born on 21 June 1973. Like most people, I don't remember anything about the first few years of life and, like most children, I went through a phase of driving my dad mad by asking 'Why?' every five seconds. With every question, the word 'dad' got longer and whinier: 'Dad, why is the sky blue?', 'Daaad, why don't worms have legs?', 'Daaaaaaaad, where do babies come from?' Eventually, my dad could take no more and whacked me around the face with a golf club.[1]

My torrent of questions reflected the natural curiosity that children have: we all begin our voyage through life as inquisitive little scientists. At the age of 3, I was at my friend Obe's party (just before he left England to return to Nigeria, much to my distress). It was a hot day, and there was an electric fan blowing cold air around the room. My 'curious little scientist' brain was working through what seemed like a particularly pressing question: 'What happens when you stick your finger in a fan?' The answer, as it turned out, was that it hurts – a lot.[2] At the age of 3, we intuitively know that to answer questions you need to collect data, even if it causes us pain.

My curiosity to explain the world never went away, which is why I'm a scientist. The fact that you're reading this book means that the inquisitive 3-year-old in you is alive and well and wants to answer new and exciting questions, too. To answer these questions you need 'science' and science has a **pilot fish** called 'statistics' that hides under its belly eating ectoparasites. That's why your evil lecturer is forcing you to learn statistics. Statistics is a bit like sticking your finger into a revolving fan blade: sometimes it's very painful, but it does give you answers to interesting questions. I'm going to try to convince you in this chapter that statistics are an important part of doing research. We will overview the whole research process, from why we conduct research in the first place, through how theories are generated, to why we need data to test these theories. If that doesn't convince you to read on then maybe the fact that we discover whether Coca-Cola kills sperm will. Or perhaps not.

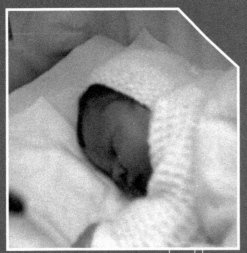

Figure 1.1 When I grow up, please don't let me be a statistics lecturer

1 He was practising in the garden when I unexpectedly wandered behind him at the exact moment he took a back swing. It's rare that a parent enjoys the sound of their child crying, but, on this day, it filled my dad with joy because my wailing was tangible evidence that he hadn't killed me, which he thought he might have done. Had he hit me with the club end rather than the shaft he probably would have. Fortunately (for me, but not for you), I survived, although some might argue that this incident explains the way my brain functions.
2 In the 1970s, fans didn't have helpful protective cages around them to prevent idiotic 3-year-olds sticking their fingers into the blades.

1.2 What the hell am I doing here? I don't belong here ▮▮▮

You're probably wondering why you have bought this book. Maybe you liked the pictures, maybe you fancied doing some weight training (it *is* heavy), or perhaps you needed to reach something in a high place (it *is* thick). The chances are, though, that given the choice of spending your hard-earned cash on a statistics book or something more entertaining (a nice novel, a trip to the cinema, etc.), you'd choose the latter. So, why have you bought the book (or downloaded an illegal PDF of it from someone who has way too much time on their hands if they're scanning 900 pages for fun)? It's likely that you obtained it because you're doing a course on statistics, or you're doing some research, and you need to know how to analyse data. It's possible that you didn't realize when you started your course or research that you'd have to know about statistics but now find yourself inexplicably wading, neck high, through the Victorian sewer that is data analysis. The reason why you're in the mess that you find yourself in is that you have a curious mind. You might have asked yourself questions like why people behave the way they do (psychology) or why behaviours differ across cultures (anthropology), how businesses maximize their profit (business), how the dinosaurs died (palaeontology), whether eating tomatoes protects you against cancer (medicine, biology), whether it is possible to build a quantum computer (physics, chemistry), whether the planet is hotter than it used to be and in what regions (geography, environmental studies). Whatever it is you're studying or researching, the reason why you're studying it is probably that you're interested in answering questions. Scientists are curious people, and you probably are too. However, it might not have occurred to you that to answer interesting questions, you need data and explanations for those data.

The answer to 'What the hell are you doing here?' is simple: to answer interesting questions you need data. One of the reasons why your evil statistics lecturer is forcing you to learn about numbers is that they are a form of data and are vital to the research process. Of course, there are forms of data other than numbers that can be used to test and generate theories. When numbers are involved, the research involves **quantitative methods**, but you can also generate and test theories by analysing language (such as conversations, magazine articles and media broadcasts). This involves **qualitative methods** and it is a topic for another book not written by me. People can get quite passionate about which of these methods is *best*, which is a bit silly because they are complementary, not competing, approaches and there are much more important issues in the world to get upset about. Having said that, all qualitative research is rubbish.[3]

1.3 The research process ▮▮▮

How do you go about answering an interesting question? The research process is broadly summarized in Figure 1.2. You begin with an observation that you want to understand, and this observation could be anecdotal (you've noticed that your cat watches birds when they're on TV but not when jellyfish are on)[4] or could be based on some data (you've got several cat owners to keep diaries of their cat's TV habits and noticed that lots of them watch birds). From your initial observation you consult relevant theories and generate explanations (hypotheses) for those observations, from which you can make predictions. To

How do I do research?

---

3   This is a joke. Like many of my jokes, there are people who won't find it remotely funny. Passions run high between qualitative and quantitative researchers, so its inclusion will likely result in me being hunted down, locked in a room and forced to do discourse analysis by a horde of rabid qualitative researchers.
4   In his younger days my cat actually did climb up and stare at the TV when birds were being shown.

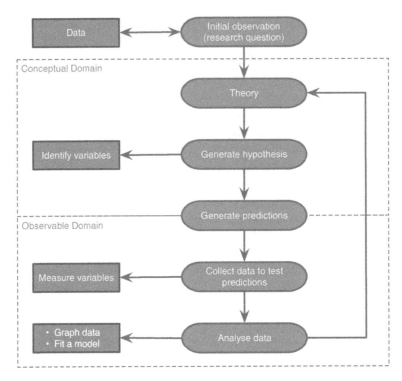

Figure 1.2 The research process

test your predictions you need data. First you collect some relevant data (and to do that you need to identify things that can be measured) and then you analyse those data. The analysis of the data may support your hypothesis, or generate a new one, which, in turn, might lead you to revise the theory. As such, the processes of data collection and analysis and generating theories are intrinsically linked: theories lead to data collection/analysis and data collection/analysis informs theories. This chapter explains this research process in more detail.

1.4 Initial observation: finding something that needs explaining ▐▌▐▌

The first step in Figure 1.2 was to come up with a question that needs an answer. I spend rather more time than I should watching reality TV. Over many years, I used to swear that I wouldn't get hooked on reality TV, and yet year upon year I would find myself glued to the TV screen waiting for the next contestant's meltdown (I am a psychologist, so really this is just research). I used to wonder why there is so much arguing in these shows, and why so many contestants have really unpleasant personalities (my money is on narcissistic personality disorder).[5] A lot of scientific endeavour starts this way: not by watching reality TV, but by observing something in the world and wondering why it happens.

Having made a casual observation about the world (reality TV contestants on the whole have extreme personalities and argue a lot), I need to collect some data to see whether this observation is true (and not a biased observation). To do this, I need to define one or more **variables** to measure that quantify the thing

---

5 This disorder is characterized by (among other things) a grandiose sense of self-importance, arrogance, lack of empathy for others, envy of others and belief that others envy them, excessive fantasies of brilliance or beauty, the need for excessive admiration, and exploitation of others.

I'm trying to measure. There's one variable in this example: the personality of the contestant. I could measure this variable by giving them one of the many well-established questionnaires that measure personality characteristics. Let's say that I did this and I found that 75% of contestants did have narcissistic personality disorder. These data support my observation: a lot of reality TV contestants have extreme personalities.

1.5 Generating and testing theories and hypotheses ▌▌▌▌

The next logical thing to do is to explain these data (Figure 1.2). The first step is to look for relevant theories. A **theory** is an explanation or set of principles that is well substantiated by repeated testing and explains a broad phenomenon. We might begin by looking at theories of narcissistic personality disorder, of which there are currently very few. One theory of personality disorders in general links them to early attachment (put simplistically, the bond formed between a child and their main caregiver). Broadly speaking, a child can form a secure (a good thing) or an insecure (not so good) attachment to their caregiver, and the theory goes that insecure attachment explains later personality disorders (Levy, Johnson, Clouthier, Scala, & Temes, 2015). This is a theory because it is a set of principles (early problems in forming interpersonal bonds) that explains a general broad phenomenon (disorders characterized by dysfunctional interpersonal relations). There is also a critical mass of evidence to support the idea. Theory also tells us that those with narcissistic personality disorder tend to engage in conflict with others despite craving their attention, which perhaps explains their difficulty in forming close bonds.

Given this theory, we might generate a **hypothesis** about our earlier observation (see Jane Superbrain Box 1.1). A hypothesis is a proposed explanation for a fairly narrow phenomenon or set of observations. It is not a guess, but an informed, theory-driven attempt to explain what has been observed. Both theories and hypotheses seek to explain the world, but a theory explains a wide set of phenomena with a small set of well-established principles, whereas a hypothesis typically seeks to explain a narrower phenomenon and is, as yet, untested. Both theories and hypotheses exist in the conceptual domain, and you cannot observe them directly.

To continue the example, having studied the attachment theory of personality disorders, we might decide that this theory implies that people with personality disorders seek out the attention that a TV appearance provides because they lack close interpersonal relationships. From this we can generate a hypothesis: people with narcissistic personality disorder use reality TV to satisfy their craving for attention from others. This is a conceptual statement that explains our original observation (that rates of narcissistic personality disorder are high on reality TV shows).

To test this hypothesis, we need to move from the conceptual domain into the observable domain. That is, we need to operationalize our hypothesis in a way that enables us to collect and analyse data that have a bearing on the hypothesis (Figure 1.2). We do this using predictions. Predictions emerge from a hypothesis (Misconception Mutt 1.1), and transform it from something unobservable into something that is. If our hypothesis is that people with narcissistic personality disorder use reality TV to satisfy their craving for attention from others, then a prediction we could make based on this hypothesis is that people with narcissistic personality disorder are more likely to audition for reality TV than those without. In making this prediction we can move from the conceptual domain into the observable domain, where we can collect evidence.

In this example, our prediction is that people with narcissistic personality disorder are more likely to audition for reality TV than those without. We can measure this prediction by getting a team of clinical psychologists to interview each person at a reality TV audition and diagnose them as having narcissistic personality disorder or not. The population rates of narcissistic personality disorder are

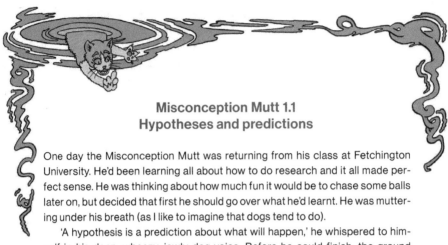

Misconception Mutt 1.1
Hypotheses and predictions

One day the Misconception Mutt was returning from his class at Fetchington University. He'd been learning all about how to do research and it all made perfect sense. He was thinking about how much fun it would be to chase some balls later on, but decided that first he should go over what he'd learnt. He was muttering under his breath (as I like to imagine that dogs tend to do).

'A hypothesis is a prediction about what will happen,' he whispered to himself in his deep, wheezy, jowly dog voice. Before he could finish, the ground before him became viscous, as though the earth had transformed into liquid. A slightly irritated-looking ginger cat rose slowly from the puddle.

'Don't even think about chasing me,' he said in his whiny cat voice.

The mutt twitched as he inhibited the urge to chase the cat. 'Who are you?' he asked.

'I am the Correcting Cat,' said the cat wearily. 'I travel the ether trying to correct people's statistical misconceptions. It's very hard work, there are a lot of misconceptions about.'

The dog raised an eyebrow.

'For example,' continued the cat, 'you just said that a hypothesis is a prediction, but it is not.' The dog looked puzzled. 'A hypothesis is an explanatory statement about something, it is not itself observable. The prediction is not the hypothesis, it is something derived from the hypothesis that operationalizes it so that you can observe things that help you to determine the plausibility of the hypothesis.' With that, the cat descended back into the ground.

'What a smart-arse,' the dog thought to himself. 'I hope I never see him again.'

about 1%, so we'd be able to see whether the ratio of narcissistic personality disorder to not is higher at the audition than in the general population. If it is higher then our prediction is correct: a disproportionate number of people with narcissistic personality disorder turned up at the audition. Our prediction, in turn, tells us something about the hypothesis from which it derived.

This is tricky stuff, so let's look at another example. Imagine that, based on a different theory, we generated a different hypothesis. I mentioned earlier that people with narcissistic personality disorder tend to engage in conflict, so a different hypothesis is that producers of reality TV shows select people who have narcissistic personality disorder to be contestants because they believe that conflict makes good TV. As before, to test this hypothesis we need to bring it into the observable domain by generating a prediction from it. The prediction would be that (assuming no bias in the number of people with narcissistic personality disorder applying for the show) a disproportionate number of people with narcissistic personality disorder will be selected by producers to go on the show.

Jane Superbrain 1.1
When is a prediction not a prediction? ▮▮▮▮

A good theory should allow us to make statements about the state of the world. Statements about the world are good things: they allow us to make sense of our world, and to make decisions that affect our future. One current example is global warming. Being able to make a definitive statement that global warming is happening, and that it is caused by certain practices in society, allows us to change these practices and, hopefully, avert catastrophe. However, not all statements can be tested using science. Scientific statements are ones that can be verified with reference to empirical evidence, whereas non-scientific statements are ones that cannot be empirically tested. So, statements such as 'The Led Zeppelin reunion concert in London in 2007 was the best gig ever,'[6] 'Lindt chocolate is the best food' and 'This is the worst statistics book in the world' are all non-scientific; they cannot be proved or disproved. Scientific statements can be confirmed or disconfirmed empirically. 'Watching *Curb Your Enthusiasm* makes you happy,' 'Having sex increases levels of the neurotransmitter dopamine' and 'Velociraptors ate meat' are all things that can be tested empirically (provided you can quantify and measure the variables concerned). Non-scientific statements can sometimes be altered to become scientific statements, so 'The Beatles were the most influential band ever' is non-scientific (because it is probably impossible to quantify 'influence' in any meaningful way) but by changing the statement to 'The Beatles were the best-selling band ever,' it becomes testable (we can collect data about worldwide album sales and establish whether the Beatles have, in fact, sold more records than any other music artist). Karl Popper, the famous philosopher of science, believed that non-scientific statements were nonsense and had no place in science. Good theories and hypotheses should, therefore, produce predictions that are scientific statements.

Imagine we collected the data in Table 1.1, which shows how many people auditioning to be on a reality TV show had narcissistic personality disorder or not. In total, 7662 people turned up for the audition. Our first prediction (derived from our first hypothesis) was that the percentage of people with narcissistic personality disorder will be higher at the audition than the general level in the population. We can see in the table that of the 7662 people at the audition, 854 were diagnosed with the disorder; this is about 11% (854/7662 × 100), which is much higher than the 1% we'd expect in the general

Table 1.1   The number of people at the TV audition split by whether they had narcissistic personality disorder and whether they were selected as contestants by the producers

	No Disorder	Disorder	Total
Selected	3	9	12
Rejected	6805	845	7650
Total	6808	854	7662

6 It was pretty awesome actually.

population. Therefore, prediction 1 is correct, which in turn supports hypothesis 1. The second prediction was that the producers of reality TV have a bias towards choosing people with narcissistic personality disorder. If we look at the 12 contestants that they selected, 9 of them had the disorder (a massive 75%). If the producers did not have a bias we would have expected only 11% of the contestants to have the disorder (the same rate as was found when we considered everyone who turned up for the audition). The data are in line with prediction 2 which supports our second hypothesis. Therefore, my initial observation that contestants have personality disorders was verified by data, and then using theory I generated specific hypotheses that were operationalized by generating predictions that could be tested using data. Data are *very* important.

I would now be smugly sitting in my office with a contented grin on my face because my hypotheses were well supported by the data. Perhaps I would quit while I was ahead and retire. It's more likely, though, that having solved one great mystery, my excited mind would turn to another. I would lock myself in a room to watch more reality TV. I might wonder at why contestants with narcissistic personality disorder, despite their obvious character flaws, enter a situation that will put them under intense public scrutiny.[7] Days later, the door would open, and a stale odour would waft out like steam rising from the New York subway. Through this green cloud, my bearded face would emerge, my eyes squinting at the shards of light that cut into my pupils. Stumbling forwards, I would open my mouth to lay waste to my scientific rivals with my latest profound hypothesis: 'Contestants with narcissistic personality disorder believe that they will win'. I would croak before collapsing on the floor. The prediction from this hypothesis is that if I ask the contestants if they think that they will win, the people with a personality disorder will say 'yes'.

Let's imagine I tested my hypothesis by measuring contestants' expectations of success in the show, by asking them, 'Do you think you will win?' Let's say that 7 of 9 contestants with narcissistic personality disorder said that they thought that they would win, which confirms my hypothesis. At this point I might start to try to bring my hypotheses together into a theory of reality TV contestants that revolves around the idea that people with narcissistic personalities are drawn towards this kind of show because it fulfils their need for approval and they have unrealistic expectations about their likely success because they don't realize how unpleasant their personalities are to other people. In parallel, producers tend to select contestants with narcissistic tendencies because they tend to generate interpersonal conflict.

One part of my theory is untested, which is the bit about contestants with narcissistic personalities not realizing how others perceive their personality. I could operationalize this hypothesis through a prediction that if I ask these contestants whether their personalities were different from those of other people they would say 'no'. As before, I would collect more data and ask the contestants with narcissistic personality disorder whether they believed that their personalities were different from the norm. Imagine that all 9 of them said that they thought their personalities *were* different from the norm. These data contradict my hypothesis. This is known as **falsification**, which is the act of disproving a hypothesis or theory.

It's unlikely that we would be the only people interested in why individuals who go on reality TV have extreme personalities. Imagine that these other researchers discovered that: (1) people with narcissistic personality disorder think that they are more interesting than others; (2) they also think that they deserve success more than others; and (3) they also think that others like them because they have 'special' personalities.

This additional research is even worse news for my theory: if contestants didn't realize that they had a personality different from the norm, then you wouldn't expect them to think that they were more interesting than others, and you certainly wouldn't expect them to think that others will *like* their unusual personalities. In general, this means that this part of my theory sucks: it cannot explain all of the data,

---

7 One of the things I like about many reality TV shows in the UK is that the winners are very often nice people, and the odious people tend to get voted out quickly, which gives me faith that humanity favours the nice.

predictions from the theory are not supported by subsequent data, and it cannot explain other research findings. At this point I would start to feel intellectually inadequate and people would find me curled up on my desk in floods of tears, wailing and moaning about my failing career (no change there then).

At this point, a rival scientist, Fester Ingpant-Stain, appears on the scene adapting my theory to suggest that the problem is not that personality-disordered contestants don't realize that they have a personality disorder (or at least a personality that is unusual), but that they falsely believe that this special personality is perceived positively by other people. One prediction from this model is that if personality-disordered contestants are asked to evaluate what other people think of them, then they will overestimate other people's positive perceptions. You guessed it, Fester Ingpant-Stain collected yet more data. He asked each contestant to fill out a questionnaire evaluating all of the other contestants' personalities, and also to complete the questionnaire about themselves but answering from the perspective of each of their housemates. (So, for every contestant there is a measure of what they thought of every other contestant, and also a measure of what they believed every other contestant thought of them.) He found out that the contestants with personality disorders did overestimate their housemates' opinions of them; conversely, the contestants without personality disorders had relatively accurate impressions of what others thought of them. These data, irritating as it would be for me, support Fester Ingpant-Stain's theory more than mine: contestants with personality disorders do realize that they have unusual personalities but believe that these characteristics are ones that others would feel positive about. Fester Ingpant-Stain's theory is quite good: it explains the initial observations and brings together a range of research findings. The end result of this whole process (and my career) is that we should be able to make a general statement about the state of the world. In this case we could state 'Reality TV contestants who have personality disorders overestimate how much other people like their personality characteristics'.

SELF TEST

Based on what you have read in this section,
what qualities do you think a scientific theory should have?

1.6 Collecting data: measurement ▎▎▎▎

In looking at the process of generating theories and hypotheses, we have seen the importance of data in testing those hypotheses or deciding between competing theories. This section looks at data collection in more detail. First we'll look at measurement.

1.6.1 Independent and dependent variables ▎▎▎▎

To test hypotheses we need to measure variables. Variables are things that can change (or vary); they might vary between people (e.g., IQ, behaviour) or locations (e.g., unemployment) or even time (e.g., mood, profit, number of cancerous cells). Most hypotheses can be expressed in terms of two variables: a proposed cause and a proposed outcome. For example, if we take the scientific statement, 'Coca-Cola is an effective spermicide'[8] then the proposed cause is 'Coca-Cola' and the proposed effect is dead

---

8 Actually, there is a long-standing urban myth that a post-coital douche with the contents of a bottle of Coke is an effective contraceptive. Unbelievably, this hypothesis has been tested and Coke does affect sperm motility (movement), and some types of Coke are more effective than others – Diet Coke is best, apparently (Umpierre, Hill & Anderson, 1985). In case you decide to try this method out, I feel it worth mentioning that despite the effects on sperm motility a Coke douche is ineffective at preventing pregnancy.

Cramming Sam's Tips
Variables

When doing and reading research you're likely to encounter these terms:

- *Independent variable*: A variable thought to be the cause of some effect. This term is usually used in experimental research to describe a variable that the experimenter has manipulated.
- *Dependent variable*: A variable thought to be affected by changes in an independent variable. You can think of this variable as an outcome.
- *Predictor variable*: A variable thought to predict an outcome variable. This term is basically another way of saying 'independent variable'. (Although some people won't like me saying that; I think life would be easier if we talked only about predictors and outcomes.)
- *Outcome variable*: A variable thought to change as a function of changes in a predictor variable. For the sake of an easy life this term could be synonymous with 'dependent variable'.

sperm. Both the cause and the outcome are variables: for the cause we could vary the type of drink, and for the outcome, these drinks will kill different amounts of sperm. The key to testing scientific statements is to measure these two variables.

A variable that we think is a cause is known as an **independent variable** (because its value does not depend on any other variables). A variable that we think is an effect is called a **dependent variable** because the value of this variable depends on the cause (independent variable). These terms are very closely tied to experimental methods in which the cause is manipulated by the experimenter (as we will see in Section 1.7.2). However, researchers can't always manipulate variables (for example, if you wanted see whether smoking causes lung cancer you wouldn't lock a bunch of people in a room for 30 years and force them to smoke). Instead, they sometimes use correlational methods (Section 1.7), for which it doesn't make sense to talk of dependent and independent variables because all variables are essentially dependent variables. I prefer to use the terms **predictor variable** and **outcome variable** in place of dependent and independent variable. This is not a personal whimsy: in experimental work the cause (independent variable) is a predictor, and the effect (dependent variable) is an outcome, and in correlational work we can talk of one or more (predictor) variables predicting (statistically at least) one or more outcome variables.

1.6.2 Levels of measurement ▌▌▌

Variables can take on many different forms and levels of sophistication. The relationship between what is being measured and the numbers that represent what is being measured is known as the **level of measurement**. Broadly speaking, variables can be categorical or continuous, and can have different levels of measurement.

A **categorical variable** is made up of categories. A categorical variable that you should be familiar with already is your species (e.g., human, domestic cat, fruit bat, etc.). You are a human or a cat or a fruit bat: you cannot be a bit of a cat and a bit of a bat, and neither a batman nor (despite many fantasies to the contrary) a catwoman exist (not even one in a PVC suit). A categorical variable is one that names distinct entities. In its simplest form it names just two distinct types of things, for example male or female. This is known as a **binary variable**. Other examples of binary variables are being alive or dead, pregnant or not, and responding 'yes' or 'no' to a question. In all cases there are just two categories and an entity can be placed into only one of the two categories. When two things that are equivalent in some sense are given the same name (or number), but there are more than two possibilities, the variable is said to be a **nominal variable**.

It should be obvious that if the variable is made up of names it is pointless to do arithmetic on them (if you multiply a human by a cat, you do not get a hat). However, sometimes numbers are used to denote categories. For example, the numbers worn by players in a sports team. In rugby, the numbers on shirts denote specific field positions, so the number 10 is always worn by the fly-half[9] and the number 2 is always the hooker (the ugly-looking player at the front of the scrum). These numbers do not tell us anything other than what position the player plays. We could equally have shirts with FH and H instead of 10 and 2. A number 10 player is not necessarily better than a number 2 (most managers would not want their fly-half stuck in the front of the scrum!). It is equally daft to try to do arithmetic with nominal scales where the categories are denoted by numbers: the number 10 takes penalty kicks, and if the coach found that his number 10 was injured, he would not get his number 4 to give number 6

Jane Superbrain 1.2
Self-report data ▌▌▌▌

A lot of self-report data are ordinal. Imagine two judges on *The X Factor* were asked to rate Billie's singing on a 10-point scale. We might be confident that a judge who gives a rating of 10 found Billie more talented than one who gave a rating of 2, but can we be certain that the first judge found her five times more talented than the second? What if both judges gave a rating of 8; could we be sure that they found her equally talented? Probably not: their ratings will depend on their subjective feelings about what constitutes talent (the quality of singing? showmanship? dancing?). For these reasons, in any situation in which we ask people to rate something subjective (e.g., their preference for a product, their confidence about an answer, how much they have understood some medical instructions) we should probably regard these data as ordinal, although many scientists do not.

---

9 Unlike, for example, NFL football where a quarterback could wear any number from 1 to 19.

a piggy-back and then take the kick. The only way that nominal data can be used is to consider frequencies. For example, we could look at how frequently number 10s score compared to number 4s.

So far, the categorical variables we have considered have been unordered (e.g., different brands of Coke with which you're trying to kill sperm), but they can be ordered too (e.g., increasing concentrations of Coke with which you're trying to skill sperm). When categories are ordered, the variable is known as an **ordinal variable**. Ordinal data tell us not only that things have occurred, but also the order in which they occurred. However, these data tell us nothing about the differences between values. In TV shows like *The X Factor, American Idol*, and *The Voice*, hopeful singers compete to win a recording contract. They are hugely popular shows, which could (if you take a depressing view) reflect the fact that Western society values 'luck' more than hard work.[10] Imagine that the three winners of a particular *X Factor* series were Billie, Freema and Elizabeth. The names of the winners don't provide any information about where they came in the contest; however, labelling them according to their performance does – first, second and third. These categories are ordered. In using ordered categories we now know that the woman who won was better than the women who came second and third. We still know nothing about the differences between categories, though. We don't, for example, know how much better the winner was than the runners-up: Billie might have been an easy victor, getting many more votes than Freema and Elizabeth, or it might have been a very close contest that she won by only a single vote. Ordinal data, therefore, tell us more than nominal data (they tell us the order in which things happened) but they still do not tell us about the differences between points on a scale.

The next level of measurement moves us away from categorical variables and into continuous variables. A **continuous variable** is one that gives us a score for each person and can take on any value on the measurement scale that we are using. The first type of continuous variable that you might encounter is an **interval variable**. Interval data are considerably more useful than ordinal data, and most of the statistical tests in this book rely on having data measured at this level at least. To say that data are interval, we must be certain that equal intervals on the scale represent equal differences in the property being measured. For example, on www.ratemyprofessors.com, students are encouraged to rate their lecturers on several dimensions (some of the lecturers' rebuttals of their negative evaluations are worth a look). Each dimension (helpfulness, clarity, etc.) is evaluated using a 5-point scale. For this scale to be interval it must be the case that the difference between helpfulness ratings of 1 and 2 is the same as the difference between (say) 3 and 4, or 4 and 5. Similarly, the difference in helpfulness between ratings of 1 and 3 should be identical to the difference between ratings of 3 and 5. Variables like this that look interval (and are treated as interval) are often ordinal – see Jane Superbrain Box 1.2.

Ratio variables go a step further than interval data by requiring that in addition to the measurement scale meeting the requirements of an interval variable, the ratios of values along the scale should be meaningful. For this to be true, the scale must have a true and meaningful zero point. In our lecturer ratings this would mean that a lecturer rated as 4 would be twice as helpful as a lecturer rated with a 2 (who would, in turn, be twice as helpful as a lecturer rated as 1). The time to respond to something is a good example of a ratio variable. When we measure a reaction time, not only is it true that, say, the difference between 300 and 350 ms (a difference of 50 ms) is the same as the difference between 210 and 260 ms or between 422 and 472 ms, but it is also true that distances along the scale are divisible: a reaction time of 200 ms is twice as long as a reaction time of 100 ms and half as long as a reaction time of 400 ms. Time also has a meaningful zero point: 0 ms does mean a complete absence of time.

Continuous variables can be, well, continuous (obviously) but also discrete. This is quite a tricky distinction (Jane Superbrain Box 1.3). A truly continuous variable can be measured to any level of

---

10 I am in no way bitter about spending years learning musical instruments and trying to create original music, only to be beaten to musical fame and fortune by 15-year-olds who can sing, sort of.

precision, whereas a **discrete variable** can take on only certain values (usually whole numbers) on the scale. What does this actually mean? Well, our example of rating lecturers on a 5-point scale is an example of a discrete variable. The range of the scale is 1–5, but you can enter only values of 1, 2, 3, 4 or 5; you cannot enter a value of 4.32 or 2.18. Although a continuum exists underneath the scale (i.e., a rating of 3.24 makes sense), the actual values that the variable takes on are limited. A continuous variable would be something like age, which can be measured at an infinite level of precision (you could be 34 years, 7 months, 21 days, 10 hours, 55 minutes, 10 seconds, 100 milliseconds, 63 microseconds, 1 nanosecond old).

1.6.3 Measurement error ▮▮▮▮

It's one thing to measure variables, but it's another thing to measure them accurately. Ideally we want our measure to be calibrated such that values have the same meaning over time and across situations. Weight is one example: we would expect to weigh the same amount regardless of who weighs us, or where we take the measurement (assuming it's on Earth and not in an anti-gravity chamber). Sometimes, variables can be measured directly (profit, weight, height) but in other cases we are forced to use indirect measures such as self-report, questionnaires, and computerized tasks (to name a few).

It's been a while since I mentioned sperm, so let's go back to our Coke as a spermicide example. Imagine we took some Coke and some water and added them to two test tubes of sperm. After several minutes, we measured the motility (movement) of the sperm in the two samples and discovered no difference. A few years passed, as you might expect given that Coke and sperm rarely top scientists' research lists, before another scientist, Dr Jack Q. Late, replicated the study. Dr Late found that sperm motility

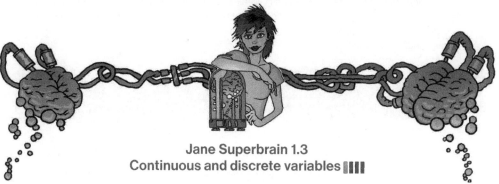

Jane Superbrain 1.3
Continuous and discrete variables ▮▮▮▮

The distinction between continuous and discrete variables can be blurred. For one thing, continuous variables can be measured in discrete terms; for example, when we measure age we rarely use nanoseconds but use years (or possibly years and months). In doing so we turn a continuous variable into a discrete one (the only acceptable values are years). Also, we often treat discrete variables as if they were continuous. For example, the number of boyfriends/girlfriends that you have had is a discrete variable (it will be, in all but the very weirdest cases, a whole number). However, you might read a magazine that says 'The average number of boyfriends that women in their 20s have has increased from 4.6 to 8.9'. This assumes that the variable is continuous, and of course these averages are meaningless: no one in their sample actually had 8.9 boyfriends.

Cramming Sam's Tips
Levels of measurement

- Variables can be split into categorical and continuous, and within these types there are different levels of measurement:
- Categorical (entities are divided into distinct categories):

  ○ Binary variable: There are only two categories (e.g., dead or alive).
  ○ Nominal variable: There are more than two categories (e.g., whether someone is an omnivore, vegetarian, vegan, or fruitarian).
  ○ Ordinal variable: The same as a nominal variable but the categories have a logical order (e.g., whether people got a fail, a pass, a merit or a distinction in their exam).

- Continuous (entities get a distinct score):

  ○ Interval variable: Equal intervals on the variable represent equal differences in the property being measured (e.g., the difference between 6 and 8 is equivalent to the difference between 13 and 15).
  ○ Ratio variable: The same as an interval variable, but the ratios of scores on the scale must also make sense (e.g., a score of 16 on an anxiety scale means that the person is, in reality, twice as anxious as someone scoring 8). For this to be true, the scale must have a meaningful zero point.

was worse in the Coke sample. There are two measurement-related issues that could explain his success and our failure: (1) Dr Late might have used more Coke in the test tubes (sperm might need a critical mass of Coke before they are affected); (2) Dr Late measured the outcome (motility) differently than us.

The former point explains why chemists and physicists have devoted many hours to developing standard units of measurement. If you had reported that you'd used 100ml of Coke and 5ml of sperm, then Dr Late could have ensured that he had used the same amount – because millilitres are a standard unit of measurement – we would know that Dr Late used exactly the same amount of Coke that we used. Direct measurements such as the millilitre provide an objective standard: 100ml of a liquid is known to be twice as much as only 50ml.

The second reason for the difference in results between the studies could have been to do with how sperm motility was measured. Perhaps in our original study we measured motility using absorption spectrophotometry, whereas Dr Late used laser light-scattering techniques.[11] Perhaps his measure is more sensitive than ours.

---

11 In the course of writing this chapter I have discovered more than I think is healthy about the measurement of sperm motility.

There will often be a discrepancy between the numbers we use to represent the thing we're measuring and the actual value of the thing we're measuring (i.e., the value we would get if we could measure it directly). This discrepancy is known as **measurement error**. For example, imagine that you know as an absolute truth that you weigh 83kg. One day you step on the bathroom scales and they read 80kg. There is a difference of 3kg between your actual weight and the weight given by your measurement tool (the scales): this is a measurement error of 3kg. Although properly calibrated bathroom scales should produce only very small measurement errors (despite what we might want to believe when it says we have gained 3kg), self-report measures will produce larger measurement error because factors other than the one you're trying to measure will influence how people respond to our measures. For example, if you were completing a questionnaire that asked you whether you had stolen from a shop, would you admit it, or might you be tempted to conceal this fact?

1.6.4 Validity and reliability ▍▍▍▍

One way to try to ensure that measurement error is kept to a minimum is to determine properties of the measure that give us confidence that it is doing its job properly. The first property is **validity**, which is whether an instrument measures what it sets out to measure. The second is **reliability**, which is whether an instrument can be interpreted consistently across different situations.

Validity refers to whether an instrument measures what it was designed to measure (e.g., does your lecturer helpfulness rating scale actually measure lecturers' helpfulness?); a device for measuring sperm *motility* that actually measures sperm *count* is not valid. Things like reaction times and physiological measures are valid in the sense that a reaction time does, in fact, measure the time taken to react and skin conductance does measure the conductivity of your skin. However, if we're using these things to infer other things (e.g., using skin conductance to measure anxiety), then they will be valid only if there are no other factors other than the one we're interested in that can influence them.

Criterion validity is whether you can establish that an instrument measures what it claims to measure through comparison to objective criteria. In an ideal world, you assess this by relating scores on your measure to real-world observations. For example, we could take an objective measure of how helpful lecturers were and compare these observations to students' ratings of helpfulness on ratemyprofessor.com. When data are recorded simultaneously using the new instrument and existing criteria, then this is said to assess **concurrent validity**; when data from the new instrument are used to predict observations at a later point in time, this is said to assess **predictive validity**.

Assessing criterion validity (whether concurrently or predictively) is often impractical because objective criteria that can be measured easily may not exist. Also, with measuring attitudes, you might be interested in the person's perception of reality and not reality itself (you might not care whether a person *is* a psychopath but whether they *think* they are a psychopath). With self-report measures/ questionnaires we can also assess the degree to which individual items represent the construct being measured, and cover the full range of the construct (**content validity**).

Validity is a necessary but not sufficient condition of a measure. A second consideration is reliability, which is the ability of the measure to produce the same results under the same conditions. To be valid the instrument must first be reliable. The easiest way to assess reliability is to test the same group of people twice: a reliable instrument will produce similar scores at both points in time (**test–retest reliability**). Sometimes, however, you will want to measure something that does vary over time (e.g., moods, blood-sugar levels, productivity). Statistical methods can also be used to determine reliability (we will discover these in Chapter 18).

SELF TEST
What is the difference between reliability and validity?

1.7 Collecting data: research design ▮▮▮▮

We've looked at the question of *what* to measure and discovered that to answer scientific questions we measure variables (which can be collections of numbers or words). We also saw that to get accurate answers we need accurate measures. We move on now to look at research design: *how* data are collected. If we simplify things quite a lot then there are two ways to test a hypothesis: either by observing what naturally happens, or by manipulating some aspect of the environment and observing the effect it has on the variable that interests us. In **correlational** or **cross-sectional research** we observe what naturally goes on in the world without directly interfering with it, whereas in **experimental research** we manipulate one variable to see its effect on another.

1.7.1 Correlational research methods ▮▮▮▮

In correlational research we observe natural events; we can do this by either taking a snapshot of many variables at a single point in time, or by measuring variables repeatedly at different time points (known as **longitudinal research**). For example, we might measure pollution levels in a stream and the numbers of certain types of fish living there; lifestyle variables (smoking, exercise, food intake) and disease (cancer, diabetes); workers' job satisfaction under different managers; or children's school performance across regions with different demographics. Correlational research provides a very natural view of the question we're researching because we're not influencing what happens and the measures of the variables should not be biased by the researcher being there (this is an important aspect of **ecological validity**).

What's the difference between experimental and correlational research?

At the risk of sounding like I'm absolutely obsessed with using Coke as a contraceptive (I'm not, but my discovery that people in the 1950s and 1960s actually tried this has, I admit, intrigued me), let's return to that example. If we wanted to answer the question, 'Is Coke an effective contraceptive?' we could administer questionnaires about sexual practices (quantity of sexual activity, use of contraceptives, use of fizzy drinks as contraceptives, pregnancy, etc.). By looking at these variables, we could see which variables correlate with pregnancy and, in particular, whether those reliant on Coca-Cola as a form of contraceptive were more likely to end up pregnant than those using other contraceptives, and less likely than those using no contraceptives at all. This is the only way to answer a question like this because we cannot manipulate any of these variables particularly easily. Even if we could, it would be totally unethical to insist on some people using Coke as a contraceptive (or indeed to do anything that would make a person likely to produce a child that they didn't intend to produce). However, there is a price to pay, which relates to causality: correlational research tells us nothing about the causal influence of variables.

1.7.2 Experimental research methods ▮▮▮▮

Most scientific questions imply a causal link between variables; we have seen already that dependent and independent variables are named such that a causal connection is implied (the dependent variable *depends* on the independent variable). Sometimes the causal link is very obvious in the research question, 'Does low self-esteem cause dating anxiety?' Sometimes the implication might be subtler; for example, in 'Is dating anxiety all in the mind?' the implication is that a person's mental outlook causes them to be anxious when dating. Even when the cause–effect relationship is not explicitly stated, most research questions can be broken down into a proposed cause (in this case, mental outlook) and a proposed outcome (dating anxiety). Both the cause and the outcome are variables: for the cause, some people will perceive themselves in a negative way (so it is something that varies); and, for the outcome, some people will get more anxious on dates than others (again, this is something that varies). The key to answering the research question is to uncover how the proposed cause and the proposed outcome relate to each other; are the people who have a low opinion of themselves the same people who are more anxious on dates?

David Hume, an influential philosopher, defined a cause as 'An object precedent and contiguous to another, and where all the objects resembling the former are placed in like relations of precedency and contiguity to those objects that resemble the latter' (1739–40/1965).[12] This definition implies that (1) the cause needs to precede the effect, and (2) causality is equated to high degrees of correlation between contiguous events. In our dating example, to infer that low self-esteem caused dating anxiety, it would be sufficient to find that low self-esteem and feeling anxious when on a date co-occur, and that the low self-esteem emerged before the dating anxiety did.

In correlational research variables are often measured simultaneously. The first problem with doing this is that it provides no information about the contiguity between different variables: we might find from a questionnaire study that people with low self-esteem also have dating anxiety but we wouldn't know whether it was the low self-esteem or the dating anxiety that came first. Longitudinal research addresses this issue to some extent, but there is still a problem with Hume's idea that causality can be inferred from corroborating evidence, which is that it doesn't distinguish between what you might call an 'accidental' conjunction and a causal one. For example, it could be that both low self-esteem and dating anxiety are caused by a third variable (e.g., poor social skills which might make you feel generally worthless but also puts pressure on you in dating situations). Therefore, low self-esteem and dating anxiety do always co-occur (meeting Hume's definition of cause) but only because poor social skills causes them both.

This example illustrates an important limitation of correlational research: the **tertium quid** ('A third person or thing of indeterminate character'). For example, a correlation has been found between having breast implants and suicide (Koot, Peeters, Granath, Grobbee, & Nyren, 2003). However, it is unlikely that having breast implants causes you to commit suicide – presumably, there is an external factor (or factors) that causes both; for example, low self-esteem might lead you to have breast implants and also attempt suicide. These extraneous factors are sometimes called **confounding variables**, or confounds for short.

The shortcomings of Hume's definition led John Stuart Mill (1865) to suggest that, in addition to a correlation between events, all other explanations of the cause–effect relationship must be ruled out. To rule out confounding variables, Mill proposed that an effect should be present when the cause is present and that when the cause is absent, the effect should be absent also. In other words, the only way to infer causality is through comparing two controlled situations: one in which the cause is present and one in which the cause is absent. This is what *experimental methods* strive to do: to provide a comparison of situations (usually called *treatments* or *conditions*) in which the proposed cause is present or absent.

---

12 As you might imagine, his view was a lot more complicated than this definition alone, but let's not get sucked down that particular wormhole.

As a simple case, we might want to look at the effect of feedback style on learning about statistics. I might, therefore, randomly split[13] some students into three different groups, in which I change my style of feedback in the seminars on my course:

- **Group 1 (supportive feedback):** During seminars I congratulate all students in this group on their hard work and success. Even when they get things wrong, I am supportive and say things like 'that was very nearly the right answer, you're coming along really well' and then give them a nice piece of chocolate.
- **Group 2 (harsh feedback):** This group receives seminars in which I give relentless verbal abuse to all of the students even when they give the correct answer. I demean their contributions and am patronizing and dismissive of everything they say. I tell students that they are stupid, worthless, and shouldn't be doing the course at all. In other words, this group receives normal university-style seminars.☺
- **Group 3 (no feedback):** Students are not praised or punished, instead I give them no feedback at all.

The thing that I have manipulated is the feedback style (supportive, harsh or none). As we have seen, this variable is known as the independent variable and, in this situation, it is said to have three levels, because it has been manipulated in three ways (i.e., the feedback style has been split into three types: supportive, harsh and none). The outcome in which I am interested is statistical ability, and I could measure this variable using a statistics exam after the last seminar. As we have seen, this outcome variable is the dependent variable because we assume that these scores will depend upon the type of teaching method used (the independent variable). The critical thing here is the inclusion of the 'no feedback' group because this is a group in which our proposed cause (feedback) is absent, and we can compare the outcome in this group against the two situations in which the proposed cause is present. If the statistics scores are different in each of the feedback groups (cause is present) compared to the group for which no feedback was given (cause is absent), then this difference can be attributed to the type of feedback used. In other words, the style of feedback used caused a difference in statistics scores (Jane Superbrain Box 1.4).

1.7.3 Two methods of data collection ▌▌▌

When we use an experiment to collect data, there are two ways to manipulate the independent variable. The first is to test different entities. This method is the one described above, in which different groups of entities take part in each experimental condition (a **between-groups, between-subjects,** or **independent design**). An alternative is to manipulate the independent variable using the same entities. In our motivation example, this means that we give a group of students supportive feedback for a few weeks and test their statistical abilities and then give this same group harsh feedback for a few weeks before testing them again and, then, finally, give them no feedback and test them for a third time (a **within-subject** or **repeated-measures design**). As you will discover, the way in which the data are collected determines the type of test that is used to analyse the data.

1.7.4 Two types of variation ▌▌▌

Imagine we were trying to see whether you could train chimpanzees to run the economy. In one training phase they are sat in front of a chimp-friendly computer and press buttons that change various parameters of the economy; once these parameters have been changed a figure appears on the screen

---

13 This random assignment of students is important, but we'll get to that later.

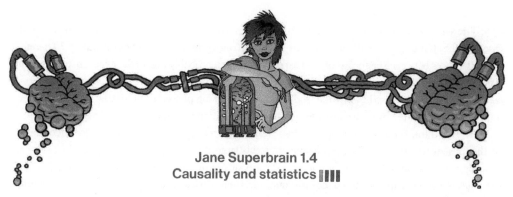

Jane Superbrain 1.4
Causality and statistics ▮▮▮▮

People sometimes get confused and think that certain statistical procedures allow causal inferences and others don't. This isn't true, it's the fact that in experiments we manipulate the causal variable systematically to see its effect on an outcome (the effect). In correlational research we observe the co-occurrence of variables; we do not manipulate the causal variable first and then measure the effect, therefore we cannot compare the effect when the causal variable is present against when it is absent. In short, we cannot say which variable causes a change in the other; we can merely say that the variables co-occur in a certain way. The reason why some people think that certain statistical tests allow causal inferences is that, historically, certain tests (e.g., ANOVA, t-tests, etc.) have been used to analyse experimental research, whereas others (e.g., regression, correlation) have been used to analyse correlational research (Cronbach, 1957). As you'll discover, these statistical procedures are, in fact, mathematically identical.

indicating the economic growth resulting from those parameters. Now, chimps can't read (I don't think) so this feedback is meaningless. A second training phase is the same, except that if the economic growth is good, they get a banana (if growth is bad they do not) – this feedback is valuable to the average chimp. This is a repeated-measures design with two conditions: the same chimps participate in condition 1 *and* in condition 2.

Let's take a step back and think what would happen if we did *not* introduce an experimental manipulation (i.e., there were no bananas in the second training phase, so condition 1 and condition 2 were identical). If there is no experimental manipulation then we expect a chimp's behaviour to be similar in both conditions. We expect this because external factors such as age, sex, IQ, motivation and arousal will be the same for both conditions (a chimp's biological sex, etc. will not change from when they are tested in condition 1 to when they are tested in condition 2). If the performance measure (i.e., our test of how well they run the economy) is reliable, and the variable or characteristic that we are measuring (in this case ability to run an economy) remains stable over time, then a participant's performance in condition 1 should be very highly related to their performance in condition 2. So, chimps who score highly in condition 1 will also score highly in condition 2, and those who have low scores for condition 1 will have low scores in condition 2. However, performance won't be *identical*, there will be small differences in performance created by unknown factors. This variation in performance is known as **unsystematic variation**.

If we introduce an experimental manipulation (i.e., provide bananas as feedback in one of the training sessions), then we do something different to participants in condition 1 than in condition 2. So, the *only* difference between conditions 1 and 2 is the manipulation that the experimenter has made (in this case that the chimps get bananas as a positive reward in one condition but not in the other).[14] Therefore, any differences between the means of the two conditions are probably due to the experimental manipulation. So, if the chimps perform better in one training phase than in the other, this *has* to be due to the fact that bananas were used to provide feedback in one training phase but not in the other. Differences in performance created by a specific experimental manipulation are known as **systematic variation**.

Now let's think about what happens when we use different participants – an independent design. In this design we still have two conditions, but this time different participants participate in each condition. Going back to our example, one group of chimps receives training without feedback, whereas a second group of different chimps does receive feedback on their performance via bananas.[15] Imagine again that we didn't have an experimental manipulation. If we did nothing to the groups, then we would still find some variation in behaviour between the groups because they contain different chimps who will vary in their ability, motivation, propensity to get distracted from running the economy by throwing their own faeces, and other factors. In short, the factors that were held constant in the repeated-measures design are free to vary in the independent design. So, the unsystematic variation will be bigger than for a repeated-measures design. As before, if we introduce a manipulation (i.e., bananas), then we will see additional variation created by this manipulation. As such, in both the repeated-measures design and the independent design there are always two sources of variation:

- **Systematic variation**: This variation is due to the experimenter doing something in one condition but not in the other condition.
- **Unsystematic variation**: This variation results from random factors that exist between the experimental conditions (such as natural differences in ability, the time of day, etc.).

Statistical tests are often based on the idea of estimating how much variation there is in performance, and comparing how much of this is systematic to how much is unsystematic.

In a repeated-measures design, differences between two conditions can be caused by only two things: (1) the manipulation that was carried out on the participants, or (2) any other factor that might affect the way in which an entity performs from one time to the next. The latter factor is likely to be fairly minor compared to the influence of the experimental manipulation. In an independent design, differences between the two conditions can also be caused by one of two things: (1) the manipulation that was carried out on the participants, or (2) differences between the characteristics of the entities allocated to each of the groups. The latter factor, in this instance, is likely to create considerable random variation both within each condition and between them. When we look at the effect of our experimental manipulation, it is always against a background of 'noise' created by random, uncontrollable differences between our conditions. In a repeated-measures design this 'noise' is kept to a minimum and so the effect of the experiment is more likely to show up. This means that, other things being equal, repeated-measures designs are more sensitive to detect effects than independent designs.

1.7.5 Randomization ▮▮▮

In both repeated-measures and independent designs it is important to try to keep the unsystematic variation to a minimum. By keeping the unsystematic variation as small as possible we get a more

---

14 Actually, this isn't the only difference because, by condition 2, they have had some practice (in condition 1) at running the economy; however, we will see shortly that these practice effects are easily eradicated.

15 Obviously I mean that they receive a banana as a reward for their correct response and not that the bananas develop little banana mouths that sing them a little congratulatory song.

sensitive measure of the experimental manipulation. Generally, scientists use the **randomization** of entities to treatment conditions to achieve this goal. Many statistical tests work by identifying the systematic and unsystematic sources of variation and then comparing them. This comparison allows us to see whether the experiment has generated considerably more variation than we would have got had we just tested participants without the experimental manipulation. Randomization is important because it eliminates most other sources of systematic variation, which allows us to be sure that any systematic variation between experimental conditions is due to the manipulation of the independent variable. We can use randomization in two different ways depending on whether we have an independent or repeated-measures design.

Let's look at a repeated-measures design first. I mentioned earlier (in a footnote) that when the same entities participate in more than one experimental condition they are naive during the first experimental condition but they come to the second experimental condition with prior experience of what is expected of them. At the very least they will be familiar with the dependent measure (e.g., the task they're performing). The two most important sources of systematic variation in this type of design are:

- **Practice effects**: Participants may perform differently in the second condition because of familiarity with the experimental situation and/or the measures being used.
- **Boredom effects**: Participants may perform differently in the second condition because they are tired or bored from having completed the first condition.

Although these effects are impossible to eliminate completely, we can ensure that they produce no systematic variation between our conditions by **counterbalancing** the order in which a person participates in a condition.

We can use randomization to determine in which order the conditions are completed. That is, we randomly determine whether a participant completes condition 1 before condition 2, or condition 2 before condition 1. Let's look at the teaching method example and imagine that there were just two conditions: no feedback and harsh feedback. If the same participants were used in all conditions, then we might find that statistical ability was higher after the harsh feedback. However, if every student experienced the harsh feedback after the no feedback seminars then they would enter the harsh condition already having a better knowledge of statistics than when they began the no feedback condition. So, the apparent improvement after harsh feedback would not be due to the experimental manipulation (i.e., it's not because harsh feedback works), but because participants had attended more statistics seminars by the end of the harsh feedback condition compared to the no feedback one. We can use randomization to ensure that the number of statistics seminars does not introduce a systematic bias by randomly assigning students to have the harsh feedback seminars first or the no feedback seminars first.

If we turn our attention to independent designs, a similar argument can be applied. We know that participants in different experimental conditions will differ in many respects (their IQ, attention span, etc.). Although we know that these confounding variables contribute to the variation between conditions, we need to make sure that these variables contribute to the unsystematic variation and *not* to the systematic variation. A good example is the effects of alcohol on behaviour. You might give one group of people 5 pints of beer, and keep a second group sober, and then count how many times you can persuade them to do a fish impersonation. The effect that alcohol has varies because people differ in their tolerance: teetotal people can become drunk on a small amount, while alcoholics need to consume vast quantities before the alcohol affects them. If you allocated a bunch of hardened drinkers to the condition that consumed alcohol, and teetotal people to the no alcohol condition, then you might find that alcohol doesn't increase the number of fish impersonations you get. However, this finding could be because (1) alcohol does not make people engage in frivolous activities, or (2) the hardened drinkers were unaffected by the dose of alcohol. You have no way to dissociate these explanations because the groups varied not just on dose of alcohol but also on their tolerance of alcohol (the systematic variation created by their past experience with alcohol cannot be separated from the effect of the experimental manipulation). The best way to reduce this eventuality is to randomly allocate participants to conditions: by doing so you minimize the risk that groups differ on variables other than the one you want to manipulate.

SELF TEST

Why is randomization important?

1.8 Analysing data ▌▌▌

The final stage of the research process is to analyse the data you have collected. When the data are quantitative this involves both looking at your data graphically (Chapter 5) to see what the general trends in the data are, and also fitting statistical models to the data (all other chapters). Given that the rest of the book is dedicated to this process, we'll begin here by looking at a few fairly basic ways to look at and summarize the data you have collected.

1.8.1 Frequency distributions ▌▌▌

What is frequency distribution and when is it normal?

Once you've collected some data a very useful thing to do is to plot a graph of how many times each score occurs. This is known as a **frequency distribution**, or **histogram**, which is a graph plotting values of observations on the horizontal axis, with a bar showing how many times each value occurred in the data set. Frequency distributions can be very useful for assessing properties of the distribution of scores. We will find out how to create these types of charts in Chapter 5.

Frequency distributions come in many different shapes and sizes. It is quite important, therefore, to have some general descriptions for common types of distributions. In an ideal world our data would be distributed symmetrically around the centre of all scores. As such, if we drew a vertical line through the centre of the distribution then it should look the same on both sides. This is known as a **normal distribution** and is characterized by the bell-shaped curve with which you might already be familiar. This shape implies that the majority of scores lie around the centre of the distribution (so the largest bars on the histogram are around the central value). Also, as we get further away from the centre, the bars get smaller, implying that as scores start to deviate from the centre their frequency is decreasing. As we move still further away from the centre our scores become very infrequent (the bars are very short). Many naturally occurring things have this shape of distribution. For example, most men in the UK are around 175 cm tall;[16] some are a bit taller or shorter, but most cluster around this value. There will be very few men who are really tall (i.e., above 205 cm) or really short (i.e., under 145 cm). An example of a normal distribution is shown in Figure 1.3.

---

16 I am exactly 180 cm tall. In my home country this makes me smugly above average. However, I often visit the Netherlands, where the average male height is 185 cm (a little over 6ft, and a massive 10 cm higher than the UK), and where I feel like a bit of a dwarf.

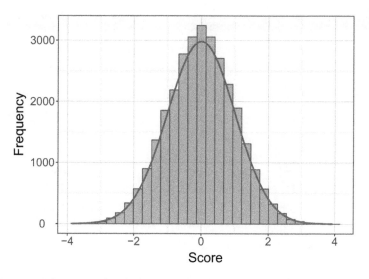

Figure 1.3   A 'normal' distribution (the curve shows the idealized shape)

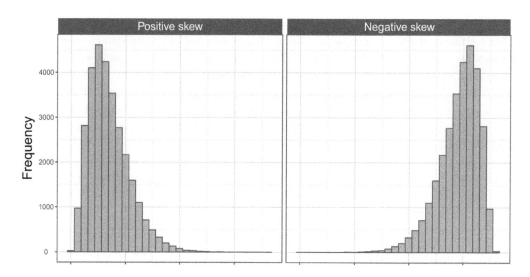

Figure 1.4   A positively (left) and negatively (right) skewed distribution

There are two main ways in which a distribution can deviate from normal: (1) lack of symmetry (called **skew**) and (2) pointyness (called **kurtosis**). Skewed distributions are not symmetrical and instead most frequent scores (the tall bars on the graph) are clustered at one end of the scale. So, the typical pattern is a cluster of frequent scores at one end of the scale and the frequency of scores tailing off towards the other end of the scale. A skewed distribution can be either *positively skewed* (the frequent scores are clustered at the lower end and the tail points towards the higher or more positive scores) or *negatively skewed* (the frequent scores are clustered at the higher end and the tail points towards the lower or more negative scores). Figure 1.4 shows examples of these distributions.

Distributions also vary in their kurtosis. Kurtosis, despite sounding like some kind of exotic disease, refers to the degree to which scores cluster at the ends of the distribution (known as the *tails*)

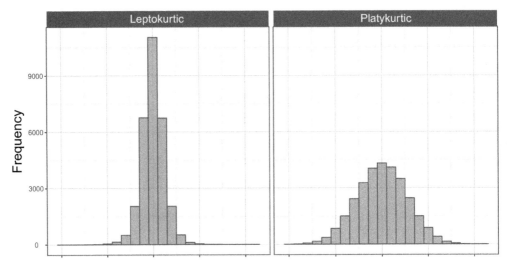

Figure 1.5   Distributions with positive kurtosis (leptokurtic, left) and negative kurtosis (platykurtic, right)

and this tends to express itself in how pointy a distribution is (but there are other factors that can affect how pointy the distribution looks – see Jane Superbrain Box 1.5). A distribution with *positive kurtosis* has many scores in the tails (a so-called heavy-tailed distribution) and is pointy. This is known as a **leptokurtic** distribution. In contrast, a distribution with *negative kurtosis* is relatively thin in the tails (has light tails) and tends to be flatter than normal. This distribution is called **platykurtic**. Ideally, we want our data to be normally distributed (i.e., not too skewed, and not too many or too few scores at the extremes). For everything there is to know about kurtosis, read DeCarlo (1997).

In a normal distribution the values of skew and kurtosis are 0 (i.e., the tails of the distribution are as they should be).[17] If a distribution has values of skew or kurtosis above or below 0 then this indicates a deviation from normal: Figure 1.5 shows distributions with kurtosis values of +2.6 (left panel) and −0.09 (right panel).

1.8.2 The mode ▌▌▌▌

We can calculate where the centre of a frequency distribution lies (known as the **central tendency**) using three measures commonly used: the mean, the mode and the median. Other methods exist, but these three are the ones you're most likely to come across.

The **mode** is the score that occurs most frequently in the data set. This is easy to spot in a frequency distribution because it will be the tallest bar. To calculate the mode, place the data in ascending order (to make life easier), count how many times each score occurs, and the score that occurs the most is the mode. One problem with the mode is that it can take on several values. For example, Figure 1.6 shows an example of a distribution with two modes (there are two bars that are the highest), which is said to be **bimodal**, and three modes (data sets with more than two modes are **multimodal**). Also, if the frequencies of certain scores are very similar, then the mode can be influenced by only a small number of cases.

---

17 Sometimes no kurtosis is expressed as 3 rather than 0, but SPSS uses 0 to denote no excess kurtosis.

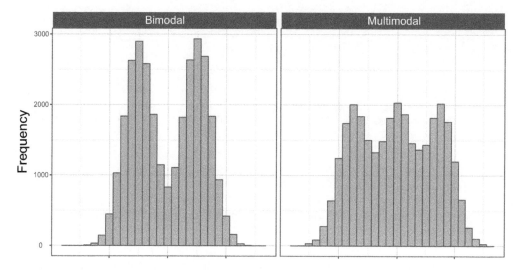

Figure 1.6 Examples of bimodal (left) and multimodal (right) distributions

1.8.3 The median ▌▌▌▌

Another way to quantify the centre of a distribution is to look for the middle score when scores are ranked in order of magnitude. This is called the **median**. Imagine we looked at the number of friends that 11 users of the social networking website Facebook had. Figure 1.7 shows the number of friends for each of the 11 users: 57, 40, 103, 234, 93, 53, 116, 98, 108, 121, 22.

To calculate the median, we first arrange these scores into ascending order: 22, 40, 53, 57, 93, 98, 103, 108, 116, 121, 234.

Next, we find the position of the middle score by counting the number of scores we have collected (n), adding 1 to this value, and then dividing by 2. With 11 scores, this gives us $(n + 1)/2 = (11 + 1)/2 = 12/2 = 6$. Then, we find the score that is positioned at the location we have just calculated. So, in this example, we find the sixth score (see Figure 1.7).

This process works very nicely when we have an odd number of scores (as in this example), but when we have an even number of scores there won't be a middle value. Let's imagine that we decided that because the highest score was so big (almost twice as large as the next biggest number), we would

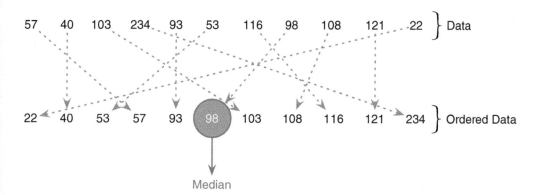

Figure 1.7 The median is simply the middle score when you order the data

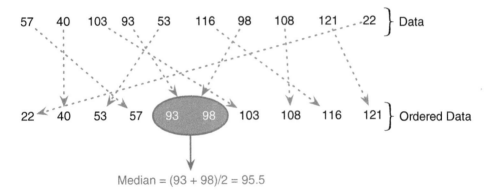

Figure 1.8 When the data contain an even number of scores, the median is the average of the middle two values

ignore it. (For one thing, this person is far too popular and we hate them.) We have only 10 scores now. Figure 1.8 shows this situation. As before, we rank-order these scores: 22, 40, 53, 57, 93, 98, 103, 108, 116, 121. We then calculate the position of the middle score, but this time it is $(n + 1)/2 = 11/2 = 5.5$, which means that the median is halfway between the fifth and sixth scores. To get the median we add these two scores and divide by 2. In this example, the fifth score in the ordered list was 93 and the sixth score was 98. We add these together ($93 + 98 = 191$) and then divide this value by 2 ($191/2 = 95.5$). The median number of friends was, therefore, 95.5.

The median is relatively unaffected by extreme scores at either end of the distribution: the median changed only from 98 to 95.5 when we removed the extreme score of 234. The median is also relatively unaffected by skewed distributions and can be used with ordinal, interval and ratio data (it cannot, however, be used with nominal data because these data have no numerical order).

1.8.4 The mean ▊▊▊

The **mean** is the measure of central tendency that you are most likely to have heard of because it is the average score, and the media love an average score.[18] To calculate the mean we add up all of the scores and then divide by the total number of scores we have. We can write this in equation form as:

$$\overline{X} = \frac{\sum_{i=1}^{n} x_i}{n} \tag{1.1}$$

This equation may look complicated, but the top half simply means 'add up all of the scores' (the x_i means 'the score of a particular person'; we could replace the letter i with each person's name instead), and the bottom bit means, 'divide this total by the number of scores you have got (n)'. Let's calculate the mean for the Facebook data. First, we add up all the scores:

$$\sum_{i=1}^{n} x_i = 22 + 40 + 53 + 57 + 93 + 98 + 103 + 108 + 116 + 121 + 234 = 1045 \tag{1.2}$$

---

18 I wrote this on 15 February, and to prove my point, the BBC website ran a headline today about how PayPal estimates that Britons will spend an average of £71.25 each on Valentine's Day gifts. However, uSwitch.com said that the average spend would be only £22.69. Always remember that the media is full of lies and contradictions.

We then divide by the number of scores (in this case 11) as in equation (1.3):

$$\overline{X} = \frac{\sum_{i=1}^{n} x_i}{n} = \frac{1045}{11} = 95 \qquad\qquad (1.3)$$

The mean is 95 friends, which is not a value we observed in our actual data. In this sense the mean is a statistical model – more on this in the next chapter.

SELF TEST

Compute the mean but excluding the score of 234.

If you calculate the mean without our most popular person (i.e., excluding the value 234), the mean drops to 81.1 friends. This reduction illustrates one disadvantage of the mean: it can be influenced by extreme scores. In this case, the person with 234 friends on Facebook increased the mean by about 14 friends; compare this difference with that of the median. Remember that the median changed very little – from 98 to 95.5 – when we excluded the score of 234, which illustrates how the median is typically less affected by extreme scores than the mean. While we're being negative about the mean, it is also affected by skewed distributions and can be used only with interval or ratio data.

If the mean is so lousy then why do we use it so often? One very important reason is that it uses every score (the mode and median ignore most of the scores in a data set). Also, the mean tends to be stable in different samples (more on that later too).

Cramming Sam's Tips
Central tendency

- The mean is the sum of all scores divided by the number of scores. The value of the mean can be influenced quite heavily by extreme scores.
- The median is the middle score when the scores are placed in ascending order. It is not as influenced by extreme scores as the mean.
- The mode is the score that occurs most frequently.

1.8.5 The dispersion in a distribution ▌▌▌

It can also be interesting to quantify the spread, or dispersion, of scores. The easiest way to look at dispersion is to take the largest score and subtract from it the smallest score. This is known as the **range** of scores. For our Facebook data we saw that if we order the scores we get 22, 40, 53, 57, 93, 98, 103, 108, 116, 121, 234. The highest score is 234 and the lowest is 22; therefore, the range is 234–22 = 212. One problem with the range is that because it uses only the highest and lowest score, it is affected dramatically by extreme scores.

Compute the range but excluding the score of 234.

If you have done the self-test task you'll see that without the extreme score the range drops from 212 to 99 – less than half the size.

One way around this problem is to calculate the range but excluding values at the extremes of the distribution. One convention is to cut off the top and bottom 25% of scores and calculate the range of the middle 50% of scores – known as the **interquartile range**. Let's do this with the Facebook data. First, we need to calculate what are called **quartiles**. Quartiles are the three values that split the sorted data into four equal parts. First we calculate the median, which is also called the *second quartile*, which splits our data into two equal parts. We already know that the median for these data is 98. The **lower quartile** is the median of the lower half of the data and the **upper quartile** is the median of the upper half of the data. As a rule of thumb the median is not included in the two halves when they are split (this is convenient if you have an odd number of values), but you can include it (although which half you put it in is another question). Figure 1.9 shows how we would calculate these values for the Facebook data. Like the median, if each half of the data had an even number of values in it, then the upper and lower quartiles would be the average of two values in the data set (therefore, the upper and lower quartile need not be values that actually appear in the data). Once we have worked out the values of the quartiles, we can calculate the interquartile range, which is the difference between the upper and lower quartile. For the Facebook data this value would be 116–53 = 63. The advantage of the interquartile range is that it isn't affected by extreme scores at either end of the distribution. However, the problem with it is that you lose a lot of data (half of it, in fact).

It's worth noting here that quartiles are special cases of things called **quantiles**. Quantiles are values that split a data set into equal portions. Quartiles are quantiles that split the data into four

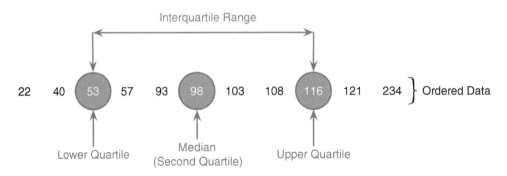

Figure 1.9 Calculating quartiles and the interquartile range

equal parts, but there are other quantiles such as **percentiles** (points that split the data into 100 equal parts), **noniles** (points that split the data into nine equal parts) and so on.

Twenty-one heavy smokers were put on a treadmill at the fastest setting. The time in seconds was measured until they fell off from exhaustion:

18, 16, 18, 24, 23, 22, 22, 23, 26, 29, 32, 34, 34, 36, 36, 43, 42, 49, 46, 46, 57

Compute the mode, median, mean, upper and lower quartiles, range and interquartile range.

If we want to use all the data rather than half of it, we can calculate the spread of scores by looking at how different each score is from the centre of the distribution. If we use the mean as a measure of the centre of a distribution, then we can calculate the difference between each score and the mean, which is known as the **deviance** (Eq. 1.4):

$$\text{deviance} = x_i - \bar{x} \tag{1.4}$$

If we want to know the total deviance then we could add up the deviances for each data point. In equation form, this would be:

$$\text{total deviance} = \sum_{i=1}^{n} (x_i - \bar{x}) \tag{1.5}$$

The sigma symbol (Σ) means 'add up all of what comes after', and the 'what comes after' in this case is the deviances. So, this equation simply means 'add up all of the deviances'.

Let's try this with the Facebook data. Table 1.2 shows the number of friends for each person in the Facebook data, the mean, and the difference between the two. Note that because the mean is at the centre of the distribution, some of the deviations are positive (scores greater than the mean) and some are negative (scores smaller than the mean). Consequently, when we add the scores up, the total is zero. Therefore, the 'total spread' is nothing. This conclusion is as silly as a tapeworm thinking they can have a coffee with the Queen of England if they don a bowler hat and pretend to be human. Everyone knows that the Queen drinks tea.

To overcome this problem, we could ignore the minus signs when we add the deviations up. There's nothing wrong with doing this, but people tend to square the deviations, which has a similar effect (because a negative number multiplied by another negative number becomes positive). The final column of Table 1.2 shows these squared deviances. We can add these squared deviances up to get the **sum of squared errors, SS** (often just called the *sum of squares*); unless your scores are all exactly the same, the resulting value will be bigger than zero, indicating that there is some deviance from the mean. As an equation, we would write: equation (1.6), in which the sigma symbol means 'add up all of the things that follow' and what follows is the squared deviances (or *squared errors* as they're more commonly known):

$$\text{sum of squared errors (SS)} = \sum_{i=1}^{n} (x_i - \bar{x})^2 \tag{1.6}$$

We can use the sum of squares as an indicator of the total dispersion, or total deviance of scores from the mean. The problem with using the total is that its size will depend on how many scores we have in

Table 1.2 Table showing the deviations of each score from the mean

Number of Friends (x_i)	Mean $(\bar{x})$	Deviance $(x_i-\bar{x})$	Deviance squared $(x_i-\bar{x})^2$
22	95	-73	5329
40	95	-55	3025
53	95	-42	1764
57	95	-38	1444
93	95	-2	4
98	95	3	9
103	95	8	64
108	95	13	169
116	95	21	441
121	95	26	676
234	95	139	19321

$$\sum_{i=1}^{n} x_i - \bar{x} = 0 \qquad \sum_{i=1}^{n} (x_i - \bar{x})^2 = 32246$$

the data. The sum of squares for the Facebook data is 32,246, but if we added another 11 scores that value would increase (other things being equal, it will more or less double in size). The total dispersion is a bit of a nuisance then because we can't compare it across samples that differ in size. Therefore, it can be useful to work not with the *total* dispersion, but the *average* dispersion, which is also known as the **variance**. We have seen that an average is the total of scores divided by the number of scores, therefore, the variance is simply the sum of squares divided by the number of observations (N). Actually, we normally divide the SS by the number of observations minus 1 as in equation (1.7) (the reason why is explained in the next chapter and Jane Superbrain Box 2.2):

$$\text{variance}\left(s^2\right) = \frac{\text{SS}}{N-1} = \frac{\sum_{i=1}^{n} (x_i - \bar{x})^2}{N-1} = \frac{32,246}{10} = 3224.6 \qquad (1.7)$$

As we have seen, the variance is the average error between the mean and the observations made. There is one problem with the variance as a measure: it gives us a measure in units squared (because we squared each error in the calculation). In our example we would have to say that the average error in our data was 3224.6 friends squared. It makes very little sense to talk about friends squared, so we often take the square root of the variance (which ensures that the measure of average error is in the same units as the original measure). This measure is known as the **standard deviation** and is the square root of the variance (Eq. 1.8).

$$\begin{aligned} s &= \sqrt{\frac{\sum_{i=1}^{n} (x_i - \bar{x})^2}{N-1}} \\ &= \sqrt{3224.6} \\ &= 56.79 \end{aligned} \qquad (1.8)$$

The sum of squares, variance and standard deviation are all measures of the dispersion or spread of data around the mean. A small standard deviation (relative to the value of the mean itself)

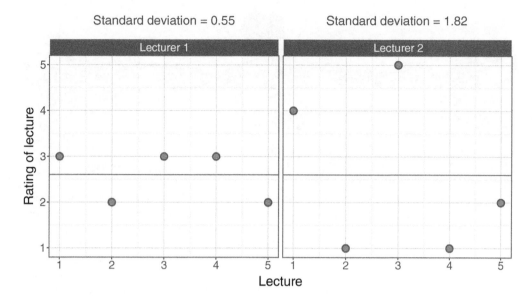

Figure 1.10   Graphs illustrating data that have the same mean but different standard deviations

indicates that the data points are close to the mean. A large standard deviation (relative to the mean) indicates that the data points are distant from the mean. A standard deviation of 0 would mean that all the scores were the same. Figure 1.10 shows the overall ratings (on a 5-point scale) of two lecturers after each of five different lectures. Both lecturers had an average rating of 2.6 out of 5 across the lectures. However, the first lecturer had a standard deviation of 0.55 (relatively small compared to the mean). It should be clear from the left-hand graph that ratings for this lecturer were consistently close to the mean rating. There was a small fluctuation, but generally her lectures did not vary in popularity. Put another way, the scores are not spread too widely around the mean. The second lecturer, however, had a standard deviation of 1.82 (relatively high compared to the mean). The ratings for this second lecturer are more spread from the mean than the first: for some lectures she received very high ratings, and for others her ratings were appalling.

1.8.6 Using a frequency distribution to go beyond the data ▮▮▮

Another way to think about frequency distributions is not in terms of how often scores actually occurred, but how likely it is that a score would occur (i.e., probability). The word 'probability' causes most people's brains to overheat (myself included) so it seems fitting that we use an example about throwing buckets of ice over our heads. Internet memes tend to follow the shape of a normal distribution, which we discussed a while back. A good example of this is the ice bucket challenge from 2014. You can check Wikipedia for the full story, but it all started (arguably) with golfer Chris Kennedy tipping a bucket of iced water on his head to raise awareness of the disease amyotrophic lateral sclerosis (ALS, also known as Lou Gehrig's disease).[19] The idea is that you are challenged and have 24 hours to post a video of you having a bucket of iced water poured over your head; in

---

19 Chris Kennedy did not invent the challenge, but he's believed to be the first to link it to ALS. There are
    earlier reports of people doing things with ice-cold water in the name of charity, but I'm focusing on the
    ALS challenge because it is the one that spread as a meme.

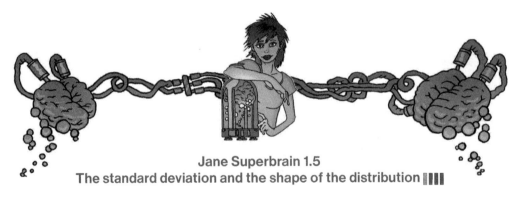

Jane Superbrain 1.5
The standard deviation and the shape of the distribution ▍▍▍

The variance and standard deviation tell us about the shape of the distribution of scores. If the mean represents the data well then most of the scores will cluster close to the mean and the resulting standard deviation is small relative to the mean. When the mean is a worse representation of the data, the scores cluster more widely around the mean and the standard deviation is larger. Figure 1.11 shows two distributions that have the same mean (50) but different standard deviations. One has a large standard deviation relative to the mean (SD = 25) and this results in a flatter distribution that is more spread out, whereas the other has a small standard deviation relative to the mean (SD = 15) resulting in a pointier distribution in which scores close to the mean are very frequent but scores further from the mean become increasingly infrequent. The message is that as the standard deviation gets larger, the distribution gets fatter. This can make distributions look platykurtic or leptokurtic when, in fact, they are not.

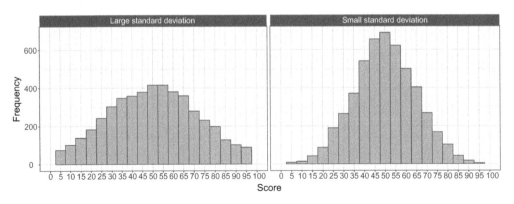

Figure 1.11   Two distributions with the same mean, but large and small standard deviations

this video you also challenge at least three other people. If you fail to complete the challenge your forfeit is to donate to charity (in this case, ALS). In reality many people completed the challenge *and* made donations.

The ice bucket challenge is a good example of a meme: it ended up generating something like 2.4 million videos on Facebook and 2.3 million on YouTube. I mentioned that memes often follow a normal distribution, and Figure 1.12 shows this: the insert shows the 'interest' score from Google Trends

Labcoat Leni's Real Research 1.1

Is Friday 13th unlucky? ▌▌▌▌

Scanlon, T. J., et al. (1993). *British Medical Journal, 307,* 1584–1586.

Many of us are superstitious, and a common superstition is that Friday the 13th is unlucky. Most of us don't literally think that someone in a hockey mask is going to kill us, but some people are wary. Scanlon and colleagues, in a tongue-in-cheek study (Scanlon, Luben, Scanlon, & Singleton, 1993), looked at accident statistics at hospitals in the south-west Thames region of the UK. They took statistics both for Friday the 13th and Friday the 6th (the week before) in different months in 1989, 1990, 1991 and 1992. They looked at both emergency admissions of accidents and poisoning, and also transport accidents.

Date	Accidents and Poisoning		Traffic Accidents	
	Friday 6th	Friday 13th	Friday 6th	Friday 13th
October 1989	4	7	9	13
July 1990	6	6	6	12
September 1991	1	5	11	14
December 1991	9	5	11	10
March 1992	9	7	3	4
November 1992	1	6	5	12

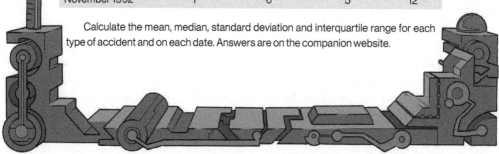

Calculate the mean, median, standard deviation and interquartile range for each type of accident and on each date. Answers are on the companion website.

for the phrase 'ice bucket challenge' from August to September 2014.[20] The 'interest' score that Google calculates is a bit hard to unpick but essentially reflects the relative number of times that the term 'ice bucket challenge' was searched for on Google. It's not the total number of searches, but the relative number. In a sense it shows the trend of the popularity of searching for 'ice bucket challenge'. Compare the line with the perfect normal distribution in Figure 1.3 – they look fairly similar, don't

---

20 You can generate the insert graph for yourself by going to Google Trends, entering the search term 'ice bucket challenge' and restricting the dates shown to August 2014 to September 2014.

Cramming Sam's Tips
Dispersion

- The deviance or error is the distance of each score from the mean.
- The sum of squared errors is the total amount of error in the mean. The errors/deviances are squared before adding them up.
- The variance is the average distance of scores from the mean. It is the sum of squares divided by the number of scores. It tells us about how widely dispersed scores are around the mean.
- The standard deviation is the *square root of the variance*. It is the variance converted back to the original units of measurement of the scores used to compute it. Large standard deviations relative to the mean suggest data are widely spread around the mean, whereas small standard deviations suggest data are closely packed around the mean.
- The range is the distance between the highest and lowest score.
- The interquartile range is the range of the middle 50% of the scores.

they? Once it got going (about 2–3 weeks after the first video) it went viral, and popularity increased rapidly, reaching a peak at around 21 August (about 36 days after Chris Kennedy got the ball rolling). After this peak, popularity rapidly declines as people tire of the meme.

The main histogram in Figure 1.12 shows the same pattern but reflects something a bit more tangible than 'interest scores'. It shows the number of videos posted on YouTube relating to the ice bucket challenge on each day after Chris Kennedy's initial challenge. There were 2323 thousand in total (2.32 million) during the period shown. In a sense it shows approximately how many people took up the challenge each day.[21] You can see that nothing much happened for 20 days, and early on relatively few people took up the challenge. By about 30 days after the initial challenge things are hotting up (well, cooling down, really) as the number of videos rapidly accelerated from 29,000 on day 30 to 196,000 on day 35. At day 36, the challenge hits its peak (204,000 videos posted) after which the decline sets in as it becomes 'yesterday's news'. By day 50 it's only the type of people like me, and statistics lectures more generally, who don't check Facebook for 50 days, who suddenly become aware of the meme and want to get in on the action to prove how down with the kids we are. It's too late, though: people at that end of the curve are uncool, and the trendsetters who posted videos on day 25 call us lame and look at us dismissively. It's OK though, because we can plot sick histograms like the one in Figure 1.12; take that, hipster scum!

---

21 Very very approximately indeed. I have converted the Google interest data into videos posted on YouTube by using the fact that I know that 2.33 million videos were posted during this period and by making the (not unreasonable) assumption that behaviour on YouTube will have followed the same pattern over time as the Google interest score for the challenge.

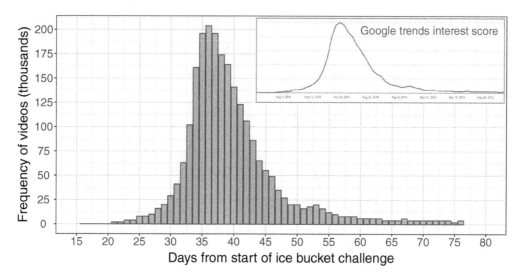

Figure 1.12 Frequency distribution showing the number of ice bucket challenge videos on YouTube by day since the first video (the insert shows the actual Google Trends data on which this example is based)

I digress. We can think of frequency distributions in terms of probability. To explain this, imagine that someone asked you 'How likely is it that a person posted an ice bucket video after 60 days?' What would your answer be? Remember that the height of the bars on the histogram reflects how many videos were posted. Therefore, if you looked at the frequency distribution before answering the question you might respond 'not very likely' because the bars are very short after 60 days (i.e., relatively few videos were posted). What if someone asked you 'How likely is it that a video was posted 35 days after the challenge started?' Using the histogram, you might say 'It's relatively likely' because the bar is very high on day 35 (so quite a few videos were posted). Your inquisitive friend is on a roll and asks 'How likely is it that someone posted a video 35 to 40 days after the challenge started?' The bars representing these days are shaded orange in Figure 1.12. The question about the likelihood of a video being posted 35–40 days into the challenge is really asking 'How big is the orange area of Figure 1.12 compared to the total size of all bars?' We can find out the size of the dark blue region by adding the values of the bars (196 + 204 + 196 + 174 + 164 + 141 = 1075); therefore, the orange area represents 1075 thousand videos. The total size of all bars is the total number of videos posted (i.e., 2323 thousand). If the orange area represents 1075 thousand videos, and the total area represents 2323 thousand videos, then if we compare the orange area to the total area we get 1075/2323 = 0.46. This proportion can be converted to a percentage by multiplying by 100, which gives us 46%. Therefore, our answer might be 'It's quite likely that someone posted a video 35–40 days into the challenge because 46% of all videos were posted during those 6 days'. A very important point here is that the size of the bars relates directly to the probability of an event occurring.

Hopefully these illustrations show that we can use the frequencies of different scores, and the area of a frequency distribution, to estimate the probability that a particular score will occur. A probability value can range from 0 (there's no chance whatsoever of the event happening) to 1 (the event will definitely happen). So, for example, when I talk to my publishers I tell them there's a probability of 1 that I will have completed the revisions to this book by July. However, when I talk to anyone else, I might, more realistically, tell them that there's a 0.10 probability of me finishing the revisions on time (or put another way, a 10% chance, or 1 in 10 chance that I'll complete the book in time). In reality, the

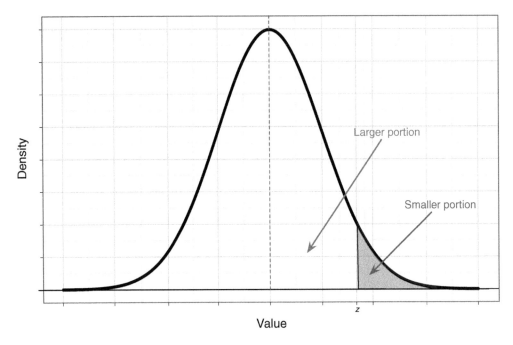

Figure 1.13 The normal probability distribution

probability of my meeting the deadline is 0 (not a chance in hell). If probabilities don't make sense to you then you're not alone; just ignore the decimal point and think of them as percentages instead (i.e., a 0.10 probability that something will happen is a 10% chance that something will happen) or read the chapter on probability in my other excellent textbook (Field, 2016).

I've talked in vague terms about how frequency distributions can be used to get a rough idea of the probability of a score occurring. However, we can be precise. For any distribution of scores we could, in theory, calculate the probability of obtaining a score of a certain size – it would be incredibly tedious and complex to do it, but we could. To spare our sanity, statisticians have identified several common distributions. For each one they have worked out mathematical formulae (known as **probability density functions, PDF**) that specify idealized versions of these distributions. We could draw such a function by plotting the value of the variable (x) against the probability of it occurring (y).[22] The resulting curve is known as a **probability distribution**; for a normal distribution (Section 1.8.1) it would look like Figure 1.13, which has the characteristic bell shape that we saw already in Figure 1.3.

A probability distribution is just like a histogram except that the lumps and bumps have been smoothed out so that we see a nice smooth curve. However, like a frequency distribution, the area under this curve tells us something about the probability of a value occurring. Just like we did in our ice bucket example, we could use the area under the curve between two values to tell us how likely it is that a score fell within a particular range. For example, the blue shaded region in Figure 1.13 corresponds to the probability of a score being z or greater. The normal distribution is not the only distribution that has been precisely specified by people with enormous brains. There are many distributions that have characteristic shapes and have been specified with a probability density function. We'll encounter some of these other distributions throughout the book, for example the t-distribution, chi-square (χ^2) distribution, and F-distribution. For now, the important thing to remember is that all of

---

22 Actually we usually plot something called the *density*, which is closely related to the probability.

these distributions have something in common: they are all defined by an equation that enables us to calculate precisely the probability of obtaining a given score.

As we have seen, distributions can have different means and standard deviations. This isn't a problem for the probability density function – it will still give us the probability of a given value occurring – but it is a problem for us because probability density functions are difficult enough to spell, let alone use to compute probabilities. Therefore, to avoid a brain meltdown we often use a normal distribution with a mean of 0 and a standard deviation of 1 as a standard. This has the advantage that we can pretend that the probability density function doesn't exist and use tabulated probabilities (as in the Appendix) instead. The obvious problem is that not all of the data we collect will have a mean of 0 and a standard deviation of 1. For example, for the ice bucket data the mean is 39.68 and the standard deviation is 7.74. However, any data set can be converted into a data set that has a mean of 0 and a standard deviation of 1. First, to centre the data around zero, we take each score (X) and subtract from it the mean of all scores ($\bar{X}$). To ensure the data have a standard deviation of 1, we divide the resulting score by the standard deviation (s), which we recently encountered. The resulting scores are denoted by the letter z and are known as z-scores. In equation form, the conversion that I've just described is:

What is a z-score?

$$z = \frac{X - \bar{X}}{s} \tag{1.9}$$

The table of probability values that have been calculated for the standard normal distribution is shown in the Appendix. Why is this table important? Well, if we look at our ice bucket data, we can answer the question 'What's the probability that someone posted a video on day 60 or later?' First, we convert 60 into a z-score. We saw that the mean was 39.68 and the standard deviation was 7.74, so our score of 60 expressed as a z-score is 2.63 (Eq. 1.10):

$$z = \frac{60 - 39.68}{7.74} = 2.63 \tag{1.10}$$

We can now use this value, rather than the original value of 60, to compute an answer to our question.

Figure 1.14 shows (an edited version of) the tabulated values of the standard normal distribution from the Appendix of this book. This table gives us a list of values of z, and the density (y) for each value of z, but, most important, it splits the distribution at the value of z and tells us the size of the two areas under the curve that this division creates. For example, when z is 0, we are at the mean or centre of the distribution so it splits the area under the curve exactly in half. Consequently, both areas have a size of 0.5 (or 50%). However, any value of z that is not zero will create different sized areas, and the table tells us the size of the larger and smaller portions. For example, if we look up our z-score of 2.63, we find that the smaller portion (i.e., the area above this value, or the blue area in Figure 1.14) is 0.0043, or only 0.43%. I explained before that these areas relate to probabilities, so in this case we could say that there is only a 0.43% chance that a video was posted 60 days or more after the challenge started. By looking at the larger portion (the area below 2.63) we get 0.9957, or put another way, there's a 99.57% chance that an ice bucket video was posted on YouTube within 60 days of the challenge starting. Note that these two proportions add up to 1 (or 100%), so the total area under the curve is 1.

Another useful thing we can do (you'll find out just how useful in due course) is to work out limits within which a certain percentage of scores fall. With our ice bucket example, we looked at how likely it was that a video was posted between 35 and 40 days after the challenge started; we could ask a similar question such as 'What is the range of days between which the middle 95% of videos were posted?' To answer this question we need to use the table the opposite way around. We know that the

A.1. Table of the standard normal distribution

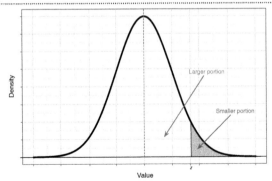

z	Larger Portion	Smaller Portion	y	z	Larger Portion	Smaller Portion	y
.00	.50000	.50000	.3989	.12	.54776	.45224	.3961
.01	.50399	.49601	.3989	.13	.55172	.44828	.3956
.02	.50798	.49202	.3989	.14	.55567	.44433	.3951
.03	.51197	.48803	.3988	.15	.55962	.44038	.3945
.04	.51595	.48405	.3986	.16	.56356	.43644	.3939
1.56	.94062	.05938	.1182	1.86	.96856	.03144	.0707
1.57	.94179	.05821	.1163	1.87	.96926	.03074	.0694
1.58	.94295	.05705	.1145	1.88	.96995	.03005	.0681
1.59	.94408	.05592	.1127	1.89	.97062	.02938	.0669
1.60	.94520	.05480	.1109	1.90	.97128	.02872	.0656
1.61	.94630	.05370	.1092	1.91	.97193	.02807	.0644
1.62	.94738	.05262	.1074	1.92	.97257	.02743	.0632
1.63	.94845	.05155	.1057	1.93	.97320	.02680	.0620
1.64	.94950	.05050	.1040	1.94	.97381	.02619	.0608
1.65	.95053	.04947	.1023	1.95	.97441	.02559	.0596
1.66	.95154	.04846	.1006	1.96	.97500	.02500	.0584
1.67	.95254	.04746	.0989	1.97	.97558	.02442	.0573
1.68	.95352	.04648	.0973	1.98	.97615	.02385	.0562
2.27	.98840	.01160	.0303	2.57	.99492	.00508	.0147
2.28	.98870	.01130	.0297	2.58	.99506	.00494	.0143
2.29	.98899	.01101	.0290	2.59	.99520	.00480	.0139
2.30	.98928	.01072	.0283	2.60	.99534	.00466	.0136
2.31	.98956	.01044	.0277	2.61	.99547	.00453	.0132
2.32	.98983	.01017	.0270	2.62	.99560	.00440	.0129
2.33	.99010	.00990	.0264	2.63	.99573	.00427	.0126

Figure 1.14   Using tabulated values of the standard normal distribution

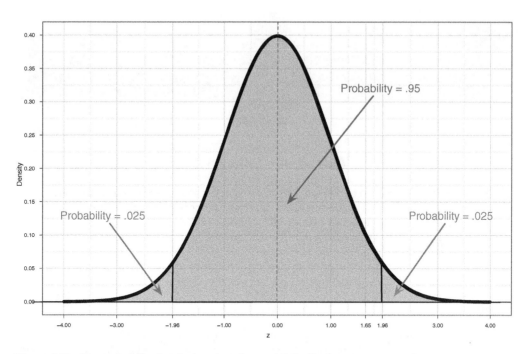

Figure 1.15 The probability density function of a normal distribution

total area under the curve is 1 (or 100%), so to discover the limits within which 95% of scores fall we're asking 'What is the value of z that cuts off 5% of the scores?' It's not quite as simple as that because if we want the *middle* 95%, then we want to cut off scores from both ends. Given the distribution is symmetrical, if we want to cut off 5% of scores overall but we want to take some from both extremes of scores, then the percentage of scores we want to cut from each end will be 5%/2 = 2.5% (or 0.025 as a proportion). If we cut off 2.5% of scores from each end then in total we'll have cut off 5% scores, leaving us with the middle 95% (or 0.95 as a proportion) – see Figure 1.15. To find out what value of z cuts off the top area of 0.025, we look down the column 'smaller portion' until we reach 0.025, we then read off the corresponding value of z. This value is 1.96 (see Figure 1.14) and because the distribution is symmetrical around zero, the value that cuts off the bottom 0.025 will be the same but a minus value (–1.96). Therefore, the middle 95% of z-scores fall between –1.96 and 1.96. If we wanted to know the limits between which the middle 99% of scores would fall, we could do the same: now we would want to cut off 1% of scores, or 0.5% from each end. This equates to a proportion of 0.005. We look up 0.005 in the *smaller portion* part of the table and the nearest value we find is 0.00494, which equates to a z-score of 2.58 (see Figure 1.14). This tells us that 99% of z-scores lie between –2.58 and 2.58. Similarly (have a go), you can show that 99.9% of them lie between –3.29 and 3.29. Remember these values (1.96, 2.58 and 3.29) because they'll crop up time and time again.

SELF TEST

Assuming the same mean and standard deviation
for the ice bucket example above, what's the probability
that someone posted a video within the first 30 days of the challenge?

Cramming Sam's Tips
Distributions and *z*-scores

- A frequency distribution can be either a table or a chart that shows each possible score on a scale of measurement along with the number of times that score occurred in the data.
- Scores are sometimes expressed in a standard form known as *z*-scores.
- To transform a score into a *z*-score you subtract from it the mean of all scores and divide the result by the standard deviation of all scores.
- The sign of the *z*-score tells us whether the original score was above or below the mean; the value of the *z*-score tells us how far the score was from the mean in standard deviation units.

1.8.7   Fitting statistical models to the data ▌▌▌▌

Having looked at your data (and there is a lot more information on different ways to do this in Chapter 5), the next step of the research process is to fit a statistical model to the data. That is to go where eagles dare, and no one should fly where eagles dare; but to become scientists we have to, so the rest of this book attempts to guide you through the various models that you can fit to the data.

1.9 Reporting data ▌▌▌▌

1.9.1   Dissemination of research ▌▌▌▌

Having established a theory and collected and started to summarize data, you might want to tell other people what you have found. This sharing of information is a fundamental part of being a scientist. As discoverers of knowledge, we have a duty of care to the world to present what we find in a clear and unambiguous way, and with enough information that others can challenge our conclusions. It is good practice, for example, to make your data available to others and to be open with the resources you used. Initiatives such as the Open Science Framework (https://osf.io) make this easy to do. Tempting as it may be to cover up the more unsavoury aspects of our results, science is about truth, openness and willingness to debate your work.

Scientists tell the world about our findings by presenting them at conferences and in articles published in scientific **journals**. A scientific journal is a collection of articles written by scientists on a vaguely similar topic. A bit like a magazine, but more tedious. These articles can describe new research, review existing research, or might put forward a new theory. Just like you have magazines such as *Modern Drummer*, which is about drumming, or *Vogue*, which is about fashion (or Madonna, I can never remember which), you get journals such as *Journal of Anxiety Disorders*, which publishes articles about anxiety disorders, and *British Medical Journal*, which publishes articles about medicine (not specifically British medicine, I hasten to add). As a scientist, you submit your work to one of these journals and they will consider publishing it. Not everything a scientist writes will be published. Typically, your manuscript will be given to an 'editor' who will be a fairly eminent scientist working in that research area who has agreed, in return for their soul, to make decisions about whether or not to publish articles. This editor will send your manuscript out to review, which means they send it to other experts in your research area and ask those experts to assess the quality of the work. Often (but not always) the reviewer is blind to who wrote the manuscript. The reviewers' role is to provide a constructive and even-handed overview of the strengths and weaknesses of your article and the research contained within it. Once these reviews are complete the editor reads them and then assimilates the comments with his or her own views on the manuscript and decides whether to publish it (in reality, you'll be asked to make revisions at least once before a final acceptance).

The review process is an excellent way to get useful feedback on what you have done, and very often throws up things that you hadn't considered. The flip side is that when people scrutinize your work, they don't always say nice things. Early on in my career I found this process quite difficult: often you have put months of work into the article and it's only natural that you want your peers to receive it well. When you do get negative feedback, and even the most respected scientists do, it can be easy to feel like you're not good enough. At those times, it's worth remembering that if you're not affected by criticism, then you're probably not human; every scientist I know has moments when they doubt themselves.

1.9.2 Knowing how to report data ▮▮▮▮

An important part of publishing your research is how you present and report your data. You will typically do this through a combination of graphs (see Chapter 5) and written descriptions of the data. Throughout this book I will give you guidance about how to present data and write up results. The difficulty is that different disciplines have different conventions. In my area of science (psychology), we typically follow the publication guidelines of the American Psychological Association or APA (American Pyschological Association, 2010), but even within psychology different journals have their own idiosyncratic rules about how to report data. Therefore, my advice will be broadly based on the APA guidelines, with a bit of my own personal opinion thrown in when there isn't a specific APA 'rule'. However, when reporting data for assignments or for publication, it is always advisable to check the specific guidelines of your tutor or the journal.

Despite the fact that some people would have you believe that if you deviate from any of the 'rules' in even the most subtle of ways then you will unleash the four horsemen of the apocalypse onto the world to obliterate humankind, the 'rules' are no substitute for common sense. Although some people treat the APA style guide like a holy sacrament, its job is not to lay down intractable laws, but to offer a guide so that everyone is consistent in what they do. It does not tell you what to do in every situation, but does offer sensible guiding principles that you can extrapolate to most situations you'll encounter.

1.9.3 Some initial guiding principles ▮▮▮▮

When reporting data, your first decision is whether to use text, a graph or a table. You want to be succinct, so you shouldn't present the same values in multiple ways: if you have a graph showing some results then don't also produce a table of the same results: it's a waste of space. The APA gives the following guidelines:

- Choose a mode of presentation that optimizes the understanding of the data.
- If you present three or fewer numbers then try using a sentence.
- If you need to present between 4 and 20 numbers consider a table.
- If you need to present more than 20 numbers then a graph is often more useful than a table.

Of these, I think the first is most important: I can think of countless situations where I would want to use a graph rather than a table to present 4–20 values because a graph will show up the pattern of data most clearly. Similarly, I can imagine some graphs presenting more than 20 numbers being an absolute mess. This takes me back to my point about rules being no substitute for common sense, and the most important thing is to present the data in a way that makes it easy for the reader to digest. We'll look at how to present graphs in Chapter 5 and we'll look at tabulating data in various chapters when we discuss how best to report the results of particular analyses.

A second general issue is how many decimal places to use when reporting numbers. The guiding principle from the APA (which I think is sensible) is that the fewer decimal places the better, which means that you should round as much as possible but bear in mind the precision of the measure you're reporting. This principle again reflects making it easy for the reader to understand the data. Let's look at an example. Sometimes when a person doesn't respond to someone, they will ask 'What's wrong, has the cat got your tongue?' Actually, my cat had a large collection of carefully preserved human tongues that he kept in a box under the stairs. Periodically, he'd get one out, pop it in his mouth and wander around the neighbourhood scaring people with his big tongue. If I measured the difference in length between his actual tongue and his fake human tongue, I might report this difference as 0.0425 metres, 4.25 centimetres, or 42.5 millimetres. This example illustrates three points: (1) I needed a different number of decimal places (4, 2 and 1, respectively) to convey the same information in each case; (2) 4.25 cm is probably easier for someone to digest than 0.0425 m because it uses fewer decimal places; and (3) my cat was odd. The first point demonstrates that it's not the case that you should always use, say, two decimal places; you should use however many you need in a particular situation. The second point implies that if you have a very small measure it's worth considering whether you can use a different scale to make the numbers more palatable.

Finally, every set of guidelines will include advice on how to report specific analyses and statistics. For example, when describing data with a measure of central tendency, the APA suggests you use M (capital M in italics) to represent the mean but is fine with you using the mathematical notation ($\bar{X}$) too. However, you should be consistent: if you use M to represent the mean you should do so throughout your article. There is also a sensible principle that if you report a summary of the data such as the mean, you should also report the appropriate measure of the spread of scores. Then people know not just the central location of the data, but also how spread out they were. Therefore, whenever we report the mean, we typically report the standard deviation also. The standard deviation is usually denoted by SD, but it is also common to simply place it in parentheses as long as you indicate that you're doing so in the text. Here are some examples from this chapter:

- ✓ Andy has 2 friends on Facebook. On average, a sample of other users ($N = 11$), had considerably more, $M = 95$, $SD = 56.79$.
- ✓ The average number of days it took someone to post a video of the ice bucket challenge was $\bar{X} = 39.68$, $SD = 7.74$.

✓ By reading this chapter we discovered that (*SD* in parentheses), on average, people have 95 (56.79) friends on Facebook and on average it took people 39.68 (7.74) days to post a video of them throwing a bucket of iced water over themselves.

Note that in the first example, I used *N* to denote the size of the sample. This is a common abbreviation: a capital *N* represents the entire sample and a lower-case *n* represents a subsample (e.g., the number of cases within a particular group).

Similarly, when we report medians, there is a specific notation (the APA suggests *Mdn*) and we should report the range or interquartile range as well (the APA does not have an abbreviation for either of these terms, but IQR is commonly used for the interquartile range). Therefore, we could report:

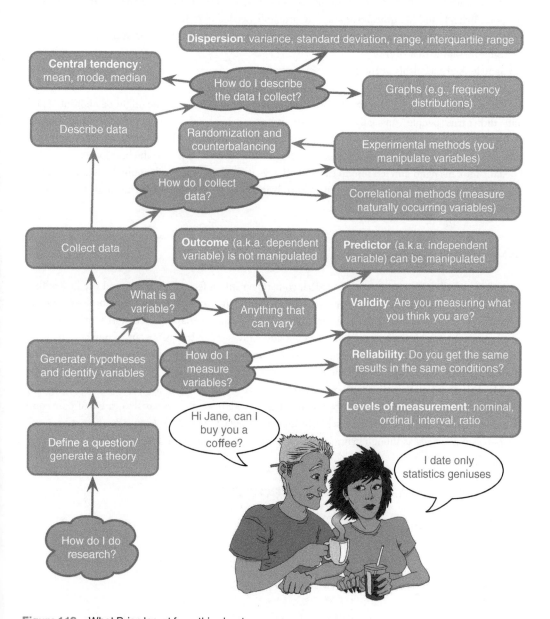

Figure 1.16 What Brian learnt from this chapter

✓ Andy has 2 friends on Facebook. A sample of other users (*N* = 11) typically had more, *Mdn* = 98, *IQR* = 63.
✓ Andy has 2 friends on Facebook. A sample of other users (*N* = 11) typically had more, *Mdn* = 98, *range* = 212.

1.10 Brian's attempt to woo Jane ▮▮▮

Brian had a crush on Jane. He'd seen her around campus a lot, always rushing with a big bag and looking sheepish. People called her a weirdo, but her reputation for genius was well earned. She was mysterious, no one had ever spoken to her or knew why she scuttled around the campus with such purpose. Brian found her quirkiness sexy. He probably needed to reflect on that someday.

As she passed him on the library stairs, Brian caught her shoulder. She looked horrified.

'Sup,' he said with a smile.

Jane looked sheepishly at the bag she was carrying.

'Fancy a brew?' Brian asked.

Jane looked Brian up and down. He was handsome, but he looked like he might be an idiot … and Jane didn't trust people, especially guys. To her surprise, Brian tried to woo her with what he'd learnt in his statistics lecture that morning. Maybe she was wrong about his idiocy, maybe he was a statistics guy … that would make him more appealing, after all stats guys always told the best jokes.

Jane took his hand and led him to the Statistics section of the library. She pulled out a book called *An Adventure in Statistics* and handed it to him. Brian liked the cover. Jane turned and strolled away enigmatically.

1.11 What next? ▮▮▮

It is all very well discovering that if you stick your finger into a fan or get hit around the face with a golf club it hurts, but what if these are isolated incidents? It's better if we can somehow extrapolate from our data and draw more general conclusions. Even better, perhaps we can start to make predictions about the world: if we can predict when a golf club is going to appear out of nowhere then we can better move our faces. The next chapter looks at fitting models to the data and using these models to draw conclusions that go beyond the data we collected.

My early childhood wasn't all full of pain, on the contrary it was filled with a lot of fun: the nightly 'from how far away can I jump into bed' competition (which sometimes involved a bit of pain) and being carried by my brother and dad to bed as they hummed Chopin's *Marche Funèbre* before lowering me between two beds as though being buried in a grave. It was more fun than it sounds.

1.12 Key terms that I've discovered

Between-groups design	Central tendency	Counterbalancing
Between-subjects design	Concurrent validity	Criterion validity
Bimodal	Confounding variable	Cross-sectional research
Binary variable	Content validity	Dependent variable
Boredom effect	Continuous variable	Deviance
Categorical variable	Correlational research	Discrete variable

Ecological validity	Multimodal	Range
Experimental research	Negative skew	Ratio variable
Falsification	Nominal variable	Reliability
Frequency distribution	Nonile	Repeated-measures design
Histogram	Normal distribution	Second quartile
Hypothesis	Ordinal variable	Skew
Independent design	Outcome variable	Standard deviation
Independent variable	Percentile	Sum of squared errors
Interquartile range	Platykurtic	Systematic variation
Interval variable	Positive skew	*Tertium quid*
Journal	Practice effect	Test–retest reliability
Kurtosis	Predictive validity	Theory
Leptokurtic	Predictor variable	Unsystematic variance
Level of measurement	Probability density function (PDF)	Upper quartile
Longitudinal research	Probability distribution	Validity
Lower quartile	Qualitative methods	Variables
Mean	Quantile	Variance
Measurement error	Quantitative methods	Within-subject design
Median	Quartile	*z*-scores
Mode	Randomization	

Smart Alex's tasks

Smart Alex knows everything there is to know about statistics and IBM SPSS Statistics. She also likes nothing more than to ask people stats questions just so that she can be smug about how much she knows. So, why not really annoy her and get all of the answers right!

- **Task 1**: What are (broadly speaking) the five stages of the research process? ▮▮▮▮
- **Task 2**: What is the fundamental difference between experimental and correlational research? ▮▮▮▮
- **Task 3**: What is the level of measurement of the following variables? ▮▮▮▮

  - The number of downloads of different bands' songs on iTunes
  - The names of the bands that were downloaded
  - Their positions in the download chart
  - The money earned by the bands from the downloads
  - The weight of drugs bought by the bands with their royalties
  - The type of drugs bought by the bands with their royalties
  - The phone numbers that the bands obtained because of their fame

○ The gender of the people giving the bands their phone numbers

○ The instruments played by the band members

○ The time they had spent learning to play their instruments

- **Task 4**: Say I own 857 CDs. My friend has written a computer program that uses a webcam to scan the shelves in my house where I keep my CDs and measure how many I have. His program says that I have 863 CDs. Define measurement error. What is the measurement error in my friend's CD-counting device? ▌▌▌

- **Task 5**: Sketch the shape of a normal distribution, a positively skewed distribution and a negatively skewed distribution. ▌▌▌

- **Task 6**: In 2011 I got married and we went to Disney World in Florida for our honeymoon. We bought some bride and groom Mickey Mouse hats and wore them around the parks. The staff at Disney are really nice and, upon seeing our hats, would say 'Congratulations' to us. We counted how many times people said congratulations over 7 days of the honeymoon: 5, 13, 7, 14, 11, 9, 17. Calculate the mean, median, sum of squares, variance, and standard deviation of these data. ▌▌▌

- **Task 7**: In this chapter we used an example of the time taken for 21 heavy smokers to fall off a treadmill at the fastest setting (18, 16, 18, 24, 23, 22, 22, 23, 26, 29, 32, 34, 34, 36, 36, 43, 42, 49, 46, 46, 57). Calculate the sum of squares, variance and standard deviation of these data. ▌▌▌

- **Task 8**: Sports scientists sometimes talk of a 'red zone', which is a period during which players in a team are more likely to pick up injuries because they are fatigued. When a player hits the red zone it is a good idea to rest them for a game or two. At a prominent London football club that I support, they measured how many consecutive games the 11 first-team players could manage before hitting the red zone: 10, 16, 8, 9, 6, 8, 9, 11, 12, 19, 5. Calculate the mean, standard deviation, median, range and interquartile range. ▌▌▌

- **Task 9**: Celebrities always seem to be getting divorced. The (approximate) lengths of some celebrity marriages in days are: 240 (J-Lo and Cris Judd), 144 (Charlie Sheen and Donna Peele), 143 (Pamela Anderson and Kid Rock), 72 (Kim Kardashian, if you can call her a celebrity), 30 (Drew Barrymore and Jeremy Thomas), 26 (W. Axl Rose and Erin Everly), 2 (Britney Spears and Jason Alexander), 150 (Drew Barrymore again, but this time with Tom Green), 14 (Eddie Murphy and Tracy Edmonds), 150 (Renée Zellweger and Kenny Chesney), 1657 (Jennifer Aniston and Brad Pitt). Compute the mean, median, standard deviation, range and interquartile range for these lengths of celebrity marriages. ▌▌▌

- **Task 10**: Repeat Task 9 but excluding Jennifer Anniston and Brad Pitt's marriage. How does this affect the mean, median, range, interquartile range, and standard deviation? What do the differences in values between Tasks 9 and 10 tell us about the influence of unusual scores on these measures? ▌▌▌

Answers & additional resources are available on the book's website at
https://edge.sagepub.com/field5e